THE FAMILY ENCYCLOPEDIA OF CHILD PSYCHOLOGY AND DEVELOPMENT

Other books by Frank J. Bruno

The Story of Psychology (1972)

Think Yourself Thin (1972)

Psychology: A Life-Centered Approach (1974)

Born to Be Slim (1978)

Behavior and Life (1980)

Adjustment and Personal Growth (1983)

Dictionary of Key Words in Psychology (1986)

The Family Mental Health Encyclopedia (1989)

THE FAMILY ENCYCLOPEDIA OF CHILD PSYCHOLOGY AND DEVELOPMENT

Frank J. Bruno, Ph.D.

JOHN WILEY & SONS, INC.

New York • Chichester • Brisbane • Toronto • Singapore

Library of Congress Cataloging-in-Publication Data

Bruno, Frank Joe, 1930–
    The family encyclopedia of child psychology and development
/ by Frank J. Bruno.
        p.   cm.
    Includes bibliographical references and index.
    ISBN 0-471-52793-9
    1. Child psychology—Encyclopedias.   2. Child development—
Encyclopedias.   I. Title.
BF721.B7157   1992   91-25322
155.4'03—dc20

Printed in the United States of America

10   9   8   7   6   5   4   3   2   1

Printed and bound by the Courier Companies, Inc.

For F. J. and all children

PREFACE

Our most important are our earliest years.

William Cowper (1731–1800), English author

How will *The Family Encyclopedia of Child Psychology and Development* be useful to you?

If you are a parent, teacher, or similar caregiver, you will find within these pages a broad spectrum of information. The kind of information provided will help you make your own decisions, and find your own answers, in response to the many challenges associated with nurturing, instructing, and rearing children in general. The encyclopedia is a convenient reference book providing facts, concepts, and discussions about almost any aspect of the thoughts, feelings, and actions of the growing child or adolescent.

Unfortunately, the path of development is not always smooth and serene. Children and adolescents display a wide range of biological impairments, mental and behavioral disorders, emotional problems, and learning disabilities. Examples include excessive aggressiveness, alcohol and other drug abuse in adolescence, alienation, autistic disorder, birth defects, cheating, schizophrenia, disobedience and rebelliousness, eating disorders, failure to thrive in infancy, gender identity confusion, hyperkinetic behavior, lying, mental retardation, night terrors and night-mares, overdependent behavior, reading difficulties, using undesirable language, shyness, stuttering, and truancy. These, and more, are addressed in the encyclopedia. Entries relating to troubled children and abnormal behavior discuss problems from the point of view of their signs and symptoms, causes and explanations, and a range of options available to responsible adult caregivers. No categorical advice is given. Instead, concepts and principles are provided that make it possible to find an effective way of coping with a difficulty in terms your own personality, attitudes, and values.

Sometimes a child's problem is beyond a parent's coping abilities. In some cases, professional help is required. The encyclopedia has a number of entries on such subjects as drug therapy, counseling, and psychotherapy. This information will help you evaluate help that is available outside of the home.

Professional persons such as pediatricians, child and school psychologists, child psychiatrists, neurologists, counselors, psychiatric nurses, and social workers often use a specialized, unfamiliar vocabulary. In your conferences and discussions with them, you may find yourself hearing about attention-deficit hyperactivity disorder, bidirectionality of influence, cephalocaudal development, convergent thinking, exceptional children, foreclosure of identity, learned helplessness, mainstreaming, norms of development, Oedipus complex, self-actualization, and so forth. This book is a reliable guide to the meaning of such terms.

Every time you look up information about a developmental subject, you learn just a bit more about children and their often unique way of perceiving and behaving in the world.

In order to provide you with a *useful* reference book, the encyclopedia contains several important features.

Subject entries. The core of the encyclopedia consists of approximately 600 subject entries based on both traditional concepts and recent research. The subject entries vary in length from a single paragraph to short articles. A wide range of developmental topics are included, all of them of practical interest.

Writing style. Every effort was made to make the writing clear and to the point. Although many specialized terms and subjects are both defined and discussed, they are dealt with in ordinary language. The unfamiliar is made intelligible through the pathway of the familiar. Where necessary, examples are used.

Technical terms. When technical terms appear in the body of a subject entry, they are always italicized and defined at the point of use. Again, the focus is on making developmental concepts clear and intelligible.

Name entries. There are a number of name entries for persons who have made significant contributions to the study of child development. The focus is not on biographical aspects of their lives but on their teachings—valuable information can be learned from them.

Cross-references. Almost every entry ends with several cross-references directing you to relevant collateral information elsewhere in the encyclopedia. Thus, subjects do not stand in isolation but are supported by a network of associated facts and ideas.

Index of authorities. At the end of the encyclopedia, you will find an index of authorities. Its purpose is to guide you to specific pages where the ideas and discoveries of thinkers and researchers who have made important contributions to the field of child development are cited.

In short, *The Family Encyclopedia of Child Psychology and Development* is a home reference book filled with practical information. The kind of material contained in it is, of course, of general interest. However, the encyclopedia will be of particular value to you during times of crisis with a child or adolescent, times when you need facts and principles at your fingertips.

Above all, the encyclopedia is *useful.*

FRANK J. BRUNO

ACKNOWLEDGMENTS

A number of people have helped me make *The Family Encyclopedia of Child Psychology and Development* a reality. My thanks are expressed to:

Herb Reich, Senior Editor at John Wiley & Sons, for recognizing the merits of the book and for being an encouraging and creative editor.

Linda Jones, Editorial Assistant to Herb Reich, for her practical assistance during the preparation phase of the manuscript.

Judith Cardanha for excellent copy editing.

Marcia Samuels for skillfully managing the project.

Maggie Dana for carefully supervising the production process of this book.

My wife, Jeanne, for our many meaningful discussions about children and their behavior.

My son, Franklin, for our conversations about words, language, and meaning.

My father and mother, Joe and Josephine Bruno, for being effective, loving parents.

My colleague George K. Zaharopoulos for his steadfast encouragement of my writing projects.

F.J.B.

A

abnormal development: A pattern of development that deviates from an expected course. *Development* itself refers to patterns of growth, maturation, and learning taking place over time. Thus, most children go through certain stages at certain ages. If the behavior associated with a certain stage does not appear, or appears in greatly modified form, one can speak of abnormal development.

For example, according to Erikson's psychosocial theory, a toddler has a great need for autonomy. This need often expresses itself in a negative way, in the form of resistance or disobedience. Thus, parents often speak informally of "the terrible twos." Assuming Erikson's theory is correct, if expressions of the need for autonomy do not appear shortly after infancy is over, then social development is abnormal. Toddlers who are excessively withdrawn and inhibited are displaying signs of abnormal development.

Numerous examples of abnormal development can be given. These include difficulties in learning to walk, talk, control the bladder and bowels, read, take instruction, and interact with others. Such conditions and problems as autistic disorder (infantile autism), mental retardation, stuttering, and attention-deficit hyperactivity disorder are just a few of the conditions and problems associated with abnormal development.

The general problem of abnormal development is indicated by the fact that various surveys and studies suggest that about one in ten children has emotional problems meriting some degree of adult concern.

From a statistical point of view, any deviation from an expectation is abnormal. Thus, a gifted child could be thought of as "abnormal" in a literal sense. This is not, however, the common, or recommended, usage. In practice, the word *abnormal* has become associated with both statistical deviation *and* pathology (i.e., "sickness").

See also *ages-stages theories; developmental psychology; Erikson, Erik Homburger; giftedness; psychosocial development.*

abusibility: A general aspect of behavior suggesting that certain children tend to elicit child abuse. Specific behaviors associated with the concept of abusibility are excessive displays of traits such as fussiness in an infant, defiance, whining, rebellion, and so forth. Children likely to invite abuse may suffer from a condition such as autistic disorder or mental retardation. Or they may have a problem such as stuttering or enuresis (bedwetting). Troubled children frustrate parents, and this frustration may bring out aggressive behavior on the part of the parents.

The concept of abusibility is of limited validity because it suggests that an abused child is somehow to blame for the abuse. First, it should be understood that only an emotionally immature parent will abuse a child because of the child's frustrating behavior. The mature parent looks for effective ways to cope with a troubled child's problems. Second, it should be realized that a child's behavior is more often than not a reaction to behavior initiated by a parent. Thus, children are almost never to be blamed for their difficulties.

See also *child abuse.*

abusing parent: A parent who has abused a child.

See *abusibility; child abuse.*

accommodation: In Piaget's theory of cognitive development, the restructuring of a schema in order to make it congruent with external reality. (The word *schema* is similar in meaning to the more familiar *concept.*) For example, suppose that 4-year-old Veronica believes that her favorite doll has thoughts and feelings just as Veronica herself has. Many facts suggest that this is not so. The taking in of these facts is a process of *assimilation,* not accommodation. When

Veronica finally realizes that the doll is just an inert object without consciousness, accommodation has taken place.

See also *assimilation; cognitive development; Piaget, Jean; schema.*

acculturation: The process by which children acquire the norms, standards, expectations, and moral values of the culture and the family to which they belong. Thus, the *acculturated child* "fits in" and displays socially appropriate behavior. Parents can foster acculturation by presenting consistent role models and by granting recognition and approval for valued behaviors.

See also *alienation; moral development; prosocial behavior; superego.*

achievement test: A paper-and-pencil test, usually given in a school setting, designed to assess a child's level of learning. The learning of interest is associated with familiar subject areas such as vocabulary, spelling, reading, the use of language, and mathematics. The basic purpose of an achievement test is to evaluate a child's performance with regard to other children with the same grade placement. For example, if Douglas has been placed in a fifth-grade class, he should be able to perform at least as well on an achievement test for the fifth grade as average children in that grade.

Percentile scores, based on percentages, are used to report a child's level of achievement. If Douglas scores at the 50th percentile, then he has a median score because one-half of children in a standardized group are below him and one-half are above him. However, if Douglas scores at the 80th percentile, he is a child with a high achievement score. Only 20 percent of children are performing better than he is.

Achievement tests are *not* tests of intelligence. It is said that they are designed to measure *performance*, not ability. The formal distinction between intelligence and performance is somewhat difficult to sustain. In practice, it is clear that children with high intelligence tend to also have high achievement. However, the distinction between intelligence and performance is not completely artificial. For example, some children are said to be *underachievers*. They work below their measured intelligence levels.

See also *intelligence; intelligence quotient (IQ); intelligence tests; Scholastic Aptitude Test (SAT); underachievement in school.*

acquired immune deficiency syndrome (AIDS): A pathological condition of the immune system attributed to infection by the *human immunodeficiency virus (HIV)*. It is estimated that approximately one percent of AIDS cases occur in babies born to women who have the disease. It is also possible for babies to contract the virus from mothers who test positive for the virus but who do not have a clinical case of AIDS.

Babies can be born with AIDS, or infected with HIV, because it is possible for the virus to cross over to the unborn child through the placenta.

See also *fetus; neonate; sexually transmitted diseases (STDs)*.

acting out: The expression of prohibited thoughts and emotional impulses in the form of motor behavior (i.e., actions). For example, if 7-year-old Duane strikes his 3-year-old sister because he is jealous, he is said to be acting out his jealousy. Or if 6-year-old Laine hurls an obscenity at her mother, then she is acting out her hostility.

Sometimes the term is used in the context of play therapy. A child is allowed to strike a doll or hit a punching bag as a way of discharging pent-up emotions. Frequently, the child's behavior is interpreted to the child with the aim of helping the child gain both an understanding of negative emotional states and better control of impulsive behavior.

Both children and adults are prone to act out occasionally. However, if a child acts out on a regular and frequent basis, then the child can be regarded as having significant problems with becoming socialized.

It is usually counterproductive to cope with acting out by taking harsh, punitive measures. This will probably make the child more hostile and aggressive. The use of behavior-modification techniques is more likely to be effective in the long run.

See also *aggressiveness; behavior modification; play therapy; socialization.*

active awake state in an infant: See *states of consciousness in an infant.*

active sleep state in an infant: See *states of consciousness in an infant.*

active vocabulary: The vocabulary that is actually used by a child in daily speech and in written communication. The active vocabulary is spontaneous and flows freely as a part of a child's verbal behavior. The active vocabulary is to be contrasted with the child's *passive vocabulary* (or *recognition vocabulary*), which comes into play, for example, when paying attention to what someone else is saying, listening to the radio or watching television, studying, or reading in general. The passive vocabulary is substantially greater in size than the active vocabulary.

Estimates concerning the size of a child's passive vocabulary vary. A classic study conducted by M. E. Smith in the 1920s suggests that an average passive vocabulary for 6-year-old children is about 2,500 words. More recent studies suggest that the average is quite a bit larger.

See also *babbling; language acquisition device (LAD); language development.*

addiction: See *drug abuse in adolescence.*

Adler, Alfred (1870–1937): Father of a school of psychology and psychotherapy known as *individual psychology.* Adler was an early associate of Sigmund Freud but broke off professional relations with Freud in a dispute over the primacy of the sexual drive. Freud saw sexual problems as the principal source of neurotic disorders. Adler, borrowing from the teachings of the philosopher Friedrich Nietzsche, contended that the frustration of the will to power was a primary cause of neurosis in childhood.

Adler asserted that the *will to power* is an inborn drive in the direction of competence, mastery, and superiority over others. When a child's will to power cannot overcome obstacles in its path, the result will be an *inferiority complex*, a set of related ideas making the child feel inadequate and incompetent in some important area of personality development. For example, one can have an inferiority complex concerning one's mathematical ability, one's athletic ability, or one's ability to make friends.

In addition to the will to power and the inferiority complex, Adler introduced a number of other important concepts into developmental psychology, such as sibling rivalry, the impact of birth order on personality development, compensation, dethroning, the spoiled child, and the superiority complex.

Two of Adler's books are *Problems of Neurosis* (1929) and *Social Interest* (1939).

See also *birth order*; *childhood neurosis*; *compensation*; *dethroning*; *inferiority complex*; *sibling rivalry*; *spoiled child*; *superiority complex*; *will to power*.

adolescence: From the point of view of biological development, a span of time starting with puberty and concluding with maturity. Chronologically, this is usually from about 12 or 13 to 18 or 19 years of age. (Consequently, there are the informal terms *teenage years* and *teenager*.) Some authorities suggest that adolescence ends for females at about the age of 21 and for males at about the age of 22.

From the psychological and social point of view, adolescence as it is popularly known is to some extent an artifact of an industrialized civilization. Primitive tribes frequently have no concept of adolescence. With the onset of puberty, there are often rites of passage, and the child becomes an adult in terms of both status and responsibility. The increased affluence associated with industrialization makes possible the prolonged period of dependence and learning that is associated with adolescence.

G. Stanley Hall, one of the principal founders of developmental psychology in the United States, called adolescence a time of "storm and stress" during which the individual was thrown about by opposites such as action versus inaction, excitement versus calm, elation versus depression, self-confidence versus doubts about self-esteem, and the need for authority versus the need to rebel against authority. Although some recent studies have suggested that adolescence is not necessarily a time of storm and stress and that there are many exceptions to the rule, Hall's way of looking at adolescence has prevailed. On the whole, it is thought of as a period of unusual emotional turbulence.

An adolescent is challenged to make a number of adjustments. With the onset of puberty, the former child becomes capable of reproduction. (In terms of Freud's psychosexual theory, this is termed the *genital stage*.) The question of how to deal with the capacity for reproduction and its associated desires is one that every adolescent must cope with. The self-image changes greatly with the appearance of pubic hair in both sexes, the development of breasts in females, and the first signs of a beard in males. The average female grows about 4 inches and gains about 33 pounds. The average male grows about 9 inches and gains about 55 pounds.

Erik Erikson has proposed that the principal task of an adolescent in terms of social development is to form a clear *identity* consisting of a robust sense of self and an image of one's future direction. Problems often arise in the adolescent's struggle to complete this task, and it is possible to speak of an *identity crisis*.

From the point of view of cognitive development, the adolescent becomes capable of *formal operations*, consisting of the ability to use symbols with flexibility and think in abstract terms.

See also *adolescent sex relations; adolescent suicide; cognitive development; drug abuse in adolescence; generation gap; Hall, Granville Stanley; identity crisis; identity versus role confusion; psychosexual development; psychosocial development.*

adolescent sex relations: Sexual activity, including intercourse, during the adolescent years. The implication of the phrase *adolescent sex relations* is that the individuals are not married. Adolescents have reached the genital stage of psychosexual development and, from the biological point of view, are ready for sexual relations and procreation. Of course, from the psychological and social points of view, they are seldom ready for long-term relationships and parenthood. Although most families, religious groups, and society in general tend to frown on sex relations between unmarried adolescents, the behavior has been on the rise for the past several decades.

Surveys conducted in the 1960s suggested that about 40 percent of adolescent females and about 60 percent of males were sexually active. It is presently estimated that close to 80 percent of adolescents of both sexes engage in sex relations at some time.

The high frequency of adolescent sex relations has spawned a set of problems such as emotional disturbances associated with broken relationships, unwanted pregnancies, decisions with regard to the pros and cons of abortion, decisions with regard to keeping or placing an infant for adoption, sexually transmitted diseases, and poorly planned marriages.

Adults and parents should not conclude from the survey figures that adolescents have gone sexually "wild" and that "anything goes" these days. Research suggests that most of the sexual activity takes place in the context of fairly stable, long-term relationships. There seems to be a reluctance, particularly among females, to engage in sex relations on a totally promiscuous basis.

See also *adolescence; homosexuality; masturbation; psychosexual development; sexually transmitted diseases.*

adolescent suicide: The act of an adolescent killing himself or herself; self-murder. As a cause of death among adolescents and young adults, suicide ranks third. Accidents and acts of violence (including murder) rank first and second, respectively. Overall, for both sexes and all age groups, suicide ranks tenth as a cause of death in the United States.

One should not conclude from the statistics that adolescents have gone on some sort of suicide spree. The statistics are somewhat misleading unless interpreted. The fact is that elderly persons (over 75 years of age) are more likely to take their own lives than are adolescents and young adults. Suicide has a high ranking as a cause of death for younger persons because they are less prone to serious illness than are older persons.

In the United States, the incidence of suicide is about 1 or 2 persons per 10,000 per year, and it is about the same for adolescents. Stated this way, the actual probability of any person dying by suicide during his or her adolescent years is relatively low. (If adolescence is thought of as spanning almost 10 years and the rate of suicide is set at 2 per 10,000 adolescents, the incidence over the 10 years turns out to be about 20 suicides per 10,000 adolescents; that is, the chance of a person committing suicide during adolescence is 0.2 percent.)

If a suicide takes place during adolescence, it is more likely to take place during the later, rather than earlier, adolescent years. Also, college students, on the borderline between adolescence and young adulthood, have about double the suicide rate of noncollege peers.

Why do some adolescents take their own lives? There is no single answer to this question. However, a number of theories have been advanced, and a number of causal factors have been identified. Taken together, some understanding of adolescent suicide emerges.

Psychoanalysis, a viewpoint that stresses the importance of unconscious motives and emotional conflicts, sees suicide not only in self-destructive terms, but also as a destructive act directed toward others. A suicide victim punishes others. Sometimes the act is a way of saying, "Look what you've done to me. Now cry and suffer the way you've made me cry and suffer." Common targets are former romantic partners and parents.

Humanistic psychology, a viewpoint that stresses the importance of willing and thinking, views suicide in common-sense terms. When adolescents find themselves frustrated in obtaining important personal goals, such as being well liked and having friends, developing adequate self-esteem, forming a well-defined sense of identity, finding a steady partner, obtaining adequate grades, achieving athletic success, and so forth, they become depressed and sometimes self-destructive. When an adolescent is convinced that existence has lost its meaning, that life is closing in, and that there are no roads leading to future happiness, then suicide may begin to look like an answer to the problems of life.

The theory of learned helplessness advanced by behavioral psychology contributes to the understanding of suicide. If an adolescent learns that he or she is helpless in situation A, then he or she may feel helpless in situation B. The person is not actually helpless in situation B but *believes* that he or she is. In consequence, the adolescent will not act in a constructive manner. An adolescent who has a history of academic, social, or other personal failures may very well feel that he or she will always be a victim of life. Learned helplessness has been shown to play a role in chronic depression. Chronic depression in turn has been shown to play a role in suicide.

The theories and causal factors identified are not mutually exclusive. They overlap and give a general view of the kinds of processes involved in suicide.

In recent years, a great deal of effort has been directed toward suicide prevention. Suicide prevention can be divided into two general categories. These are (1) general preventive measures and (2) crisis intervention. General preventive measures include effective parenting aimed at raising children and adolescents with high self-esteem, helping adolescents overcome depression, discovering ways to cope with aggressive and self-aggressive impulses, developing ways to deal with learned helplessness, and so forth.

Crisis intervention has led to the establishment of suicide and crisis-intervention centers. Many cities and large communities have hot lines to these centers. Trained volunteers answer telephones 24 hours a day. A professional staff of psychiatrists and clinical psychologists backs up the volunteer crew. The parent of an adolescent who is particularly despondent or seems to be thinking of suicide should seriously consider consulting a crisis service. In 1966, the Center for Studies of Suicide Prevention was established by an agency of the federal government, and a broad network of support is in place.

Warning signs sometimes associated with suicidal tendencies include (1) a prior attempt at suicide, (2) withdrawal from others, (3) inability to hold a job or to be an effective student, (4) alienation from parents and the rest of the family, and (5) chronic depression. Each of these signs provides an example of what has been called "a cry for help."

A cry for help should not be ignored. Sometimes parents and other family members are convinced that the signs associated with suicide are an effort to manipulate them or seek attention. However, even if this is so, the manipulative behavior itself is a sign that the adolescent is troubled and having problems in adjustment. Such an adolescent is in need of help in order to find more mature ways of coping with life.

See also *adolescence*; *depression*; *identity crisis*; *learned helplessness*.

adopted child: A child received by a parent, or parents, into a relationship such that the child is treated as one's own biological offspring. Formal adoption requires legal action.

Although there are many pros and cons concerning adoption, and many attitudes expressed toward it, one thing is clear. If the choice is between long-term institutional care for an orphaned, neglected, or abandoned child and adoption, adoption is definitely more desirable. Assuming that the adoptive parents are reasonable people with the best of motives, the adopted child will usually display development that is superior in almost all areas to that of the institutionalized child.

On the whole, the earlier that adoption takes place, the better. The bonding of an infant with a parent appears to foster optimal social development. This does not mean that adoption after infancy is impractical or ineffective. Research suggests that late adoption, although it presents more problems in the area of parent-child interactions, has a beneficial impact on the child's development.

Adoption has advantages for both children and adults. It tends to foster optimal development in children, as indicated above. It gives childless individuals the opportunity to experience the rich and rewarding role of parent. On the other hand, one should not be a Pollyanna about adoption. Realistically, there are often problems. Irving B. Weiner and David Elkind, developmental psychologists, point out that an adopted child's undesirable behavior is sometimes blamed on "bad genes." This "cause" of a child's behavior is not usually found in one's own biological children. These authors also point out that adopted children are somewhat more likely than biological children to be referred to child-care agencies for personal problems.

See also *adoptive parent; attachment; bonding of parent and child.*

adoptive parent: A person who has adopted a child and who has, consequently, taken on the role usually reserved for a biological parent.

See also *adopted child.*

Adult ego state: See *ego state.*

adulthood: From the point of view of biological development, a span of time starting when adolescence ends and concluding with death. Chronologically, the beginning of adulthood is associated with the ages between 18 to 21 years. From the point of view of law, adulthood begins when one attains a legal majority—usually associated with emancipation from one's parents, the right to hold property in one's name, the right to vote, and so forth.

It is possible for an individual to be an adult from the biological point of view and still remain an adolescent from the point of view of emotional maturity. Indeed, more than one observer of the contemporary social scene has argued that as a psychological stage adolescence is often extended to about 25 years of age for middle-class youth.

It is now recognized that development does not cease when one becomes an adult. There are developmental tasks and important psychological transitions that occur in adulthood. A spotlight is thrown on these challenges to the individual by Erik Erikson's psychosocial theory.

See also *adolescence; Erikson, Erik Homburger; psychosocial development.*

aesthetic needs: See *self-actualization.*

affectional drive: See *attachment.*

affective development: See *emotional states.*

ages-stages theories: Theories that describe development in terms of a series of discontinuous steps that stretch over discrete chronological periods. The chronological periods are the "ages" (e.g., infancy, early childhood, late childhood, and adolescence). The stages are the steps, each one representing a temporary plateau. One example of a stage is *latency*, during which a child has little conscious interest in sex, associated with Freud's theory of psychosexual development. This stage is hypothesized to last from about 6 to 12 years of age. Another example of a stage is the *preoperational stage*, during which a child thinks in magical terms, associated with Piaget's theory of cognitive development. This stage is associated with early childhood and lasts from about 2 to 7 years of age.

Ages-stages theories play an important role in developmental psychology, and there are several important ones. They summarize large amounts of data into organized systems, giving meaning to many random observations. However, it should be realized that their grand sweep can sometimes be misleading, giving the false impression that more has been explained than in fact has been explained.

See also *cognitive development; moral development; psychosexual development; psychosocial development; theories of development.*

aggressiveness: A behavioral trait characterized by a hostile attack, usually upon someone or something else. However, it is possible to speak of self-aggression, in which one attacks oneself. Aggressiveness can be overt, or clearly observed. A child who strikes another is said to be "acting out" his or her aggression. Overt aggressiveness is quite common in both early and late childhood.

With socialization, aggressiveness often becomes covert, or hidden. A snide remark that is subject to two interpretations or a betrayal are examples of disguised aggressiveness. When a child performs poorly in school or fails to live up to parental expectations, the general behavior is often described as *passive aggression*, suggesting that the child is striking out against a parent or other authority figures in a covert way.

Excessive aggressiveness plays a role in several disorders associated with childhood. Children who suffer from *autistic disorder* are often very self-aggressive, biting their fingers or banging their heads against walls. Children with a *conduct disorder* or an *attention-deficit hyperactivity disorder* frequently act out aggressiveness in a direct, unpleasant way. They may scream insults, break things, hit other children, and so forth.

There are several theories of aggression, each of which provides a partial explanation of destructive behavior.

1. Freud postulated that there is an *inborn aggressive drive*. It is a part of the *id*, or primitive personality, and it seeks some form of expression. Thus, children just have a natural urge at times to break thinks, burn things, shoot at birds, and insult their friends. Freud's suggestion is a part of classical psychoanalytic theory; however, it is not accepted by all behavioral scientists.

2. The *frustration-aggression hypothesis* suggests that aggression is a reaction to frustration. When, for example, a child is blocked in attaining a positive goal or blocked in avoiding a negative outcome, the emotional reaction is some form of anger (ranging from irritation to rage). The behavioral component of anger is aggressive behavior. Thus, children who act overly aggressive are unhappy, frustrated children.

3. The *behavioral hypothesis* states that the probability of acting in an aggressive manner is increased if the action is reinforced (i.e., pays off in some desirable way). If a bully strikes a younger child, steals candy, and escapes without penalty, then the likelihood increases that the bully will repeat such an action.

4. *Social learning theory* states that aggressive behavior is often learned from models, individuals who demonstrate hostile acts. If a child admires a stronger, seemingly more competent peer, and if that peer frequently demonstrates aggressive behavior, then the first child is likely to try out aggressive behavior. Or, in a more unfortunate case, if a parent is a violent, abusive person, the parent may provide the undesirable model.

Adults need to realize that some level of aggressiveness is considered normal in children. There has to be some margin of error and region of adult acceptance. Only if aggressiveness is chronic and is used by the child in many situations as an ineffective way of coping with life should the child be thought of as "having a problem" with aggressiveness.

See also *attention-deficit hyperactivity disorder (ADHD); autistic disorder; conduct disorder; id; social learning.*

AIDS: See *acquired immune deficiency syndrome.*

alcohol abuse in adolescence: The improper or excessive consumption of alcohol during adolescence. Such consumption is associated with behaviors described as either self-defeating or self-destructive. It is estimated that somewhat over one million adolescents abuse alcohol. Translated into percentages, this is about 3 to 4 percent of teenagers. Therefore, alcohol abuse in adolescence is a social problem of substantial proportions.

Here are some features of adolescent alcoholic consumption:

1. About two-thirds of adolescents have tried an alcoholic beverage at least once.
2. Beer is consumed more often than other alcoholic beverages.
3. Many, perhaps most, teenagers who abuse alcohol begin doing so in early adolescence.
4. The adolescent's own residence is the most common place where alcohol is consumed.
5. Excessive drinking often takes place when socializing with friends.
6. Alcohol is a complicating factor in many adolescent auto accidents, including deaths.
7. Alcohol abuse among adolescents has been on the rise in recent years.

Psychological and social factors contributing to adolescent alcohol abuse include parents who abuse alcohol, the belief that drinking will help one deal with life's problems, low self-esteem, the influence of friends, the need to seek relief from anxiety, the desire to have fun, the wish to take risks for excitement, self-directed anger leading to self-destructive behavior, the need to flirt with forbidden behaviors, and a society that uses alcohol for recreation and celebrations. A particular adolescent may be affected by one or several of these factors.

It has also been hypothesized that a genetic predisposition to become easily addicted to alcohol exists in some people. There are studies that support this hypothesis. However, even if a genetic factor does exist, it is unlikely that it is sufficient in itself to cause alcohol abuse. It seems likely, however, that it might play a part in aggravating the effect of psychological and social factors.

There is hope for adolescents who abuse alcohol. Alcoholics Anonymous (AA) and Alateen offer helpful programs. Most telephone books in urban areas have listings for these organizations. Also, counseling and psychotherapy are often effective.

See also *adolescence; adolescent suicide; drug abuse in adolescence; genetic predisposition; juvenile delinquency; self-esteem.*

alcoholic parent: A parent who is dependent upon, is addicted to, or chronically abuses alcohol. The prevalence of alcoholism is somewhat difficult to estimate because of differing opinions concerning its correct definition. If *alcoholism* is defined as "the frequent abuse of alcohol," then perhaps 5 to 10 percent of parents are alcoholics. But, if the definition is restricted to "hard core compulsive drinking on a regular basis," then the incidence is probably on the order of 1 percent to 2 percent of parents. In any event, the abuse of alcohol is a major health problem touching many families.

The excessive use of alcohol by a parent can be a contributing factor to child abuse. This is so because alcohol has a tendency to reduce impulse control; and an intoxicated parent is more likely, when frustrated by a child, to lash out in an aggressive manner. In a similar way, alcohol abuse can play a role in lack of appropriate emotional involvement with a child and irrational methods of discipline. Sometimes alcohol is a factor in sexual molestation by a parent.

Through the process of social (i.e., observational) learning, alcohol abuse by a parent may be a contributing cause to eventual alcohol abuse by a child.

A major problem associated with alcoholic parents is fetal alcohol syndrome.

See also *child abuse; discipline; drug abuse in adolescence; fetal alcohol syndrome (FAS); parental style; sexual molestation; social learning.*

alienation: A feeling that one does not belong to a given reference group. Thus, children or adolescents can feel alienated from their families, from their friends, from their religion, and so forth. Note that alienation is always alienation *from.* The literal roots of the word *alienation* mean "without ties." Alienated individuals, in a sense, are not tied to groups to which they were formerly tied.

Alienation as a psychological problem may be aggravated by the trials and tribulations of adolescence. It is not unusual for a teenager to feel lonely and apart both at school and at home. Alienation plays a significant role in adolescent depression, self-destructive behavior, and suicide.

However, it should be recognized that a certain level of adolescent alienation is to be expected and is normal. Adolescents are in the process of creating an identity and need to place a certain amount of psychological distance between themselves and their families.

The popular term *generation gap* reflects the idea that it is common for adolescents and young adults to be alienated from their families to some degree. The problem for parents is to evaluate the difference between normal and pathological alienation. There are, of course, no exact criteria. But there are a few guidelines. Pathological alienation is indicated if the child or adolescent (1) wants almost nothing to do with the family, even on holidays and special occasions; (2) has no friends and does not identify with a given peer group; (3) takes no interest in school; (4) is generally hostile and insulting; (5) seems in general to have a negative attitude toward life; (6) speaks only when spoken to; (7) appears to have no regard for conventional values or traditions.

See also *adolescence; adolescent suicide; generation gap; identity crisis.*

altruism: Unselfish concern for the well-being of others. Altruism is the psychological underpinning for benevolent actions in which people place the welfare of others before their own. Altruism is considered a form of prosocial behavior, meaning behavior that benefits the family, a club, a nation, or other meaningful group.

Altruism generally does not make its appearance until late childhood or early adolescence. In infancy and early childhood, individuals are egocentric, thinking and acting as if they are at the hub of the world.

Sociobiologists suggest that there is a genetic basis for altruism. They indicate that altruism emerges with maturation because it has survival value. A family or tribe with altruistic members is more likely to be effective and successful than a group in which its members care only for themselves. Alfred Adler, a major figure in early psychoanalysis, believed that social interest is inborn in human beings; that is, human beings are naturally gregarious and interested in companionship. The views of the sociobiologists and Adler are in agreement.

See also *Adler, Alfred; egocentric thinking; prosocial behavior; sociobiology.*

ambidexterity: The ability to use the right hand or the left hand with equal skill. An ambidextrous child performs manual skills without regard to handedness, the dominance of one hand over the other. For example, such a child may be seen to dry dishes one day with a dish towel in the left hand, and on another day with the dish towel in the right hand. There is probably a genetic basis for ambidexterity. Ambidextrous children are more likely than other children to have parents, grandparents, or other blood relatives with the same trait. Ambidexterity is real, but it is rare.

See also *heredity; motor development.*

amniocentesis: A method of obtaining sample cells of a fetus. In amniocentesis, a syringe and needle are used to withdraw a small amount of amniotic fluid, the fluid surrounding the fetus in the womb. (The needle is introduced through the abdominal wall.) The amniotic fluid contains free-floating fetal cells, cells that have flaked off the fetus. Therefore, the sample is not taken directly from the fetus.

The most common purpose of amniocentesis is to evaluate the status of a suspected genetic problem. For example, amniocentesis can be used to determine if a fetus has three chromosomes on the 21st pair of chromosomes, a condition known as *Trisomy 21*. If this is the case, the child will usually have Down's syndrome. Assuming that the evaluation takes place early in the pregnancy, and also assuming that the parents live in a state that allows abortions under the conditions described, they may decide on a medical abortion.

Amniocentesis can also be used to determine the fetus' blood type and sex.

There is some risk associated with amniocentesis. The likelihood of inducing an unwanted abortive process is about 1 in 200. Also, there is the possibility of infection. Therefore, amniocentesis is not a routine testing method. Its use is reserved for females who are evaluated as having a higher than average likelihood of having a child with Down's syndrome, Tay-Sachs disease, or other genetic problems.

An alternative method to amniocentesis is *chorionic villus sampling*, in which the placenta is used to provide tissue. The *chorionic villi* are hairlike structures on the placenta, and they have the same genetic structure as the fetus. Samples are obtained through the use of a syringe and a needle that is inserted through the abdominal wall. An alternative method is to obtain a sample by the introduction of a hollow reedlike sampling tube through the vagina.

See also *Down's syndrome; genetic anomaly; Tay-Sachs disease.*

anaclitic depression: A depressive syndrome associated with infancy, approximately the first 18 to 24 months of life. An infant suffering from anaclitic depression is listless and apathetic. Weight loss, poor physical and mental development, and in some cases even death have all been associated with anaclitic depression. The overall condition of an infant suffering from anaclitic depression is described as a *marasmus*, meaning "an emaciation and gradual wasting away of the body."

The principal cause of anaclitic depression is separation from a parent, usually the mother. The depression is aggravated if the child is isolated, receiving inadequate social stimulation. Even if physical care is quite adequate, the syndrome may appear.

Anaclitic depression is much more common in institutions than it is in a home setting. For this reason, it is sometimes referred to as *hospitalism*. Pioneer investigations conducted in foundling homes by researcher René A. Spitz established the reality of anaclitic depression. The syndrome can, of course, appear in a home setting when there is gross neglect of an infant. Under these circumstances, the syndrome is referred to as *attachment disorder*, or, more completely, *attachment disorder of infancy or early childhood*. Unfortunately, such cases do occur. However, in the vast majority of homes, there is little risk that an infant will develop anaclitic depression.

See also *attachment; bonding of parent and child; deprived environment; infant.*

anal stage: In Freud's theory, the second stage of psychosexual development, the stage associated with toddlerhood, the time from approximately 18 to 36 months of age. This is also the time frame during which toilet training takes place. According to Freud, the way in which a parent manages or mismanages toilet training can have a significant effect on the formation of a child's personality. Although Freud's hypothesis tends to be taken as a truism in psychoanalytic theory, there is no general consensus among psychiatrists and psychologists concerning its general importance.

See also *anal-expulsive character; anal-retentive character; character; Freud, Sigmund; psychosexual development; toilet training.*

anal-expulsive character: A personality type characterized by traits such as generosity, messiness, and agreeableness. An individual with an anal-expulsive character tends to be giving with both affection and money. According to Freud's psychosexual theory, an anal-expulsive character in adulthood is caused primarily by pleasure associated with the expulsion of fecal bulk during the anal stage of development.

Although the term *anal-expulsive character* does identify a recognizable personality type, it is open to question whether or not this type is caused primarily by experiences during the anal stage of development.

See also *anal-retentive character; anal stage; character; Freud, Sigmund; psychosexual development; toilet training.*

anal-retentive character: A personality type characterized by excessive orderliness, stinginess, and obstinacy. An individual with an anal-retentive character holds back both affection and money. The miser Scrooge in *A Christmas Carol* by Charles Dickens captures in fictional form the essence of the anal-retentive character.

According to Freud's psychosexual theory, an anal-retentive character in adulthood is caused primarily by emotional difficulties experienced during the anal stage of development. If parents are particularly harsh and punitive in their efforts to toilet train a child, this can lead to fixations of libido (i.e., psychosexual energy) in the anal zone. Preoccupations with holding back and metering out something valuable (i.e., fecal bulk) generalize through unconscious mechanisms to produce an anal-retentive character in adulthood.

Although the term *anal-retentive character* does identify a recognizable personality type, it is open to question whether or not this type is caused mainly by toilet-training procedures. Present thinking suggests that toilet training may be one causal factor among others.

See also *anal-expulsive character; anal stage; character; Freud, Sigmund; psychosexual development; toilet training.*

androgen hormones (androgens): Hormones that play an important part in the development of secondary masculine characteristics, such as the growth of a beard, muscle development, and the lowering of the voice's pitch. Androgens are produced in the male by the testes, and their level increases during and after puberty. In the female, androgens are produced in small amounts by the ovaries.

See also *estrogen hormones; hormone; ovaries; testes; testosterone; virilism.*

animistic thinking: The primitive belief that all objects and events have a soul or spirit. Thus,, in accordance with animistic thinking, a rock and a thunderstorm both have a vital quality that goes beyond mere existence. For example, they might have feelings or awareness. (Words such as *animistic, animal,* and *animate* are derived from the Latin word *anima,* meaning "soul.")

Animistic thinking tends to appear spontaneously in children, usually during toddlerhood. It is quite natural for them to think that a stone experiences pain if it breaks in two or that the world is crying when it is raining. It seems quite likely that animistic thinking is a simple generalization from children's own experience. Children know that they themselves have feelings and consciousness. Without sufficient analysis, they naturally expect that everything else is like them.

See also *anthropomorphic thinking; cognitive development; egocentric thinking; Piaget, Jean; preoperational stage.*

anorexia nervosa: An eating disorder characterized primarily by the refusal to eat enough food for the maintenance of a normal body weight. Although *anorexia* literally means "loss of appetite," the individual with anorexia nervosa usually *does* have an appetite. The refusal to eat is just that, a *refusal*; it is an act of will related in most cases to a dread of obesity.

The victim of anorexia nervosa is, in the vast majority of cases (about 95 percent), a female. The high-risk time period for the disorder is adolescence.

Other common symptoms of anorexia nervosa include:

1. *A confused body image.* The victim perceives herself as fat even when she is skinny or emaciated. She may look in a mirror and say in disgust, "I'm as fat as a pig."

2. *Amenorrhea.* Amenorrhea is a cessation of the menstrual flow. This is an early symptom of anorexia nervosa and often is in evidence prior to substantial weight reduction.

3. *Lanugo.* The term *lanugo* is used to describe the growth of a fine covering of hair on the body resembling that of a newborn child.

4. *Psychosexual disturbance.* Adolescents with the disorder are often behind others in their sexual development. Adults with the disorder tend to lose interest in sexual activity.

5. *The cooking of meals.* It is common for the victim to cook meals for others, insisting they eat well.

Anorexia nervosa is a serious disorder. Its victims may very well die of complications associated with emaciation. The American Psychiatric Association's *Diagnostic and Statistical Manual* states that the mortality rates for anorexia nervosa may be as high as between 5 and 18 percent. Therefore, the disorder must be taken very seriously.

It is difficult to estimate with any accuracy the general frequency of anorexia nervosa. In some studies, the incidence is very low—

close to one-tenth of one percent. In other studies, the incidence is higher—approximately one percent. The great variability in results is due to differences in groups sampled and methods of sampling.

Anorexia nervosa appears to be caused primarily by an interaction of psychosocial factors. Some of these factors are (1) overcontrolling parents, (2) a strong-willed adolescent, (3) an upwardly mobile family, and (4) a culture that overvalues a thin female body. When the adolescent female diets to an extreme, parents often react with stern lectures and warnings. The issue becomes "Who is in control?" A battle of wills ensues. Not eating becomes a symbol of the adolescent's ability to exercise autonomy. This analysis is an oversimplification, of course. The psychology of anorexia nervosa is a large subject in itself. However, it is correct that in broad general terms a process like the one described above is commonly found.

The treatment of anorexia nervosa often requires hospitalization for the medical aspects of the disorder. Sometimes the victim must be force-fed just to keep her alive. This, of course, increases her resentment and makes long-term therapy more difficult. Recovery usually requires both individual psychotherapy for the patient and group therapy for the family. Both the victim of anorexia nervosa and members of her family need to see ways in which they can stop working against each other.

See also *bulimia nervosa; obesity; pica; rumination disorder of infancy.*

anoxia: An insufficient supply of oxygen to the tissues of the body. The term *hypoxia* is used to indicate that there is some oxygen supply, but that it is inadequate. Sometimes neonates are subjected to a deprivation of oxygen because of a long and difficult delivery or other complications. The effect can be some degree of damage, ranging from slight to extreme, to the brain and nervous system. Some of the possible long-term behavioral effects associated with either anoxia or hypoxia during the birthing process are hyperactive behavior and impaired mental abilities.

See also *attention-deficit hyperactivity disorder (ADHD); birth trauma; mental retardation.*

anthropomorphic thinking: A primitive kind of thinking character-ized by a tendency to explain natural events in terms of human characteristics. Saying that Mother Nature is making the sun shine, that Jack Frost is painting the leaves pretty colors, or that Thor is making thunder by throwing his hammer are all examples of anthropomorphic thinking.

Anthropomorphic thinking is particularly appealing to toddlers and preschoolers. They more readily appreciate explanations couched in terms of human behavior than they do explanations couched in terms of impersonal cause and effect. The idea that an invisible giant pulls an airplane up into the air makes more sense to a very young child than does an explanation of the differences in air pressure on the top and bottom of a wing.

This question arises: Is it a disservice to children when they ask questions to explain physical events in anthropomorphic terms? Might this not retard their correct understanding of cause and effect? The answer is that occasional anthropomorphic explanations from the ages of about 2 to 5 or 6 probably do no harm. The odds are that they help the child to perceive the world as a sensible, meaningful place. However, older children, certainly after the age of 7 in most cases, will benefit by, and prefer, explanations in terms of known natural principles. They will feel misled by anthropomorphic explanations.

See also *cognitive development; Piaget, Jean; preoperational stage.*

antidepressant drugs: See *drug therapy.*

antipsychotic drugs: See *drug therapy.*

antisocial behavior: Behavior that works against the needs and functions of a social group, such as the family, church, tribe, school, club, or, on a larger scale, the nation. Antisocial behavior consists of such attributes as lack of concern for the welfare of others, unwillingness to cooperate, hostility, refusal to be helpful, irresponsibility, and untrustworthiness. Often there is an absence of guilt feelings for offensive actions. From the point of view of parents and adults in general, antisocial behavior is deemed undesirable and is an important sign of a general breakdown in the socialization of the child or adolescent. Consequently, caregivers should seek ways to discourage, modify, or extinguish it. The application of behavior modification and communication skills can be helpful.

Antisocial behavior is an aspect of problem behaviors and disorders included in the following cross-referenced entries.

See also *behavior disorder; behavior modification; cheating; communication skills; conduct disorder; juvenile delinquency; lying; moral development; oppositional defiant disorder; prosocial behavior; socialization; stealing; truancy.*

anxiety: A vague feeling of dread or apprehension. Anxiety is a state similar in terms of physiological arousal to fear. Fear, however, has a specific source (e.g., a gun or a barking dog). Anxiety has no readily identifiable source. (It is, of course, possible to speak of realistic anxiety. This usage is identical in meaning to fear.)

In psychoanalytic theory, anxiety has its source in the individual's awareness that he or she may act on forbidden sexual or aggressive impulses. Therefore, one would not expect anxiety in an infant or a toddler. However, when a child is somewhat older and has developed a sense of right and wrong, anxiety may appear. One would logically expect some anxiety in the "good" child, one that does not often act out forbidden wishes.

It should be noted that anxiety is not always manifest. Sometimes it is latent and expresses itself in the form of phobias, obsessional thoughts, and compulsive behaviors. These may be thought of as attempts to manage anxiety. Children who suffer from chronic anxiety are entitled to a certain amount of understanding. Parents and responsible adults should avoid discounting anxiety as "silly" or "foolish."

See also *childhood neurosis; fear; phobia; separation anxiety disorder.*

Apgar scale: A rating scale consisting of five signs used to determine the general state of health of a neonate. The scale was developed by Virginia Apgar, an anesthesiologist. The five signs are (1) hue and cast of the skin in terms of blood supply, (2) rate and steadiness of the pulse, (3) tone of the muscles, (4) quality and rate of respirations, and (5) state of the reflexes. Each sign is rated with 0, 1, or 2. The highest score a neonate can obtain is 10. Scores of 7 or 8 suggest good health. Scores of 3 or 4 suggest the neonate may be in danger and require medical attention.

See also *Neonatal Behavioral Assessment Scale; neonatal reflexes; neonatal scales; neonate.*

apnea: See *sudden infant death syndrome (SIDS)*.

assimilation: In Piaget's theory of cognitive development, the taking in of information, or facts, without making a corresponding change in existing schemata (i.e., conceptual outlines). For example, suppose that 4-year-old Patricia is told that a nickel is worth more than three pennies. She is asked an hour later, "What's worth more—three pennies or a nickel?" She correctly answers, "A nickel." Now she is given a choice of either three pennies or a nickel. She "incorrectly" takes the three pennies. She has assimilated the fact that she has been told, but she has not accommodated to that fact.

See also *accommodation; cognitive development; Piaget, Jean; schema.*

associative play: A kind of social play characterized by a willingness to share toys and other objects. For example, Margaret and Victoria are coloring different pictures at the same table and sharing, without conflict, a single box of crayons. Each child is absorbed in her own project. However, there is a kind of low-level social interaction.

See also *cooperative play; ludic behavior; onlooker play; parallel play; play; solitary play.*

attachment: An emotional bond. When applied to child development, attachment usually refers to the bond between a parent and an infant. (Most of the studies of attachment focus on the mother, not the father.) Although attachment is a two-way psychological street, psychologists have been particularly interested in the question of why the infant becomes attached to the mother.

Freud theorized that a mother meets an infant's biological needs (e.g., hunger, thirst). The satisfaction of these needs strengthens positive feelings for the mother. Although Watson, the father of behaviorism, had very little use for Freud and his theories, he expounded a similar view. An infant becomes attached to the mother because of association. A learned link is made between being held by one's mother and being fed by one's mother. Thus, attachment is a form of conditioning.

In the 1950s, Harry Harlow, one of the presidents of the American Psychological Association, using rhesus monkeys as his subjects, suggested that attachment arises from an inborn *affectional drive*. The infant needs the mother in a psychological-emotional sense. If deprived of affection in infancy, there will be retarded mental and social development. Harlow's research suggests that one of the important ways in which the affectional drive is met in infancy is by comfortable contact with the caregiver. This supports the age-old value of holding, cuddling, and rocking an infant. Harlow's view has prevailed over Freud's and Watson's.

More recently, John Bowlby, a scientist with an evolutionary perspective, has proposed that an infant's attachment to the mother has a survival value. Therefore, most normal infants have a strong inborn tendency to bond to the mother. It is important to note that Bowlby's viewpoint does not contradict Harlow's, but builds on it.

See also *anaclitic depression; bidirectionality of influence; breastfeeding; Harlow, Harry F.; imprinting.*

attachment disorder: See *anaclitic depression.*

attention-deficit hyperactivity disorder (ADHD): A disorder in children characterized by such behavioral problems as seldom completing tasks, not listening, being distracted easily, and not concentrating on school assignments. These difficulties are summarized in the single word *inattention*. Combined with inattention is an *impulsive pattern*. The child may jump arbitrarily from one activity to another one. Acting without sufficient thought is common.

Hyperactivity is characterized by a lot of running about and/or climbing on objects. Staying seated will be a problem. Such a child seems to always have his or her "motor" running. Described more formally, there is a chronic high state of arousal.

Although both sexes can suffer from the disorder, male children tend to suffer from it more frequently than do female children.

Attention-deficit hyperactivity disorder is not to be confused with other problems such as mental retardation, conduct disorder, schizophrenia, or the normal exuberance of childhood.

The disorder usually makes its first appearance before the age of 7 and often continues well into adolescence. It is believed that many adults with a mild form of antisocial personality disorder may have suffered from ADHD as children. It *is*, however, encouraging to note that both Thomas Alva Edison and Winston Churchill are suspected to have been hyperkinetic as children.

One of the suspected causes of attention-deficit hyperactivity disorder is minimal brain dysfunction (MBD). Another factor is heredity; it is suspected that some children are somewhat more prone by temperament to be restless and impulsive. It has also been suggested that some children are allergic to certain food additives (see *Feingold hypothesis*), and this may adversely affect their ability to concentrate.

The principal drug treatment for ADHD is the prescription of a stimulant such as methylphenidate. (Two trade names for methylphenidate are Methidate and Ritalin). Stimulants normally increase arousal. However, they often have a paradoxical effect on children with attention-deficit hyperactivity disorder and often lower arousal. In mild cases, coffee, because it contains the stimulant caffeine, has a therapeutic effect.

The principal psychological treatment for the disorder is behavior therapy.

See also *antisocial behavior; behavior therapy; drug therapy; Feingold hypothesis; methylphenidate; minimal brain dysfunction (MBD); temperament.*

attribution: See *self-expectations.*

authoritarian parent: A parent who tends to be dominating and overcontrolling without sufficient regard for a child's thoughts and feelings. The parent seems to take the attitude that he or she is always in the right merely because he or she is the parent. Phrases such as "Because I told you so" or "You'll do what I say as long as you're under my roof and I pay the bills" fall easily from the lips of the authoritarian parent.

Does the authoritarian style backfire eventually on the parent? The answer is not a simple yes or no. If the parent is both authoritarian and affectionate, the child will often work hard to earn the parent's approval. A number of psychologists believe that this set of factors contributes to neurotic tendencies in children. On the other hand, if the parent is authoritarian and emotionally cold, the child will often reject the parent and become alienated. A number of psychologists believe that this set of factors contributes to conduct disorders in children.

See also *love*; *parental style*; *tough love*.

authoritative parent: A parental style characterized by a well-defined set of values and limits on both acceptable and unacceptable behavior. The term *authoritative* is used to suggest a broader spectrum of parental flexibility than does the term *authoritarian*, which is associated with a parental style that is overcontrolling and excessively demanding.

See also *authoritarian parent; parental style*.

autistic disorder (infantile autism): A very serious developmental disorder characterized by a lack of social interest, mutism or speech problems, and self-destructiveness. The disorder was first identified by the psychiatrist Leo Kanner in 1943. The reason the word *infantile* is sometimes used is because the disorder usually starts in infancy or early childhood. However, it tends to remain a problem as the child matures. *Autism* refers to the fact that these children seem to be living in their own private dream world. They pay attention to themselves and have almost no concern for others.

It is often said that autistic disorder is not a form a mental retardation. Nonetheless, most children with autistic disorder perform very poorly on standardized intelligence tests. It is very difficult to reliably measure their intelligence because they tend to be uncooperative. In fact, it is estimated that about three-fourths of autistic children are mentally retarded.

Autistic disorder (autism) tends to be a lifelong problem. It is not easily cured. However, it is treatable. The most effective approach seems to be behavior therapy aimed at helping the child live in a family setting. The goal is to avoid years of institutionalization.

It used to be thought that autistic disorder was the result of parental coldness (i.e., a rejecting attitude and lack of interest in the infant). Today, there is a consensus that it is a *biogenetic disorder*, one that is primarily due to inborn factors. Evidence suggests that the brain of an autistic individual does not process information like most other brains do.

It is important to discriminate autistic disorder from early-onset schizophrenia. At one time the two disorders were thought to be identical. Children can develop schizophrenia, but it is not autism. Schizophrenia in childhood tends to appear after a period of normal development (e.g., at the age of 7), not in infancy or early childhood. Schizophrenic children may have delusions or even sometimes hallucinations. Autistic children do not.

Fortunately, infantile autism is a relatively rare disorder. It appears to affect 1 or 2 children per 5,000. Approximately three males have the disorder for every female that has it.

See also *behavior therapy; developmental disorders; childhood schizophrenia; mental retardation.*

autonomy versus shame and doubt: In Erikson's theory, the second stage of psychosocial development, the stage associated with toddlerhood, the time from 18 months to 3 years of age. If toddlers are allowed to explore and do things for themselves within their capacities, they will develop the positive personality trait of *autonomy*, a sense that they have some degree of control over their own lives. It is the feeling that "I can do it all by myself" or "I don't always need help." On the other hand, say that 2-year-old Betty is not allowed to handle a fork or pick up a glass because "she makes such a mess!" This will cause her to feel *shame* and *doubt*, a lack of confidence in her own abilities. If the parent makes a habit of blocking the expression of autonomy, the child may form the negative traits of shame and doubt.

Often one hears the phrase "the terrible twos" in connection with toddlerhood because the need for autonomy often expresses itself in a negative way. Children may say "No!" when you make a reasonable request. Or they may run away when you try to dress them. Instead of looking on this as "bad" behavior, the thoughtful parent will recognize that the motivation arises from the need for autonomy. This does not mean that unacceptable behavior should be allowed; it should be corrected in a realistic way. However, the child does not need to be shamed into compliance.

See also *Erikson, Erik Homburger; psychosexual development; psychosocial development.*

autonomy-control dimension: See *parental style.*

autosomes: The chromosomes in 22 of the 23 pairs of chromosomes in the nucleus of every cell of the human body. The autosomes are distinguished from the chromosomes in the 23rd pair, which are the *sex chromosomes*.

See also *chromosomes; gene; sex chromosomes.*

aversive conditioning: A kind of classical conditioning in which a previously neutral stimulus produces an aversive, unpleasant, or otherwise negative response. For example, suppose that 6-year-old Valerie eats a small green apple and shortly later has a stomachache because the apple was not ripe. If she associates the apple with digestive pain, then the sight of similar apples in the future may produce twinges of nausea or some similar hint of gastric distress. And, logically, Valerie will avoid eating small green apples.

Aversive conditioning can occur in natural settings as described above, or it can be produced in the laboratory. John Watson, the father of behaviorism, and his assistant Rosalie Raynor used an aversive conditioning procedure with an infant known in the psychological literature as Little Albert to demonstrate how a fear can be acquired by learning.

See also *classical conditioning; conditioning; Little Albert; Watson, John Broadus.*

B

babbling: The tendency of infants to spontaneously give voice, at first seemingly at random, to all of the basic phonemes (i.e., individual sounds) used in human speech. Babbling is a part of the *prespeech stage* of language development and is associated with the first year of life.

Although the voicing of phonemes appears to be random to adults, this is not correct. In early infancy, more vowel sounds are uttered than consonants. Babbling is not imitation because even infants with impaired hearing babble in about the same way as infants with normal hearing.

Depending upon the native language of the infant's family, the infant is reinforced for certain sounds with smiles, touches, and other forms of attention. Around the age of 6 months this has a selective effect on the infant's utterances so that the sounds are gradually shaped in such a way that their frequency reflects their likelihood of appearance in the child's native language.

Thus, it is asserted that babbling is the seed from which language grows.

See also *holophrase; language development; morpheme.*

Babinski reflex: A reflex present in most newborn infants and characterized by (1) a fanning out of all five toes and (2) the stretching forward of the big toe. The Babinski reflex is a sign that the infant is neurologically normal. When the infant is about 1 year old, the Babinski reflex vanishes and remains absent. It cannot be elicited in the older child or adult even during sleep. However, the Babinski reflex may reappear when a person is in a coma and is one sign used to ascertain whether or not a person has entered this state.

See also *neonatal reflexes.*

Babkin reflex: One of the reflexes that is present in the neonate and that is characterized by an involuntary opening of the neonate's mouth if pressure is applied to the palms of the hands. The presence of the reflex is one of the signs that the newborn is neurologically normal.

See also *neonatal reflexes.*

"bad" language: See *undesirable language.*

Bandura, Albert (1925–   ): A research psychologist and learning theorist. Bandura was born in Canada, earned a Ph.D. degree from the University of Iowa in 1952, has been a member of the psychology faculty at Stanford University for a number of years, and was a president of the American Psychological Association (1973). Bandura is known primarily for his contributions to the understanding of social (i.e., observational) learning. He has made clear its relation to the acquisition of both prosocial and antisocial behavior during childhood. He conducted important experiments demonstrating how aggressive behavior can be sometimes acquired by watching a model act in an aggressive manner. He has also made important applications of behavior-modification principles, applications of practical value to parents, other caregivers, and behavior therapists.

Two of Bandura's books are *Principles of Behavior Modification* (1969) and *Aggression: A Social Learning Analysis* (1973).

See also *aggressiveness; antisocial behavior; behavior modification; operant conditioning; prosocial behavior; social learning; socialization; television and aggression.*

battered child syndrome: A pattern of injury to a child caused by such acts as punching, slapping, cutting, kicking, and the twisting of limbs. Characteristic injuries are bruises, sprains, and broken bones. Such physical violence against the child is commonly inflicted by the child's parents or principal caretakers. It is estimated that three or four parents out of every hundred sometimes batter a child.

See also *child abuse.*

Bayley Scales of Infant Development: A test used to evaluate the intellectual and developmental level of infants and toddlers. The suitable age range for the test is between the ages of 2 and 30 months. The overall test consists of three individual scales. First, the Mental Scale is used to evaluate the child's ability to remember, learn, speak, and solve simple problems. Second, the Motor Scale is used to evaluate the child's ability to grasp objects, sit or stand, and coordinate muscle activities. Third, the Infant Behavior Record evaluates social and emotional development.

See also *Apgar scale; developmental quotient (DQ); Gesell, Arnold Lucius; Gesell Developmental Schedules; McCarthy Scales of Children's Abilities (MSCA).*

bedwetting: See *enuresis.*

behavior disorder: A disorder characterized by maladaptive behavior. The term *behavior disorder* tends to focus on what is observable in contrast to the more familiar term *mental disorder.* There is, in fact, no formal clinical distinction that can be made between the two terms. Therefore, they are, for all practical purposes, synonyms.

However, it should be noted that some therapists, particularly those who emphasize behavior therapy, prefer "behavior disorder" to "mental disorder." They argue that many troubled persons have no significant mental problems. Their thinking is not grossly disturbed. It is traditional, nonetheless, to include all behavioral pathology in the general category of *mental disorders.*

See also *maladjusted child; mental disorder.*

behavior modification: Applied to children and adolescents, a general term for a set of techniques useful in helping them give up maladaptive behaviors and acquire more adaptive ones. Behavior modification is broadly based on operant conditioning, a kind of learning in which actions are shaped by their own consequences. At the practical level, this simply means that children will tend to give up behaviors that provide few if any reinforcers. Conversely, they will tend to repeat behaviors that bring reinforcers.

A *reinforcer* is similar, but not identical, to a reward. In general, a reinforcer is the consequence of an act that tends to increase the likelihood that the act will be repeated. A reinforcer is valued by the receiver. A *reward*, on the other hand, is valued by the giver. It may or may not have the effect of increasing the likelihood that an act will be repeated. (For a more complete discussion of these points, see *reinforcer*.)

A parent or responsible adult who wants to use behavior modification to improve a child's behavior (e.g., to make it more socialized) will seek ways to reinforce acceptable behavior and avoid ways of inadvertently reinforcing unacceptable behaviors.

Suppose that 4-year-old Garrett has developed the bad habit of acting aggressive and irritated when he wants his mother's attention. Inadvertently, she reinforces the habit every time she responds to impolite behavior on his part. The application of behavior modification requires that the mother be sensitive to Barry's social behavior. She should give him prompt attention when his requests are made in a reasonable manner. This will reinforce acceptable behavior. She should give as little attention and status as possible to impolite behavior. This should eventually produce a decrease in its frequency.

See also *behavior therapy; operant conditioning; punishment; reinforcer; response-cost punishment; time-out procedure.*

behavior therapy: A kind of therapy based on learning principles. The two main kinds of behavior therapy applied to troubled children are behavior modification and systematic desensitization. Behavior modification has been used primarily to help children acquire prosocial behaviors and give up antisocial ones. It has also been used with some success to help children break "bad" (i.e., undesirable) habits. Systematic desensitization has been used primarily to help children cope with anxiety and phobias. It has also been applied with some success to the treatment of stuttering.

The behavior therapist concentrates on what children *do* and *how* they can change. The child's past is usually not explored beyond the minimum requirements necessary to establish a general understanding of the presenting problem. Concepts such as *insight, self-under-*

standing, and *unconscious motivation* are not of great importance to the behavior therapist. Instead, concepts such as *conditioning, learning, change,* and *action* are stressed. The behavior therapist is oriented to the present and what can be done fairly quickly to help a troubled child.

See also *antisocial behavior; behavior modification; cognitive-behavior modification; phobia; prosocial behavior; systematic desensitization.*

behaviorism: A school of psychology asserting that behavior itself, not the mind or consciousness, is the proper subject matter of psychology. The father of behaviorism is John B. Watson, and the school first came into clear existence in the middle of the 1910s.

Behaviorism, unlike psychoanalysis, focuses on learning rather than on motivational and emotional states. Applied to children, it sees their problems in adjustment as failures to acquire adaptive behaviors, behaviors that will be useful to them, their family, and general culture.

Behaviorism was the dominant force in American academic psychology from the 1910s until the 1950s. It is still very influential. However, today's behaviorism is different in some respects from the behaviorism of John Watson. In particular, Watson avoided any talk about what children think. The processes of consciousness, such as perception and thinking, were off limits to Watson because they were not observable to the objective scientist. In contrast, many of today's behaviorists are willing to define thinking as a kind of behavior. And this has led to applications of learning principles to therapy that were not previously possible. In particular, there is now a kind of behavior therapy known as cognitive-behavior modification, in which a direct attempt is made to help children think more clearly and effectively.

See also *behavior therapy; cognitive-behavior modification; psychoanalysis; Watson, John Broadus.*

belongingness and love needs: According to Abraham Maslow, a category of fundamental psychological and emotional needs. Within the category are included (1) *affiliation,* the need to make social and personal contact with others; (2) *acceptance,* the need to be approved of by others; and (3) *affection,* the need to be cared about by others.

These needs are inborn and begin to express themselves early in infancy. They operate as *deficiency needs*, needs that are activated when there is an absence of the desired social stimulus. Belongingness and love needs remain active throughout childhood and life. The needs for love and belongingness are never outgrown. However, if the needs are adequately met, they become rungs on the ladder toward a higher level of social and emotional maturity.

See also *aesthetic needs; cognitive needs; esteem needs; Maslow, Abraham Harold; physiological needs; safety needs; self-actualization.*

Berne, Eric (1910–1970): The father of transactional analysis, a theory of personality and a kind of psychotherapy. Berne was born in Canada and received his M.D. degree there in 1935. He studied psychiatry at the Yale University School of Medicine and continued to reside and work in the United States.

Berne trained to be a psychoanalyst after he became a psychiatrist. However, he broke off an instructional analysis with the famous psychoanalyst Erik Erikson and went on to found his own distinctive approach to therapy. It is evident that transactional analysis owes much to psychoanalysis. In particular, Berne's formulation of the Parent, Adult, and Child ego states bears substantial similarity to Freud's concept of the superego, the ego, and the id. The difference, Berne argued, is that the three ego states are experienced personal realities. In contrast, the agents of the personality identified by psychoanalysis are abstractions.

The really distinctive contribution made by Berne was his focus on the importance of the communication process in human relations. Pathological patterns of communication that repeated themselves over and over, and that kept people from becoming emotionally close, he called *games*. The principal thrust of transactional analysis was to help people exchange thoughts and feelings in a more effective manner. The psychiatrist Harry Stack Sullivan is usually identified as the principal forerunner of the interpersonal approach in psychotherapy, the approach Berne favored. The interpersonal approach is of particular value in understanding dysfunctional families and in applications of family therapy.

Berne had a flair for popular writing, and his ideas came to the attention of the general public. Also, he often gave his concepts colloquial terms in order to give them a striking, memorable quality. Thus, a person with low self-esteem was called a *frog*. A person with high self-esteem was a *prince* or a *princess*. An expression of recognition was a *stroke*. For the reasons cited, Berne was sometimes not taken too seriously by many mental health professionals. However, substantial numbers of psychiatrists, clinical psychologists, and social workers do find merit in Berne's ideas.

Among Berne's books are *Transactional Analysis in Psychotherapy* (1961), *Games People Play* (1964), and *What Do You Say After You Say Hello?* (1972). The last book has much to say about family interactions and their effects on the developing child.

See also *dysfunctional family; ego; ego state; Erikson, Erik Homburger; family therapy; Freud, Sigmund; id; psychoanalysis; self-esteem; stroke; Sullivan, Harry Stack; superego; transactional analysis.*

Bettelheim, Bruno (1903–1990): A psychoanalyst and educational psychologist. Bettelheim was associated for a major part of his professional career with the University of Chicago and its orthogenic school, a care facility for emotionally disturbed children. Working in the setting of the school, he made important contributions to child psychotherapy.

Bettelheim asserted that love for a child by a parent was not in and of itself enough to assure normal development in the child. Instead, a parent needs to be aware of a child's perceptions of the parent's intentions and expectations. Consequently, the parent needs to develop skills in order to be effective.

Also, as a part of development, children need to confront their fears and forbidden impulses. Bettelheim believed that fairy tales and similar stories for children helped them to do this.

Among Bettelheim's books are *Love Is Not Enough: The Treatment of Emotionally Disturbed Children* (1950) and *The Uses of Enchantment: Meaning and Importance of Fairy Tales* (1978).

See also *child psychotherapy; communication skills; educational psychology; fairy tales; parent effectiveness training (PET); parental style; psychoanalysis.*

bidirectionality of influence: The tendency of the relationship between parent and child to be a two-way emotional street. Much has been written on the way in which parental style and emotional attitude affect the personal and social development of children. Less obvious is the fact that the personality of a child elicits certain kinds of behaviors on the part of parents. For example, suppose that 4-year-old Matthew is an "easy" child. He is agreeable and responds well to reasonable correction. This will elicit from his parents a parental style characterized by a democratic attitude and displays of spontaneous affection. On the other hand, suppose that 4-year-old Andrew is a "difficult" child. He is strong-willed and resists correction. This will elicit from his parents a parental style characterized by an authoritarian attitude and the withholding, or manipulation, of affection.

The theory of the bidirectionality of influence has been applied to explain the behavior patterns associated with the parents of autistic children, particularly the mother. It used to be thought that the mothers of autistic children were "cold" and rejecting mothers. This was seen as a primary cause of infantile autism. On the other hand, it is now generally agreed that infantile autism is a biogenic disorder and appears without significant parental provocation in the predisposed child. Autistic infants do not cling affectionately to the mother; they avoid eye contact; they hate to be touched; and so forth. It is easy to imagine how these behaviors on the part of an infant may quickly make a mother "cold."

See also *attachment; attachment disorder; authoritarian parent; autistic disorder; parental style.*

Binet, Alfred (1857–1911): The principal author of the first practical intelligence tests. Binet was a French researcher who, in collaboration with his colleague Theodore Simon (1873-1961), developed at the request of the French government a way of evaluating the intelligence of children. The collaboration led to the eventual publication of the Binet-Simon Intelligence Scale and the introduction of the concept of mental age.

The concept of *intelligence quotient* (IQ) was not introduced by Binet and Simon but was suggested instead by Wilhelm Stern (1871-1938), a German psychologist. IQ is based on a comparison of mental age with chronological age.

Prior efforts to test intelligence had failed because the researchers attempted to make direct assessments of biological capacities. For example, the English scientist Sir Francis Galton (1822–1911) thought intelligence might be related to the quickness of one's reflexes. It turns out that it is difficult to show any clear one-to-one link between biological measurements and intelligence.

Instead, Binet took the very practical road of measuring a child's actual performance on intellectual tasks. Thus, a child was asked to answer questions having to do with vocabulary, arithmetic, comprehension, and recognition of familiar objects. Binet assumed that intelligence *is* as intelligence *does*.

The Binet-Simon Scale was adapted for use in the United States by the Stanford psychologist Lewis Terman and was eventually published as the Stanford-Binet Scale. The Stanford-Binet Scale is generally regarded as the first practical intelligence test used in the United States.

See also *chronological age (CA); Galton, Francis; intelligence; intelligence quotient (IQ); mental age (MA); Stanford-Binet Intelligence Scale; Terman, Lewis Madison.*

biogenic factors: Factors that play a role in development and are assumed to have an inborn, or genetic, basis. Biogenic factors are of particular importance in our efforts to understand severe mental disturbances such as mental retardation, infantile autism, and childhood schizophrenia. All three of these conditions appear to be caused in large part by inborn predispositions.

To a smaller extent, biogenic factors can also be referred to in explanations of personality development in general. Various studies suggest that temperament is to a large extent inborn and relatively stable over time.

See also *autistic disorder; childhood schizophrenia; mental retardation; psychogenic factors; temperament.*

biological drives: A group of inborn drives that induce organisms to (1) respond to physiological needs and (2) avoid tissue destruction. The biological drives include such drives as hunger, thirst, the need for sleep, temperature maintenance, oxygen hunger, and pain avoidance. They are sometimes called the "energizers of behavior," and they represent the foundation of our motivational structure.

With some qualifications, the biological drives tend to follow the principle of *homeostasis*, a tendency to maintain an optimal constant level. A prime example is the hunger drive. When blood sugar is too low a person feels hungry and seeks food. When blood sugar is too high, one feels sated and avoids food. Infants cry for milk when they are hungry and turn away from the breast or bottle when they have had enough.

As indicated above, the biological drives are present at birth and tend to function on a person's behalf throughout life.

See also *id; physiological needs; primary reinforcer.*

biological parent: A parent who contributed one-half of a child's genetic constitution. In the case of the biological mother, this is contributed through the ovum. In the case of the biological father, this is contributed through the sperm.

Sometimes one hears the term *surrogate mother* used to describe a woman who has been impregnated by artificial insemination in order to provide a childless couple with a baby. Strictly speaking, she is not a surrogate mother if she provides the ovum. She is the biological mother. However, if the female member of the childless couple provides her own ovum, if fertilization takes place *in vitro* (i.e, "in glass" outside of the mother's body), or if a second female acts as host to an implanted embryo, then it is appropriate to speak of her as a surrogate mother.

The importance of biological parents in child development is becoming increasingly obvious. A number of studies have shown that adopted children who have had little or no contact since infancy with their biological parents often show remarkable similarities to them in some of their personality traits. Also, if a biological parent has a mental disorder such as schizophrenia, the child of that parent is at somewhat greater risk than average to become a victim of the disorder. Again, this is true even of adopted children.

See also *adoptive parent; genetic predisposition;* in vitro *fertilization.*

bipolar disorder: See *mood stabilizing drugs.*

birth defects: Biological imperfections that are readily detectable in a neonate. These are also known as *congenital defects.* Approximately one percent of newborn children have a serious birth defect that requires medical attention. Another one percent have minor defects.

The most common birth defect is heart disease. Approximately 7 out of every 1,000 neonates are born with a significant heart problem. Other common birth defects include mental retardation, inadequate brain development, spina bifida (i.e., exposure of the spinal cord), Down's syndrome, and cleft palate. Less common birth defects include impaired hearing, cystic fibrosis, and Turner's syndrome.

There is a spectrum of causal factors that contribute to birth defects. These include genetic anomalies, the toxic effects of drugs (including alcohol) taken during pregnancy, and infections (e.g., rubella).

See also *fetal alcohol syndrome (FAS); genetic anomaly; mental retardation; rubella; Turner's syndrome.*

birth order: The sequence in which siblings are born. Such familiar phrases as "the firstborn child," "the oldest daughter," "the middle child," and "the baby of the family" suggest a high level of conscious awareness of the importance of birth order in family status.

Alfred Adler, an important figure in the early history of psychoanalysis, hypothesized that birth order was a major causal factor in personality development. The firstborn child is for a time an only child. He or she basks in the undivided love of the parents and is a little prince or princess. Then the child is dethroned and becomes concerned with regaining lost status. For these reasons, the firstborn tends to become somewhat power-oriented.

The secondborn child often attempts to copy the behavior of the older sibling. As a consequence, this child becomes achievement-oriented. The child who is born last is sometimes "spoiled" and is not expected to do too much. This may lead to an overly passive attitude toward life.

Adler based his conclusions on astute clinical observations. A number of studies have attempted to evaluate the impact of birth order on personality, and Adler's clear-cut hypotheses have not been supported. There *is* a relationship between birth order and development, but it is complex and involves a number of factors. So it is difficult to make blunt statements about personality derived simply from birth order. In general, however, it can be said that studies tend to support, with many exceptions, a tendency for firstborn children to have a somewhat higher need to achieve than other children in the family. (This finding is somewhat at odds with Adler's observations.) Also, related to the need for achievement, firstborn children tend to receive somewhat better grades in school than do their siblings.

See also *Adler, Alfred; dethroning; inferiority complex; only child; sibling rivalry.*

birth trauma: A term that has acquired two meanings; that is, (1) in general, the gross disturbance experienced by infants when they are forced to make the relatively abrupt transition from the comfort and security of the womb to the harsher demands of an external existence; and (2) according to the hypothesis of Otto Rank, the physical and emotional pain of being born as the individual's first encounter with anxiety. If the birth is particulary painful, Rank, a member of Freud's inner circle in the early years of psychoanalysis, believed that this might translate into a general and relatively enduring fear of life. Although Freud accepted the importance of the birth trauma, he believed that Rank had exaggerated its importance as a causal factor in personality development.

Although the significance of the birth trauma is debatable, it stands to reason that anything that can be done in a practical way to reduce an infant's pain and discomfort upon its first encounter with the world in which it will live for many years should be done.

See also *Lamaze method; Leboyer method; Rank, Otto.*

bladder control: See *toilet training.*

blindness: See *visual impairment.*

blink reflex: One of the reflexes that is present in the neonate and that is characterized by an involuntary blink if the neonate's eyes are subjected to a sudden burst of light, an abrupt concentration of air pressure, or the too-rapid approach of an object. The obvious purpose of this reflex is to protect the eyes against potential injury. The blink reflex is never outgrown, and it retains the described pattern for life.

See also *neonatal reflexes.*

body type: An individual's kind of physical constitution. According to the personality theorist William H. Sheldon, there are three dimensions that contribute to body type. These are endomorphy, mesomorphy, and ectomorphy. Each is innately determined and is due to a genetic predisposition in the individual. *Endomorphy* is associated with a soft, round, flabby body. *Mesomorphy* is associated with a hard, muscular, athletic body. *Ectomorphy* is associated with a slim, frail, thin body. A person's combined rating on the three dimensions is his or her *somatotype*, or body type.

Sheldon contended that his research indicated that there are three inborn traits of temperament associated with the three dimensions. These are viscerotonia, somatotonia, and cerebrotonia. *Viscerotonia* is associated with endomorphy and suggests a self-indulgent person who loves to relax and enjoy the good things of life. *Somatotonia* is associated with mesomorphy and suggests a highly assertive person who constantly craves action and adventure. *Cerebrotonia* is associated with ectomorphy and suggests an inhibited, introverted person with a preference for solitary activities.

If correct, Sheldon's research has important implications for child rearing because it says that to a large extent the child's temperament, a major component of personality, is inborn. Consequently, the thoughtful parent will accept the child as he or she is and work with, not against, the inborn temperament. It is important to note, however, that there is no consensus in psychology that Sheldon's work is basically descriptive of the nature of temperament. On the contrary, it is believed by many psychologists that body type, if it is linked to temperament, is simply one factor among others.

See also *genetic predisposition; innate; nativism; personality development; temperament; trait.*

bonding of parent and child: See *attachment.*

bowel control: See *toilet training.*

brain damage: Injury to the brain as a result of a trauma, an infection, or a tumor. Chromosomal anomalies may interfere with the normal development of the brain and nervous system during the fetal period. Also, inherited disorders can impair normal brain functioning.

Brain damage can be a cause or a complicating factor in a variety of childhood difficulties, including hearing impairment, visual impairment, various learning disabilities, motor-coordination problems, attention-deficit hyperactivity disorder, and mental retardation.

Examples of traumata (i.e., "wounds") are oxygen deprivation associated with the birthing process (see *anoxia*), a head injury sustained as the result of an accident, and fetal alcohol syndrome. Examples of infections that can cause brain damage are congenital syphilis, rubella (i.e., German measles) during pregnancy, and bacterial meningitis. *Tumors* are abnormal growths and can be benign or malignant. However, even benign, or noncancerous, tumors can cause brain damage.

Examples of disorders associated with chromosomal anomalies are Down's syndrome, Turner's syndrome, and super males (i.e., males with an extra Y chromosome). One of the common effects of these disorders is to impair intelligence. Examples of inherited defects that have an adverse effect on brain functioning are phenylketonuria (PKU) and Tay-Sachs disease.

See also *anoxia; attention-deficit hyperactivity disorder (ADHD); chromosomal anomalies; Down's syndrome; fetal alcohol syndrome (FAS); fetal development; hearing impairment; mental retardation; motor development; phenylketonuria (PKU); rubella; sexually transmitted diseases (STDs); super males; Tay-Sachs disease; Turner's syndrome.*

Brazelton neonatal scale: See *Neonatal Behavioral Assessment Scale (NBAS)*.

breastfeeding: The way in which mammalian mothers feed their infants. So basic to survival is the process of breastfeeding that one of the neonatal reflexes is the *rooting reflex*, a turning of the head, with associated sucking, in the direction of the breast when the cheek is stroked by the nipple. Aside from its nutritional value, mother's milk provides antibodies that help an infant ward off infectious illnesses.

From the psychological point of view, it is usually noted that breastfeeding fosters attachment of an infant to its mother. However, it seems evident that it is not breastfeeding in and of itself that fosters attachment, but the holding of the infant combined with attention and expressions of affection. This can also be accomplished during bottlefeeding and is one of the ways in which infants can become attached to their fathers.

If possible, an infant should be breastfed. On the other hand, if breastfeeding is difficult or impossible, for medical or other reasons, infants who are bottlefed normally thrive quite well.

See also *attachment; oral stage; rooting reflex.*

Bruner, Jerome S. (1915–): A research psychologist associated for a number of years with Harvard University, and a former director of its Center for Cognitive Studies. Bruner has made important investigations into both cognitive development and language development. His findings have had important implications for educational psychology and the rearing of children. He is recognized for his formulation of the distinction between enactive, iconic, and symbolic modes of thought.

Among books written by Bruner, or in collaboration with other authors, are *A Study of Thinking* (1956), *Toward a Theory of Instruction* (1966), and *Child's Talk: Learning to Use Language* (1983).

See also *cognitive development; educational psychology; enactive mode of thought; iconic mode of thought; language development; symbolic mode of thought.*

bulimia nervosa: An eating disorder characterized by alternate phases of compulsive binge eating and desperate purge attempts, the latter in order to undo the effects of the binge. Like anorexia nervosa, the victims of bulimia nervosa tend to be young females. Often the origins of the disorder in an individual case can be traced back to behaviors that first appeared in adolescence. Males can and do suffer from bulimia nervosa, but females with it outnumber males by about eight to one. According to various studies, the incidence of bulimia is between 1 and 3 percent of the young middle-class female population.

During the binge-eating phase of bulimia nervosa, the individual may eat two or three times the amount of food normally consumed at a meal. Often the binge eating takes place between meals, secretly, and may consist of easy-to-eat foods with high caloric density. During the purge phase, the individual may go on a severe diet, avoid food altogether for two or three days, engage in compulsive exercise, or find ways to cause vomiting after eating.

Bulimia nervosa tends to be a chronic disorder, one that afflicts the individual for a number of years. Usually, individuals with the disease function fairly well as students or employees. However, the disease takes a physical toll. In the case of those who purge by vomiting, there is often damage to the teeth because gastric juices tend to be destructive to the enamel. In addition, the erratic eating pattern may adversely affect levels of important electrolytes in the body. Irregular heart patterns and other negative signs can be a result. A tendency toward hypoglycemia (i.e., low blood sugar) can be aggravated.

Causal factors in bulimia nervosa are several. Studies have shown that victims often have obese parents or siblings. Thus, the binge eater often has a fear of obesity. A culture that stresses the value of being a thin woman has been blamed. The compulsive eating of food is used to satisfy more than one emotional need (e.g., the need for love, the need to express anger). If the person has a tendency toward compulsive eating and at the same time has a strong desire to avoid obesity, the unsatisfactory psychological compromise between the two opposing tendencies is bulimia nervosa.

The treatment of choice for bulimia nervosa is psychotherapy. Usually the therapist stresses insight into the unconscious motives for wanting to binge. This approach is combined with behavior modification to help the individual cope with self-defeating habits. Victims of the disease often make good candidates for psychotherapy because they are well aware that they are suffering and would like to be rid of their affliction.

See also *anorexia nervosa; eating disorders; pica; rumination disorder of infancy.*

C

canalization: In the psychological domain, an inherited tendency to learn certain kinds of behaviors easily. Certain behaviors are weakly canalized. Others are strongly canalized. Learning to swim may be said to be weakly canalized, or perhaps not canalized at all, in human beings because many people never learn to swim. On the other hand, learning to talk may be said to be strongly canalized because almost all human beings acquire the behavior.

The concept of canalization is somewhat more sophisticated than the concept of an instinct because it includes the impact of experience on the expression of inborn tendencies.

See also *genetic predisposition; innate; instinct; language acquisition device (LAD).*

cannabis: See *marijuana.*

carbamazepine: See *mood stabilizing drugs.*

caretaker speech: A way of talking in which a responsible adult (e.g., a parent, a teacher) simplifies language in order to match the level of development of a child. Caretaker speech is almost universally used when speaking to toddlers and preschoolers. It should not be thought of as "talking down" to the child, because its purpose is to facilitate communication and foster language development. Distinguishing features of caretaker speech include sentences of relatively few words, a restricted vocabulary, and a greater than usual range of facial and emotional expressiveness.

See also *active vocabulary*; *language development*; *speech therapy*.

castration complex: In psychoanalysis, a set of repressed ideas surrounding a fear of the loss of one's genitals. The term *castration complex* is applicable to males only and may form in early childhood (around the age of 5) as a result of incest wishes toward the mother and a perceived threat from the father. At the conscious level, a castration complex expresses itself as a fear of losing a part of the body superficially resembling the penis, such as a finger, a toe, a limb, or one's nose. The castration complex is a part of a more pervasive complex known as the Oedipus complex. Although it is doubtful that all boys form a castration complex, it seems defensible to assert that some do.

See also *Oedipus complex; penis envy.*

Cattell, James McKeen (1860–1944): One of the early researchers into the subject of psychological testing and a professor of psychology at Columbia University for more than 25 years. Cattell made major contributions to the methods used in the standardization of psychological tests, including intelligence tests.

In his student years, Cattell did graduate work under Wilhelm Wundt (1832-1920) at the University of Leipzig in Germany. Wundt is recognized as the founder in 1879 of the world's first scientific laboratory dedicated to the study of psychological subjects. Cattell was reluctant to follow in Wundt's footsteps and investigate the nature of human consciousness, one of Wundt's principal interests. Instead, Cattell was curious about individual differences. Pursuing this interest, he spent some time in England exploring ways of evaluating human abilities with Francis Galton, a pioneer researcher in the area of testing and measurement.

In 1895, Cattell was elected the president of the American Psychological Association. He was a principal founder in 1924 of the Psychological Corporation, a major publisher of psychological tests. Cattell is considered be one of the principal persons responsible for the strong tendency in the United States for psychology to be both practical and applied.

See also *correlation; Galton, Francis; individual differences; intelligence; intelligence tests; reliability of a test; validity of a test.*

cephalocaudal development: A strong tendency for the processes of growth and maturation to proceed in a downward direction, with the first important changes taking place in the head. (The literal meaning of the word *cephalocaudal* is "head-to-tail.") This is evident in fetal development. The eyes and brain are well formed in advance of the lower extremities.

Cephalocaudal development is also evident after birth. Infants acquire the ability to turn the head and pay attention before they can successfully grasp objects. And they can grasp objects before they can crawl or walk.

See also *fetal development; proximodistal development; walking alone.*

cerebral palsy: An impairment in the ability to move arising from brain damage during the fetal period or shortly after birth. The vast majority of cerebral palsy cases are due to an inadequate oxygen supply to the fetus. Other causes during pregnancy include infections and biochemical imbalances. After birth, injuries to the head or infections are relatively infrequent causes. It is estimated that 1 or 2 infants out of every 500 have cerebral palsy.

Three different ways to classify cerebral palsy are diplegia, hemiplegia, and quadriplegia. In *diplegia,* the greatest impairment is associated with the legs. In *hemiplegia,* the greatest impairment is associated with either the right or left half of the body, and the impairment of the arm is greater than that of the leg. In *quadriplegia,* both the arms and the legs are impaired. It is also possible in a general way to classify cerebral palsy as *mild* or *severe.*

Although mental retardation is often associated with cerebral palsy, this is not necessarily the case for all individuals. Persons with cerebral palsy often have normal intelligence and should be treated accordingly.

Cerebral palsy is a permanent affliction. It can be treated, but not cured. Thus, its victims can, through physical therapy, learn to make maximum use of whatever abilities they possess. From the psychological point of view, it is important to accept the disability of children with cerebral palsy without making them feel they are at fault in some way. It is essential to do whatever can be done to build self-esteem. Many children with cerebral palsy grow up to live productive, rewarding lives.

See also *anoxia; birth defects; fetal development; mental retardation.*

cesarean section (cesarean operation): The making of an incision in both the abdominal wall and the uterus of a pregnant woman in order to give birth to a child. Legend states that the Roman general Julius Caesar (ca. 104–44 B.C.) was born in this manner. An equally plausible possibility is that the term *cesarean* is derived from a Latin word meaning "to cut."

The principal reason to perform a cesarean section is to avoid a stressful birth that presents a high risk to the infant and/or the mother. Causes of stressful birth include a breech position, a pelvic opening that is inadequate, and a placenta that is pressed too tightly against the cervix. Sometimes a cesarean section is performed in an attempt to avoid a herpes infection in the infant if the mother is already infected. Approximately 25 percent of deliveries in the United States are through cesarean section.

Avoiding a stressful birth through cesarean section may save an infant from loss of oxygen and, thus, damage to the brain and nervous system and/or other medical complications.

Some critics of contemporary medical practice believe that cesarean sections have become too common. They assert that some cesarean sections are performed mainly to avoid potential lawsuits or for other borderline considerations. Obviously, there is nothing routine about a cesarean section, and it should be performed only for sound medical reasons. On the other hand, it is essential to balance criticism and recognize that many mothers and infants have benefited by the use of the cesarean section.

See also *birth defects; birth trauma; Lamaze method; Leboyer method; sexually transmitted diseases (STDs).*

character: Those traits of personality that stand out and readily stamp one as an individual; the outer manifestations of one's personality.

William James, the dean of American psychologists, said that the character is completely formed by young adulthood. After that, he suggested that it is set "like plaster" and is next to unchangeable.

Even if James was overly pessimistic about the malleability of one's character, it certainly seems evident that children have more flexibility and plasticity of character than do adults. For this reason, most responsible parents are concerned about ways to mold a child's character in a positive direction. In general, a child with a "good" character (or sometimes simply "with character") is conceived of as being responsible, having good study habits, and exhibiting a large range of prosocial behaviors.

See also *James, William; personality development; prosocial behavior; socialization.*

cheating: Applied to the classroom, using dishonest means to improve one's performance on an examination. Almost everyone is familiar with the principal methods of cheating: copying homework, handing in reports or papers done by someone else, sneaking a look at someone else's paper, whispering answers in response to the questions of another student, or using a crib sheet. Everyone is familiar with these methods because cheating is very common among both children and adolescents. Although cheating cannot be condoned, if a child cheats, it is not a sign of complete moral degeneration. Studies have shown that cheating is not a pervasive personality trait. It is almost entirely situational and is elicited to some extent from the child by a desire to excel and win adult approval.

The best way to curb cheating in the classroom is for a teacher to effectively proctor an examination and to convince students of any age that they will not be able to cheat without getting caught. It is *not* a good idea to tell students that they are trusted, that they are on "their honor," and that minimal supervision will be exercised. This is flying in the face of reality.

If a child is caught cheating, an example of a proper response is for the child to receive an *F* on the examination in question. If the child does passing work on a future examination, then the child will have earned the right to repeat the failed examination under proper supervision. The child should be made to feel that the cheating was an unsuccessful ploy and that it is unlikely to succeed in the future. And a constructive opportunity should be offered. Neither teachers nor parents need to use excessive punishment and lengthy moral messages. These are likely to alienate the child and have the opposite effect from the one intended.

See also *antisocial behavior; character; open classroom; school achievement.*

child: In the context of developmental psychology, a human being between the approximate ages of 2 and 12. The time span approximately from ages 2 to 6 is called *early childhood.* The time span approximately from ages 6 to 10 is called *middle childhood.* The time span approximately from ages 10 to 12 is called *late childhood* or *preadolescence.*

A parent may properly speak of a son or daughter as "my child" no matter how old the offspring is.

See also *adolescence; latency stage; toddlerhood.*

child abuse: A pattern of behavior in which the adults in a child's life batter, exploit, molest, or otherwise mistreat the child. As indicated, the pattern of abuse need not be physical. Negligence and insults can also be forms of abuse.

Child neglect can be thought of as a kind of passive abuse and refers to not meeting the child's biological, psychological, and emotional needs. Examples of child neglect include inadequate diets leading to malnutrition, social isolation, and lack of love and affection. Such neglect may have a highly adverse impact on the child's physical, mental, and social development.

Unfortunately, abusers are often parents. There are many causes of abusive behavior. Some of the factors that have been identified in abusive parents are these: youth, low intelligence, mental disorders, criminal background, marriage difficulties, poverty, job instability, and a personal history of having been abused.

Child abuse can have highly adverse effects on both a child's physical and emotional development. Mental health problems in an adult may stem in part from abuse as a child.

Adults who abuse children are subject to criminal prosecution.

See also *battered child syndrome; discipline; latchkey children; parental style.*

Child ego state: See *ego state.*

child neglect: See *child abuse.*

child psychology: The study of the behavior of children. As presently conceived by a majority of behavioral scientists, psychology includes the study of both covert and overt behavior. *Covert* behavior includes thoughts, perceptions, and feelings. *Overt* behavior refers to observable actions. Thus, contemporary researchers in child psychology explore not only what children do, but what children think and feel.

It is possible to think of child psychology as a subcategory of developmental psychology. Developmental psychology studies all aspects of the individual's growth and behavior from the moment of conception to death. Child psychology focuses on a briefer time frame, usually from conception to the end of adolescence.

See also *developmental psychology; theories of development.*

child psychotherapy: The application of the principles and techniques of psychotherapy to the treatment of troubled children. There is nothing unique about child psychotherapy in and of itself. It is best understood in the larger context of general psychotherapy. The literal meaning of *psychotherapy* is "healing the self." Sometimes psychotherapy is called the "talking cure" because it is a process that takes place without drugs or other medical intervention. Today's psychotherapy may be broadly conceived as the application of psychological principles to the treatment of personal problems and mental disorders.

There are several approaches to psychotherapy, and these are generally described as psychodynamic, behavioral, humanistic, cognitive, and interpersonal. The *psychodynamic* approach assumes that the personality is a battlefield of conflicting motivational forces. The *behavioral* approach assumes that most personal difficulties have their roots in the learning process. The *humanistic* approach assumes that many personal problems arise when the natural growth of the self is inhibited or blocked. The *cognitive* approach assumes that confused and illogical thoughts reside behind many personal problems.

• 53 •

The *interpersonal* approach assumes that emotional and behavioral problems often arise in the context of a relationship between two or more people. Each of these general approaches has spawned a number of specific kinds of psychotherapy within it. It is important to realize that these approaches are not necessarily mutually exclusive. Many psychotherapists, perhaps most, prefer to pick and choose among the identified approaches. These psychotherapists use their own judgment in such a way as to be of practical, effective help to their patients and clients without allegiance to a single viewpoint.

Two of the early pioneers in child psychotherapy were Anna Freud and Melanie Klein.

See also *behavior modification; behavior therapy; cognitive-behavior modification; Freud, Anna; Klein, Melanie; psychoanalysis; systematic desensitization.*

childhood: See *child.*

childhood masturbation: See *masturbation.*

childhood neurosis: In classical psychoanalytical theory, emotional difficulties experienced in childhood as a result of anxiety associated with unconscious motives and ideas. The child with a neurosis has good reality contact and is not demented or lacking in intelligence. On the contrary, the child is usually bright and socialized. Informally, the child may be described as "nervous" and usually displays the "good little boy" or "good little girl" pattern. Such a child is anxious to please the parent and tends to repress personal feelings.

Psychological and psychiatric language has evolved over the years, and it is no longer technically correct to diagnose a child or adult as having "a neurosis." The American Psychiatric Association's *Diagnostic and Statistical Manual of Mental Disorders* does not recognize neurosis as a specific disorder. However, it continues to be correct to speak of a neurotic process. A *neurotic process* takes place when, as indicated in the first paragraph, the individual is the victim of intense emotional conflict. Therefore, a neurotic process is one of the causal factors in a number of specific behavioral problems such as phobias, sleep disturbances, skin rashes, stuttering, obsessions, compulsions, and chronic worry.

See also *anxiety; phobia; psychoanalysis; sleep patterns; sleepwalking disorder; stuttering.*

childhood schizophrenia: Traditionally, the appearance of schizophrenia during middle childhood after a period of development in infancy and early childhood that appeared to be normal. *Schizophrenia* itself is a severe mental disorder characterized by a gross impairment in the ability to think in logical and rational terms. Related symptoms frequently include delusions, hallucinations, odd use of language, and loss of touch with reality as most people understand it. The behavior of persons suffering from this disorder is often, but not always, bizarre. Schizophrenia represents what has been informally called "madness" in the Western world.

The term *childhood schizophrenia* has only informal meaning now because it no longer appears as a diagnostic category in the *Diagnostic and Statistical Manual of Mental Disorders* published by the American Psychiatric Association. The reason for its absence is because a substantial amount of research has failed to establish a clear connection between mental confusion, delusions, hallucinations, and other associated states in children. It is now recommended that what used to be called "childhood schizophrenia" be referred to as a profound *developmental disorder.*

A number of psychiatrists and clinical psychologists remain willing to make a connection between childhood and schizophrenia. If this is done, it is considered somewhat preferable to use such expressions as *schizophrenia with onset in childhood* or *early-onset schizophrenia* instead of "childhood schizophrenia." The aim is to indicate that "childhood schizophrenia" is not a unique disease in and of itself.

The incidence of early-onset schizophrenia is very low. It is estimated to be somewhat lower than autistic disorder, which has an incidence of approximately 1 or 2 children per 5,000. Two-thirds of children who suffer from schizophrenia are males.

It is widely recognized that schizophrenia tends to make its first appearance in adolescence or young adulthood. During this chronological period, the disorder is not considered to be rare, but relatively common. The overall rate of schizophrenia, including adults, is approximately 1 percent. A practical measure that is applied to prognosis and recovery is called the "rule of thirds." About one third of patients will become chronic cases, about one third will have off and on bouts with their disorder, and about one third will make a full recovery. Males and females are affected in equal numbers.

Schizophrenia is thought of as a functional disorder, not an organic one. It is usually said to be the most severe kind of functional mental disorder. It is classified as functional, however, *not* because biological and organic factors are absent, but because their presence and action are subtle. As research evidence has been gathering, the importance of biological and organic factors is becoming increasingly evident. Therefore, one cannot really say that this disorder is clearly and simply functional in nature.

A tremendous amount of thought and research has gone into attempting to explain schizophrenia. Below are listed some of the principal explanations. However, it should be realized that the explanations overlap. Also, multiple causal factors may be operating in a given case.

1. It is possible that schizophrenia has a *genetic basis*. Studies of families have clearly revealed that if one identical twin has schizophrenia, a second identical twin is more likely to have the disorder than a nontwin sibling. Because identical twins have identical hereditary structures, this suggests strongly that genetic factors make a contribution to this disorder.

2. It is possible that an *inherited defect in the brain* of persons with schizophrenia makes it difficult for them to process information in the same way as normal persons.

3. There is evidence to suggest that one of the causal factors in schizophrenia is *excessive activity of the neurotransmitter dopamine*. This is known as the *dopamine hypothesis.*

4. Psychoanalysis suggests that *fixations of libido at the oral stage* of development may contribute to the formation of schizophrenia. The oral stage is the most primitive level of psychosexual development, and much of the behavior of persons with schizophrenia is regressive and infantile.

5. There is some research data to suggest that some *parents are schizophrenogenic*; that is, they inadvertently do things to bring

out the disorder. They mix up and confuse the child during the developmental years. In particular, it is believed that they tend to use double-bind communication patterns that create insolvable psychological problems for their children.

6. *Severe psychosocial stressors* may be important precipitating factors in schizophrenia. If a person believes that he or she cannot cope with reality, then the individual may take flight into a fantasy world.

As indicated before, a substantial amount of effort has been expended in an attempt to explain schizophrenia. An equally great effort has gone into treatment. Although there is no "cure" for schizophrenia, treatments are often effective and can ameliorate the worst symptoms of a given patient's disorder. The two principal approaches to treatment are (1) drug therapy, in which antipsychotic drugs are prescribed, and (2) behavior therapy, in which applications of behavior modification are made. Electroconvulsive therapy (ECT) was frequently used in the past to treat schizophrenia. It is sometimes still used, but infrequently. In most cases, a patient with schizophrenia will not be a resident of a mental hospital for life but will be helped through treatment to live in the larger world.

See also *autistic disorder; behavior modification; dementia praecox; developmental disorders; drug therapy; echolalia; genetic predisposition; oral stage.*

child-rearing practices: The specific techniques and methods used by parents, or persons serving in parental roles, to raise children. These include the whole range of things adults do to influence child behavior and development, ranging from rewards to punishments, from acceptance to rejection, from speaking rationally to tongue lashings, and from keeping one's temper to losing it. Various studies of child-rearing practices suggest that they vary greatly from family to family and from culture to culture. Against all psychological logic, it seems that children grow up reasonably well across a broad range of methods. It seems that it is not possible to pinpoint a distinct set of optimal methods for raising children.

However, it can be said with a reasonable degree of confidence that the child needs a basic foundation of parental affection and acceptance. The unloved child has difficulty thriving. This, however, is not a method, but a basic orientation on the parent's part.

See also *behavior modification; communication skills; discipline; parental style.*

Chomsky, Noam Avram (1928–   ): An innovative researcher in the area of linguistics. Chomsky earned a Ph.D. degree from the University of Pennsylvania and became a member of the faculty of the Massachusetts Institute of Technology (M.I.T.) in 1955. Chomsky's theories have had an influence on studies of both language development and cognitive development.

Unlike behavioristic psychologists, such as John Watson and B. F. Skinner, who focus on the learning process, Chomsky stresses the importance of inborn tendencies to acquire and use language. This is summarized in his concept of a *language acquisition device (LAD).* Chomsky's general approach to language development reflects nativism in contrast to empiricism.

Chomsky does not, of course, assert that learning is of no importance in language development. He indicates, however, that inborn tendencies to speak are primary. They provide a foundation upon which learning builds a psychological house.

Among Chomsky's books are *Language and the Mind* (1968) and *Reflections of Language* (1975).

See also *cognitive development; empiricism; language acquisition device (LAD); language development; nativism; Skinner, Burrhus Frederic; Watson, John Broadus.*

chorionic villus sampling: See *amniocentesis.*

chromosomal anomalies: Abnormal chromosome patterns. There are 23 pairs of chromosomes in the normal fertilized ovum. Sometimes a given pair has an extra chromosome, a condition known as *trisomy.* Sometimes a member is missing from a pair. The individual that develops from an ovum with a chromosomal anomaly will often display an abnormal pattern of development. One example is Trisomy 21, in which there is an extra chromosome on the 21st pair. This combination is responsible for children with Down's syndrome. If an ovum has a single X chromosome on the 23rd pair, the associated disorder is called Turner's syndrome. A number of chromosomal anomalies and their associated syndromes have been identified.

See also *Down's syndrome; gene; trisomy; Turner's syndrome.*

chromosomes: Bodies that carry genes. The literal meaning of the word *chromosome* is "colored body." They are so named because when stained they are visible under a microscope. Located in a cell nucleus, chromosomes are relatively large and carry many genes. The relationship of a chromosome to a set of genes can be roughly compared to the relationship of a ship to a crew. The ship (i.e., the chromosome) carries the crew (i.e., the genes), who do all of the actual work. There are 23 pairs of chromosomes in the nucleus of a normal cell.

See also *chromosomes; gene; heredity.*

chronological age (CA): A person's actual age in terms of measured time (e.g., days, months, and years). Chronological age is useful in establishing norms of development. A certain level of maturation, learning, and growth is expected in association with a given chronological age. The concept of chronological age also played an important part in the original formulation of the concept of the intelligence quotient. In its first form, an intelligence quotient was a ratio derived from a comparison of a child's mental age with the child's chronological age.

See also *intelligence quotient (IQ); mental age (MA); norms of development.*

circular reactions: Behavior patterns that stimulate their own repetition; in other words, a chain of self-stimulating action. According to Piaget, circular reactions in infancy play an important part in providing a foundation for later cognitive development. He identifies three types of circular reactions, each one indicating a somewhat higher level of development and maturity than the prior one. *Primary circular reactions* focus on the self. Examples include sucking on a pacifier or the thumb or playing with the feet. *Secondary circular reactions* focus on the external world. Examples include shaking a rattle over and over again and rolling a ball back and forth on a high-chair tray. *Tertiary circular reactions* also focus on the external world and involve the discovery of causes and effects. Examples include turning a light switch on and off and opening and closing a little door on a "busy box" in order to reveal and conceal a mirror.

See also *cognitive development; Piaget, Jean; sensorimotor stage.*

circumcision: In males, cutting off a portion of the foreskin of the penis; in females, circumcision refers to surgical excision of a portion of the clitoris or other genital structures.

Circumcision (i.e., a "circular cut") in newborn males is common and is performed for religious and/or hygienic reasons. Males of Jewish or Muslim background have traditionally been circumcised. In the United States, circumcisions have been routinely performed because it prevents the likelihood of an infection and irritations in the area of the glans penis (i.e., the sensitive tip of the penis).

Some sexologists assert that sexual relations with a foreskin in place are more pleasurable than sexual relations without a foreskin. A number of physicians believe that the hygienic value of circumcision in males has been overstated. For these reasons, the performance of routine circumcisions is being re-evaluated. As far as is known, neither circumcision nor noncircumcision makes any predictable contribution to psychosexual development or to eventual sexual and social adjustment. At present, if parents are offered an alternative when a child is born, they must make a choice based on their own religious training, other beliefs, and personal standards of hygiene.

Circumcision in females is rare in the United States. However, it has been common in a number of countries in Africa. Reasons for female circumcision have included religious beliefs and cultural attitudes. Most physicians and mental health professionals in the United States believe that routine female circumcision is without merit.

See also *genitals; penis envy; psychosexual development.*

classical conditioning: A basic kind of learning first studied experimentally by the Russian physiologist Ivan Pavlov. In classical conditioning, a previously neutral stimulus is paired with one that elicits an innate reflex. In Pavlov's experiments, dogs were trained to salivate when they heard a tone of a particular pitch. This was accomplished by pairing the tone in training trials with the presentation of food.

Here is an example of classical conditioning in an infant. A buzzer is sounded and a moment later the sucking reflex is elicited with the presentation of the nipple of a bottle or the breast. After a number of pairings, the sounding of the buzzer elicits the sucking reflex even though no nipple is presented. Although Pavlov rejected psychological explanations and preferred to speak in strictly physiological terms, an informal analysis of the above example suggests that the infant associates the buzzer with being fed and *anticipates* the presentation of the bottle or breast.

Four important terms in classical conditioning are the unconditioned reflex (UCR), the unconditioned stimulus (UCS), the conditioned stimulus (CS), and the conditioned reflex (CR). The *unconditioned reflex* is a reflex to which there is an inborn response. All of the neonatal reflexes are unconditioned reflexes, and the sucking reflex is a specific example. Unconditioned reflexes make up the foundation stones upon which conditioned reflexes are built. The *unconditioned stimulus* is a stimulus that elicits an unconditioned reflex. For example, the nipple normally elicits the sucking reflex. The *conditioned stimulus* is the stimulus to which there is a learned reflex. If a buzzer can acquire the ability to elicit the sucking response, the buzzer has become a conditioned stimulus. The *conditioned reflex* is a learned reflex. Sucking in response to a buzzer is a conditioned reflex.

Pavlov referred to classical conditioning as a "signaling system," and it seems fairly evident that its purpose is to help individuals learn their way about in the world. Infants and toddlers acquire some of their learned behaviors, and augment the range of their reflexes, through classical conditioning.

See also *behaviorism; conditioning; operant conditioning; Pavlov, Ivan Petrovich; stimulus-response theory.*

clowning: See *silliness.*

cognitive development: The development of the ability to think. The thinking process includes a set of subprocesses, including perception, reflection, concept formation, and memory. According to Piaget, there are four stages of cognitive development.

1. The *sensorimotor stage*: This is associated with infancy. During this stage, the infant acquires the basic foundation upon which the ability to think will be built.

2. The *preoperational stage*: This is associated with toddlerhood and the preschool age. During this stage, the young child uses intuition and magical thinking as a stepping stone toward more mature thought.

3. The *concrete operations stage*: This is associated with the elementary school-age child (about 7 to 12 years of age). During this stage, the older child acquires the ability to think in cause-and-effect terms and to reason in simple, direct terms.

4. The *formal operations stage*: This is associated with adolescence. During this stage, the adolescent acquires the ability to use abstract logic and to think about thinking. (Adults continue in this stage.)

Although Piaget's theory of cognitive development has been criticized in some of its details, the broad outline presented above has been accepted by a majority of psychologists and researchers. A more detailed description of the four stages is presented in appropriate entries elsewhere in the encyclopedia.

See also *concrete operations stage; formal operations stage; Piaget, Jean; preoperational stage; sensorimotor stage.*

cognitive giftedness: See *giftedness.*

cognitive needs: According to Maslow, a set of needs just below the need for self-actualization. An example of a cognitive need is the need to *know*, that is, the need to gather information and possess facts about life and the world. Children display the need to know when they become interested in a set of facts about insects, the stars, or plants. Another cognitive need, and related to the need to know, is the need to *understand.* Children display the need to understand when they ask, "Why is the sky blue?" and "Why do I have to wash my face?" Cognitive needs fall into the general category that Maslow called *growth needs*. In order for children eventually to attain cognitive maturity, it is important that their cognitive needs be met. Their requests for information and explanations are not silly, but essential.

See also *cognitive development; Maslow, Abraham; self-actualization.*

cognitive restructuring: See *cognitive-behavior modification.*

cognitive-behavior modification: A relatively recent innovation in behavior therapy that assumes that cognitions (i.e., thoughts, ideas) are learned just like other behaviors. If this is so, then cognitions are subject to all of the known laws of learning, including those that affect modification of observable behavior. This general approach has led to the formulation and application of several cognitive-behavior modification skills, and these can be used to help children and adolescents cope with the challenges of life.

Three important cognitive-behavior modification skills are stress-inoculation training, cognitive restructuring, and self-instructional training. In *stress-inoculation training*, subjects are trained to make mental preparations for stressful situations. For example, 14-year-old Marjorie worries excessively about her school work and experiences a substantial amount of test anxiety. Suppose she is scheduled to take an algebra examination. Using stress-inoculation training, the day before the examination she can reassure herself that she is well prepared, that moderate anxiety will not hurt, that she has performed well on past examinations, and that she is familiar with the testing procedure.

In *cognitive restructuring*, subjects are taught to change the form and content of their ideas. Say that 9-year-old Henry has the idea, "Nobody likes me." Using cognitive structuring, a behavior therapist would ask Henry to make a rational examination of his idea. Is it true that *nobody* likes him? Henry admits that he has a best friend and two or three other friends in school. Also, his first cousin Tom likes him. The old thought is replaced with the new thought, "A few people like me." This helps Henry realize that he can become well liked and have more friends.

In *self-instructional training*, subjects are taught that through a process of talking out loud they can change ineffective ideas. For example, 5-year-old Peggy is afraid of the dark. She reveals to a therapist that behind her fear is the idea, "A monster might get me." She herself thinks that her fear is silly and wants to learn to sleep without a light. A behavior therapist might teach her to say, out loud at first, "Monsters aren't real. There's nothing to be afraid of. I'm safe and snug in my own bed in my own room." After a number of nights, she can whisper the sentences. Eventually, she will just think them and she will feel better.

The methods described above are similar and overlap to some degree because all three refer to the general process of cognition.

See also *behavior modification; behavior therapy; child psychotherapy.*

colic: In infants, a set of signs and symptoms characterized by irritation, crying, screaming, a facial flush, a tightening of the muscles, and flatulence. The general medical consensus assigns colic, in the absence of known organic problems, to involuntary intestinal contractions and digestive distress. It is possible that colic is caused or aggravated by a disturbed sleep pattern, milk that has been overheated, fatigue, emotional rejection by a parent, and an allergy to the kind of milk being used (e.g., cow's milk).

Approximately 10 percent of infants suffer from colic. It is somewhat more common in males and firstborn children. In most cases, colic is not a problem after approximately three to five months. Common colic is not an indication of a long-range health problem.

Parents can cope with colic in several ways. Methods that can be effective some of the time are rocking the infant, offering a pacifier, rubbing the infant's shoulders, going out for a little trip, walking and singing to the infant, running a device with an electric motor that makes a humming sound (e.g., a fan or air conditioning unit), and making sure that the baby is cozy and warm. Sometimes pediatricians recommend using a different kind of milk (e.g., goat's milk or a milk substitute).

See also *attachment; infant; oral stage; sleep patterns; trust versus mistrust.*

communication skills: As applied to rearing children, a set of skills useful to parents and other responsible adults. The general aim of communication skills is to facilitate understanding between adults and children. It is believed that this in turn will make children more cooperative and more readily socialized. Here are several communication skills:

1. *Have respect for a child's feelings.* Children feel understood when their feelings are taken seriously. They should not be told that they are silly or foolish when they say that they are mad or disappointed or afraid. This does not, of course, suggest that children should be allowed to act on feelings in an irresponsible way.

2. *Limit criticism to actions.* Everyone knows that criticism of any kind hurts. If a child must be criticized, it is better to direct the criticism toward the child's actions than toward the child's personality. If Alvin spills his milk at the dinner table, it is constructive to say, "Place your milk to the left of your plate. Then it won't get in the way when you reach with your right hand for food." It is not helpful to say, "You're so sloppy and careless."

3. *Limit praise to actions.* Although it is clear that criticism stings, it seems to many people that praise is always good. However, praise can be laid on too thickly. It is better to praise a specific action rather than the child's personality. If Joy is taking piano lessons, it is constructive to say, "I enjoyed the way you captured the mood of the piece you just played." It is not helpful to say, "You're so talented, dear. You have an incomparable gift." These statements place Joy in a corner and make her feel trapped.

4. *Address the child's rational side.* Remember that children can think. Studies of cognitive development suggest that even toddlers and preschoolers have some rational capacities. In the Western world, 7 is the traditional age of reason. Speak to children in a calm, reasonable tone of voice. If they ask why they have to do something, offer at least one sensible explanation before relying on adult authority.

See also *authoritarian parent; cognitive development; parental style; permissive parent.*

compensation: One of the ego defense mechanisms, in which the ego attempts to offset a real or imagined sense of inferiority in one area of the personality with superiority striving in another area. Compensation is one of the ways in which children maintain self-esteem.

For example, 14-year-old Meg suffers from chronic shyness. She is a talented writer of stories. She pours her heart and soul into creative writing as a way of counterbalancing the inadequacies she experiences in her social relations. Or 7-year-old James is short for his age. He develops a tough, feisty exterior with other children in order to make himself feel "as big as they are."

The concept of compensation was first introduced into the literature of psychoanalysis by Alfred Adler when he was a member of Freud's study circle.

See also *Adler, Alfred; ego defense mechanisms; inferiority complex; self-esteem.*

competitiveness: A behavioral trait characterized by striving against others in order to obtain a goal not available to all. The goal can be tangible, such as a trophy. Or the goal can be intangible, such as higher status in the family. It is likely that competitiveness is natural in human beings, arising from the general struggle for survival. Competitiveness is seen in children when they try to win a race or place first in a spelling contest. Competitiveness is also seen when children display sibling rivalry in the home. Each child may, in his or her own way, seek to be first in the eyes of the parents.

Several studies have suggested that in childhood boys are more competitive, and less cooperative, than girls. Some researchers have hypothesized that this is a natural trait in boys, perhaps related to androgens. Others have hypothesized that male-female differences in competitiveness are largely due to culture, training, and social expectations.

See also *androgen hormones; antisocial behavior; prosocial behavior; sibling rivalry.*

concept formation: The learning process by which a *concept*, a cognitive, or mental, class created by the thinking process, is acquired. A concept's aim is to organize perceptions and concepts less complex than itself into meaningful groups. As a consequence, it involves many of the general processes of learning, such as both classical and operant conditioning, social (i.e., observational) learning, and reinforcers.

An example of a basic concept used by children in the early years is a *conjunctive concept*. Conjunctive concepts are formed by associations, or conjunctions, of perceived attributes. These are readily connected by the familiar word *and*. For example, a preschooler's concept of a bird might be that it is a creature that *sings* and *flies* and *builds nests* and *eats worms*. Many similar conjunctive concepts make it possible for toddlers and preschoolers to build up a rich and meaningful perceptual world.

See also *classical conditioning; cognitive development; learning; operant conditioning; reinforcer; social learning.*

concrete operations stage: The third stage in Piaget's theory of cognitive development, the stage associated with the ages of about 7 to 12 and characterized by *operational thinking*, thinking that is relatively mature and only one step below the abstract thinking abilities of the adolescent and adult.

The stage of concrete operations is characterized by a set of several distinct attributes. Four of these attributes are identified below.

1. The child develops the ability to understand the principle of *cause and effect*. No longer are events explained in terms of magic or anthropomorphism. The child now appreciates that a light bulb goes on because the opening of a switch allows an electric current to flow to the bulb.

2. The child develops the capacity of *conservation*, the ability to appreciate that changes of form in substances do not affect their total quantity. For example, a handful of clay is understood to be the same amount of clay in the form of a ball or a long sausage-like shape.

3. The child develops the capacity to appreciate *numbers and their operations*. Therefore, grammar school children benefit from instruction in addition, subtraction, multiplication, and division. However, they often have a difficult time appreciating the importance of variables and the operations of algebra. The idea that the numeral "2" stands for two beans or two coins is readily appreciated. However, the idea that the variable x stands for *any* quantity is usually beyond the cognitive abilities of the preadolescent child.

4. Children in the stage of concrete operations readily appreciate the idea of *categories and subcategories*. For example, they can understand that birds belong to the larger class "animals." And they can also understand that robins, hawks, and parakeets are subcategories of birds. Children acquire many hierarchical structures like the one described, and these structures help them give order and meaning to their perceived worlds.

In brief, concrete operations represents a fairly sophisticated form of thought and, as such, is an important stepping stone to the fully adult stage of formal operations.

See also *anthropomorphic thinking; cognitive development; formal operations stage; Piaget, Jean.*

conditioned reflex: See *classical conditioning.*

conditioned stimulus: See *classical conditioning.*

conditioning: A kind of learning in which cognitive processes (i.e., thinking, insight, and conscious problem solving) play little or no role. Conditioning is thought of as a more or less automatic, or "mechanical," process. (This viewpoint is open to debate.) The study of conditioning has been dominated by such ancillary concepts as *trial-and-error* and *reinforcement.* The two principal kinds of conditioning are classical (i.e., respondent) and operant (i.e., instrumental). *Classical conditioning*, frequently associated with the work of Ivan Pavlov, traditionally involves the capacity of new and novel stimuli (e.g., a light or a sound) to elicit involuntary reflexes. *Operant conditioning*, frequently associated with the work of B. F. Skinner, traditionally involves the shaping of observable actions through the use of reinforcers.

See also *classical conditioning; operant conditioning; Pavlov, Ivan Petrovich; reinforcer; Skinner, Burrhus Frederick.*

conduct disorder: A disorder of childhood or adolescence characterized by such behaviors as (1) sneak thievery, (2) running away from home, (3) chronic lying, (4) setting fires, and (5) truancy. The oddness and pathology of the behavior is quite beyond the normal impishness and playfulness of childhood.

The *Diagnostic and Statistical Manual of Mental Disorders* published by the American Psychiatric Association distinguishes three kinds of conduct disorders. These are (1) group type, (2) solitary aggressive type, and (3) undifferentiated type. The *group type* is characterized by pathological behavior in association with friends and peers. The child or adolescent in question "goes along with the gang." The *solitary type* is characterized by pathological behavior on an individual basis without the necessity of group support. The *undifferentiated type* displays characteristics common to the other two types, and no clear clinical picture emerges.

There are many causal factors involved in the conduct disorders. Some of these are a history of attention-deficit hyperactivity disorder, emotionally cold parents, too much punishment, absence of a stable home environment, and living in an institution. The incidence of conduct disorder in child and adolescent males is estimated to be about 9 percent. In females, the incidence is estimated to be about 2 percent.

It is impossible to make a general statement about the prognosis for children and adolescents with conduct disorders. On a specific basis, if the behavioral signs are relatively mild, the troubled young person may improve substantially. Treatment consists of behavior therapy and general psychotherapy. A therapeutic approach in which the troubled child or adolescent is helped to see the adverse long-run consequences of pathological behavior may be helpful.

See also *attention-deficit hyperactivity disorder (ADHD); behavior therapy; child psychotherapy; lying; oppositional defiant disorder; psychotherapy; pyromania; running away; stealing; truancy.*

conformity: A trait characterized by behaving in a manner that is similar to the behavior of other members of a group. For example, if most children in a particular classroom raise a hand when they want to ask a question, the conforming child will do the same. On the whole, conformity is a desirable trait because it represents a willingness to cooperate and is positive evidence that a child is becoming socialized.

There are, however, times when conformity can be distressing. If a child or adolescent identifies with members of a peer group or other subgroup that is at variance with the general standards and expectations of the family or larger culture, conformity to the behavior of the subgroup may be a source of conflict and/or alienation between the younger person and parents, teachers, and other authority figures. Conformity is, of course, relative to a reference group. From the point of view of a subgroup, one might be conforming. From the point of view of the family, one might not be conforming.

Also, it should be noted that not all nonconformity to the expectations of a traditional group is "bad" by definition. A certain amount of nonconformity plays a role in such positive processes as autonomy, creative thinking, and self-actualization.

See also *alienation; autonomy versus shame and doubt; creative thinking; peer group; self-actualization; socialization; trait.*

congenital defects: See *birth defects.*

conjunctive concept: See *concept formation.*

conscience: Traditionally, the part of the human personality that tells the individual what is right and what is wrong. It is the agent of the moral self. This usage is preserved in Freudian theory, and the conscience is thought of as a part of the superego.

Over the centuries, the source of the conscience has been discussed without reaching a satisfactory consensus. One view is that the conscience is inborn in human beings, placed in the soul or personality by God or nature. This view is held by the philosophers Plato and Immanuel Kant. In modified form, it is reflected in the work of Carl Jung, Alfred Adler, and, to a less explicit extent, in the recently developed discipline of *sociobiology.* (One of the key doctrines of sociobiology is that much of our social behavior is genetically determined.)

Freud held to the view that the conscience is acquired by developmental experiences. The sense of right and wrong is learned in the context of the family. Forbidden wishes combined with the both shame and the fear of punishment induce most normal children to internalize moral standards.

See also *Adler, Alfred; Jung, Carl Gustav; Kohlberg, Lawrence; moral development; socialization; superego.*

conservation: See *concrete operations stage* and *preoperational stage.*

conventional stage: See *moral development.*

convergent thinking: Thinking in which the lines of logic lead to a single best answer or solution. It is the kind of thinking that underlies most rational thought, and it plays a dominant role in intelligence. The ability to define words, recite information, perceive similarities among common objects, and use arithmetic are all examples of convergent thinking in action.

See also *creative thinking; divergent thinking; intelligence; productive thinking.*

cooperative play: Play characterized by the ability to follow the rules of a game. The capacity for cooperative play is required for a host of games played in childhood, ranging from jacks to baseball to Monopoly. Toddlers have little or no capacity for cooperative play. However, as children approach the age of 4, their capacity for such play increases significantly.

See also *onlooker play; parallel play; play; solitary play.*

coprolalia: See *Tourette's disorder.*

correlation: The magnitude of the relationship between two or more variables. A common measure of the magnitude is the *correlation coefficient,* which can be readily computed by a formula devised a number of years ago by the mathematician Karl Pearson working in conjunction with the scientist Francis Galton. Correlation coefficients have a limited range from -1.00 to +1.00, and coefficients anywhere in between are also possible (e.g., -0.49, 0, and +.53). Minus correlation coefficients represent *negative correlations.* Suppose one variable is designated as X and a second variable as Y. If Y decreases when X increases, there is a negative correlation. For example, let Y stand for the amount of money in a checking account. Let X stand for the number of checks written. Assuming no deposits are made, the more checks that are written, the less money will remain in the account.

Plus correlation coefficients represent *positive correlations*. If *Y* increases when *X* increases, there is a positive correlation. For example, let *Y* stand for the height of a homeowner's grass. Let *X* stand for the amount of water given the grass. Assuming the grass is not cut frequently, the more water that is given, the taller will be the grass.

All of this may seem fairly remote from the concerns of child behavior and development. However, the correlation coefficient is a valuable statistical tool useful in research. For example, by using the correlation coefficient, it is possible to evaluate the role of genetics as a contributing factor to various traits and behaviors. To illustrate, if identical twins separated at birth and raised in different homes show a correlation in traits of temperament or mental disorders as adults, this suggests the important role played by genetic factors.

Also, correlation coefficients are used to evaluate the reliability and validity of psychological tests. A test item is considered *reliable* if it shows a high positive correlation with other items on the same test. The test itself is considered *valid* if it shows a high positive correlation with other related measures of performance. For example, an intelligence test is considered valid if it demonstrates a high positive correlation with grades earned in school.

See also *Galton, Francis; genetic predisposition; reliability of a test; validity of a test.*

counterconditioning: One of the methods used to extinguish conditioned responses. In counterconditioning, a natural response is elicited that is antagonistic to an unwanted conditioned response. For example, relaxation is antagonistic to fear. In helping a child get over phobias, or irrational fears, it is helpful to reassure the child, hold the child, or allow the child to have a cup of hot chocolate in order to induce relaxation before encouraging the child to face the fearful situation or stimulus. The principle of counterconditioning is taken advantage of in systematic desensitization, a kind of behavior therapy.

See also *behavior therapy; classical conditioning; fear; Little Albert; phobia; systematic desensitization.*

couvade syndrome: Labor pains and other signs and symptoms of childbirth demonstrated by a father-to-be. The male's distress can be intense and is not an indication of acting or any other voluntary action. The term *couvade* refers to a tradition in some cultures in which the male participates in the birth of his children by going to bed and acting out the delivery experience. In Western culture, couvade syndrome appears to be induced by factors such as identification with the mother-to-be, suggestibility, a vivid imagination, strong nurturing tendencies, and empathy. Full-blown couvade syndrome is uncommon. However, weaker versions of it, in which the male may experience mild physiological distress. are not uncommon.

See also *birth trauma; Lamaze method; Leboyer method.*

crawling: A form of locomotion characterized by a horizontal position and the use of all four limbs. In a normal sequence of motor development, crawling will appear between 9 and 11 months of age. It is a stepping stone leading to standing and walking alone. Most children, given the opportunity, will go through the crawling stage. However, some children do not crawl. Children raised in institutions under conditions of stimulus deprivation sometimes do not crawl. Children who are allowed early motility with wheeled toys may not crawl as much as other children. And some children prefer various forms of scooting to crawling.

Normal crawling involves a sequence of motor movements that are easily recognized. The left hand and the left knee are close together when the right hand and the right knee are far apart. With locomotion, the positions go through a series of alternating exchanges. It has been hypothesized that this typical pattern of crawling plays an important role in "programming" the brain and nervous system, building a foundation for future forms of perceptual-motor learning.

A consensus does not exist, but it has been suggested by some theorists that lack of patterned crawling during infancy plays a role in subsequent learning disabilities, including reading difficulties. Some therapists recommend a set of crawling exercises for children with reading problems.

See also *developmental reading disorder; motor development; scooting.*

creative thinking: The ability to think in novel, original ways. Creative thinking is useful when there is no standard solution to a problem. It also plays an essential role in creative writing, musical composition, and invention. A prime example of creative thinking is Thomas A. Edison's invention of the phonograph. If various biographical accounts are accurate, there was little or no prior work on the recording of sound before Edison's efforts. He seems to have recognized in a set of creative insights that it would be possible to preserve the basic patterns of sound waves on an appropriately prepared rotating cylinder. He also invented a speaker that would allow for the audible reconstruction of the preserved waves.

An important aspect of creative thinking is its divergent quality, a tendency to avoid old, overworked mental pathways.

Some critics of modern education have pointed out that creative thinking is important for humankind's progress. They argue that our schools overly reinforce convergent thinking and pay scant attention to creative thinking. Indeed, children who display too much creative thinking are often thought of as "smart alecks" and "brats." Some of Edison's teachers thought of him as an incorrigible child, apparently because his thought processes were too creative for the traditional classroom.

See also *convergent thinking; creativity tests; divergent thinking.*

creativity tests: In most cases, standardized paper-and-pencil tests designed to assess a child's capacity to think in a creative way. One well-known creativity test is the Torrance Test of Creative Thinking. Here is an example of the kind of question that might be asked on a creativity test: "What are some of the things you can do with an unlined sheet of paper about 8 x 11 inches in size?" A child might be instructed to write down a list of the possibilities. The list can then be scored by an examiner on several dimensions of creativity, such as originality, flexibility, and fluency. *Originality* refers to how unusual, or unexpected, an answer is. If a child answers, "Write a letter on it," this is not a very original response. (Note that it *is* an intelligent one.) On the other hand, if the child answers, "Cut a snowflake pattern out of it," this is a fairly original response.

Flexibility refers to how many conceptual shifts the child makes. If, after a first response, the child moves to a different domain of interest, then flexibility is shown. Saying first that one can write a letter on a piece of paper and then saying that one can make a paper airplane demonstrates flexibility. Saying first that one can write a letter and then saying that one can write a story shows limited flexibility.

Fluency refers to the sheer number of answers given to a question. If a child gives two or three responses, low fluency is shown. If a child gives seven, eight, or more responses, high fluency is shown. See also *cognitive development; creative thinking; intelligence.*

creeping: See *crawling.*

cretinism: A pathological condition traceable to thyroid difficulties in the mother during the fetal period. The infant and child suffering from cretinism is often mentally retarded and the victim of various physical problems, such as skin abnormalities, poor skeletal development, and a large, round belly. Thyroid imbalances are sometimes caused by iodine deficiencies in the diet. The advent of iodized salt and better nutrition has resulted in a reduction in the incidence of cretinism.

See also *birth defects; fetal development; fetus; hormone; mental retardation.*

crib death: See *sudden infant death syndrome (SIDS).*

critical period (sensitive period): A time period of relatively short duration early in an organism's development when it is particularly sensitive to certain kinds of stimuli. The concept of critical periods arose in connection with the research of Konrad Lorenz, an ethologist, on the following behavior of goslings and ducklings. (*Ethology* is the study of both innate and learned behavior through the use of the method of natural observation.) Lorenz found that a gosling or a duckling will acquire the ability to follow its mother only if exposed to her during the critical period.

The discovery of critical periods in animals suggested that perhaps human beings also have critical periods. The idea of critical periods has been applied to behaviors as diverse as smiling, attachment to a parent, and reading. In general, it can be said that if human beings have critical periods, they are neither as well defined nor as explicit as they are in geese and ducks. Also, the concept is more accurately applied to a basic behavior such as social smiling in infancy than it is to a complex behavior such as learning to read.

See also *attachment; ethology; smiling.*

cross-sectional study: See *longitudinal study.*

crying and fussing in an infant: Behavior characterized by such signs as tears, excessive excitement, and general distress. There are numerous causes of crying and fussing in an infant. These include hunger, thirst, an uncomfortable room temperature, soiled diapers, diaper rash, a need for attention or affection, an undiagnosed childhood disease, an infection, and colic. The suggestions given in connection with the entry for colic are useful for calming a fussy infant in the absence of a significant medical problem.

See also *colic.*

culture-fair test: A psychological test, such as an intelligence test, that does not give extra advantage to members of its own culture. Thus, a comprehension question such as "What is the principal advantage of a microwave oven?" will be useless in attempting to assess the intelligence of a child from a home where a microwave oven is unknown. However, a test item requiring a child to recite several random digits is closer to being fair because it requires only general, not specific, knowledge. The same would be true of an item requiring the assembly of blocks into a pattern.

It is, however, in practice next to impossible to design a completely culture-fair test. Even the use of random digits, for example, assumes some familiarity with the concept of number. Therefore, the effort in test construction is to produce tests that are as culture-fair as possible.

Particularly in the case of intelligence testing, some standardized tests have been criticized with the assertion that they place some children from racial and ethnic minorities at a disadvantage. Tests have been revised and improved with these considerations in mind.

See also *intelligence tests.*

curiosity drive: See *ludic behavior.*

cursing: See *undesirable language.*

D

Darwinian reflex: See *palmar grasp reflex.*

day care: The care of infants, toddlers, and preschoolers during the day in the absence of their parents. Adequate day-care facilities provide meals, a place to play, an opportunity to interact with other children, safety, and parent surrogates in the form of the staff members. More and more parents are employed outside of the household. And there are an increasing number of one-parent families. In view of these facts, the question of the effects of day care on development has become of substantial interest.

In general, it can be said that if the day-care facility has enough caregivers and is intelligently managed, there will be no significant adverse effects on the child. Having said this, it nonetheless seems sensible, in view of studies of attachment, that day care not start until after infancy if at all possible. Even this generalization is a weak one. Infants who spend time in day care generally *do not* come to have more affection for their caretakers than for their actual parents. And they generally do not have low developmental quotients.

Toddlers and preschoolers who are only children may very well derive social benefit from interacting with peers. Studies suggest that the cognitive and emotional development (see *emotional states*) of children reared exclusively at home and children who have spent significant time in day care are essentially comparable. The body of available data suggests that parents do not have to feel guilty for depending upon a certain amount of day care, particularly if this seems to be an economic necessity. However, the *adequacy* of the facility must be carefully evaluated. The parents need to be convinced that their children are in good hands.

See also *attachment; cognitive development; developmental quotient; emotional states; one-parent family; peer group.*

daydreaming: A series of fanciful thoughts and images occurring when one is awake. Often, daydreams represent idle wishes or a need to escape from everyday constraints. Daydreaming is normal in both children and adults and often plays an important role in creative thinking.

Daydreaming is a problem behavior in a child only if the child uses this means regularly as a way to not pay attention to parents or teachers or to avoid homework or as a means of procrastination. Under these conditions, daydreaming overlaps with the ego defense mechanism known as fantasy.

In most cases, excessive daydreaming in childhood will diminish with increasing age and maturation. Parents can cope if there is a moderate problem by the application of behavior modification and communication skills. If the problem is severe, it may be a sign of a more profound difficulty, such as chronic anxiety or depression, and professional treatment with psychotherapy may be recommended. It is important to realize that daydreaming in and of itself is *not* a behavioral disorder. Again, it is common. And quite a bit of daydreaming in children should be tolerated by parents and other caregivers.

See also *anxiety; creative thinking; depression; fantasy; procrastination; psychotherapy.*

deafness: See *hearing impairment.*

deductive thinking: A kind of thinking in which conclusions are reached by the evaluation and comparison of propositions. Assume that you say to a child, "All ducks like to quack. Donald is a duck. What is one of the things that Donald likes to do?" Suppose that the child answers, "Donald likes to quack! Because all ducks like to quack!" Then the child is displaying the capacity for deductive thinking. The ability to think in this way is absent in toddlers but may begin to appear in preschool children. The ability to reason deductively is an important part of intelligence and is in fact evaluated by standardized intelligence tests.

Deductive thinking is often confused with *inductive thinking*, a kind of thinking in which conclusions are reached by the evaluation and comparison of facts or observations. For example, a detective who gathers several clues all pointing to one suspect is using inductive, not deductive, thinking. In the Sherlock Holmes stories, the associate Dr. Watson is frequently puzzled by how Holmes cracked a case. Holmes was likely to reply in a lofty manner, "Deduction, my dear Dr. Watson. Deduction." Technically, Holmes was wrong in the description of his own mental processes.

The development of the capacity for both deductive thinking and inductive thinking is an important step forward in a child's cognitive development.

See also *cognitive development; creative thinking; intelligence tests; reasoning.*

defense mechanisms: See *ego defense mechanisms.*

dementia praecox: An outdated term for schizophrenia. The familiar word *precocious*, suggesting advanced or premature development, is derived from the Latin word *praecox.* Thus, *dementia praecox* has a literal meaning indicating "an early onset of mental decline." The German psychiatrist Emil Kraepelin (1856–1926) favored the term because schizophrenic disorders often make their first appearance in adolescence or young adulthood. The Swiss psychiatrist Eugen Bleuler (1857–1939) introduced the term *schizophrenia* in the early 1900s, and it has remained the preferred usage since that time.

See also *childhood schizophrenia.*

deoxyribonucleic acid (DNA): A complex organic molecule that forms the basis of the genetic code. Interwoven strands of DNA form the basis of genes, found as part of the structure of chromosomes. *Replication*, the ability to make an accurate copy of itself, is one of the chief characteristics of DNA. And this is what makes the reproduction of organisms possible at all. DNA molecules are somewhat like pages of instruction in an operation manual. These instructions provide the data foundation used to build organisms ranging from snails to fish, from cats to human beings. Four bases (adenine, thymine, guanine, and cytosine) make up the larger DNA molecule, and these act somewhat like letters of the alphabet. In varying, highly complex combinations, they create the "words" underlying the genetic code.

The discovery of the structure of DNA is considered to be one of the outstanding scientific achievements of the 20th century. James Watson, Francis Crick, and Maurice Wilkins were awarded a Nobel prize for their analysis of the characteristics of DNA in 1953.

See also *chromosomes; gene; genetic endowment; genetic predisposition.*

deep-sleep state: See *sleep patterns.*

deep structure of a sentence: According to the linguist Noam Chomsky, the second of the two levels of a sentence. The first level is the *surface structure.* The surface structure is the actual shape of the words, the manifest order and arrangements chosen. The deep structure is what the sentence actually means.

For example, assume that one child says, "I want no more milk." Now assume that a second child says, "I don't want any more milk." Although the surface structure of the two sentences is somewhat different, the actual meaning is the same in both cases. In Spanish, double negatives are used correctly in a single sentence to communicate a single negation. Therefore, it is good form in Spanish to say, "I do not want no more milk." This indicates, translated into English, a lack of desire for more milk. However, a *literal* (and incorrect) translation suggests a desire for more milk because of the double negation, which in standard English is self-contradictory. In most cases, the actual meaning, or deep structure, is quite evident in spite of superficial differences.

The existence of a deep structure in sentences and the ready capacity of children to recognize these structures from early ages suggests to Chomsky that inborn cognitive capacities play a significant role in language acquisition.

See also *Chomsky, Noam Avram; language acquisition device; language development; syntax.*

deficiency motivation: The motivation to act in response to what Abraham Maslow calls deficiency needs.
See also *deficiency needs.*

deficiency needs: According to Abraham Maslow, a founder of humanistic psychology, one of the two sets of needs into which human needs can be grouped. The other set of needs is growth needs. Deficiency needs are "lower" on the ladder of human motivation than growth needs. The first deficiency need is *physiological.* A person must have food, water, air, a liveable temperature, and so forth, in order to be able to survive at all. The second deficiency need is *safety.* A person is motivated to preserve his or her body by avoiding accidents and infections. The infant and the child must be protected from harm. The third deficiency need is *belongingness.* Belongingness includes the need to be loved. There is very good evidence to suggest that infants who are deprived of adequate amounts of attention and affection fail to thrive. The fourth deficiency need is *esteem.* People need to have others look upon them as persons with worth and value.

People never outgrow their deficiency needs. They remain throughout life. However, they are of particular importance in infancy and childhood because if they are not met, or are met inadequately, the resulting physical, psychological, and emotional deprivation will have an adverse effect on the course of development.

See also *anaclitic depression; growth needs; Maslow, Abraham Harold; self-actualization.*

delayed walking: See *walking alone.*

delinquency: See *juvenile delinquency.*

denial of reality: An ego defense mechanism characterized by a refusal to face unpleasant facts. Five-year-old Opal has just been told that a planned family picnic is canceled because it is raining heavily. She looks out of the window and tells her mother, "I think it's going to stop pretty soon." There is no evidence for her statement. Seven-year-old Harold comes in last in a school race. He is somewhat overweight. On the way home he tells a friend, "Tomorrow I'll win."

Although adults also use denial of reality, children are particulary prone to use it. It is one of the least complex and most direct of the several ego defense mechanisms.

See also *ego defense mechanisms.*

depressant drugs: Drugs that decrease alertness and central nervous system arousal. These include sedatives and narcotics.

See also *sedatives; narcotic drugs.*

depression: A negative emotional state characterized by sadness, self-doubt, and a loss of interest in daily living. Although people like to think of childhood as a golden period of life, it is widely recognized by psychiatrists, clinical psychologists, and other mental-health professionals that both children and adolescents can suffer from depression. Although some specific details may vary, as a psychological and emotional problem, there is no essential conceptual difference between depression in childhood, adolescence, and adulthood.

Depression plays a part in a number of mental disorders, particularly the mood disorders (e.g., bipolar disorder) and the eating disorders (e.g., anorexia nervosa). Along with anxiety, depression is one of the most frequent complaints heard by therapists. It has been called "the common cold of mental illness." The portrait of depression can be greatly enriched by listing some of the symptoms often associated with it. In children, these include dejection, poor self-image, crying, inability to laugh, pessimism, suicidal thoughts and impulses, withdrawal from others, and fatigue. With adolescents, it is possible to add loss of interest in sexual activity.

A first way to classify depression is as either endogenous or exogenous. *Endogenous depression* is depression that arises from within. It has no known external cause in present circumstances. Such depression may be biological in nature (i.e., genetic or biochemical). Or it may be due to psychological factors with roots in negative experiences in infancy and early childhood (e.g., neglect of an infant and child abuse). *Exogenous depression* is depression that arises from without. It is sometimes called *reactive depression.* It has a known external cause in present circumstances, such as poor school performance, an inability to make friends, lack of a talent or poor athletic ability, or the death of a parent or sibling. If it is mild in severity, it is thought of as normal.

A second way to classify depression is as either neurotic or psychotic. In *neurotic depression*, the child maintains contact with reality. He or she maintains stable perceptions of time, space, and the external world. In *psychotic depression* the child has impaired reality contact. There is great mental confusion, and there may be delusions. Such depression may be associated with a severe developmental disorder. (Do not identify the word *neurotic* with "mild." Neurotic depression can be severe and can in some cases lead to suicide.)

A third way to classify depression is in terms of severity. The range is from mild to moderate to severe. In *mild depression*, the child or adolescent may complain that most activities are not fun any more, that he or she needs a lot or rest, and so forth. Although the depression is irritating, the individual is able to continue functioning and carries out school assignments and other responsibilities without too much difficulty. In *moderate depression*, the person may feel that familiar pleasures such as reading, watching television, and working on a hobby have become very boring. There is a lack of interest in other people; good grooming and neatness become unimportant; and there may be suicidal fantasies. The child or adolescent can usually live up to responsibilities, but with a great effort of will. In *severe depression,* the individual may be convinced that nothing makes any sense at all, that life is totally without meaning, and that he or she is not loved or lovable. There is great apathy about almost everything, and there may be suicidal attempts.

Explanations of depression tend to fall into three major categories. These are biological, psychological, and existential. The *biological explanation* states that depression is caused by genetic or biochemical factors. It is hypothesized that some children are predisposed to depression in terms of their inborn temperament. There is evidence, for example, to suggest that in bipolar disorder, genetic factors probably play a role. A biochemical deficit, such as a lack of normal levels of the neurotransmitter norepinephrine, may contribute to depression. Biological explanations are used primarily to help in the understanding of endogenous depressions.

The *psychological explanation* states that depression has its roots in the individual's developmental history. Classical psychoanalysis suggests two principal factors play a role. First, the "good little boy" or "good little girl" is taught to repress aggressive responses. They are not "nice." Second, such a child may also acquire a very moral and high-minded outlook on life. In Freudian terms, this means the individual has a very strict superego. Thus, whenever, even as an adult, normal aggressive responses want to surface, they are repressed by the superego. The inability to express real feelings, particularly aggressive ones, in a normal way leads to depression. In brief, psychoanalysis looks upon depression as bottled-up anger.

It should be noted that the psychological explanation does not end with psychoanalysis. Another major psychological explanation is the one offered by learning theory. Learning theory states that depression is an acquired response pattern, a kind of emotional habit. For example, a child raised in a household with a depressed parent may, through the process of social (i.e., observational) learning, imitate and acquire depression as a maladaptive way of coping with the stress of life. Another possibility is a phenomenon known as *learned helplessness*. A series of failure experiences may lead the individual to generalize and believe that he or she is helpless in situations where this is not in fact so.

The *existential explanation* states that depression is inescapable. It is a part of life. Everyone knows that he or she may have losses and experience illnesses and will eventually die. Any person of normal intelligence who profoundly contemplates the nature of existence can hardly escape some feelings of depression. This cause of depression tends to surface first in early adolescence when the individual becomes more reflective. And it may plague a person on and off for many years. Psychotherapy with an existential orientation can help a person to minimize the impact of existential depression by developing an attitude of courage toward the very real hardships of life.

Depression can be treated with drugs or psychotherapy. If it is believed that the depression is both biological and endogenous in nature, then drug therapy is the treatment of choice. If these two conditions are not met, then the treatment of choice is psychotherapy.

See also *anaclitic depression; anorexia nervosa; bipolar disorder; childhood neurosis; developmental disorders; drug therapy; learned helplessness; psychotherapy; social learning; superego; temperament.*

deprivation: See *emotional deprivation; deprived environment.*

deprivation of privileges: See *response-cost punishment.*

deprived environment: An environment that inadequately meets a child's biological, psychological, and emotional needs. Deficient nutrition for a prolonged period may lead to stunted growth or improper development of the brain and nervous system.

Research has demonstrated that deprivation of affection and social contacts during infancy and early childhood may lead to mental retardation and emotional disturbances.

See also *anaclitic depression; emotional deprivation; failure to thrive; feral child; malnutrition; short stature.*

desensitization therapy: See *systematic desensitization.*

destructiveness: In childhood, a tendency to break things or to do property damage. Sometimes children are destructive because they are clumsy or inattentive. However, the principal problem of concern to parents is willful destructiveness. Destructiveness of this kind is a sign of emotional distress. The breaking of things can be seen as an expression of anger and general unhappiness.

Coping with destructiveness requires (1) some insight into the specific reasons a child is emotionally upset, (2) the setting of realistic limits, and (3) practical strategies designed to modify the child's behavior.

It is possible, of course, to extend the concept of destructiveness beyond property damage. An adolescent or adult may manifest destructiveness in human relations, sabotaging friendships or a marriage. Also, it is possible to speak of *self-destructiveness.* Sometimes emotional distress is turned on the self and may play a role in such behaviors as alcohol and drug abuse, heavy smoking, and compulsive overeating. It is evident that children do not just automatically outgrow childhood destructiveness. For this reason, it is important to help the child modify destructive behavior when it is first displayed.

See also *acting out; aggressiveness; behavior modification; displacement.*

dethroning: According to Adler, a loss of status of a firstborn child when a second child is born. The magnitude of the loss varies as a function of such factors as the emotional security and the age of the firstborn. It is common for firstborn children to make various kinds of attempts to reclaim the seemingly lost throne. Examples of such attempts are demanding more attention, becoming willful or stubborn, regression in toilet habits, throwing tantrums, and so forth. Usually attempts to reclaim lost status are of the childish variety indicated in the examples and, consequently, are counterproductive. It is helpful for a parent to know the firstborn's goal. Then it is possible to cope with the seemingly irrational behavior in a meaningful way. The firstborn needs a certain amount of attention and recognition and cannot be emotionally neglected, even temporarily, in favor of a secondborn infant.

See also *Adler, Alfred; birth order; inferiority complex; regression; sibling rivalry; superiority complex; will to power.*

developmental arithmetic disorder: See *developmental disorders.*

developmental disorders: Disorders of infancy, childhood, or adolescence characterized by impairment of the maturation process. There are two broad ways to categorize such disorders. These are pervasive developmental disorders and specific developmental disorders. *Pervasive developmental disorders* affect all aspects of the child's functioning in a profound way. Thinking, perception, social skills, and motor control are all affected. *Autistic disorder* is the principal pervasive developmental disorder, and it is distinguished by an absence of normal interest in other people.

Specific developmental disorders affect a given area of a child's functioning. In *developmental reading disorder,* there are substantial problems in the child's ability to comprehend written words and sentences. The term *dyslexia* is sometimes applied to this disorder. In *developmental arithmetic disorder,* there are substantial problems in the child's ability to grasp basic concepts of number and the processes of addition, subtraction, multiplication, and division. In *developmental language disorder,* there are substantial problems in the child's ability to comprehend what is said and to express thoughts in speech.

It is believed that the principal causal factors in the pervasive disorders are biological in nature. There may be a genetic predisposition, or the child may have some degree of mental retardation complicating the developmental picture. In the case of the specific disorders, it is believed that environment plays a more significant role. Ineffective parenting involving such behaviors as abuse, neglect, overcontrol, or emotional coldness may contribute to the formation of these disorders.

Behavior therapy has been shown to be of some value in the treatment of pervasive developmental disorders. Various training and educational procedures are of value in treating the specific developmental disorders.

See also *autistic disorder; behavior therapy; developmental reading disorder; mental retardation.*

developmental language disorder: See *developmental disorders.*

developmental norms: See *norms of development.*

developmental psychology: The study of changes in behavior over time. Changes in behavior include those that are influenced by physical growth, maturation, learning, and aging. Developmental psychology does not limit itself to the study of childhood and adolescence but includes as its domain of interest the entire life span. Thus, such subjects as middle-age crisis and integrity in old age are included in developmental psychology. Child psychology should be thought of as a subcategory of developmental psychology, the larger field of study.

Developmental psychology, taking a chronological approach to life, lends itself readily to thinking in terms of ages and stages. *Ages* refers to chronological periods (e.g., infancy or toddlerhood). *Stages* refers to characteristic kinds of behavior displayed (e.g., autonomy or concern with one's identity) in association with specific ages.

See also *ages-stages theories; autonomy; child psychology; identity crisis.*

developmental quotient (DQ): A quotient obtained by dividing a child's chronological age into his or her developmental age. *Chronological age (CA)* is the actual age in months or years. *Developmental age (DA)* is a measure of the child's perceptual, motor, and cognitive abilities in comparison to standardized age norms based on large samples of data. The formula for calculating a developmental quotient is:

$$DQ = DA/CA \times 100$$

For example, Rose's DA is 11 months. Her CA is 9 months. Using the formula, $11/9 \times 100$, or $1.22 \times 100 = 122$. Thus, Rose's DQ is 122, somewhat above average. For a second example, Oscar's DA is 9 months. His CA is 10 months. Thus, Oscar's DQ is $9/10 \times 100$, or $0.90 \times 100 = 90$, somewhat below average.

Note that if the DA is higher than the CA, the DQ is above average. If the DA is lower than the CA, the DQ is below average. Also note that if the DA and CA are identical, the DQ will automatically be 100, or average.

The concept of developmental quotient is of particular value when applied to infancy and early childhood. It is used in connection with standardized tests of development.

See also *Bayley Scales of Infant Development; Gesell Developmental Schedules; intelligence quotient (IQ)*.

developmental reading disorder (dyslexia): A behavioral disorder characterized by difficulties in acquiring the ability to read with facility. A developmental reading disorder does *not* suggest mental retardation or gross organic brain damage. On the contrary, the child's reading level is usually below what might be expected in terms of an IQ score.

A child suffering from developmental reading disorder will display such behaviors as hesitant oral reading, leaving out words, modifying words, not recognizing words, reversing the perception or reproduction of letters, and general lack of reading comprehension. Frequently, children with this disorder also suffer from attention-deficit hyperactivity disorder. The disorder is more common in males than in females.

Reading instruction using special techniques can benefit the child with developmental reading disorder. Often the child seems to have what has been described as *word blindness*, an inability to perceive words correctly. Thus, a technique such as having the child trace his or her finger over sandpaper letters glued to blocks of wood can be helpful. While tracing a letter, the child can also say it aloud. The child thus sees the letter while, at the same time, making motor movements (i.e., moving the hand and speaking). Thus, an improved sensorimotor connection may form between seeing letters (and words) and their reproduction by the child in speech or writing.

Parents who have a child suffering from a developmental reading disorder should take heart. Much improvement can result if the child receives the proper instruction.

Sometimes developmental reading disorder is called *dyslexia*. The literal meaning of the term is a "defective understanding of words."

See also *attention-deficit hyperactivity disorder (ADHD); intelligence quotient (IQ); language development.*

Dewey, John (1859–1952): A philosopher and educational psychologist. Dewey received his Ph.D. degree from Johns Hopkins University in 1884, became a member of the faculty of the University of Chicago in 1894, and was elected a president of the American Psychological Association in 1899. He was a leading advocate of functionalism, a school of psychology asserting that the study of mental life should focus on its *useful* faculties, such as intelligence, memory, perception, thinking, and the will. The father of this point of view is usually said to be William James.

Dewey's interest in functionalism naturally led him to think of the education of children in practical, applied terms. Consequently, Dewey argued that much of classical education, in which students study subjects such as Latin and geometry in a kind of psychological vacuum, tends to be an idle, and not too useful, exercise in learning. Students tend to be bored by abstract subjects detached from life, do not pay attention, and may lose interest in learning. Instead, Dewey argued that subjects should be presented in a direct, useful way so that students could see their importance and connection to life as it is actually lived. One of Dewey's most important points is that children learn by doing. They learn best when they are active and solving a problem, not when they are passive and listening politely. In this regard, he shared the viewpoint of Maria Montessori, an influential Italian educator. Dewey's educational philosophy is referred to as *instrumentalism*. It has also been called *progressive education.*

See also *cognitive development; educational psychology; intelligence; James, William; Montessori method; open classroom; school achievement.*

differential emotions theory: See *emotional states.*

discipline: A loosely organized set of methods used by parents, teachers, and other caretakers to manage the behavior of children, particularly their social behavior. Frequently, discipline is overly equated with the concepts of *punishment* and *restriction.* It is worth pointing out that discipline is related to the word *disciple.* Fitzhugh Dodson, a child psychologist, has pointed out that to discipline a child is to make the child one's disciple (i.e., one's "follower"). Taking this viewpoint, the responsible adult looks for ways to discipline in an effective and constructive manner. The principles associated with operant conditioning and behavior modification generate a number of practical methods of discipline, particularly with toddlers and preschoolers.

Effective discipline is, of course, an art, not a science. It involves bringing to bear upon the socialization of the child all that one knows about child development. Communication skills, for example, are of great importance.

Disciplinary measures that discount a child's feelings, that are harsh and arbitrary, and that reflect hostility on the part of a parent are, on the whole, ineffective. They do not foster self-esteem and may create substantial amounts of resentment. And children who are overly resentful may act out their aggressions in various antisocial ways.

See also *acting out; aggressiveness; antisocial behavior; authoritarian parent; behavior modification; communication skills; operant conditioning; parental style; punishment; self-esteem; socialization.*

disobedience: Lack of compliance with a request or order given by a parent or other authority figure. Although disobedience is generally unacceptable to parents, it is important to realize that occasional disobedience is to be expected in both children and adolescents. It is one of the ways in which they express their autonomy and prove to themselves that they are individuals. Regular disobedience can, of course, be a significant problem. It can be a sign of chronic anxiety, depression, or undersocialization. And it can play a causal role in such behavioral disorders as conduct disorder and oppositional defiant disorder.

Parents can cope with occasional disobedience by using behavior modification and communication skills. Regular disobedience is a sign of a behavioral disorder, and may require professional intervention or psychotherapy.

See also *antisocial behavior; anxiety; autonomy versus shame and doubt; behavior modification; communication skills; conduct disorder; discipline; depression; oppositional defiant disorder.*

displacement: A defense mechanism in which a child's ego is protected by directing toward a second source an emotional reaction that is actually associated with a first source. The most common kind of displacement is *displacement of aggression.* For example, 8-year-old Karen is criticized during breakfast by her mother for slurping when she eats her milk and cereal. Karen believes that her mother is being unfair and overly harsh, but Karen is overtly agreeable and says, "I'm sorry, Mother." Later at school, she starts out the day badly by being mean and rude to her best friend. Her best friend has become, innocently, the scapegoat for the hostile feelings Karen kept back from her mother.

It should be noted the expression of aggression can take objective or symbolic form. Breaking something or hitting someone are examples of objective expressions. Insults and snide remarks are examples of symbolic expressions.

See also *acting out; aggressiveness; ego defense mechanisms.*

displacement in language: The use of language to refer to the past, the future, or other places. One can speak of the days when Abraham Lincoln was president of the United States, of "the world of tomorrow" when human beings travel to the stars, or of the fact that people in Europe are sleeping when people in North America are awake. These expressions, which seem so easy to adults, are a result of cognitive maturity. Although language includes displacement as one of its built-in characteristics, toddlers are incapable of taking advantage of it because they appear to live to a large extent in the world of the here and now. However, language abilities develop rapidly in human beings, and the great majority of preschoolers apply the displacement function with ease.

See also *meaning in language; productiveness in language.*

divergent thinking: Thinking in which the lines of reasoning lead to various answers or solutions. Informally, it is thinking that departs from the main road and takes interesting detours. Divergent thinking underlies most original thought, and it plays a dominant role in creativity. Thus, it is an important factor in such behaviors as writing poetry or fiction, composing music, making scientific discoveries, and inventing new products.

See also *convergent thinking; creative thinking; creativity tests.*

diving reflex: A reflex that is present in the neonate and that is characterized by slowing of the pulse and an increase in the blood supply to the brain if cool water is splashed on the infant's face. It is possible that the function of the diving reflex is to prepare the infant to cope physiologically if submerged. Although strong at first, the reflex tends to fade out to some extent over time.

See also *neonatal reflexes.*

divorce: The legal dissolution of a marriage. Divorce is about seven times more common today than it was at the beginning of the century. Across the United States, if current trends continue, about 40 to 50 percent of recent marriages will end in divorce. It is estimated that almost one-half of children will spend a significant amount of time being raised by one parent. In 90 percent of cases, this parent will be the mother. The social impact of divorce is great, and it only natural to ask: What is the impact on the development of children? The question is complex and does not lend itself to a simple answer. The age of the child at the time of divorce, the attitude of both parents, the amount of emotional support given the child, and similar factors all need to be considered. Taking as many factors into account as possible, some observations can be made.

In general, children usually react with strong emotions to a divorce. They frequently experience fear, anger, resentment, helplessness, and depression. The emotional distress is often aggravated by the idea that if they had been "better," then the divorce would not have taken place. They often think that they are to blame. Parents need to provide reassurance that this is not so. Unfortunately, parents are often wrapped up in their own emotional states during the divorce process and may find it difficult to simultaneously meet the needs of children. Nonetheless, parents need to be aware of these points and make an effort to act constructively on the behalf of their offspring.

Toddlers and preschoolers may react to a divorce with confusion. A frequent reaction is regression to a more infantile level of development. For example, a child who is toilet trained may fail to function reliably in this area for a time. A fear of meeting new people and excessive shyness are common. Other problems such as enuresis or stuttering may be aggravated by a divorce.

Somewhat older children may react to a divorce with a superficial acceptance, responding in a rational way to the reasons parents give for the necessity of the divorce. Nonetheless, below the surface, there are usually strong negative emotional responses. Various studies suggest that children of divorce may, at least for a time, suffer from lowered self-esteem and lack of interest in school work.

The adverse impact of a divorce on a child's development is not an argument in favor of continuing to endure a severely troubled marriage in noble self-sacrifice for the "welfare of the children." A chronically unhappy couple will have a difficult time playing the required roles of nurturing, effective parents. A relatively stable one-parent household probably provides more emotional reassurance in the long run than an unstable household with two parents.

A high divorce rate is a fact of modern life. Divorcing parents share the responsibility to (1) recognize that a divorce will have some adverse impact on their children and (2) seek effective ways to minimize the effects of this adverse impact.

If divorced parents take responsibility and act intelligently, the long-run adjustment, intelligence, and personality of their children should be well within normal bounds.

See also *dysfunctional family; enuresis; extended family; nuclear family; one-parent family; regression; socialization; stuttering.*

dominant gene: A gene that exerts its influence on the phenotype independent of the information arising from a second gene with which it is paired. In practical terms, what this means is that if an individual has a dominant gene for a given characteristic on the first member of a pair of chromosomes and a recessive gene for that same characteristic on the second member, the individual will display only the attributes associated with the dominant gene.

For example, suppose that Kathy has a gene for brown eyes. The gene for brown eyes is dominant and is usually symbolized B. (The capital letter is used to indicate *dominant*; lower case is used to indicated *recessive*.) Kathy also has a recessive gene for blue eyes (b). The gene pair is Bb, and Kathy will have brown eyes.

A knowledge of how dominant genes exert their influence is of particular importance in the case of a disease caused by such a gene. Huntington's chorea is an example of this kind of disease.

See also *gene; genotype; Huntington's chorea; phenotype; recessive gene.*

Down's syndrome: A set of related symptoms, both mental and organic, caused by an extra chromosome in the 21st pair of chromosomes (i.e., Trisomy 21). An older name for Down's syndrome was *mongolism* because the person with the syndrome has almond-shaped eyes and flattened features. Because of overtones of racial bias, the more neutral term *Down's syndrome* is the preferred one. The syndrome was originally studied by Langdon Down in the 1880s.

A principal feature of Down's syndrome is mental retardation. The range of retardation is usually from moderate to severe; this is an IQ range from about 20 to 49. The incidence of Down's syndrome is 1 in every 600 infants. This translates into somewhat over 400,000 people with the syndrome in the United States. It has been long known that the risk of having an infant with Down's syndrome increases with the mother's age. Contemporary studies also suggests the father's age may be a factor.

Children with Down's syndrome tend to respond well to instruction. They can learn to help themselves in many ways and often develop quite remarkable social skills. On the whole, they are affectionate and oriented toward people.

In addition to the almond-shaped eyes, a constellation of physical features are signs of Down's syndrome. These include short fingers, a fold of skin on the inner side of the eye, a very small amount of hair on the face and body, a large tongue, a short neck, and a curved little finger. Cataracts are common in children with Down's syndrome. The life expectancy for an infant with Down's syndrome is 16 years. Compare this with a general expectancy of 70 to 75 years, and one sees that Down's syndrome is associated with significant health problems.

Genetic counseling is one way to reduce the risk of having an infant with Down's syndrome. Another way is for parents to be relatively young. If an infant is born with the syndrome, treatment consists of good medical care, parental affection, and the special training available for a retarded person. Ideally, intervention with special training should come early in the child's development.

See also *birth defects; chromosomal anomalies; genetic counseling; mental retardation.*

drug abuse in adolescence: The improper or excessive use of drugs, such as hallucinogens, inhalants, narcotics, and stimulants during adolescence. Such use is associated with behaviors described as either self-defeating or self-destructive. The use and abuse of drugs in adolescence is common. If one includes legal and socially acceptable drugs such as nicotine and alcohol in a survey of drug use, it is clear that a majority of adolescents have experimented with drugs. It is also estimated that 80 to 90 percent of adults addicted to drugs were introduced to these substances in adolescence. The most common drugs used by adolescents are nicotine, alcohol, marijuana, and inhalants. The term *gateway drugs* is used to describe them because such drugs provide an entrance into the eventual abuse of narcotics, sedatives, and hallucinogens.

A formal distinction should be made among drug use, drug abuse, and drug addiction. *Drug use* in and of itself neither implies abuse nor dependence. The user may try a drug once and never try it again. Or sometimes there is a "take it or leave it" attitude toward a drug. The use of some drugs may be recreational and infrequent. However, it should be noted that it is impossible to abuse drugs unless one is first a drug user.

Drug abuse involves using a drug in a way that is either self-defeating or self-destructive. The abuse of a drug may lead to problems in living, including poor school performance, to injury to the body, or even to death. *Drug addiction* suggests a physiological or psychological dependence on the drug. The person cannot stop taking the drug by an act of will. Obviously, use, abuse, and addiction are overlapping concepts.

There are several causal factors involved in adolescent drug abuse. First, this is a society that uses drugs. Adolescents hear a lot about drugs, and drugs are readily available. Second, peers who already use drugs exert a significant influence on those who have not yet tried drugs. Third, the adolescent subculture in some schools and neighborhoods may send the message that one is neither an effective nor interesting person unless one uses drugs. Fourth, parents often provide models for drug abuse. Adolescents may begin to use drugs in part because of observational learning. Fifth, anxiety, depression, shyness, low self-esteem, and similar problems in personal and social adjustment tend to make an adolescent somewhat more susceptible to drug abuse. Drugs are used as an escape from negative emotional states and doubts about oneself.

There is no easy answer to the problem of drug abuse in adolescence. However, concerned parents have some options open to them. They should make children aware from an early age of the hazards of drug abuse by providing realistic *information*, not by moralizing or preaching. If parents are convinced that an adolescent is actually abusing drugs, they should not deny reality. They should air their concerns with the teenager. They should also set limits, defining both acceptable and unacceptable behavior. The concept of *tough love* comes into play here. Parents need to love their children enough to be firm with them and attach response costs to unacceptable behavior. Also, parents need to help adolescents with their problems in personal and social adjustment if at all possible. If parents are overwhelmed and unable to help the adolescent, they should turn to mental health professionals and community resources, such as school counselors, psychologists, social workers, psychiatrists, family clinics, and hospitals.

See also *depressant drugs; hallucinogens; inhalant drugs; narcotic drugs; sedatives; stimulant drugs; tough love.*

drug therapy: In psychiatry, the prescription of drugs to help individuals with behavioral difficulties, emotional problems, or mental disorders. The clinical term for drug therapy in psychiatry is *psychopharmacology*. The use of drug therapy with troubled children and adolescents has generated a certain amount of debate among both lay persons and mental health professionals. However, on the whole, a consensus appears to exist suggesting that drug therapy with children and adolescents is appropriate if certain guidelines are met. These guidelines include the following:

1. The problem or mental disorder does not respond to psychotherapy or behavior modification alone.

2. Doses of the medication should be as small as is practical for effectiveness.
3. Potential adverse side effects must be carefully evaluated.
4. A long-term plan for eventual withdrawal from the drug is considered.
5. The drug should not be seen as a cure-all for the child's problems.

Prescription drugs for behavioral problems and mental disorders fall into one of several principal classes.

1. *Antianxiety drugs* or *minor tranquilizers* are used to treat anxiety disorders, tension, convulsive conditions, and insomnia.
2. *Antipsychotic drugs (major tranquilizers; neuroleptic drugs)* are used to treat the symptoms of psychotic disorders. They are of particular value in treating the delusions and hallucinations associated with schizophrenia. Antipsychotic drugs are often prescribed to treat such disorders in children and adolescents as conduct disorder, pervasive developmental disorders (e.g., autistic disorder), and Tourette's disorder. In addition, these drugs are also sometimes prescribed for chronic behavioral problems such as aggressiveness, impulsiveness, and rage.
3. *Antidepressant drugs* are used to treat unipolar disorder and other depressive conditions.
4. There is a single *antimanic drug*. The generic name of this drug is *lithium carbonate,* and it is used to treat manic episodes associated with bipolar disorder.
5. *Stimulants* are used to treat attention-deficit hyperactivity disorder, narcolepsy, and obesity.
6. *Sedatives* depress the activity of the central nervous system and are sometimes used to treat sleep difficulties such as insomnia, night terrors, or nightmares. Both alcohol and barbiturates are kinds of sedatives, and it is, of course, barbiturates that are prescribed. Barbiturates have a high potential for physiological addiction and may produce many unwanted side effects, such as abrupt emotional changes, poor motor coordination, slurred speech, memory problems, and difficulties in understanding ideas. Therefore, they should be administered with the utmost care and concern.

Some of the problems and mental disorders treated with drugs in children and adolescents are identified in the following cross-referenced entries.

See also *aggressiveness; anorexia nervosa; anxiety; attention-deficit hyperactivity disorder (ADHD); bulimia nervosa; childhood schizophrenia; conduct disorder; depression; enuresis; impulsiveness; insomnia; night terror; nightmare; pervasive developmental disorders; psychotic disorders; separation anxiety disorder; Tourette's disorder.*

dwarfism: See *short stature.*

dysfunctional family: A family that is not meeting the psychological and emotional needs of its members. Causal factors that tend to interplay in a dysfunctional family are numerous and may include parents who abuse alcohol and other drugs, child abuse, ineffective discipline, a single parent, inability to communicate effectively, poverty, lack of parental affection, a child who suffers from a behavioral disorder (e.g., a conduct disorder), temperamental differences between parents and children, and so forth. An important treatment for the kind of dysfunction described here is family therapy.

See also *abusing parent; alcoholic parent; authoritarian parent; child abuse; communication skills; conduct disorder; discipline; family therapy; juvenile delinquency; parental style.*

dyslexia: See *developmental reading disorder.*

dyssocial behavior: Behavior that does not fit in well with the standards and norms of the conventional society or culture. Both antisocial and dyssocial behavior are similar in this regard. However, the individual displaying dyssocial behavior functions as if he or she is socialized in the context of a gang or other group representing a subculture. For example, adolescents who are members of gangs often display such prosocial traits as courage, honesty, and loyalty to other gang members. Unfortunately, this means they may also steal or inflict bodily injury on others as part of their subgroup behavior. Therefore, they cannot be considered socialized.

See also *antisocial behavior; prosocial behavior; socialization.*

E

early childhood: See *child*.

eating disorders: A set of related disorders distinguished by abnormal eating behavior. These disorders commonly make their first appearance in infancy, childhood, or adolescence; and anorexia nervosa and bulimia are more common among females than males. There are four principal eating disorders.

1. *Anorexia nervosa* is characterized by a fear of becoming fat and a tendency toward self-imposed eating restrictions.
2. *Bulimia nervosa* is characterized by eating binges and purges.
3. *Pica* is characterized by the eating of substances without nutritional value, such as clay or paint.
4. *Rumination disorder of infancy* is characterized by bringing back into the mouth previously swallowed food.

These disorders can have quite serious consequences, such as biochemical imbalances, emaciation from undereating, obesity from overeating, and death from self-imposed starvation.

Eating disorders associated with infancy and early childhood are usually treated with behavior therapy. In the case of older children and adolescents, the approach is usually two-pronged. First, the individual is helped with verbal psychotherapy to understand *why* he or she abuses food. Second, the individual is aided with behavior-modification strategies revealing *how* eating behavior can become more normal.

See also *anorexia nervosa; bulimia nervosa; obesity; pica; rumination disorder of infancy.*

echolalia: A tendency of one person to repeat portions of the statements of a second person. Thus, the first person "echoes" the second person. Repetitions are sometimes described as *parrotlike*, suggesting that they are meaningless imitation. For example, a nurse says to an institutionalized child suffering from autistic disorder, "Your mother telephoned and told me she wants to take you out for a pizza for lunch today." And the child picks up and repeats, "Told me she wants, told me she wants." No sensible response is given to the nurse's comment.

In some cases, echolalia can be caused by a neurological defect. Echolalia sometimes appears in children who are suffering from autistic disorder, childhood schizophrenia, and mental retardation caused or complicated by organic factors.

See also *autistic disorder; childhood schizophrenia; developmental disorders; mental retardation.*

educational psychology: An applied field of psychology that concerns itself with ways in which to improve the school learning process. Such subjects as learning, memory, cognitive development, intelligence, and motivation are presented as a part of teacher training. The effective classroom teacher is expected to make use of a substantial range of knowledge in these areas.

The scope of educational psychology is quite large, and includes such areas of interest as (1) social interactions in the classroom, (2) the maturation and developmental levels of students, (3) classroom management, (4) effective teaching methods, (5) behavior modification, (6) creativity of students, and (7) the construction of valid and reliable examinations.

See also *developmental psychology; Dewey, John; Montessori, Maria; Montessori method; Pygmalion effect; Scholastic Aptitude Test (SAT); school achievement; Thorndike, Edward Lee; Wertheimer, Max.*

egg cell: See *ovum.*

ego: According to Freud, the second principal part of the personality to emerge during development, the other two being the id and the superego. The ego is the "I" of the personality. (The Latin word for *I* is *ego.*) It is reality oriented and is said to follow the *reality principle.* It is the ego that takes on the difficult task of mediating differences between the emotional demands of the id and the moralistic supervision of the superego. When the ego is not up to its job, when there is inadequate ego strength, symptoms of mental disorders may appear.

According to classical Freudian theory, the ego forms out of the id around the time that infancy ends and toddlerhood begins. When children can make declarations such as, "I want milk" or "I don't like Billy," it can be assumed from their correct usage of the pronoun *I* that a primitive ego has formed. In early childhood, the ego is weak, self-esteem is easily threatened, and the child has a high degree of emotional vulnerability.

Sometimes the word *ego* is used as a synonym for the word *self.* Although this usage is common, it blurs the conceptual distinction between the ego and the whole personality. It is probably best to say that the ego is the *conscious self.* This suggests that the ego is at the center of the personality and that the whole self revolves around it.

The term *ego* is often used as a prefix, and, immediately following this entry, there are six entries where this is the case.

See also *Freud; id; psychoanalysis; superego.*

ego defense mechanisms: A set of involuntary psychological processes that protect the individual against the harsher aspects of reality. Defense mechanisms, arranged unconsciously by the ego, provide a buffer between unpleasant facts and threats to the integrity of the personality.

Defense mechanisms play a significant role in psychoanalytic theory. If used to a moderate degree, they are seen as normal and useful in maintaining the health of the personality. If they are used excessively, they contribute to neurotic tendencies and personality disorders. If they stop functioning, the person is left without protection, and there may be a collapse of the personality. Schizophrenic disorders can be conceptualized in this way.

The ego defense mechanisms were first identified and described by Freud. Later they were studied more extensively by his daughter, Anna Freud, a leading psychoanalyst and child psychologist of her day.

Ego defense mechanisms make their first appearance in early childhood. A common one used by preschoolers is denial of reality. It is a primitive attempt to say that something *is not* so just because one *wishes* that it were not so. Another common defense mechanism in early childhood is regression. For example, toddlers who are already toilet trained may begin to act like infants again in this regard upon the arrival of a sibling or being exposed to severe marital discord.

Older children and adolescents use subtle, more complex defense mechanisms, such as reaction formation or rationalization.

See also *denial of reality; fantasy; Freud, Anna; Freud, Sigmund; narcissism; projection; rationalization; reaction formation; regression; repression; sublimation.*

ego identity: See *identity.*

ego integrity: See *integrity versus despair.*

ego state: In transactional analysis, a way in which the personality expresses itself at a given moment. According to the psychiatrist Eric Berne, father of transactional analysis, a person employs three ego states. These are the Parent, the Adult, and the Child. (In transactional analysis, ego states are capitalized in order to discriminate them from actual parents, adults, and children.)

The Parent ego state tends to be value oriented. It is often judgmental and authoritarian. When one finds oneself quoting proverbs or repeating attitudes observed previously in one's own parents, then the Parent ego state is active.

The Adult ego state is the computer of the personality. It is logical and rational. When one is solving a problem or talking with another person in a reasonable manner, then one is in an Adult ego state.

The Child ego state is the emotional side of the personality. It seeks recognition in the form of love, affection, and attention. It also rebels and acts out aggressively when frustrated or when recognition cannot be obtained in a constructive way. This is called the *Rebellious Child ego state*.

According to Berne, one can manifest any ego state at any age. Five-year-old Tammy puts her hands on her hips and tells her pet dog, "I'm sending you to bed without supper. You've been a very bad boy today." She is in her Parent ego state. A 25-year-old husband begins to act toward his wife like the bully he was in grammar school. He is in his Child ego state. (In psychoanalytic terms, this can also be thought of as regression.)

Using the formulation of the three ego states, many problems in adjustment can be seen as the activity of the Child ego state at times when it would be better for the Adult ego state to be active.

See also *Berne, Eric; regression; script; stroke; transactional analysis.*

egocentric thinking: A way of thinking about the external world in such a way that it seems to revolve around one's ego. A child with an egocentric orientation tends to see the whole world, including other people, revolving around his or her personality.

It is natural for children between the ages of about 2 and 7 to be egocentric. They perceive themselves as being at the center of the universe, and it is very difficult for them to imagine any viewpoint other than their own. For example, 4-year-old Galen has a pain in his arm. He tells his mother, "It hurts, Mommy." He then moves his arm up and down saying, "See what I mean." It seems that he thinks his mother feels the pain. On the other hand, when a few days later his mother says, "Let me take a nap, Galen. Don't bother me for a while. I have a headache," he is unable to really understand. He examines his own experience, feels no pain, and cannot grasp how it is possible for his mother to be hurting.

There are many examples of egocentric thinking in the behavior of young children. A common example is that they often think the moon is following the family car at night. The moon even seems to start and stop when the car starts and stops. Another common example is the mental confusion that arises when a child learns the Earth is round. How can people on the other side of the world be right-side up? They must be upside down. When the child is told that they are right-side up *to themselves* but upside down *to us*, the situation seems hopeless. Egocentric thinking does not allow the child to shift subjective frames of reference.

See also *cognitive development; Piaget, Jean; preoperational stage.*

egocentrism: The point of view that one's ego is at the center of the universe.

See also *egocentric thinking.*

elaborated language codes: See *language codes.*

elective mutism: A childhood behavioral disorder characterized by a stubborn unwillingness to speak. The child *can* speak but will not cooperate with parents and teachers. The cause of the disorder is *not* mental retardation. In most cases the child's intelligence is normal. The disorder is usually first evident at approximately 5 years of age.

Causal factors in the disorder include a shy temperament, lack of friends, hostility to parents and other caregivers, a history of being sickly, and overprotection. The incidence of the disorder is low. Elective mutism is associated with less than 1 percent of clinical cases seen by mental health professionals.

The majority of children with the disorder manifest it for a relatively short time. If the disorder persists, child psychotherapy and family therapy are recommended.

See also *mutism.*

Electra complex: Another name for the *Oedipus complex.* The term *Electra complex* is sometimes used when this particular complex refers to females. However, it correct to use the single term *Oedipus complex* when referring to either males or females.

The name *Electra complex* is derived from an ancient Greek tragedy by Sophocles in which Electra urges her brother to kill their mother.

See also *Oedipus complex.*

eliciting stimulus: A stimulus that evokes, or "brings out," a reflex. For example, if an infant's cheek is stroked with a nipple or a finger, the infant will turn toward the source and make sucking motions. This is known as the *rooting reflex*. In this case, *stroking of the cheek* is the eliciting stimulus.

See also *neonatal reflexes; rooting reflex.*

embracing reflex: See *Moro reflex.*

embryo: A prenatal organism in the early stages of its development. The embryonic stage follows immediately after the stage of the *zygote* and just before the stage of the *fetus.* In human beings, the embryonic stage lasts about eight weeks. The embryo is approximately one inch in length toward the end of the eighth week and is a formed individual with a face and internal organs.

See also *fetal development; fetus; neonate; ovum; sperm cell; zygote.*

emotional deprivation: In infancy and early childhood, deprivation of attention and affection. The child who is emotionally deprived may have a difficult time building a sense of trust, may feel anxious and insecure, and may also have a difficult time becoming attached to parents. Such children also may demonstrate a low developmental quotient and be subject to an excessive number of health problems. Meeting the emotional needs of infants and young children appears to be almost as important as meeting their needs for food and water.

See also *anaclitic depression; attachment; developmental quotient (DQ); feral child; institutionalized children; trust versus mistrust.*

emotional development: See *emotional states.*

emotional states: States characterized by (1) significant changes in central nervous system arousal and associated physiological activity and (2) displays of behavior suggesting the presence of these changes. There are four basic emotional states, and these are derived from the two primary emotional dimensions. The emotional dimensions are bipolar in nature and are identified as (1) pleasure-distress and (2) excitement-calm. Pleasure-distress is called the *hedonic* dimension. Excitement-calm is called the *arousal* dimension.

The four basic states are, therefore, (1) pleasure with excitement, (2) distress with excitement, (3) pleasure with calm, and (4) distress with calm. The four basic states can be readily identified in infancy. They become more articulated and detailed in early childhood, and this is the process known as *emotional development*. By late childhood the individual is possessed of a complete emotional range. Emotional states such as *ecstasy, joy,* and *delight* reflect pleasure with excitement. Emotional states such as *rage, anger,* and *anxiety* reflect distress with excitement. Emotional states such as *tranquillity, bliss,* and *serenity* reflect pleasure with calm. Emotional states such as *depression, apathy,* and *dejection* reflect distress with calm.

The process described above reflects an approach to emotional development known as *differential emotions theory*. As is evident, this theory hypothesizes that the more subtle, complex emotions are born out of the basic emotional states. Both learning and maturation are involved in emotional development.

Emotional development is sometimes also referred to as *affective development*. The term *affect* in psychology has become more or less synonymous with the word *emotion*. A technical distinction is sometimes made indicating that *affect* is the *display* of an emotion in contrast to the emotion itself.

See also *anxiety; depression; emotional deprivation; emotional trauma.*

emotional trauma: An emotional wound that leaves an individual feeling rejected, inferior, unloved, or otherwise psychologically damaged. (The word *trauma* is the Greek word for "wound"; *traumata* is the plural form.) Emotional traumata, or wounds, are of particular importance in the early years because children with their limited cognitive abilities can make very little sense out of personal mistreatment. Therefore, repeated emotional wounds experienced in childhood can have a severely negative impact on personality development. Psychoanalysis considers a pattern of emotional wounds to be one of the principal causal factors in the formation of neurotic tendencies and maladjustment in general.

See also *childhood neurosis; maladjusted child; psychoanalysis.*

empiricism: In philosophy and psychology, the point of view that everything known to the mind is acquired through experience. The most well-known version of this is the philosopher John Locke's doctrine of the *tabula rasa* (i.e., "blank slate"). According to Locke, the infant has no inborn ideas, no inborn knowledge. The mind at birth is a blank slate. Experience, like a piece of chalk, writes on the slate. Therefore, a child's moral sense, attitudes, beliefs, concepts, and all knowledge are acquired through learning.

A 20th-century version of empiricism is to be found in the teachings of John B. Watson, the father of behaviorism. He asserted that, aside from a few inborn reflexes, the infant has no inborn ideas and probably very few behavioral tendencies as well. The developing personality of the child is due almost entirely to conditioning. Habits, not inborn tendencies, explain behavioral traits.

The situation is not as clear-cut as Locke and Watson asserted. It now appears that some behavioral dispositions, particularly temperament, are to some extent inborn. *Nativism* is the point of view that opposes empiricism.

See also *conditioning; innate; learning; nativism; temperament; Watson, John Broadus.*

empty nest syndrome: A group of adverse psychological and emotional reactions characterized by depression, a sense of loss, the conviction that life has lost much of its meaning, lack of immediate purpose and psychological structure, and loneliness precipitated by the last child moving out of the home on a permanent basis. The syndrome can affect a single parent or one or both members of a couple. The empty nest syndrome is common, and the symptoms can range from mild to severe. In the vast majority of cases, the symptoms are temporary and tend to resolve themselves within a few months. The syndrome is likely to take its greatest toll on mothers who have made full-time homemaking their principal vocation for a number of years.

A futile way to cope with the empty nest syndrome is to barrage the absent child with visits, phone calls, letters, gifts, and invitations. Naturally, a meaningful and loving contact should be maintained. But excessive interest and overinvolvement in the child's life will be perceived as an attempt to manipulate and control, and it will be resented.

A parent can cope effectively with milder forms of the empty nest syndrome by investing psychological energy in activities that appear to have value in terms of what Erikson calls *generativity*. Such activities contribute to the welfare of humankind and, in a sense, the long-range interests of children in general. The most obvious example is volunteer work with children in schools and/or hospitals. However, in a more general way, any work, paid or unpaid, that has value to others satisfies the basic criterion of generativity.

If the syndrome becomes chronic, it is likely that deeper causal factors are involved, such as a long-standing tendency toward depression. In this instance, the empty nest is an aggravating cause of depression, but not its principal cause. In such a case, psychotherapy can be helpful.

See also *depression; Erikson, Erik Homburger; generativity versus self-absorption; psychosocial development; psychotherapy.*

enactive mode of thought: As described by the cognitive psychologist Jerome Bruner, a mode of thought in which reality is represented in the form of action. It is a way of processing information and tends to be associated with the sensory and motor capacities of infants and toddlers. To a very young child, a nipple is simply something that can be sucked, a rattle is an object that can be grabbed and shaken, and a ball is a thing that can be bounced. The enactive mode of thought is preverbal but is important because it forms the foundation for more complex cognitive skills that come with subsequent development.

One does not outgrow the enactive mode of thought. It plays a prime role in the use of tools—objects that enhance our ability to *do*, to *act*, to *have an effect* upon the world.

See also *Bruner, Jerome S.; iconic mode of thought; symbolic mode of thought.*

encopresis: The involuntary expulsion of fecal bulk. The term is usually used to describe the behavior of children who have not learned either adequate or appropriate control of their bowel movements. (*Soiling* is an informal word often used to describe the effect of encopresis.) For example, a 4-year-old child who defecates while sleeping or playing with friends may be said to be suffering from encopresis.

Organic encopresis has a biological basis and requires medical treatment. *Functional encopresis* has an emotional, or psychological, basis. Causal factors in functional encopresis include inadequate toilet-training procedures and hostility toward the parents. The problem of encopresis is similar in nature to the problem of enuresis. Treatment consists of psychotherapy aimed at helping the child resolve emotional conflicts. This is combined with training procedures designed to help the child gain greater voluntary control of the anal sphincter. The prognosis for functional encopresis is good. Most children outgrow the problem by late childhood.

See also *enuresis*.

enuresis: A behavioral disorder characterized by the uncontrolled release of urine. It is possible to discriminate organic enuresis from functional enuresis. *Organic enuresis* is due to pathology at a biological level and requires medical treatment. *Functional enuresis* is basically psychological in nature and is the type that is discussed below.

If enuresis occurs in the day, it is known as *diurnal enuresis*. If enuresis takes place during sleep, it is known as *nocturnal enuresis* and is the most common kind. Nocturnal enuresis usually takes place during deep sleep. (The popular term for nocturnal enuresis is *bedwetting*.)

About 7 percent of boys and 3 percent of girls 5 years of age suffer from the disorder. In adults, functional enuresis is very rare.

The disorder tends to run in families. Thus, it is possible to hypothesize the existence of at least some genetic predisposition toward it. Research with identical twins tends to support this hypothesis. On the other hand, emotional factors and maladaptive habits also appear to play causal roles. For example, unconscious hostility toward a parent may aggravate the condition.

Several modes of treatment exist for enuresis. The antidepressant drug imipramine sometimes relieves symptoms. Psychotherapy aimed at helping a child resolve emotional conflicts can be of value. A pad that is wired to sound a bell when the pad is wet with urine has been found to be very useful. The pad-bell method is based on conditioning principles and was developed by O. Hobart Mowrer, a former president of the American Psychological Association.

See also *encopresis*.

epigenesis: The process by which new characteristics emerge in the developing organism. The basic idea of epigenesis is that information contained in a young organism makes its appearance in more mature form according to a biological timetable. The idea was originally associated with biology. Thus, the information that will make a man have a beard is contained in the genes present on the chromosomes at conception. An infant boy does not have a beard, but, through epigenesis, the boy will eventually develop one.

The concept of epigenesis has been generalized to cover larger phenomena such as cognitive development. According to Piaget, children's minds mature in a series of predictable stages. The unfolding of certain mental abilities, somewhat independently of environmental influence, is a case of epigenesis at the psychological level.

See also *cognitive development; maturation; Piaget, Jean.*

epilepsy: A disorder in which pathological functioning of the brain causes a variety of symptoms, such as seizures, odd actions, and altered states of consciousness. It is a neurologic disorder, not a mental one. About 1,500,000 people in the United States suffer from epilepsy. Although the disorder is not associated exclusively with either children or adults, it usually makes its first appearance in an individual in the early developmental years, usually not later than adolescence. Epilepsy follows an informal rule of thirds. About one-third of children with epilepsy simply do not suffer from it once they become adults. Another third have a moderate case of the disorder, one that is readily controlled with medication. A final third find the disorder a chronic problem.

General causes of epilepsy in children include damage to the brain and nervous system at the time of birth, head wounds, infections of the central nervous system, and tumors in the brain. (Fetal alcohol syndrome is one example of how the brain and nervous system can be damaged before birth.) However, the cause of epilepsy in a given individual is often obscure. In *idiopathic epilepsy,* there is no distinct organic basis for the symptoms. In *symptomatic epilepsy*, there is an identifiable organic brain pathology. Only 25 percent of cases fall in this category.

In addition to the distinction made above between idiopathic and symptomatic epilepsy, four basic kinds of epilepsy are identified: grand mal, petit mal, Jacksonian, and psychomotor.

1. *Grand mal (major) epilepsy* is characterized by severe convulsive seizures.

2. *Petit mal (minor) epilepsy* is characterized by a lapse in consciousness. The individual seems to be unaware of what is happening or seems somewhat confused. This state is termed a *nonconvulsive seizure.* Petit mal epilepsy is more likely to affect children than adults.

3. *Jacksonian epilepsy* is characterized by involuntary movements of the body such as twitches and spasms without the loss of consciousness. Jacksonian epilepsy was identified and described by J. Hughlings Jackson (1835–1911), a neurologist.

4. *Psychomotor epilepsy* is characterized by actions that do not seem to fit the individual's normal personality. (This kind of epilepsy is also called *temporal-lobe epilepsy.*) A usually soft-spoken person may become loud and aggressive. Or an individual may begin to laugh uncontrollably without apparent cause.

(It should be noted that *narcolepsy,* a tendency to fall suddenly and involuntarily asleep, is not usually listed as a form of epilepsy.)

There is no specific cure for epilepsy. However, as already noted, many children and adolescents do not have the problem follow them into adulthood. Also, epilepsy is treatable and controllable with anticonvulsant medication. With adequate medical supervision, the life of many children suffering from epilepsy can be free, or almost free, from seizures.

See also *attention-deficit hyperactivity disorder (ADHD); birth defects; cerebral palsy.*

Erikson, Erik Homburger (1902–   ): Developed the concept of psychosocial stages as a logical extension of Freud's psychosexual stages. Erikson was born in Germany, studied under Freud, became a psychoanalyst, emigrated to the United States, and did research in association with Harvard University.

Erikson's investigations suggest that people move through eight stages of development from birth to death. The first stage is trust versus mistrust, and the last is ego integrity versus despair. Each stage presents a developmental task that challenges the individual to develop the positive attribute associated with the stage (e.g., trust or ego integrity).

It was Erikson who coined the now-famous term *identity crisis*. An identity crisis is associated with the fifth stage of psychosocial development, identity versus role confusion.

Erikson's work has done much to further understanding of the causal factors involved in the formation of both the healthy and the pathological personality. Three of Erikson's books are *Childhood and Society* (1963), *Identity: Youth and Crisis* (1968), and *Life History and the Historical Moment* (1975).

See also *adolescence; autonomy versus doubt; Freud, Sigmund; generativity versus self-absorption; identity crisis; identity versus role confusion; industry versus inferiority; initiative versus guilt; integrity versus despair; intimacy versus isolation; psychosexual development; psychosocial development; socialization; trust versus mistrust.*

esteem needs: According to Maslow, the related needs for competence, approval, and recognition. In children, the need for *competence* is the need to be able to do things well. An example of the expression of this need in childhood is the desire to be able to ride a bicycle. The need for *approval* is the need to have others place a positive value on one's accomplishments and behavior. An example of the expression of this need is the anticipation of praise from a parent for a job well done. The need for *recognition* is the need to have one's accomplishments be seen and approved of by others. An example of the expression of this need is the desire to have parents attend a performance of a school play.

If a child's esteem needs are not met by parents, teachers, and other caregivers, this may be a contributing factor to what Adler termed an *inferiority complex*. On the other hand, if a child's esteem needs are met, then this will tend to foster self-esteem in the child. It follows that self-esteem is a stepping stone on the way toward self-actualization.

See also *Adler, Alfred; inferiority complex; Maslow, Abraham Harold; self-actualization; self-esteem.*

estrogen hormones (estrogens): Hormones produced primarily by the ovaries in the female. (A small amount of estrogens are produced by the adrenal glands in both males and females.) When a female approaches puberty, she begins to secrete relatively large amounts of estrogens. Her ovaries will triple in size by the time she reaches adulthood. Estrogens play a significant role in the appearance of secondary sexual characteristics, such as breast development.

The presence of more estrogens in females than in men is associated with the fact that the adult female is about 25 percent body fat and the adult male is about 15 percent body fat. Thus, estrogens contribute to the curvaceous look of the normal-weight female in contrast to the leaner, harder look of the normal-weight male. This is the source of some dismay to some adolescent females who yearn to be ultrathin and plays a part in the psychology of anorexia nervosa.

Increased production of estrogen hormones around the time of puberty is also associated with the menarche, sexual drive, and the ability of females to bear children.

See also *androgens; menarche; sexual development; ovaries.*

ethology: The study of the behavior of animals in their own regions or usual settings. The principal method used is *naturalistic observation,* in which the organism is studied without interference from the scientist. One of the important discoveries associated with ethology is the phenomenon called *imprinting,* and this has led to important insights relative to the understanding of bonding and attachment.

See also *attachment; imprinting; naturalistic observation.*

eugenics: The application of scientific knowledge about how genes and the mechanisms of heredity work with the purpose of improving the human race. The term *eugenics* itself was introduced by Sir Francis Galton somewhat over 100 years ago and means literally "well born." Galton believed that through eugenics many undesirable traits (e.g., mental retardation) could be bred out and many desirable traits (e.g., high intelligence) could be bred in.

Eugenics has had a controversial history. On the one hand, it seems like a good idea. Through eugenics, it would be possible to eliminate, or reduce in number, many birth defects and genetic disorders. On the other hand, it seems that Hitler and his followers believed that they were using eugenics when they encouraged Caucasian gentiles of Nordic stock (i.e., Aryans) to breed with each other in the belief that they were vastly superior to other "races." The general consensus is that Nazi ideology was on the wrong track.

Voluntary genetic counseling is an enlightened approach to eugenics and provides a middle ground between total rejection of eugenics and uncritical acceptance.

See also *Galton, Francis; genetic counseling; heredity.*

exceptional children: Children who reside at either end of the scale used to measure an attribute. The term is used most frequently in school settings, and usually it refers to (1) gifted children (i.e., those with high intelligence or unusual creative ability) or (2) children with intellectual or cognitive problems (i.e., those suffering from mental retardation or significant learning disabilities). Being designated an exceptional child has its advantages and disadvantages. On the positive side, the child receives the special treatment from parents, teachers, and other caregivers that he or she requires for maximum growth and maturation. On the negative side, other children may brand the child with unappealing labels ranging from "egghead" to "dummy." Although test results are not distributed to peers, they observe that the exceptional children go to special classes.

Also, a child's self-image is affected by the use of labels. It seems fairly obvious that it would have a negative impact on a child's self-image to find out that he or she has been diagnosed as mentally retarded and that this is part of a filed record. What is less obvious is that it may be undesirable for a child to know that he or she is "gifted" or "very superior" in intelligence. These labels only suggest a potential that may come to fruition with some effort on the child's part. The mentally gifted child cannot rest on the label, and it may be tempting to do so.

See also *creative thinking; giftedness; intelligence; intelligence quotient (IQ); mental retardation.*

extended family: The larger family beyond the confines of parents and their children. In traditional terms, an extended family consists of three generations living in the same household. Informally, an extended family is thought of as a larger network, not necessarily in the same household, consisting of grandparents, aunts, uncles, cousins, and so forth. The extended family is seen in sociology and social psychology as a support system that helps the individual to find and maintain an identity, develop a sense of belongingness, and foster traditional values. It acts as a force against alienation and isolation.

The major role that can be played by the extended family is lost to a large extent when job transfers, economic conditions, a desire to live in another part of the country, or other circumstances bring about a move by the nuclear family. The nuclear family, as an isolated social unit, may find it difficult to fulfill all of the roles played by the extended family. And this is often a hardship on the developing child.

See also *alienation; family therapy; intimacy versus isolation; nuclear family.*

extinction: In conditioning, the unlearning of a conditioned response. The most reliable way to bring about extinction is to withhold reinforcement when the conditioned response is performed. Another reliable method is counterconditioning. A less reliable method, one with sometimes paradoxical results, is punishment.

Methods of extinction are of particular value in applications of behavior therapy with children. One way to look at such therapy is that it aims to help them extinguish maladaptive emotional or behavioral habits.

See also *behavior therapy; classical conditioning; conditioning; counterconditioning; operant conditioning; punishment; reinforcer.*

extraversion: As formulated by Carl Jung, a basic attitude toward the world characterized by an outgoing orientation. The extraverted child tends to have a dominant interest in the outside world of social interactions and concrete objects as opposed to the inner world of thought and the mind. Jung believed that the personality trait of extraversion is basically inborn, although it can be modified to some extent by experience. Therefore, if Jung is correct, parents should not try to convert born extraverts into introverts. They should recognize and appreciate their children's natural tendencies and help their children build on them in a positive way. Relatively recent research on temperament suggests that Jung's general approach makes sense.

See also *introversion; Jung, Carl Gustav; temperament.*

Eysenck, Hans Jurgen (1916–   ): A research psychologist with a particular interest in personality traits and behavior therapy. Eysenck was born in Germany and has lived and worked in England for many years. He earned a Ph.D. degree from the University of London in 1940 and joined its faculty in 1955.

Eysenck's research indicates that the bipolar personality dimension introversion-extraversion interacts with a second bipolar personality dimension, emotionally stable-emotionally unstable. This yields complex personality traits. For example, a child who is high in introversion and emotional stability will display traits such as *calmness, reliability, peacefulness*, and *carefulness*. On the other hand, a child who is high in introversion but low in emotional stability will display traits such as *unsociability, pessimism, rigidity*, and *moodiness*.

Eysenck has been a strong advocate of behavior therapy, a kind of therapy based on principles of learning such as classical and operant conditioning. His findings suggest that, in general, behavior therapy produces results that are more predictable and reliable in both children and adults than those produced by therapies based on psychoanalytic assumptions. This contention has been a source of vigorous debate among mental health professionals. A compromise position held by many therapists is that behavior therapy is best for certain kinds of problems (e.g., phobias) and that therapies with other orientations, such as psychoanalytic or cognitive, are best for other kinds of problems (e.g., chronic anxiety or depression).

See also *behavior therapy; emotional states; extraversion; introversion; trait.*

F

failure to thrive: In infancy, unsatisfactory developmental progress. The infant who is failing to thrive does not gain enough weight, is not growing adequately in stature, displays weak reflexes, and often seems listless and lacking in alertness. Failure to thrive is a general condition, not a specific disease or disorder. Therefore, it may be caused by a host of factors varying from heart disease to infections, from nutritional inadequacies to emotional neglect. It is, however, a very serious sign suggesting that its causes must be explored immediately.

See also *anaclitic depression*; *developmental quotient (DQ)*; *marasmus*; *rumination disorder of infancy*.

fairy tales: Incredible story usually involving elements of magic and fantastic creatures, such as witches, dragons, talking animals, and so forth. Most people are familiar with a number of classical fairy tales, such as *Cinderella*, *Snow White and the Seven Dwarfs*, and *Beauty and the Beast*. However, fairy tales should not be associated only with folklore and older writings. Contemporary authors are also writing fairy tales for children.

Fairy tales have particular appeal to children during the preoperational stage of thought, associated with the ages of about 2 to 7 years. During this stage of cognitive development, events are more readily understood in terms of magic than in terms of natural causes and effects.

Are fairy tales, particularly the classical ones with their emphasis on violence and vengeance, harmful to the developing minds of children? Should children of 4 or 5 years of age be exposed to evil witches and threatening monsters? According to Bettelheim, a leading researcher on the subject, the answer appears to be that familiarity with fairy tales helps, rather than hinders, children's adjustment to life. In the fairy tales, they have an opportunity to confront their fears and forbidden impulses in an objective, manageable form.

See also *Bettelheim, Bruno; cognitive development; creative thinking; preoperational stage.*

familial mental retardation: A kind of mental retardation without definite organic basis. It appears to be essentially functional in nature and is probably caused by a highly disadvantaged home environment. Often the parents are mentally retarded themselves and do not provide the child with sufficient stimulation of the right kind for adequate cognitive development in the early years.

Sometimes this kind of mental retardation is called *cultural-familial mental retardation* to suggest that the family itself may exist in a socially deprived setting.

Familial mental retardation accounts for the majority of mental retardation in the United States. It is hoped that in the future much retardation can be prevented by enriching the environments of deprived children. Training programs can be of great value for individuals who are already mentally retarded.

See also *mental retardation.*

family therapy: A general approach to psychotherapy in which parents and their children are treated as a single functional unit. The nuclear family itself is seen as the entity that has the pathology, not a single individual. Therefore, if a given child has a mental disorder or a significant behavioral problem, the child's difficulties are not seen as isolated events arising from something within the child. Instead, the child's difficulties are thought of as reflections of troubled interactions in the family.

For example, a child displaying a conduct disorder may be a scapegoat for aggressions associated with older siblings. The younger child's misconduct may be a way of acting out anger in the face of unfair treatment. For a second example, parents who are unhappy with each other and engage in chronic bickering may aggravate the symptoms of an attention-deficit hyperactivity disorder.

The principles applied in family therapy are general and draw from many approaches to therapy, ranging from psychoanalysis to behavior therapy. However, it should be mentioned that the focus on interpersonal psychology emphasized by such thinkers as Eric Berne and Harry S. Sullivan has had much to do with the growth of family therapy.

The convention is for a family to meet with the therapist on a regular basis at least once a week until a crisis is resolved.

See also *acting out; attention-deficit hyperactivity disorder (ADHD); Berne, Eric; conduct disorder; nuclear family; Sullivan, Harry Stack.*

fantasy: In general, a set of mental images inspired by imagination and owing no allegiance to reality. A daydream is such a fantasy. In psychoanalysis, fantasy is an ego defense mechanism. Its purpose is to protect the ego against facts that threaten its integrity. Within limits, fantasy is a normal mechanism and is often used to bolster sagging self-esteem. Thus, after having been criticized by a parent, a child may have a fantasy in which he or she is running away from home. Associated with the fantasy, the child is thinking with pleasure, "Mommy will be really sorry for what she said when she finds out she made me run away."

Fantasy can easily become excessive from an adult point of view. Thus, some children may spend a great deal of time daydreaming without constructive action. However, parents have to be somewhat understanding about this and allow some latitude. Daydreaming and fantasy are very common in middle childhood. And what might seem to an adult like an extreme amount of time spent daydreaming or reading children's books might be normal and in some ways psychologically necessary to a child.

Fantasy is an important process in childhood schizophrenia. The schizophrenic child is often more in touch with a fantasy world than the one most people agree is the real one. However, it is important to realize that vivid fantasies alone do not suggest the presence of schizophrenia. As long as a child knows that a fantasy *is* a fantasy, then there is no schizophrenic process at work. On the other hand, if a child believes that a fantasy is as real as objects such as tables and chairs, then delusional thinking and hallucinations, signs of schizophrenia, may be present.

See also *childhood schizophrenia*; *ego defense mechanisms*; *imaginary playmate.*

father: In developmental psychology, a word that has acquired two related meanings, that is, (1) a male biological parent and (2) a male who fulfills the role of parent. An adoptive parent or a stepfather may be clearly identified as a father in a child's mind. It is widely recognized that playing the role of father is as important, perhaps more important in some ways, than being a biological parent. Adopted children, when they become adolescents or adults, are sometimes heard to say something such as, "Tom was not my father. He was my biological parent—the person who sired me. He did not care about me and I almost never saw him. My real father was Harry. He loved me and took care of Mom and the other kids."

The role of father has been undergoing important changes in modern times. In the past, not as much was expected emotionally of a father. During the early decades of this century, it was common for males to work 10 to 12 hours a day, six days a week. It was enough that they "brought home the bacon" and laid down family law. The father was often seen as a stern, somewhat remote figure. An authoritarian stance was taken for granted. Today's father is expected to spend more quality time with his children and adopt a somewhat more nurturing role. This has many obvious advantages for both the father and the children. However, it also places greater burdens on the father. He must be more of a companion, more affectionate, and in general more understanding of the thoughts and feelings of his children than the stern patriarch of years gone by.

Research on child development has tended to focus on the importance of the mother's role. However, recent studies suggest that the father's role in the family, although different, is extremely important. For example, studies of infant attachment suggest that if fathers feed babies, change them, and hold them that infants definitely become attached to their fathers. It is important for fathers to appreciate that infant attachment is a foundation for subsequent emotional closeness in subsequent years.

Another way to illustrate the significance of the father's role is to note that the incidence of both male and female juvenile delinquency increases when a home has no father.

In short, today's father needs to realize that he is an integral part of the household and that he plays a significant part in the adjustment and emotional life of his children.

See also *attachment; authoritarian parent; juvenile delinquency; mother; parental style.*

fear: An emotional response to a stimulus or situation perceived as dangerous. The emotional response is characterized by excitement, a subjective feeling of displeasure, and apprehensive thoughts.

In folklore and mythology, it has often been suggested that many of our fears are inborn, possibly due to centuries of experience with certain kinds of dangers, such as poisonous snakes, dark nights, thunderstorms, and so forth. This viewpoint is, on the whole, discounted by American psychology. However, it should be noted that it is shared to some extent by Jungians.

Watson took the viewpoint that most fears are acquired through experience, that they are learned. His observations of infants suggested the existence of only two inborn fears: (1) loud noises and (2) a sudden downward motion while being held (suggesting being dropped). He and his assistant Rosalie Raynor conducted experiments with a child known in the literature as Little Albert to illustrate how fears can be acquired through classical conditioning.

Many fears are common in children and should be thought of as a relatively normal part of growing up. These include fear of heights, of strangers, of getting hurt, of the dark, of dogs, of thunder and lightning, of supernatural creatures such as werewolves, and the strange beings and situations encountered in nightmares. Some children are more fearful than others. One possibility is that due to inborn individual differences some children have a lower threshold to stimulation than do others. Another possibility is that some children are more imaginative than others. And it seems reasonable to suggest that highly imaginative children tend to acquire fears more readily than less imaginative ones.

The appropriate parental response to fears is neither to discount them nor to take them too seriously. The child should be listened to with understanding. Parents should model self-control and quiet confidence. This is reassuring to a child, and it helps them to control fears via the mechanism of observational, or social, learning.

Fear is not the same as anxiety. In fear, there is a specific, known stimulus. In anxiety, the source of danger is vague. Also, a fear needs to be distinguished from a phobia. A phobia is an irrational fear, one that has crossed realistic boundaries.

See also *anxiety; Jung, Carl Gustav; Little Albert; phobia; social learning; Watson, John Broadus.*

Feingold hypothesis: The hypothesis advanced by the pediatrician and allergist Benjamin Feingold that artificial food flavors and colors play an important role in hyperactive behavior. Feingold does not target food preservatives as problems, with the possible exception of butylated hydroxytoluene (BHT), an antioxidant used in many foods; he says that an occasional child may show a reaction to BHT. Essentially, Feingold's viewpoint is that hyperactive behavior results as a side effect of allergic reactions to artificial flavors and colors. (Although the focus of the Feingold hypothesis is on artificial colors and flavors, it can be logically extended to include allergies to chemicals naturally present in certain foods.) Feingold's hypothesis has attracted a substantial amount of interest, but there is no professional consensus concerning its importance.

The causes of hyperkinetic behavior appear to be several. And these causes may interact with each other.

See also *attention-deficit hyperactivity disorder (ADHD).*

feral child: A wild, savage child. The behavior of a feral child resembles that of an untamed animal. There are many tales of feral children in folklore and literature. In Roman mythology, Romulus and Remus, founders of Rome, were suckled and raised by a she-wolf. In *Tarzan of the Apes,* by Edgar Rice Burroughs, Tarzan was reared by a she-ape.

There are very few authenticated cases of feral children. One of the most well known is the study of the wild boy of the forest of Aveyron in France. The boy was discovered, given the name Victor, and brought into civilization when he was about 7 years old. Working in the early part of the 19th century, Jean-Marc-Gaspard Itard, a physician, made every effort to socialize the boy and teach him to talk. Victor made some progress, but very little. The conclusion from Itard's study and somewhat similar cases is that early experiences of a positive kind are essential foundations for socialization and mature cognitive functioning. In particular, early experiences play a critical role in language development.

Once in a while, children are discovered who are raised by their parents in filth or in social isolation (e.g., locked in a room). Studies of these children tend, on the whole, to confirm Itard's findings.

The discovery that it is difficult to socialize feral children has important implications for our understanding of human behavior. The idea that there is an innate goodness that will spring into existence without the corrupting influence of civilization was advanced by the philosopher Jean-Jacques Rousseau almost 200 years ago. He spoke of the "noble savage," and Rousseau's idea is reflected in the character of Tarzan. The evidence is against Rousseau's proposition. It appears that children need socializing experiences early in life in order to become social beings and in order to acquire a rich range of language abilities.

See also *cognitive development; emotional deprivation; empiricism; language development; nativism; socialization.*

fetal alcohol syndrome (FAS): A set of related symptoms present in an infant and child associated with alcohol abuse by the mother during pregnancy. Evidence suggests that in a number of cases the excessive intake of alcohol does damage to the developing fetus. Typical symptoms of FAS include a below average weight at birth, muscle weakness, heart defects, joint abnormalities, a cleft palate, brain abnormalities, mental retardation, and a short attention span. One of the key facial characteristics associated with FAS are vertical eyelid folds on the nasal side; these are called epicanthic folds.

Often when a neonate is born with fetal alcohol syndrome, he or she is also physiologically addicted to alcohol and must undergo withdrawal symptoms. It is important to note that the symptoms of FAS are not transient ones associated with birth, but chronic ones that plague the individual for years.

A common attitude toward FAS is that it will be a problem only for children whose mothers abuse alcohol. Common sense would suggest that moderate drinking will not present a problem. The situation is not quite this clearly defined. Not all women who drink to excess during pregnancy have children with FAS. On the other hand, some research suggests that the regular consumption of the equivalent of a can of beer per day might increase the likelihood of birth defects. It is not possible to state an appropriate level of alcohol consumption during pregnancy. In 1981, the U.S. Surgeon General issued a report advising that if at all possible a pregnant woman should avoid alcohol completely.

Fetal alcohol syndrome is the third principal cause of birth defects. (Down's syndrome and spina bifida, malformation of the base of the spine, are the two principal ones.)

See also *birth defects; Down's syndrome; fetal development; fetus; mental retardation.*

fetal development (prenatal development): The process of biological growth and change in an unborn child from the beginning of the ninth week of life until birth. This development associated with this span of time is known as the *fetal stage.* At the beginning of the fetal stage, the average fetus is about one inch long and weighs somewhat less than one ounce. Just before birth, the average fetus is 20 inches long and weighs 7 to 8 pounds. The internal organs of the fetus are fully formed about eight weeks before birth; at this time, the average fetus is 16 inches longs and weighs 3 to 4 pounds. Survival is often possible at this level of development in the case of premature birth.

An obvious sign of life for the mother is the detection of movement in the fetus. The term *quickening* is used to refer to this and is usually associated with the fifth month of pregnancy. Around this time, a fine covering of hair, termed a *lanugo,* appears and will be present at birth. The 6-month-old fetus has eyelids that open and close and a detectable heartbeat. From the seventh to the ninth month, the most important change is an increase in weight. As indicated above, around the beginning of the seventh month, the fetus is essentially a completely formed organism.

See also *embryo; fetal alcohol syndrome (FAS); fetus; lanugo; neonate; zygote.*

fetus: A prenatal organism in the secondary stages of its development. The fetal stage follows immediately after the stage of the embryo and just before birth. In human beings, the fetal stage lasts about 32 weeks.

See also *fetal alcohol syndrome (FAS); fetal development.*

firesetting: See *pyromania.*

fixation: In general terms, a preoccupation or an obsession. Suppose that Gus, a 16-year-old, spends an inordinate amount of time thinking and talking about Elise, a classmate. She barely acknowledges his existence. Gus spends sleepless nights wondering how he might awaken her interest. He begins to lose weight and does not feel like eating. Gus might be said to have a fixation on Elise.

A more technical meaning of *fixation* is the one associated with psychoanalysis. A fixation is the excessive attachment of libido to an erogenous zone associated with pregenital development. Thus, individuals can have oral fixations, anal fixations, or phallic fixations. Such fixations may play a complicating role in certain kinds of maladaptive behavior. For example, oral fixations may play a role in compulsive eating.

See also *anal stage; libido; Oedipus complex; oral stage; phallic stage; psychosexual development.*

foreclosure of identity: According to Erikson's theory of psychosocial development, settling on an identity too early in psychosocial development. An adolescent may make a vocational choice or become involved in a permanent relationship resulting in marriage on the basis of impulse or incomplete information. Sometimes outside pressure from peers or parents forces foreclosure of identity.

Persons who foreclosed an identity early may in subsequent years feel trapped in careers for which they have little liking or in loveless marriages. Most adolescents need to take a few years to reflect and grow before they make major life commitments.

See also *Erikson, Erik Homburger; identity; identity versus role confusion; psychosocial development.*

formal operations: In Piaget's theory of cognitive development, the last of four stages. Formal operations is associated with adolescence and adulthood. During the stage of formal operations, human beings acquire their highest cognitive powers. They can not only think, they can think about thinking. This ability is called *metacognition*.

An adolescent or adult who has attained the stage of formal operations is able to manipulate abstract symbols in such a way as to arrive at a solid conclusion. This is most easily demonstrated in the realm of mathematics. Give an 8-year-old child (in the stage of concrete operations) the equation $3 + x = 7$ and tell the child that in the equation x equals 4. Now give the child the equation: $5 + x = 11$ and ask: "How much does x equal?" The child is likely to answer that x equals 4. If you say, "No. In this case, x must equal 6," the child is likely to protest, "But you just told me that x equals 4!" The average 8-year-old child cannot manipulate an abstract symbol such as x in such a way as to recognize that it is a variable capable of taking on different values in different situations. Give the same equations to an adolescent or an adult, and the individual will usually be able to give the correct values for x even if he or she has no academic knowledge of algebra. The person in the stage of formal operations is able to think in abstract terms even without explicit instruction.

The powers of formal operational thought are many. Adolescents are capable of generalizing readily, of relating propositions to each other in order to make deductions, of entertaining abstract hypotheses, of understanding theories made up mostly of ideas, and of appreciating philosophical concepts. As far as is known, there is no higher level of cognition than formal operations.

See also *cognitive development; concrete operations stage; deductive thinking; Piaget, Jean; preoperational stage; sensorimotor stage.*

foster child: A child who is reared as a member of a family or household without being formally adopted. Foster children are sometimes orphans without living parents. However, foster children often do have living parents. Unfortunately, there is frequently a history of abandonment, abuse, or neglect. Children in various states of distress are placed by public agencies in selected foster homes, and the foster parents receive a monthly stipend for the child's care. The foster child who lives in a stable, affectionate home for many years is fortunate indeed. Unfortunately, too often the child lives in a series of homes during crucial developmental years, and this often has an adverse effect on psychological and social development. The situation of foster children has improved markedly in recent years. Social workers usually make every effort to make sure that foster parents will be loving and effective. Regular home visits provide continuing information. The loosely autobiographical novel *David Copperfield*, written in the 19th century by Charles Dickens, describes what life was like for foster children in a less enlightened age.

An interesting sidelight is the *foster-child fantasy*. This is the belief, sometimes quite strongly held, that one's parents are not in fact one's real parents. They must be foster or adoptive parents because they are so unkind, unloving, or without understanding. The fantasy appears to be a defense against real or imagined unfair treatment by biological parents.

See also *adopted child; adoptive parent;* in loco parentis; parens patriae.

fragile X syndrome: A genetic disorder characterized primarily by mental retardation. The disorder more commonly afflicts males than females. However, about one-third of children with the disorder are females, and they do display mild mental retardation. Symptoms other than mental retardation associated with the disorder include meaningless motions of the hand, self-inflicted bites, hyperactive behavior, avoidance of eye contact, and lack of social interest. Males with the disorder are often above average in height and possessed of substantial strength. They also tend to suffer from epilepsy. Females with the disorder usually appear to be physically normal.

As its name suggests, the fragile X syndrome is caused by a weak X chromosome, the female chromosome on the 23rd pair. There is a narrow place in the chromosome that is easily broken, resulting in scrambled genetic information. The incidence of the fragile X syndrome in the general population is somewhat over 1 in 1,000, and it is the second leading cause of mental retardation. (Down's syndrome is first.)

See also *birth defects; Down's syndrome; genetic anomaly; mental retardation.*

fraternal twins: See *twins.*

Freud, Anna (1885–1982): Made major contributions to techniques of child psychotherapy, to the theory of the ego defense mechanisms, and to methods of preventing mental disorders. Anna Freud was the daughter of Sigmund Freud, and was the only one of his children to become a psychoanalyst. She left Austria with her father in 1938 and continued her professional career in England. In 1947, she was appointed the director of the London Hampstead Child-Therapy Clinic and served in that position for more than 25 years.

Two of Anna Freud's books are *The Ego and the Mechanisms of Defense* (1936) and *Normality and Pathology in Childhood* (1965).

See also *child psychotherapy; ego defense mechanisms; Freud, Sigmund; psychoanalysis.*

Freud, Sigmund (1856–1939): Father of psychoanalysis, a major school of psychology. As Freud presented it, psychoanalysis is at once a developmental theory, a personality theory, and a method of psychotherapy. As a developmental theory, it introduced into psychology such concepts as stages of psychosexual development (i.e., oral, anal, phallic, latency, and genital), the Oedipus complex, the castration complex, and penis envy. These concepts advanced Freud's viewpoint that children have an erotic life with a quality all its own. Also, Freud's formulation of the personality in terms of the id, ego, and superego has a developmental basis. The id is first in time and is present in infancy. The ego then emerges from the id and is associated with toddlerhood. The superego is itself an outgrowth of the ego and takes on most of its characteristics during the preschool period and middle childhood.

Psychoanalysis has exerted an enormous amount of influence on both child-rearing practices and child psychotherapy. Its influence is rivaled only by behaviorism, upon which both behavior modification and behavior therapy are based.

Freud was born in the Austro-Hungarian empire and spent the majority of his professional career working in Vienna, Austria. His early training was in biology, and his initial ambition was to pursue a career as a professor of biology. However, he was advised by his major professor, Ernest Brücke, that his future as an academician would be limited because he was Jewish. Freud then decided on a career in medicine and earned an M.D. degree when he was 25 years of age.

Shortly after Freud's graduation from the University of Vienna in 1881, he obtained a financial grant that enabled him to study neurology under Jean Martin Charcot in France. Freud was impressed by Charcot's repeated demonstrations that the symptoms of hysteria could be temporarily removed through hypnotic suggestion. ("Hysteria" is an outdated term for what today is called *conversion disorder*, a kind of behavioral disorder characterized by an impairment of sensory and/or motor capacities, such as vision, hearing, and ability to move, without an organic basis.) Charcot's work with hypnosis confirmed for Freud that there was a deep unconscious level to mental processes, a level that could cause pathological symptoms. Charcot's observation that sexual problems were often important causal factors in hysteria was also an important influence on Freud's thinking.

When Freud returned to Austria, he set up a private practice and married his fiancee of several years, Martha Bernays, and eventually became the father of six children. One of his children, Anna Freud, became a psychoanalyst.

In his early years of medical practice, Freud was assisted with loans and patient referrals by Josef Breuer, an eminent physician. Josef Breuer told Freud about a case of hysteria he was treating with hypnosis and his own innovative methods. This case eventually because known as the case of Anna O. and is considered the first psychoanalytic case. Freud consistently gave Breuer credit for discovering psychoanalysis, or the "talking cure." Breuer discontinued his investigations, but they became a jumping off place for Freud.

Freud developed psychoanalysis over a period of years in "splendid isolation." All of its fundamental assumptions and basic concepts were developed without the assistance of colleagues. This period of time lasted about 15 years and culminated in the publication of the highly influential book *The Interpretation of Dreams* in 1900. This book brought followers to Freud, among them Carl Jung and Alfred Adler.

Little by little, psychoanalysis gathered momentum and influence, and in 1909 Freud was invited by the eminent psychologist G. Stanley Hall to give a series of lectures in the United States at Clark University in Worcester, Massachusetts. This marked the transition of psychoanalysis as a development of local Austrian interest to one of much greater status. In 1910, The International Psychoanalytic Association was formed.

The Nazi government gave Freud permission to emigrate from Austria in 1938, and he died in London in 1939.

The history of the psychoanalytic movement under Freud's guidance was turbulent. He had a number of loyal followers who always saw him as the "master." Others became impatient with Freud and defected from the ranks after a few years to form their own splinter movements. Today, Freud is regarded as the most influential single psychologist who ever lived. There is continuing debate over the value of his theories and his methods of therapy. He still has many followers—and many detractors.

The first book published in psychoanalysis was *Studies on Hysteria* (1895), written in collaboration with Josef Breuer. Among Freud's influential books are *The Interpretation of Dreams* (1900), *The Psychopathology of Everyday Life* (1901), and *The Ego and the Id* (1923).

See also *Adler, Alfred; anal stage; castration complex; child psychotherapy; ego; Freud, Anna; genital stage; Hall, Granville Stanley; id; Jung, Carl Gustav; latency stage; Oedipus complex; oral stage; penis envy; phallic stage; psychoanalysis; psychosexual development; superego.*

frustration-aggression hypothesis: See *aggressiveness.*

G

Galton, Francis (1822–1911): Made contributions to the study of genetics and the measurement of human abilities. Galton was a man with a broad range of interests who explored many regions of science. (One of his inventions was the Galton whistle, known by many as the "dog" whistle, capable of producing frequencies inaudible to the human ear.) Three years before he died, he was knighted in recognition of his discoveries, and he became Sir Francis Galton.

Galton believed that genetic factors make a paramount contribution to human behavior and account for many individual differences. He conducted studies that he believed supported these viewpoints. He was one of the first researchers to study twins in an effort to explore the role of genetic factors in behavior. Galton and the mathematician Karl Pearson, working together, developed the method of correlation.

Galton attempted to measure intelligence through the use of the *biometric method*, a method that employs a direct measurement of human abilities such as quickness of reflex or strength of grip. His efforts met with very little success, and it remained for Alfred Binet in France to discover a practical method of measuring intelligence.

From today's vantage point, Galton can be seen as a forerunner of the contemporary interest in such subjects as genetic counseling and genetic predisposition.

Two of Galton's principal books are *Hereditary Genius* (1869) and *Inquiries into the Human Faculty and Its Development* (1883).

See also *Binet, Alfred; correlation; genetic counseling; genetic endowment; genetic predisposition; giftedness; individual differences; intelligence; intelligence tests.*

gargoylism: See *Hurler's syndrome.*

gender identity: The personal perception that one is of a specific sex, either male or female. In most cases one's gender identity corresponds with one's actual biological gender. Thus, most biological males perceive themselves as males, and most biological females perceive themselves as females. However, this is not always the case.

Experiences in infancy and toddlerhood appear to be the principal factors involved in establishing a robust gender identity. These include in our culture dressing an infant boy in blue and an infant girl in pink, in the giving of masculine and feminine first names, in the different ways boys and girls are treated, and so forth. Most children have a well-defined gender identity by about the age of 3. Once established, a gender identity tends to be very stable and resistant to change.

See also *gender identity disorder of childhood; identity; sex role; transsexualism.*

gender identity disorder of childhood: A prepubertal disorder characterized by profound discontent with one's own biological gender. Usually the discontent is accompanied by an expressed wish to be of a different sex. A female with the disorder may deny reality and say that she is a boy, refuse to wear female clothing, insist that she will soon sprout a penis, and urinate standing up. A male with the disorder may deny reality and say that he is a girl, insist on wearing dresses, and find his penis disgusting. The disorder greatly interferes with personal and social adjustment.

No exact statistics are available on the incidence of the disorder. Although it is real and recognized by the American Psychiatric Association, it is also rare. More males suffer from the disorder than females.

Causal factors in the disorder include odd or deviant treatment by parents or siblings, little or no reinforcement for typical gender-linked behaviors, a single-parent home lacking a parent of the same biological gender as the child, and immoderate physical contact or almost pathological emotional involvement with the parent of the opposite sex. It is also possible that an unresolved Oedipus complex may contribute to the disorder. Although genetic factors have been hypothesized to play a role in the disorder, their action, if any, is obscure. Certainly there is no gross genetic abnormality in children with a gender identity disorder.

Although it is true that most adults who suffer from transsexualism also suffered from gender identity disorder as children, the reverse statement is not true. Most children with gender identity disorder do not suffer as adults from transsexualism. In most cases, gender identity disorder of childhood tends to resolve itself in a favorable manner and ceases to be a problem after puberty.

Treatment for the disorder consists of child psychotherapy and counseling for the parents. Parents can be helped to find ways, using behavior modification, to avoid reinforcing actions associated with the disorder.

See also *identity; Oedipus complex; transsexualism.*

gene: A discrete unit of heredity. Genes can work individually or in groups and are the means by which the biological characteristics of parents are transferred to their children. Genes are made up of interwoven strands of deoxyribonucleic acid (DNA). An average of about 50,000 genes are carried on a single chromosome.

See also *chromosomes; deoxyribonucleic acid (DNA); dominant gene; genetic anomaly; genetic counseling; genetic endowment; recessive gene.*

generation gap: An informal term, with no precise meaning, most commonly used to suggest the idea that the values, attitudes, and actions of adolescents are quite different from those of their parents. An average time span of about 30 years is considered to be a generation, and, in a rapidly changing society, there may indeed be sharp differences in the outlooks of the members of an older and of a younger generation. On the other hand, more than one study has shown that the popular idea of a huge generation gap affecting all families and social classes in the United States is both oversimplified and incorrect. Many adolescents, perhaps most, still subscribe to many of the values and attitudes of their parents. For example, most adolescents have the same religious and political affiliations as their parents.

See also *alienation; juvenile delinquency; socialization.*

generativity versus self-absorption: In Erikson's theory, the seventh stage of psychosocial development, the stage associated with middle age. The behavior of an adult manifests generativity if it is characterized by productive work and a general interest in the welfare of others. The novel *Goodbye Mr. Chips* by James Hilton provides a portrait of a person who has attained generativity. Although Mr. Chips, a teacher in a boys' school in England, never has biological children of his own, he thinks of his students as his children. It is as if he is a father, and consequently he demonstrates generativity.

The behavior of an adult manifests self-absorption if it is characterized primarily by selfish action, extreme vanity, lack of goals valued by the general culture, and no particular sense of interest in the larger social community.

See also *Erikson, Erik Homburger; prosocial behavior; psychosocial development.*

genetic abnormality: See *genetic anomaly.*

genetic anomaly (genetic abnormality): A deviation in an organism's genetic pattern from a normal, or expected, one. For example, in the usual case, all chromosomes in the nucleus of a body cell exist in pairs, and there are 23 such pairs. However, there is a genetic anomaly in which the chromosomes of what is usually the 21st pair exist as a set of three. This is a condition known as Trisomy 21, and it is the genetic basis for Down's syndrome. Genetic anomalies are responsible for a number of inherited diseases.

See also *Down's syndrome; genetic counseling; genetic endowment; genetic predisposition; Klinefelter's syndrome; Turner's syndrome.*

genetic counseling: The giving of information and guidance to a prospective parent or parents concerning the likelihood of having a child with a birth defect or a chronic inherited disorder due to an identifiable genetic factor. Genetic counseling is available through various hospitals and clinics. Members of a couple who both have a family history of hereditary diseases caused by a recessive gene are well-advised to consider genetic counseling. It is possible that they are both carriers of the disease, even if they are disease-free themselves. Examples of diseases in this category include Tay-Sach's disease and sickle-cell anemia.

In the case of Huntington's chorea, the disease is cased by a dominant gene and can be transmitted by one parent. In this particular case, genetic counseling would appear to be of particular importance.

Genetic counseling may also address itself to a current pregnancy. For example, it is possible through the use of amniocentesis to obtain a sample of fetal cells and determine the presence of genetic anomalies, such as those that contribute to Down's syndrome, Klinefelter's syndrome, and Turner's syndrome.

See also *amniocentesis; dominant gene; Down's syndrome; genetic anomaly; genetic endowment; genetic predisposition; Huntington's chorea; Klinefelter's syndrome; recessive gene; sickle-cell anemia; Tay-sach's disease; Turner's syndrome.*

genetic endowment: One's hereditary givens; what one has to work with at birth in terms of his or her own particular chromosomes and genes. An individual's genetic endowment appears to play an important causal role in the manifestation of many traits, both biological and psychological. Thus, one's adult height is the result not only of nutrition, but also of nutrition interacting with one's genetic endowment. One's adult intelligence is the result not only of experience and opportunity in childhood and adolescence, but of these factors interacting with the endowment. Traits of temperament are not the result of upbringing and social learning alone, but of these factors interacting with the endowment. Freud once said, "Biology is destiny." This statement is today considered to be too strong. Nonetheless, experience and environment alone do not determine the course of human development. The genetic endowment also plays a major role.

See also *gene; genetic anomaly; genetic counseling; genetic predisposition.*

genetic predisposition: An inborn tendency to develop along certain lines or in a given direction. The genetic predisposition is an aspect of the genetic endowment. A predisposition can refer to either undesirable traits or desirable ones. Thus, it can be hypothesized that certain children, based on their genetic endowments, might be predisposed to be artists, musicians, scientists, explorers, and so forth. Although this is a highly debatable proposition, it is a common meaning attached to a genetic predisposition.

In the case of undesirable traits, it is today believed that there is a genetic predisposition toward schizophrenia. This contention is supported by a number of studies as well as the general observation that schizophrenia is usually first evident in childhood or adolescence.

Unfortunately, the concept of a genetic predisposition is associated with the folklore concept of a "good seed" or a "bad seed." Today's consensus suggests that children are born neither good nor bad, that this is a value judgement imposed by parents and/or society on traits of behavior. Although it is true that predispositions probably exist, they are not in and of themselves either "good" or "bad."

See also *childhood schizophrenia; genes; genetic anomaly; genetic counseling; temperament.*

genital stage: In Freud's theory, the last stage of psychosexual development, the stage that begins at puberty (around 12 or 13 years of age) and continues throughout adolescence and adulthood. In psychoanalytic theory, if development is normal, during the genital stage the individual will both desire and enjoy sexual relations with members of the opposite sex.

See also *Freud, Sigmund; libido; psychosexual development.*

genitalia: See *genitals.*

genitals (genitalia): The sexual organs. At a formal level, the genitals refer to all of the organs and physiological structures involved in sexual activity and reproduction of either sex. In informal everyday usage, the term *genitals* is usually used to refer to the external, visible organs of the male. These include the penis and the testes. More accurately and completely, however, the male genitals also include such structures as the prostate gland and the seminal vesicles. The female genitals include such structures as the vagina, the clitoris, the ovaries, the fallopian tubes, and the uterus.

See also *testes; gonads; ovaries.*

genius: An individual with exceptional intelligence or creative powers. The term *genius* is not a scientific one, and no precise meaning is attached to it. It might be tempting to think of children and adolescents who score in the upper 1 or 2 percent on intelligence or creativity tests as geniuses. However, this is somewhat dubious. Often these promising high scores in the early years of life are not correlated with actual accomplishments as adults. It would seem that in order to qualify as a genius one would have to do more than display unusual powers in youth.

Thus, it would appear to be appropriate to speak of Marie Curie, the physicist, or Leo Tolstoy, the novelist, as geniuses because they combined intellectual and creative powers with great accomplishments. It does not appear to be appropriate for a parent to speak of a 10-year-old with high scores on psychological tests or exceptional grades in school as a genius. The 10-year-old's genius needs to be evaluated retrospectively *after* the individual has had a chance to function at the adult level.

The word *genius* is related to *jinni*, or *genie*. In mythology, a jinni is a spirit assigned to an individual as a guide and teacher. It is evident that the concept of genius in modern terms contains some of the ancient meaning. The genius is usually thought of as born, not made. An optimal environment may be necessary to bring out the best in the potential genius, but the environment cannot create the unusual powers. The point of view underlying the genius concept is nativism.

See also *creative thinking; creativity tests; giftedness; intelligence; intelligence quotient (IQ); intelligence tests; nativism.*

genotype: An individual's underlying genetic makeup. A genotype needs to be compared to a *phenotype*, the expression of an individual's genetic makeup. Sometimes the genotype is clearly expressed in the phenotype. At other times, the genotype is latent and is not expressed in the phenotype. A clear example of this is provided in the case of eye color. Suppose that Phyllis received a gene for blue eyes from her mother and a gene for blue eyes from her father. The lower case letter "b" is used to stand for a gene for blue eyes because this particular gene is recessive. Thus, Phyllis's genotype is written as follows: bb. Her phenotype, that which is manifest, is *blue eyes*. Therefore, both her phenotype and genotype are known by looking at Phyllis.

On the other hand, suppose that Carl received a gene for blue eyes from his mother and a gene for brown eyes from his father. The upper case letter "B" is used to stand for a gene for brown eyes because this particular gene is dominant. Thus, Carl's genotype is written as follows: Bb. His phenotype, that which is manifest, is *brown eyes*. However, Carl's genotype is not known by looking him. His appearance alone reveals that his genotype could be either Bb or BB.

The fact that an individual can have a genotype that is different from his or her phenotype is of particular importance in the case of inherited diseases caused by recessive genes. Two parents can both be carriers of an inherited disease (e.g., Tay-Sachs disease) without having the disease themselves. However, their children can have the disease if they inherit the recessive gene from both parents.

See also *dominant gene; heterozygous; homozygous; recessive gene; Tay-Sachs disease.*

German measles: See *rubella.*

Gesell, Arnold Lucius (1880–1961): Conducted important research on the subject of various stages of child development. Because of his early investigations, Gesell is sometimes referred to as the father of child psychology in the United States. He earned a Ph.D. degree from Clark University in Worcester, Massachusetts, in 1906, established the Yale Clinic of Child Development in 1911, and earned an M.D. degree from Yale University in 1915.

Among Gesell's research innovations are the use of motion picture cameras and one-way mirrored glass to record and view child behavior. Gesell's approach to human development was essentially biological in nature. He believed that the maturation of human traits and abilities follow an inborn timetable that unfolds into stages at given ages. Although this timetable is, of course, influenced by environment and learning, it is primary. Experience is secondary and plays the role of bringing the stages forth from the underlying plan. With this general viewpoint, Gesell can be placed squarely among others, such as Chomsky and Piaget, who stress nativistic factors in development.

Two of Gesell's books are *The Mental Growth of the Pre-School Child* (1925) and *Infancy and Human Growth* (1928). He coauthored with Frances L. Ilg and other authors *Infant and Child in the Culture of Today* (1942).

See also *ages-stages theories; Chomsky, Noam Avram; Gesell Developmental Schedules; motor development; nativism; Piaget, Jean.*

Gesell Developmental Schedules: A set of four schedules, or time-tables, setting forth typical behaviors at specified ages. The schedules can be used as a set of norms for evaluating the development of children. As such, they are of particular value to pediatricians, child psychologists, pediatric nurses, and other professionals who work with children. The schedules were developed at Yale by Arnold Gesell and are based on the direct observation of the behavior of many children.

The Gesell Developmental Schedules are useful for evaluating the behavior of infants, toddlers, and preschoolers. They span the first six years of life. The four kinds of behavior targeted by the schedules are (1) ability to adapt, (2) motor functioning, (3) use of language, and (4) social interaction.

See also *Bayley Scales of Infant Development; developmental quotient (DQ); Gesell, Arnold Lucius.*

gestation period: The span of time required from conception to the birth of a neonate. In human beings, the normal gestation period is 270 to 280 days, or approximately 9 months. Gestation periods significantly shorter than the normal one result in both immature births and premature births.

See also *embryo; fetal development; fetus; immature birth; neonate; perinatal period; premature birth.*

giftedness: A general attribute used to describe either exceptional intelligence or exceptional creativity. Usually, a child needs to score in the upper 1 or 2 percent on a standardized test in order to be thought of as "gifted." Although the word *gift* tends to suggest a genetic predisposition, in contemporary psychology, the concept of giftedness is detached from this implication. Giftedness exists if it is displayed. In an individual case, it may be the result of a genetic predisposition or of unusual nurturing. Or it may be the result of the interaction of both factors.

See also *creative thinking; creativity tests; empiricism; intelligence; intelligence quotient (IQ); intelligence tests; nativism.*

Goddard, Henry Herbert (1866–1957): One of the founders of clinical psychology in the United States. Goddard conducted important research on intelligence and its measurement. He authored tests of mental ability used in screening personnel in World War I, established the Vineland Training School for mentally retarded children in New Jersey in 1918, and served for approximately 20 years as a member of the faculty at Ohio State University.

Goddard was convinced that heredity makes a major contribution to intelligence and sought to establish this viewpoint with data. One of his well-known studies was of the Kallikak family (not the family's real name). The study attempted to show how mental retardation and other problems such as criminal tendencies and alcohol abuse can have a genetic basis. Today, it is believed that the methodology of the study was seriously flawed and that the study cannot in and of itself be taken as evidence in favor of a genetic hypothesis.

Goddard coined the term *moron* to identify mentally retarded individuals who could benefit from special learning programs and training. He used the term in a positive way, but it has taken on a pejorative, degrading connotation and is almost never used today as a formal part of a psychological vocabulary.

See also *genetic endowment; genetic predisposition; intelligence; intelligence tests; mental retardation; moron; Vineland Social Maturity Scale.*

golden age of childhood: The years from approximately 6 to 12 years of age. These are the school-age years and are associated with grades 1 through 6. The term *golden age* is used to capture the idea that during this time period many children tend to be relatively untroubled emotionally. The child is alert, can think, and has a high level of cognitive functioning. However, the stresses of adolescence and the responsibilities of adulthood have not yet arrived. This is the period of time when children ride bicycles, fly kites, start hobbies, spin tops, play with jacks, swim, and in general show an intense interest in the outside world.

In psychoanalytic theory, some of the behavior associated with the golden age of childhood is linked to psychosexual latency. Repression of sexual desire is compensated for by a lack of personal reflection and an investment of libido in the external world of things, not the internal world of the personality. The psychoanalytic way of looking at the golden age of childhood is open to discussion, and there is no general consensus among developmental psychologists that it provides a major explanation of the behaviors associated with this period.

See also *latency stage; play.*

gonads: The glands of reproduction. In males, the gonads are called the *testes*. In females, the gonads are called the *ovaries*. The term *gonads* is also often used to refer to undifferentiated glands of reproduction in the embryo before they can clearly be identified as testes or ovaries.

See also *ovaries; testes.*

grand mal seizures: See *epilepsy.*

growth hormone (GH): See *pituitary gland.*

growth needs: According to Maslow, a set of needs that reside at the top of the motivational hierarchy. Growth needs are also termed *metaneeds*, meaning needs beyond, or "after," basic needs. As such, growth needs have very little to do with immediate survival in terms of food and water. The two principal kinds of growth needs are cognitive needs and the need for self-actualization. Metaneeds represent, according to Maslow, the higher reaches of human nature.

See also *cognitive needs; deficiency needs; Maslow, Abraham; self-actualization.*

growth spurt: A period of unusually rapid growth. There is rapid growth during the prenatal period. However, this is seldom referred to as a growth spurt. The term tends to refer primarily to postnatal development, and there are two such periods. The first occurs in infancy and the second in adolescence. Toward the end of infancy, around the age of 2 years, the average infant is 34 inches in height and 27 pounds in weight. This represents an increase of 14 inches over an average birth weight of 20 inches and an increase of almost 20 pounds over an average birth weight of 7.5 pounds. After infancy, growth tends to continue fairly steadily and is neither sudden nor dramatic for a prolonged period of time.

The second growth spurt is associated with adolescence. Females typically begin their growth spurt around the age of 11, earlier than males. In about a seven-year period, the average female gains about 7 inches in height and about 40 pounds in weight. The average female is about 5 feet 4 inches in height when growth is almost complete at age 18.

Males begin their growth spurt around the age of 12 or 13. In about a six-year period, the average male gains about 9 to 10 inches in height and about 55 pounds in weight. The average male is about 5 feet 8.5 inches when growth is almost complete at age 18.

See also *adolescence; fetal development; infant; maturation.*

guilt: As a personal experience, the unpleasant feelings associated with the belief that one has violated one's own moral standards. There has been a running discussion in both philosophy and psychology concerning the question of the origins of guilt. Certain classical philosophers (e.g., Plato and Kant) believed that guilt arises when one violates inborn standards of moral conduct put in place by God or Nature. Other classical philosophers (e.g., Aristotle and Locke) believed that guilt arises when one violates moral standards acquired through learning.

Freud placed himself in company with the second group. He asserted that the superego, the moral agent of the personality, is acquired in early childhood due to a set of experiences revolving around forbidden incest wishes toward the parent of the opposite sex and the fear of parental punishment. Erikson, building on Freud's approach, suggested that the superego arises as a function of general social experiences in a family setting involving doubt and shame.

More recently, theorists such as Piaget and Kohlberg have suggested that moral development, and consequent feelings of guilt, require a parallel cognitive development. The child who can think clearly, who can reason, and who can evaluate consequences is likely to have more of a capacity to experience guilt than children with less cognitive maturity. Although Piaget and Kohlberg recognize the importance of experience and learning in moral development, they also assign value to the concept of maturation. Therefore, they assign some importance to both inborn and learned factors in the acquisition of the ability to feel guilt.

See also *conscience; Freud, Sigmund; initiative versus guilt; Kohlberg, Lawrence; moral development; superego.*

Guthrie test: See *phenylketonuria (PKU).*

H

habit: Loosely, a learned pattern of behavior. There are two more or less correct ways of speaking of habits. First, a habit can refer to almost any learned action or response. Thus, psychologists speak of *habit formation* even when it is applied to relatively small units of behavior such as picking up a fork correctly or capping a tube of toothpaste. Second, a habit can refer to a complex, chained sequence of learned behaviors. Consequently, it is common to speak of having a smoking habit, a habit of talking too loudly, good study habits, a habit of being neat and clean, and so forth.

(It should be noted that there is a use of the word *habit* in which learning is not implied. Behavior patterns typical of a group are often spoken of as habits, and the implication is that these may be natural, or inborn, dispositions. Thus, one might say, "It is the habit of many kinds of fish to swim in schools," "It is the habit of babies to cry," or "It is the habit of adolescents to be impulsive and seek excitement.")

The second meaning identified above in which habits are thought of as complex sequences of behavior is the most common one used in developmental psychology. Classical conditioning, operant conditioning, and social learning are the basic processes underlying the acquisition of habits.

Parents and caregivers seek to establish "good" habits (i.e., prosocial ones) and to eliminate "bad" habits (i.e., antisocial ones) in children. This is a major task associated with the rearing of children. Consequently, a study of behavior modification skills and reinforcers can be useful to responsible adults.

See also *behavior modification; classical conditioning; learning; operant conditioning; reinforcer; social learning.*

Hall, Granville Stanley (1844–1924): One of the principal founders of American psychology. Hall is credited with earning the first Ph.D. in psychology in the United States, obtaining the degree in 1878 under the sponsorship of the eminent William James. In 1887, he was responsible for the publication of the first journal of academic psychology in the United States, the *American Journal of Psychology.* Hall helped to organize the American Psychological Association and became its first president in 1892.

Hall invited Sigmund Freud and Carl Jung to lecture in the United States on psychoanalysis at Clark University in Worcester, Massachusetts, in 1909. These presentations did much to establish psychoanalysis as an important force in American psychology.

Hall's research was primarily in the areas of developmental and educational psychology. One of his methods was to explore the thinking processes of children by asking them sets of questions. Two of Hall's principal works are *The Contents of Children's Minds* (1883) and *Adolescence* (1904).

See also *developmental psychology; educational psychology; Freud, Sigmund; James, William; Jung, Carl Gustav; ontogeny recapitulates phylogeny; psychoanalysis.*

hallucinogens: Drugs capable of producing hallucinations (i.e., false perceptions). Hallucinogens are also known as *psychedelic drugs.* Hallucinations experienced under these conditions represent, in most cases, a temporary alteration in the perceptual processes.

Hallucinogens have been used in a variety of ways. First, they have been used for recreational purposes. When used in this manner, they have a substantial potential for abuse. Second, they have been used for religious purposes, as a way of opening doors to mystical experiences and "other realities." Third, they have been used in psychotherapy (primarily research projects) to help patients gain access to different viewpoints on life. At present, there is little or no use of hallucinogens in psychotherapy.

Three hallucinogens that have been cited often in connection with drug abuse in adolescence are lysergic acid diethylamide-25 (LSD), marijuana (i.e., cannabis), and phencyclidine (PCP).

See also *drug abuse in adolescence; lysergic acid diethylamide-25 (LSD); marijuana; phencyclidine (PCP).*

handedness: The tendency to regularly use one hand instead of the other for primarily single-handed tasks, such as writing with a pen, turning a doorknob, waving at someone, holding a telephone, or pounding with a hammer. Children will be right-handed for 70 to 90 percent of major tasks with or without encouragement. The tendency for the right hand to dominate appears to depend to some extent on inborn nerve pathways.

Assuming that a child shows a very strong preference for using the left hand, it is quite likely due to individual differences in the structures and functions of the brain and nervous system. Consequently, it is probably best not to use punishment or psychological force in an attempt to create a preference for the use of the right hand. It is acceptable to use encouragement and reinforcement, gentle methods, in an attempt to create such a preference. If the child is basically ambidextrous (i.e., capable of using either hand with equal skill) as a toddler, then such gentle methods may shape the behavior in the conventional direction. However, if a toddler shows a strong preference for the left hand, and about 10 percent will, it is probably best to let nature take its course. The disadvantages of being left-handed are probably more than offset by the dual benefits of emotional calm and self-esteem experienced by the child who is not pressured to conform or made to feel odd by parents.

See also *nativism; reinforcer; shaping.*

Harlow, Harry F. (1905–1981): Experimental and developmental psychologist recognized for his important contributions to both learning theory and motivational theory. Harlow's principal subjects were rhesus monkeys. He earned a Ph.D. degree from Stanford University in 1930, taught psychology at the University of Wisconsin for approximately 30 years, and was the director of Wisconsin's primate laboratory for about 10 years.

Harlow discovered that when rhesus monkeys are presented with problems, they not only learn how to solve specific problems, but in general become better at coping with similar problems. He called this phenomenon *learning to learn*. The same set of learning events takes place in human beings. This observation advances our understanding of both cognitive development and language development in children and has important implications in educational psychology.

Working with infant monkeys reared in social isolation, Harlow challenged Freud's contention that an infant's love for his or her mother grows out of association with being fed. On the contrary, Harlow's research suggested that there is an inborn affectional drive with an independent status all its own.

Harlow's research also supported the hypothesis that there is an inborn curiosity drive (see *ludic behavior*).

Among Harlow's publications are "Love in Infant Monkeys," published in the *Scientific American* (1959); "Affectional Responses in the Infant Monkey" (with R. R. Zimmerman), published in *Science* (1959), and *The Human Model: Primate Perspectives* (with C. Mears), (1979).

See also *attachment; cognitive development; educational psychology; language development; learning; ludic behavior.*

Head Start programs: Programs funded by governmental agencies and designed to provide preschool experiences to children from disadvantaged homes. Head Start programs are also referred to as *early intervention* programs. The basic assumption is that exposure to the kinds of cognitive and motor tasks available to children from advantaged homes will have a positive impact on intellectual functioning, the kind of functioning eventually required in standard grammar school settings.

The first Head Start programs were instituted in the 1960s, and there have been a number of them presented over the years in various regions of the country. A substantial body of research exists concerning the effectiveness of these programs. Some studies suggest that the effects of a Head Start program are temporary. Other studies suggest quite the opposite—that there are long term beneficial effects. The contradiction can to some extent be resolved by noting that many specific factors, such as the personality of a teacher, the quality of a particular program, the attitudes of the parents, the physical setting used for the preschool experience, and so forth, vary substantially. On the whole, it appears that Head Start programs can be of real value assuming they are implemented by educators who have a sound knowledge of both childhood development and educational psychology.

See also *cognitive development; early childhood; educational psychology; preschool experience.*

head-turning reflex: See *rooting reflex.*

hearing impairment: A significantly below-average ability to discriminate sounds, particularly those used in speech. The term *hearing impairment* is preferred to the more informal *deaf. Deaf* is an either-or word. It suggests that an individual either can or cannot hear. Cases are usually not this simple. *Hearing impairment* suggests a range of individual differences in the kind and quality of impairment experienced by different persons.

Ninety percent of hearing-impaired children were born with the condition. The other 10 percent develop the condition after they are toddlers. Causal factors in hearing impairment include fetal alcohol syndrome, genetic predispositions, infections, and child abuse.

Hearing impairment often has a highly adverse impact on a child's cognitive development. Without the ability to assimilate well-defined information, it is difficult to keep pace with other children. Language development often suffers, and the ability to express oneself with speech is also severely impaired. For these reasons, a folklore belief arose that hearing-impaired children were "dumb." This is a completely incorrect and unfortunate way to look at hearing impairment in childhood. The hearing-impaired child in most cases has as much intellectual potential as any other child.

If the hearing-impaired child is provided with a special education program designed to provide information through senses other than hearing (e.g., vision and touch), then substantial progress can be made. It is very important that hearing-impaired children be taught American Sign Language (ASL) from an early age. They can be exposed to ASL as toddlers in the same way that other children are exposed to conventional speech. Also, hearing-impaired children can learn the art of lip reading. This helps them to feel not totally excluded from ordinary social environments.

See also *child abuse; cognitive development; fetal alcohol syndrome (FAS); genetic predisposition; speech therapy; visual impairment.*

heredity: The characteristics that one has received from one's parents. The basic unit of heredity is the gene, and genes are carried on 23 pairs of chromosomes. In the case of physical characteristics such as eye color, shape of the face, and height, the effects of heredity are often well defined and fairly obvious. In the case of psychological and emotional characteristics such as intelligence, creativity, temperament, and proneness to mental disorders, the effects of heredity are somewhat more obscure and controversial. Environment interacts with heredity, and the joint effects of the two sources of variation are often difficult to assess. This has led to what is known as the *nature-nurture controversy.*

See also *canalization; chromosomes; gene; heredity and environment interaction; nature-nurture controversy.*

heredity and behavior: See *sociobiology.*

heredity and environment interaction: An interaction that exists when two (or more) variables affect each other in a complex way. The concept of an interaction is more readily understood by contrasting it with the concept of an *additive* relationship. In an additive relationship, the variables in question have an obvious relationship and do not affect each other. A basic example is taken from the field of mathematics. $2 + 3 = 5$ symbolizes an additive relationship. The sum 5 is clearly no more and no less than what is contained in the contributing numbers 2 and 3. However, $2 \times 3 = 6$ symbolizes an interaction, or multiplicative relationship. Here, the product 6 is "more than the sum of its parts."

Heredity and environment, like the multiplication example, interact to produce human characteristics. The product of this interaction is, again, "more than the sum of its parts." Complex human attributes such as intelligence, creativity, and traits of personality are determined not by heredity alone or by environment alone, but by their interaction.

See also *heredity; heredity and intelligence; nature-nurture controversy.*

heredity and intelligence: Refers to the hypothesized connection between genetic potential and intellectual achievement. There has been a running discussion in developmental psychology concerning these questions: Is intelligence due primarily to heredity? Or is it due primarily to the effects of environment? There seems to be no question that genes have some effect on intelligence. On the other hand, it seems equally obvious that an optimal environment maximizes one's genetic potential. Consequently, a disadvantaged environment tends to suppress or obscure genetic potential. Therefore, most of today's developmental psychologists are unwilling to give simple answers to the two questions asked above. The correct response to questions concerning heredity and intelligence is to say that heredity plays a significant role in intelligence. However, it interacts in a complex way with the environment; it does not act alone.

See also *heredity; heredity and environment interaction; intelligence.*

hermaphroditism: A biological condition characterized by the possession of the characteristics of both sexes. Hermaphroditism is not unknown in the plant and animal kingdoms and is sometimes normal. For example, earthworms are hermaphrodites; so are some plants. However, when the condition exists in a human being, it is considered both pathological and abnormal. True human hermaphroditism exists when the individual has both a set of ovaries and a set of testes. The condition is not at all common, and the causal factors that produce it are obscure. Usually, hermaphrodites are raised as if they are males because they have external sexual organs with a masculine appearance. (However, it should be noted that these organs are not definitely male or female.)

Pseudohermaphroditism (i.e., false hermaphroditism) occurs more frequently than true hermaphroditism. In pseudohermaphroditism, the individual has a set of testes or a set of ovaries, but not both. Thus, the individual is actually a male or a female. The principal cause of the condition is an improperly functioning endocrine system. Children with the condition need to have their correct sex determined by a physician. Then they need to be treated by an endocrinologist.

If a child suffers from either true hermaphroditism or pseudohermaphroditism, counseling and family therapy may be recommended in order to help the child make an appropriate social adjustment.

See also *androgen hormones; estrogen hormones; gender identity; gender identity disorder of childhood.*

heterozygous: A common and normal condition in which an individual's underlying genetic makeup consists of two different genes for the same characteristic. For example, suppose that Carl has a gene for blue eyes on the first of a pair of chromosomes and a gene for brown eyes on the second member of the pair. Carl is heterozygous for eye color. Consequently, about one-half of his sperm will carry a gene for blue eyes and about one-half will carry a gene for brown eyes.

See also *chromosomes; dominant gene; gene; genotype; homozygous; recessive gene.*

holding an infant: See *attachment.*

holophrase: The use by an infant or a toddler of a single word to stand for a whole sentence. For example, the child might say, "Bread." Under certain circumstances, this might mean, "I do not like this piece of bread," or "Give me some more bread," or "Put some jelly on the bread." Parents and caregivers can often tell from the child's gestures, facial expression, and the situation itself what the child is attempting to communicate. The use of holophrases is an intermediate step between babbling and the appearance of actual short sentences.

See also *babbling; Chomsky, Noam Avram; language acquisition device (LAD); language development; one-word stage.*

homosexuality: A distinct erotic attraction to, or a preference for sexual relations with, persons of one's own gender (i.e., male-male or female-female). There have been many sexual surveys, and the general incidence of homosexuality is fairly well-known. The following percentages are conservative ones.

Among adolescents, it is estimated about 9 percent have engaged in homosexual relations. Among adolescent males, it is estimated that about 12 percent have had a homosexual contact. Among adolescent females, it is estimated that about 6 percent have had such a contact.

It is further estimated that among adult males, about 4 percent have an exclusively homosexual orientation; about 10 percent have had a homosexual experience. Among females, it is estimated that about 2 or 3 percent have an exclusively homosexual orientation; about 6 or 7 percent have had a homosexual experience. When a female has homosexual desires, she is more likely to maintain bisexual behavior than is a male with homosexual desires.

The American Psychiatric Association's *Diagnostic and Statistical Manual* does not identify homosexuality as a mental disorder. Therefore, it would not seem to require explanation. However, persons with a heterosexual orientation are often puzzled by homosexuality, finding it very difficult to understand. Therefore, psychiatry and psychology do make some attempt to explain homosexuality. A number of explanations have been offered. Some of the principal ones follow. First, it is possible that there is an inherited tendency toward homosexuality. Correlational studies of identical twins give some credibility to this idea. Second, it is possible that abnormal changes in a mother's hormone levels during pregnancy may in some way affect the sexual development of the fetus; this may affect adult sexual orientation in a way that is not yet clear. Third, psychoanalysis hypothesizes that fixations of libido, caused by emotional trauma, during the phallic stage of development may be a principal cause of homosexuality. Fourth, learning theory suggests that copying the behavior of a parent of the opposite sex (e.g., a boy copying the behavior of his mother) may play a role in subsequent homosexuality.

Although homosexuality is not a mental disorder, it is of some interest to note that until fairly recently a formal distinction was made between ego-dystonic and ego-syntonic homosexuality. *Ego-dystonic homosexuality* was defined as a kind of homosexuality in which the homosexual individual was greatly distressed by his or her sexual orientation. *Ego-syntonic homosexuality* was defined as a kind of homosexuality in which the homosexual individual was content with his or her sexual orientation.

Although the distinction between ego-dystonic and ego-syntonic homosexuality no longer has any formal status, the ego-dystonic diagnosis can still be made if a clinician deems it useful or proper. This is accomplished by reference to a general category used to classify sexual disorders not otherwise identified in the American Psychiatric Association's *Diagnostic and Statistical Manual.* However, the diagnosis appears to be rarely made.

See also *gender identity disorder of childhood; identity; psychosexual development; sex role; transsexualism.*

homozygous: A common and normal condition in which an individual's underlying genetic makeup consists of two identical genes for the same characteristic. For example, suppose that Phyllis has a gene for blue eyes on the first of a pair of chromosomes and another gene for blue eyes on the second member of the pair. Phyllis is homozygous for eye color. Consequently, all of her ova, or egg cells, will carry genes for blue eyes.

See also *chromosomes; dominant gene; gene; genotype; heterozygous; recessive gene.*

hormone: A complex organic molecule secreted directly into the bloodstream by an endocrine gland. For example, the pituitary gland secretes, among other hormones, growth hormone (GH). GH is a key factor in a child's rate of growth and the eventual height that will be reached.

See also *androgen hormones; estrogen hormones; pituitary gland.*

Horney, Karen (1885–1952): One of the principal founders of psychoanalysis in the United States. Horney received her academic training in Germany; she earned an M.D. degree and obtained her psychoanalytic training at the Berlin Institute of Psychoanalysis under the guidance of the eminent psychoanalyst Karl Abraham. In 1932, Horney became a resident of the United States.

Although Horney is known as a psychoanalyst, she felt no great loyalty to Freud's specific theories. She accepted the broad concepts that mental life has unconscious roots, that ego defense mechanisms are important, and that anxiety plays an important part in neurotic conflict. However, she believed that Freud placed too much emphasis on biological factors in development and not enough emphasis on the role of interpersonal relationships and the influence of society in general. Like Erik Erikson, known for his theory of psychosocial development, Horney believed that a certain amount of neurotic anxiety can be traced back to adverse emotional experiences in early childhood causing a deficiency in the ability to trust. She is considered to be a neo-Freudian and a major revisionist of Freud's theories.

Horney was a principal founder in 1942 of the American Institute for Psychoanalysis. The Karen Horney Clinic was founded in 1955 in New York, and it became an important center for psychotherapy and the training of analysts. Horney wrote highly readable books for the general public and, through these books, exerted a wide influence. Two of her books are *The Neurotic Personality of Our Times* (1936) and *Self-Analysis* (1942).

See also *anxiety; childhood neurosis; Erikson, Erik Homburger; Freud, Sigmund; psychoanalysis; psychosocial development; trust versus mistrust.*

hospitalism: See *anaclitic depression.*

Huntington's chorea: An inherited disease of the central nervous system involving a degenerative process of neurons located in the frontal portion of the brain. (Huntington's chorea is also known as *Huntington's disease* and *hereditary chorea.* Informally, it is sometimes referred to as *Woody Guthrie's disease.*) George Huntington, a neurologist, identified the disease in 1872. Symptoms include jerky random movements of the entire body and mental deterioration. The word *chorea* is from a Greek word meaning "dance." (Note the similarity to the familiar word *choreography.*) The idea is that the person with the disease makes involuntary dancelike motions. Huntington's chorea is a progressive disease and usually leads to death in 10 to 20 years. At present, there is no known cure for the disease. Treatment consists of drugs and sometimes surgery to alleviate symptoms.

The disease is caused by a dominant gene and can be carried by either a male or a female. (The term *carrier* of a gene for an illness often suggests an individual who passes on a gene without suffering the effects of the illness. However, in the case of a *dominant* gene, the individual will be *both* a carrier and a victim of the disease.) Assume that a father is a carrier and that a mother is not. Because the gene is dominant, the statistical odds are that one-half of this couple's children will have the disease. The father, the carrier, will develop the disease himself. However, he is likely to pass it on to his children before he experiences symptoms. This is because in most cases the disease is latent until the individual is 30 or 40 years of age, or even older. It is estimated that there are presently about 50,000 latent cases in the United States.

Potential parents who suspect that they are carriers of Huntington's chorea should consider obtaining genetic counseling prior to having children. Such counseling can play a role in preventing the spread of the disease.

See also *dominant gene; genetic counseling.*

Hurler's syndrome: An inherited disorder characterized by mental retardation, shortness of stature, and chronic medical problems. The disorder used to be called *gargoylism* because its victims often suffer from facial deformities. The principal causal factor in Hurler's syndrome is an imbalance in the body's enzymes, chemicals that are important in the regulation of metabolism. The disorder is not usually evident in a neonate. However, its symptoms begin to appear early in infancy.

See also *mental retardation; phenylketonuria (PKU).*

hydrocephalus: An abnormally large head caused by excessive amounts of cerebrospinal fluid trapped within ventricles (i.e., openings) in the brain. (In terms of its Greek roots, *hydrocephalus* means "a head filled with water.") The condition may be present at birth or may develop later as a result of an infection. If untreated from infancy, the victim often develops a very large head and is mentally retarded. The mental retardation is due to brain damage caused by excessive pressure on the brain. In the case of an adult, trapped cerebrospinal fluid will not lead to an enlarged head because the skull has lost its plasticity. However, mental retardation can still result.

Treatment consists of surgery designed to drain off excessive cerebrospinal fluid. If this is done in the early years, the head will grow normally and the child will be saved from mental retardation. Adults can be treated with a similar procedure.

See also *mental retardation; microcephaly.*

hyperactivity: See *attention-deficit hyperactivity disorder (ADHD).*

hyperkinesis: Behavior characterized by excessive movement. The term *hyperkinesis* is used interchangeably with *hyperactivity.*

See also *attention-deficit hyperactivity disorder (ADHD).*

hypoxia: See *anoxia.*

I

iconic mode of thought: As described by the cognitive psychologist Jerome Bruner, a mode of thought in which reality is represented in the form of images or pictures. (An *icon* is an image, likeness, or picture.) Using the iconic mode of thought, 2-year-old Gloria might imagine in her proverbial mind's eye that if a ball is dropped on the floor, the ball will bounce. The old saying "A picture is worth a thousand words" is appropriate here. Long before Gloria can manipulate words with any kind of facility, it would seem that she can manipulate mental images in order to make rough predications. She is not thinking in words, "If I drop the ball on the floor, it will bounce back up toward my hand." Instead, she is *visualizing* the ball hitting the floor and bouncing back. She is thinking in images.

The need to think in iconic terms is not outgrown. Iconic thought is a living root from which more complex symbolic thought springs.

See also *Bruner, Jerome S.; enactive mode of thought; symbolic mode of thought.*

id: According to Freud, the foundation of the personality. The id is present at birth; therefore, it is said to be *primal*, or "first," in development. The id consists of the basic biological drives, such as hunger, thirst, pain, and sex. The relief of tension created by these drives is perceived by the individual as pleasure. Thus, it is said that the id is pleasure oriented. Also, Freud stressed the importance of aggression, which he thought of as one more inborn drive. There has been substantial debate about this point in psychology. Not all thinkers agree with Freud's point about aggression.

It was Freud's contention that the excessive repression of the drives of sex and aggression are responsible for neurotic reactions. The family and society want the individual to inhibit the sexual drive until marriage, to be faithful to one partner, and to engage in a limited range of sexual behaviors. Also, the family and society want to person to be polite, have good manners, and control outbursts of anger. Naturally, these constraints are necessary if there is to be any kind of culture or progress. However, Freud contended that neurosis is, to some extent, the price paid for civilization.

The id is impersonal and common to all of us. This, indeed, is why it is called the id. The Latin word *id* simply means "it." Thus the id is, in a sense, the "it" of the personality. In Freud's writings in German, he simply refers to the id as the *it*. However, when the psychoanalyst A. A. Brill translated Freud's works into English, he introduced the term *id*.

The other two principal agents of the personality are the ego and the superego.

See also *aggressiveness; ego; Freud, Sigmund; superego.*

identical twins: See *twins.*

identification: A kind of ego defense mechanism characterized by one individual's unconscious association with the attributes of a second individual. For example, 4-year-old Eddie might want to be "just like daddy." He might try to shave or engage in some other behavior he associates with his father. The identification of children with their parents in early childhood is seen as healthful and one of the ways in which children acquire the values of their culture.

The process of identification continues to take place in both adolescence and adulthood. For example, 14-year-old Candace admires 16-year-old Julia. Candace strives to imitate Julia's way of dressing, walking, and talking. The basic theme involves the gathering of psychological strength from the real or imagined powers of the admired individual. That is why children and adolescents with low self-esteem are likely to overuse identification. If a child has very low self-esteem, he or she may identify intensely with a seemingly more competent child. Blind following of the more dominant person may be the result.

See also *ego defense mechanisms.*

identity: A robust sense of self. Persons with a well-defined identity have the feeling that they know "who they really are." They tend to be convinced that they are on the right road in life, that their goals stand clearly before them, and that these goals have real value. These individuals associate strongly with life's various roles and vocations. They tend to think without ambivalence, "I am a mother," or "I am a father," or "I am a teacher," or "I am a master plumber."

The formation of an identity gives the individual a sense of continuity in life. There is the impression, correct or incorrect, that one is the same person that one was years ago. Also, one will be the same person in the future. Thus, the person with an identity feels strongly linked to both the past and the future.

The attainment of a positive identity, one that is valued by one's family and general culture, is a principal developmental task.

See also *identity crisis; identity disorder; identity versus role confusion; negative identity.*

identity crisis: According to Erikson, a turning point in the process of the formation of an identity. If the crisis is resolved satisfactorily, the adolescent will have an identity. If the crisis is resolved unsatisfactorily, or remains open, the adolescent will be in a state of role confusion.

See also *Erikson, Erik Homburger; identity versus role confusion; negative identity.*

identity diffusion: See *identity versus role confusion.*

identity disorder: A behavioral disorder characterized by a much more intense version of the kinds of attitudes and feelings associated with role confusion. It is important to note that the common doubts and anxieties associated with the creation of an identity are not severe enough in most cases to say that an actual disorder exists. Sixteen is the approximate age usually associated with the beginning of the disorder.

The diagnosis of an identity disorder is warranted only if symptoms are both severe and relatively long-lasting. Some of the symptoms are (1) difficulty becoming interested in a vocation, (2) inability to make a commitment to significant goals in life, (3) lack of stability in friendships, (4) religious uncertainty, (5) highly unconventional moral attitudes, (6) lack of willingness to adopt social roles approved of by the family or larger culture, (7) hostility toward conventional, traditional patterns of behavior, and (8) great anxiety concerning the choices involved in the creation of an identity.

The specific causal factors that contribute to the disorder are somewhat obscure. They seem to be related to an intensification of the kinds of general factors associated with role confusion in adolescence. It is not known whether or not one sex tends to be more frequently afflicted with the disorder than the other one. Also, there are no statistics concerning the incidence of the disorder. However, clinical experience suggests it occurs more frequently today than it did 30 or 40 years ago. This is probably due to a number of factors such as a greater range of vocational options, more open moral attitudes, a higher divorce rate, and a longer time spent in academic education than was the case in the past.

Treatment for the disorder usually consists of psychotherapy for the adolescent combined with family therapy. Sometimes an antianxiety agent is prescribed.

See also *identity; identity versus role confusion; identity crisis; negative identity.*

identity versus role confusion: In Erikson's theory, the fifth stage of psychosocial development, the stage associated with adolescence, the time from about 12 to 18 years of age. The outstanding challenge to an individual's personality during this time span is to develop a sense of identity. If the positive quality of an identity does not develop, then the adolescent will suffer from role confusion. Role confusion, also known as *identity diffusion*, is characterized by the conviction that one is lost in the maze of life, an inability to choose goals, doubt about one's vocation, and no well-defined image of the future. It is difficult to go on to the next stage of psychosocial development, intimacy versus isolation, until an identity is attained.

Loving parents who see their children in a state of role confusion usually want to be of help. Encouragement, empathy, and information may be of some value in helping the adolescent form an identity. However, it must be remembered that an identity cannot be imposed from without, even by parents. An authoritarian approach and strongly voiced convictions may actually interfere with the natural process of creating an identity.

See also *Erikson, Erik Homburger; intimacy versus isolation; psychosexual development; psychosocial development.*

idiot: An imprecise term suggesting a person who suffers from profound mental retardation. The term *idiot* has acquired negative connotations, and it is out of favor when clinical, objective language is required.

See also *imbecile; mental retardation; moron.*

idiot savant: A mentally retarded person who has a special talent such as solving mathematical problems, building ship models, singing like an opera star, memorizing reams of statistics, or playing the piano without knowing how to read music. The word *savant* means "wise person" or "person with great learning." This obviously refers to the idiot savant's special aptitude or talent. However, the term is also intended to be somewhat contradictory because it can be translated "wise fool."

Although idiot savants have been the object of both curiosity and scientific scrutiny, not a lot is known about how some of them can accomplish seemingly amazing feats (e.g., the rapid calculations of large square roots). It can be said, however, that some principle of compensation seems to be at work. What an idiot savant has lost in most cognitive areas appears to be offset to some extent by specific abilities.

See also *idiot; intelligence; mental retardation.*

imaginary playmate: An invisible friend or companion created by daydreaming. About one-half of children have such a playmate during the preschool years. Although, if challenged, most children will steadfastly deny that the playmate is unreal, they are in fact usually quite clear on the subject. They know the playmate is a kind of make-believe. Imaginary playmates usually have names and well-defined personality traits.

The existence of an imaginary playmate does not suggest that a child suffers from infantile autism or is a candidate for schizophrenia. Quite the contrary. Studies suggest that children who have an imaginary playmate are likely to be somewhat more creative than others in adolescence and adulthood. Also, such children are also somewhat less prone to violence and tend to make a satisfactory social adjustment. Children usually give up their imaginary playmates around the ages of 6 or 7 years.

See also *autistic disorder; childhood schizophrenia; daydreaming; fantasy; imaginative play.*

imaginative play: A kind of play characterized by pretending that something or someone is real that does not in fact exist. This kind of play is most common during the preschool years. For example, 3-year-old Vina is eating spaghetti wrapped around a fork. She begins to make motor noises and pretends that the forkful of spaghetti is a dirigible and that her mouth is a hanger. Five-year-old Scott is standing in front of a mirror with a large bath towel tied around his neck. He imagines that it is a cape and declares, "I'm Superman, the man of steel! Up, up, and away!"

Imaginative play is normal and should not be arbitrarily inhibited by parents. It tends to fade in both frequency and intensity with the arrival of late childhood and adolescence. This is not to say that the capacity for imaginative play is completely lost in later years. There is a well-known movie clip in which Judy Garland sings to a photograph of Clark Gable, "You made me love you." The frequent replaying of this clip suggests that it strikes a common chord. It is not difficult for most of us to understand how an adolescent can, through imagination, pretend to be loved by someone else.

See also *daydreaming; fantasy; imaginary playmate.*

imbecile: An individual with an IQ score between 20 and 50. The word *imbecile* is derived from Latin roots meaning "weak mind" and is no longer used in clinical work because of its negative connotations. The preferred term in its place is *severe mental retardation.*

See also *idiot; mental retardation; moron.*

imitation: Copying or mimicking the behavior of a model. Children often imitate the behavior of their parents, siblings, and peers. A large body of research suggests that imitation plays a significant role in social learning.

See also *Bandura, Albert; model; modeling; social imitation; social learning.*

immature birth: A birth taking place between the fifth and sixth months of pregnancy. The average birth weight under these circumstances is between one and two pounds. An immature birth usually presents difficulties and complications even greater than those associated with a premature birth. In most cases, the neonate does not survive.

See also *mature birth; premature birth.*

imprinting: The rapid acquisition of a behavior pattern in conjunction with specific early experiences during a critical period of special sensitivity. The concept of imprinting was studied in detail by the ethologist Konrad Lorenz. For example, goslings follow a mother goose shortly after hatching. However, if given the opportunity to follow a different moving object (e.g., a toy truck pulled by a string), they will follow it. Subsequently, they will not follow the mother. They have imprinted on the truck and "recognize" it as the object of perception that would normally be the mother. (Fortunately, goslings in nature almost always imprint on their own mothers, not toy trucks.)

It is possible that a process somewhat similar to imprinting operates in human beings when an infant becomes attached to a parent. If so, it is believed that the attachment, or emotional bond, forms best during a critical period associated with early infancy.

See also *attachment; bidirectionality of influence; critical period; ethology.*

impulsiveness: Acting suddenly and spontaneously without reflection or concern for consequences. It is expected that toddlers and preschoolers will be more impulsive than older children. However, if, for example, a 7-year-old child displays the kind of impulsiveness associated with the behavior of a preschooler, than the impulsiveness is classified as a kind of immature behavior. Impulsiveness is often associated with an attention-deficit hyperactivity disorder.

Causal factors in age-inappropriate impulsiveness include minimal brain dysfunction (MBD), chronic emotional distress, low self-esteem, and maladaptive social habits. Drug therapy can be useful if the impulsiveness has a biological basis. Child psychotherapy, family therapy, and behavior modification are recommended if the psychological factors are dominant.

See also *aggressiveness; attention-deficit hyperactivity disorder (ADHD); minimal brain dysfunction (MBD); spoiled child.*

in loco parentis: A legal term derived from the Latin meaning "in place of the parent." Examples of adults who often act in place of parents are teachers, school principals, chaperons, camp counselors, scout leaders, directors of a dormitory, and so forth. Through the power of *in loco parentis,* the adult caregiver has some of the rights and responsibilities of the actual parents. However, the power is temporary in that it is not formally granted by a legal action such as adoption.

See also *adopted child; adoptive parent; orphan;* parens patriae; *stepparent.*

in vitro fertilization: Fertilization outside of the human body. A container such as a petri dish (i.e., a glass container used in biological research for cultures of organic material) is used. (*In vitro* is a Latin term, meaning "in glass.") In order for *in vitro* fertilization to take place, at least one ovum must be obtained from one of the female's ovaries. (Often several ova are obtained.) Sperm donated by the father are introduced into the container. If conception occurs, the zygote (i.e., fertilized egg) is introduced into the mother through her vagina for implantation in her uterus.

The informal, and inaccurate, term *test-tube baby* is often used to identify an infant born through the process of *in vitro* fertilization.

See also *embryo; ovum; sperm cell; zygote.*

incest: Sexual relations with a close relative. The clearest examples of close relatives are (1) parents and their children and (2) siblings. There are borderline cases. If marriage between two persons is forbidden by law or custom, then sexual relations are considered incestuous. Thus, some groups might consider sexual relations between first cousins incest. Other groups would not. If a stepfather and a stepdaughter have sexual relations, is this incest? Again, this is a borderline case.

They are related by marriage, but not by blood. Some groups would consider their sexual relations incest. Again, others would not.

The actual incidence of incest is unknown because it is probably underreported to authorities. Various studies place their estimates at between 2 percent of families and one-half of 1 percent of families. But these estimates are not considered to be highly reliable. Sexual relations between brother and sister are believed to be about five times as common as between father and daughter. And sexual relations between mother and son are believed to take place very infrequently.

Although estimates suggest that the actual incidence of incest is low, Freud believed that an incest wish is fairly common, particularly in children. This hypothesis forms the basis of what is called in psychoanalysis the *Oedipus complex*.

The *incest taboo*, society's prohibition against incest, arises from good cause. If incest were practiced on a wide and regular scale, there would be a substantial increase in birth defects and recessive genetic disorders.

See also *Electra complex; Oedipus complex.*

incest wish: See *incest.*

individual differences: Traits, attributes, and characteristics that make it possible to differentiate one person from another. The list of these features is long and includes hair color, eye color, height, weight, gender, intelligence, creativity, temperament, need to achieve, social attitudes, table manners, and so forth. Some individual differences are determined primarily by genetic factors (e.g., hair color and height). Other individual differences are determined primarily by learning (e.g., social attitudes and table manners). Still other individual differences are determined by an interaction of genetic and learned factors (e.g., intelligence and creativity). In many cases, the relative contribution of inborn and learned factors to behavior is not clear and is still being researched and discussed. This is the basis of the long-running controversy between empiricism and nativism.

It is important for parents and other caregivers to recognize the important role that individual differences play in the behavior of children.

See also *creative thinking; empiricism; genetic predisposition; intelligence; learning; nativism; need to achieve; temperament.*

inductive thinking: A kind of thinking in which conclusions are reached by the evaluation and comparison of facts or observations. A general conclusion is reached after studying several particular situations. If the sums of several pairs of odd numbers were studied ($1 + 1 = 2, 5 + 7 = 12, 19 + 3 = 22, 11 + 5 = 16$), one could draw the conslusion, through inductive thinking, that the sum of two odd numbers if always an even number.

See also *deductive thinking.*

industry versus inferiority: In Erikson's theory, the fourth stage of psychosocial development, the stage associated with middle and late childhood, the time from about 5 or 6 to 11 or 12 years of age. Children who usually complete their schoolwork, do their chores, and have personal hobbies are displaying the positive personality trait of *industry*, the sense that one can start and finish a worthwhile task. The urge to be industrious appears to be a natural tendency in children. Effective parents and caregivers can encourage and reinforce it. If parents or caregivers discourage tendencies toward industry by being overly critical or showing no interest in a child's accomplishments, the negative trait of *inferiority* may develop. Children with a strong sense of inferiority may believe that they cannot do anything right, that they are stupid or incompetent, and that they are unsuited for the future challenges of life.

See also *Erikson, Erik Homburger; psychosexual development; psychosocial development.*

infant: In human beings, a child between 2 to 3 weeks of age and 18 to 24 months of age. Prior to 2 to 3 weeks of age, in technical language the child is referred to as a *neonate*. After infancy, the period of toddlerhood begins. The word *infancy* is derived from a Latin word meaning "without speech." Infants do babble, of course, but it is obvious that they do not speak an intelligible language.

See also *babbling; child; neonate; toddlerhood.*

infant states of consciousness: See *states of consciousness in an infant.*

infantile autism: See *autistic disorder.*

inferiority complex: According to Adler, a complex that arises when the will to power is blocked in a particular domain of behavior. For example, if a child strives to understand arithmetic and has significant learning problems, an inferiority complex may arise. The complex is a set of associated ideas such as "I'm no good at long division" and "I can't understand fractions" and "I always make mistakes when I add." The child can be said to have a mathematics inferiority complex. It is possible to have an inferiority complex concerning almost any important aspect of life: sex, appearance, athletic ability, speaking ability, and so forth.

An inferiority complex is made worse if parents and other caregivers make arbitrary attributions concerning the child's personality such as, "You're just like your grandfather. He was never good at arithmetic either." Caregivers can keep an inferiority complex from becoming larger by providing encouragement and reinforcement for successes.

The term *inferiority complex* is somewhat outdated and tends to be associated with both Adler and the 1930s. The comparable modern term, similar in meaning, is *low self-esteem.*

See also *Adler, Alfred; self-esteem; spoiled child; superiority complex; will to power.*

information-processing theory: The theory that human cognitive processes are similar to the information-processing capacities of a computer. Sensory processes (e.g., vision, hearing, taste, and so forth) are similar to the *input* functions of a computer. Perception, thinking, problem solving, and memory are similar to the *storage, data processing* and *retrieval* functions of a computer. Motor activities (e.g., speaking, walking, using a tool, and so forth) are similar to the *output* functions of a computer.

Behavioral scientists have found the analogy between the human mind and a computer a useful one for guiding and organizing research in cognitive development. However, it should be remembered that an analogy is, after all, only an analogy. When one says that the human mind is like a computer, one should be aware that the mind came first in the planet's history, not the computer. It is really more accurate to say that the computer is like the human mind. A person's cognitive processes are understood somewhat better by reducing them to processes that are designed, defined, and controlled in machines.

In view of the importance of the study of cognitive development in children, information-processing theory has been an important analytical tool.

See also *cognitive development; memory; motor development.*

inhalant drug: A drug that is taken into the lungs by the act of breathing in. The molecules of the drug then work their way into the bloodstream and nervous system. Inhalant drugs are used in order to obtain an altered state of consciousness, a "high" characterized by excitement and euphoria. The duration of the high is about one-half hour to two hours. Examples of inhalant drugs are some glues, solvents, polishes, gasoline, and lighter fluid. Unfortunately, these drugs are readily available in most households.

Undesirable side effects of inhalant drugs include nausea, confusion, seizures that resemble those associated with epilepsy, distorted perceptions, and damage to the brain and nervous system.

Because inhalant drugs are cheap and readily available, they are sometimes abused by preadolescent children. Parents need to be alert to this possibility. If younger children are discovered to be experimenting with inhalant drugs, their behavior should be discussed with them. They need to be provided with information concerning the dangers of using the drugs. In some cases, the easy availability of the drugs needs to be curtailed. The information included in the entries for *drug abuse in adolescence, behavior modification,* and *tough love* may be of some value.

See also *behavior modification; depressant drugs; drug abuse in adolescence; hallucinogens; narcotic drugs; stimulant drugs; tough love.*

inhibition: A restraint on behavior. Inhibition is a broad general concept with several applications to both general and developmental psychology. It is possible to make a distinction between external and internal inhibition. *External inhibition* refers to blocks or obstacles to motivated behavior, often imposed by an external agent such as a parent or other authority figure. Although this usage is correct, it is not the more common one. *Internal inhibition* refers to something that is self-imposed; and more often than not this is the usage intended.

Inhibition plays an important role in the learning process. When an undesirable habit is extinguished by withholding reinforcers or by counterconditioning, it is, in a sense, unlearned. This is sometimes referred to as *conditioned inhibition.*

Inhibition may play a role in stuttering. The desire to speak competes with an internal restraint, or inhibition, against speaking. The inhibition arises from a desire to control anxiety. For example, the stutterer may fear being laughed at or may wish too strongly for someone else's approval (see *stuttering*).

Inhibition is a contributing factor to traits and behavior patterns in children involving avoidance or withdrawal such as extreme introversion, shame, or chronic shyness.

See also *counterconditioning; extinction; introversion; reinforcer; shame; shyness; stuttering.*

initiative versus guilt: In Erikson's theory, the third stage of psychosocial development, the stage associated with the preschool period, the time from about 3 to 5 years of age. *Initiative* is characterized by self-motivated behavior involving a somewhat complex task. For example, 5-year-old Natalie announces, "I'm going to put all my big books at this end of the shelf, and I'm going to put all my little books at the other end." If preschoolers are encouraged to engage in such tasks, they will tend to develop initiative as a trait. On the other hand, if the effects of their efforts are overly criticized, discounted, or laughed at, there will be a tendency to develop the negative trait of *guilt*, the belief that they are being "bad" or doing wrong when they act without direction or instruction.

See also *Erikson, Erik Homburger; psychosexual development; psychosocial development.*

innate: Inborn. That which is innate, or inborn, is intrinsic to one's nature. At the biological level, it is evident that much is innate. Human beings have an innate structure; most have two eyes, five fingers on a hand, one heart, and so forth. Also, the neonate has a set of innate reflexes. However, at the psychological level, that which is and is not innate is somewhat debatable.

The philosopher Plato believed that human beings have innate ideas. The philosopher Immanuel Kant suggested the existence of an innate moral code. Alfred Adler asserted that human beings have an innate social interest. Carl Jung wrote that tendencies toward extraversion and introversion are innate. Sociobiology hypothesizes that some patterns of behavior have an inborn basis. Recent research indicates that some behavioral dispositions, particularly temperament, are to some extent inborn. *Nativism* is the point of view that much of our behavior is determined by innate factors. *Empiricism* is the point of view that opposes nativism.

See also *Adler, Alfred; empiricism; Jung, Carl Gustav; nativism; nature-nurture controversy; neonatal reflexes; sociobiology; temperament.*

insight learning: According to the Gestalt psychologist Wolfgang Köhler (1887–1957), a kind of learning characterized by a sudden perceptual reorganization such that a new understanding emerges. The capacity for insight learning is sometimes called the *"Ah-hah" phenomenon.* Informally, one describes the experience of insight learning by making such statements as "I get it!" or "Things connected" or "A light bulb went on in my brain."

Suppose that 11-year-old William is being taught the concept of pi in his arithmetic class. He is told that pi is defined as the ratio of the circumference of a circle to its diameter and is equal to 3.14159. . . . Then he and the class are given a set of homework problems. He is confused for a while and cannot understand the meaning of pi. While working one of the problems, he suddenly says to himself, "I get it. A circle is always about three times bigger around than it is across. That's all that pi really is." Now he continues doing his homework with a clear grasp of what he is doing. Learning without insight is called *rote learning*, a mechanical process of association or memorization. Insight learning appears to have distinct advantages over rote learning. A child is more comfortable with the content of what is to be learned if it is clearly understood. Also, material learned by insight seems to be retained for a long time.

Parents and teachers can encourage insight learning by creating conditions that tend to bring it forth. For example, in the teaching of pi, the teacher can provide a class with circular objects of various sizes, lengths of string, and rulers. By measuring and comparing the circumferences and diameters of the objects, the students are helped to grasp the actual nature of pi. Two important mental processes underlying insight learning are deductive and inductive thinking.

See also *concept formation; deductive thinking; inductive thinking; learning; Montesorri, Maria; Montesorri method; Wertheimer, Max.*

insomnia: Inability to sleep. Most children and adults have difficulty in sleeping from time to time. This is normal and requires no special coping techniques. *Chronic insomnia* is characterized by frequent difficulties in obtaining adequate sleep. Children who suffer from chronic insomnia may complain that they cannot fall asleep, that they wake up during the night and cannot get back to sleep, or that they wake up too early. During the day, symptoms of chronic insomnia include drowsiness, lethargy, acting cross and out of sorts, and inability to pay attention in school. If such symptoms are absent, it is unlikely that the child is suffering from chronic insomnia.

Sleep needs differ with age. In general, the formula is that the younger the child, the more sleep required. A toddler needs 12 to 13 hours of sleep. A preschooler needs 11 to 12 hours. During most of childhood 10 to 11 hours are needed. During adolescence 8 to 9 hours are adequate. However, it should be realized that there are substantial individual differences in sleep needs. Some preadolescent children thrive on 8 hours of sleep. Before a parent decides that a child suffers from chronic insomnia, it is a good idea to explore the question: Is the child being asked to spend too much time in bed in terms of his or her individual needs?

Causal factors in chronic insomnia include medical problems such as hyperthyroidism and minimal brain dysfunction (MBD). On the psychological level, emotional problems such as phobias, chronic anxiety, depression, anger, and low self-esteem may function as causes.

Common-sense measures for insomnia include allowing the child some say in the choice of a bedtime, making sure the bed and room are comfortable, encouraging a period of rest and relaxation before going to bed in order to reduce excitement, and providing a light bedtime snack with some milk. If the child wants to get up for 10 or 20 minutes during the night in order to get rid of restlessness and tension, this can be allowed.

If common-sense measures fail, the child should have a physical examination to make sure there are no medical problems. If there is no medical basis for the chronic insomnia, child psychotherapy may be indicated. Sometimes drug therapy is recommended. Antihistamines have been found to be useful for inducing sleep. A specific prescription drug that has been found to be helpful is flurazepam, an antianxiety agent and sedative.

See also *anxiety; depression; minimal brain dysfunction (MBD); night terror; nightmare; phobia; self-esteem; sleep patterns; sleep-walking disorder.*

instinct: An inborn tendency to perform a well-defined, complex behavioral sequence. Examples of instincts in animals are the Pacific salmon's tendency to swim upstream and return to spawning grounds, the nest-building patterns of many birds, and the highly specific kinds of webs spun by different varieties of spiders. Although the existence of instincts in animals seems obvious at a common-sense level, some behavioral scientists have been skeptical. John Watson denied that instincts exist at all. Others have suggested one should refer to *instinctive behaviors,* giving up the use of *instinct* as a noun. The gain in using this kind of language is the avoidance of simplified explanations of behavior by referring to it as a mysterious, unexplainable, and unobservable instinct lost somewhere in the organism. To say that behavior is "instinctive" is to describe a general class of behavior while avoiding facile explanations.

The ethologists prefer to speak of *species-specific behavior* in order to avoid the history of verbal and conceptual confusion surrounding the word *instinct.*

The real question of concern in reference to child development is: Do children have instincts? Or, better: Do they display instinctive behaviors? If one adopts the viewpoint that the mind at birth is *tabula rasa,* or blank slate, then the answer is "No." Watson subscribed to this doctrine, and he argued that infants are born with only a few reflexes. All other behaviors are acquired through learning.

On the other hand, if one adopts the viewpoint that there is some genetic basis for certain kinds of behavior, then, loosely speaking, it could be argued that infants and children show a variety of instinctive behaviors. Jung believed that human beings have an "instinctoid nature." By this he meant that we do not have instincts as such, but something that resembles them. Adler asserted that social interest is inborn. The sociobiologists hypothesize that many behaviors such as altruism, territoriality, and mating patterns have a genetic basis in both animals and human beings.

The pendulums swings both ways on the issue of whether or not human beings have instincts. About 100 years ago, psychologists such as William James took for granted the existence of instincts in human beings. In the 1920s and 1930s, behaviorism was at the peak of its influence, and the existence of instincts in human beings was completely denied. Today, the pendulum has returned at least halfway to its position 100 years ago. The teachings of the ethologists and sociobiologists are taken seriously, and the behavior of children is seldom explained solely in terms of experience and learning.

See also *Adler, Alfred; empiricism; ethology; James, William; Jung, Carl Gustav; nativism; sociobiology; Watson, John Broadus.*

institutionalization: See *institutionalized children.*

institutionalized children: Children who are wards of a public agency such as an orphanage, a charitable hospital, or a reform school. A number of studies have found that institutionalized children often fail to thrive. Institutionalized infants often suffer from anaclitic depression and low developmental quotients. Older children often display conduct disorders, other behavioral problems, and low IQ scores. The fault resides not necessarily in institutionalization as such, but in the way in which children are treated in many institutions. If they receive little individual attention and almost no affection, it is no wonder that they display behavioral difficulties. On the other hand, enlightened institutions are discovering ways around these difficulties, and much progress is being made in ways of giving quality care under difficult circumstances.

See also *anaclitic depression; developmental quotient (DQ); failure to thrive;* in loco parentis; *intelligence quotient (IQ);* parens patriae.

instrumental learning: See *operant conditioning.*

integrity versus despair: In Erikson's theory, the eighth and last stage of psychosocial development, the stage associated with old age. Individuals who have accepted life's responsibilities, risen to its challenges, and made a contribution to their social world are likely to experience *integrity*, a sense that one's self and one's life are whole and complete. Individuals who have not been responsible and who have failed to act constructively on their opportunities and talents are likely to experience *despair*, the belief and feeling that life has been largely wasted. The last stage is tied to earlier ones and is, to some extent, an outgrowth of successes and failures associated with them.

See also *Erikson, Erik Homburger; psychosexual development; psychosocial development.*

intellectual development: See *cognitive development.*

intellectual giftedness: See *giftedness.*

intellectualization: An ego defense mechanism in which abstract thinking is used as a way to cope with a threatening feeling. The emotional content of an experience is repressed and replaced with a cold analysis. For example, 14-year-old Dale has been battling leukemia, a potentially fatal disease, since the age of 9. He has become well-informed about the disease, has several books on it, and can speak at length about how leukemia is a form of cancer, how abnormal white blood cells attack the bone marrow, and so forth. When he discovers new information about leukemia, he says, "How interesting," with very little emotion. *Thinking* is, to some extent, antagonistic to *feeling.* Thus, Dale's anxiety is in part diminished by the process of intellectualization, at least at the conscious level. Also, being informed gives him the sense that he has some control over the disease.

Although intellectualization may be used to some extent by pre-adolescent children, it is more likely to be associated with adolescence and adulthood because it requires a fairly high level of cognitive maturity.

See also *cognitive development; ego defense mechanisms.*

intelligence: A very general concept implying the ability of an individual to think logically, solve problems, comprehend relationships, employ mathematical symbols, and grasp concepts. David Wechsler, a leading researcher and test author, defines *intelligence* as "the global capacity of the individual to act purposefully, to think rationally, and to deal effectively with the environment."

See also *heredity and intelligence; intelligence quotient (IQ); intelligence tests; Wechsler, David.*

intelligence quotient (IQ): Traditionally, the ratio of mental age (MA) to chronological age (CA). The German psychologist William Stern (1871–1938) introduced the concept of the intelligence quotient as a device for obtaining stable measurements of intelligence over a period of years. The basic formula he proposed is:

$$IQ = MA/CA \times 100$$

If a child's mental age and chronological age are the same, then MA/CA equals 1, and his or her IQ is 100, the *average IQ*. If MA is higher than CA, the IQ is above average; and if MA is lower than CA, then the IQ is below average. Note the following examples.

1. Katherine's MA is 10; her CA is 8.
   $10/8 \times 100 = 1.25 \times 100 = 125$.
   Thus, her IQ is 125, which is above average.
2. Todd's MA is 12; his CA is 13.
   $12/13 \times 100 = 0.92 \times 100 = 92$
   Todd's IQ is 92, which is below average.
3. Melba's MA is 9; her CA is 9.
   $9/9 \times 100 = 1 \times 100 = 100$
   Melba's IQ is 100, the average IQ.

The formula proposed by Stern is the original one. However, it should be noted that IQs on contemporary tests are also often arrived at by a statistical method. The statistical method utilizes a measure of variability known as the *standard deviation*. Ranges of scores under a *normal distribution curve*, a bell-shaped distribution, are used to define the IQ when this approach is taken. The statistical method does not alter the basic meaning of the IQ.

A widely used classification scheme used for IQ scores is the one proposed by the research psychologist David Wechsler:

IQ	Classification	Percent
130 and above	Very superior	2.2
120–129	Superior	6.7
110–119	Bright normal	16.1
90–109	Average	50.0
80–89	Dull normal	16.1
70–79	Borderline	6.7
69 and below	Mental defective	2.2

Thus, in the earlier example, Katherine, with an IQ score of 125, belongs to the IQ classification Superior, a group comprising 6.7 percent of a standardized population. Melba, with an IQ score of 100, and Todd, with an IQ score of 92, both belong to the IQ classification Average, a group comprising 50.0 percent of a standardized population.

It is important to realize that IQ is not intelligence itself. It is a *measure* of intelligence. Therefore, it is subject to any of the problems involved in measurement. Sometimes it is unreliable. If, for example, a child is anxious while taking the test, the IQ score may be suppressed, and the child may in fact be more intelligent than he or she appears to be in terms of the IQ obtained.

In the field of mental health, the IQ has a practical purpose. Its purpose is to assess the amount of intellectual impairment associated with a mental disorder, mental retardation, or organic brain damage. This can be useful information in arriving at an adequate treatment program for a child or an adolescent with a behavioral disorder.

See also *chronological age (CA); intelligence; intelligence tests; mental age (MA); reliability of a test; validity of a test.*

intelligence tests: Standardized tests of intellectual performance designed to measure intelligence. These tests yield an IQ score. They also provide a profile of a child's highs and lows in different areas of intelligence such as comprehension, mathematical ability, attention span, or spatial reasoning. Such a profile can be useful if the child needs counseling for a learning disability or a behavioral disorder.

Also, the profile can be of diagnostic value if the child suffers from an organic problem such as minimal brain dysfunction (MBD) or epilepsy.

The most well-known, and widely used, tests are the Stanford-Binet Intelligence Scale, the Wechsler Preschool and Primary Scale of Intelligence (WPPSI), the Wechsler Intelligence Scale for Children (WISC), and the Wechsler Adult Intelligence Scale (WAIS). (The adult scale is administered to adolescents with a chronological age of 16 or more.)

See also *epilepsy; learning disability; minimal brain dysfunction (MBD); Stanford-Binet Intelligence Scale; Wechsler intelligence scales.*

intimacy versus isolation: In Erikson's theory, the sixth stage of psychosocial development, the stage associated with young adulthood. The basically normal young adult, a person who has more or less successfully consolidated the prior five psychosocial stages, will be inclined to seek out other people. The aim of the seeking will be to establish a sense of *intimacy*, a feeling of both psychological and emotional closeness with others. A close friendship in which one is convinced "I can be myself with you" provides an example of intimacy. For the majority of individuals, the core of a sense of intimacy will consist of a loving sexual relationship with another person. If one has no close friends and no loving relationship with another person, that individual will experience a sense of *isolation*, a feeling of being an unwanted outsider.

See also *Erikson, Erik Homburger; psychosexual development; psychosocial development.*

introversion: As formulated by Carl Jung, a basic attitude toward the world characterized by an ingoing orientation. The introverted child tends to have a dominant interest in the inner world of thought, reflection, ideas, and imagination as opposed to the outer world of action, social activities, and concrete objects. Jung believed that the personality trait of introversion is basically inborn, although it can be modified to some extent by experience. Therefore, if Jung is correct, parents should not try to convert born introverts into extraverts. They should recognize and appreciate their children's natural tendencies and help their children build on them in a positive way. Relatively recent research on temperament suggests that Jung's general approach makes sense.

See also *extraversion; Jung, Carl Gustav; temperament.*

invisible companion: See *imaginary playmate.*

invulnerables: Children who are highly resistant to behavioral disturbances and mental disorders. In the same way that some children seem predisposed to develop mental health problems, there are some children who seem predisposed to be well adjusted. Several studies have identified children who have a personal and family history that greatly increases their risk of becoming troubled. Nonetheless, these same children seem to escape into adolescence and adulthood with few, if any, psychological scars. This is not to say that "invulnerables" are *completely* invulnerable. If subjected to a sufficient amount of psychological and social stress, it is expected that they too will show signs of emotional problems. Nonetheless, invulnerables have a high threshold for the kinds of psychological and emotional wounds that produce pathology in other children.

See also *emotional trauma; genetic predisposition; temperament.*

iris reflex: See *pupillary reflex.*

J

James, William (1842–1910): Highly influential psychologist and philosopher associated for many years with Harvard University. James is often referred to as the "dean of American psychologists." He is considered to be the first American psychologist, established a psychological laboratory at Harvard, and sponsored the first Ph.D. degree granted in psychology in the United States. (The recipient of this degree was Granville Stanley Hall, who made important early contributions to research in child development.)

James was the father of *functionalism*, a major school of psychology. Functionalism asserts that a principal aim of psychology is to study the mental life of human beings. It further asserts that mental life is highly conscious, that consciousness is always flowing and moving, and that this dynamic aspect of consciousness must be understood. This viewpoint was expanded upon by John Dewey and became an important part of educational psychology.

Functionalism faded into insignificance in academic psychology in the 1930s and the 1940s due to the rise of behaviorism. However, in recent times, there as been a reassertion of the importance of understanding the conscious aspects of mental life. This attitude underlies the present interest in both cognitive development and cognitive-behavior modification. James can be seen as an important forerunner of this contemporary trend.

Two of James's important works are *Principles of Psychology* (1890) and *Varieties of Religious Experience* (1902).

See also *behaviorism; cognitive development; cognitive-behavior modification; Dewey, John; educational psychology; Hall, Granville Stanley.*

Jung, Carl Gustav (1875–1961): A Swiss psychiatrist, early follower of Freud, and major personality theorist. Jung was working as a young psychiatrist in Switzerland with the eminent Eugen Bleuler when Jung became aware of Sigmund Freud and psychoanalysis. Jung visited Freud in Austria, and the two men became fast friends. For a number of years, they worked together and cooperated in the formation of psychoanalysis as an influential movement.

In 1909 Jung and Freud traveled together to Clark University in Worcester, Massachusetts, to deliver introductory lectures in psycho-analysis. (They were invited by G. Stanley Hall, a pioneer researcher into child behavior.) Due to Freud's instigation, Jung, not Freud, became in 1910 the first president of the International Psy-choanalytic Association. Freud was concerned that psychoanalysis might be rejected by a larger community of scientists because of his Jewish origins. Jung was a Christian, and his father was a clergyman.

It eventually became clear to both Jung and Freud that they differed on too many theoretical points to continue their collaboration. Jung established his own approach to therapy and personality theory, calling it *analytic psychology.*

Jung's approach has had an influence on thinking in developmental psychology. Jung stressed the importance of inborn factors in personality development; this is essentially a nativistic approach. He believed, for example, that extraversion and introversion are to a large extent givens of the human personality and will make an early appearance in the child's behavior. This he held was true of temperament and of traits in general.

Jung made a careful study of schizophrenia in his early years of research and believed that this disorder, although largely due to inborn factors, was greatly aggravated by adverse experiences in childhood, such as child abuse and emotional neglect.

Jung was a prolific writer and published many books in his lifetime. Among his important works are *Modern Man in Search of a Soul*

(1933), *Psychological Types* (1933), and *The Archetypes and the Collective Unconscious* (1936).

See also *childhood schizophrenia; extraversion; Freud, Sigmund; Hall, Granville Stanley; introversion; nativism; psychoanalysis; temperament; trait.*

junk food: An informal and imprecise term associated with foods high in sugar, high in saturated fats, high in refined carbohydrates, low in fiber, and low in nutritional content. Fast foods, foods quickly prepared in commercial establishments, are also often called "junk foods." For example, sometimes people speak of "garbage burgers."

Pizza has been identified as the favorite food of adolescents, and it is sometimes thought of as junk food. However, in most cases pizza consists of a baked bread dough with protein in the form of meat and cheese. Although pizza tends to be high in saturated fat, it is not "junk" any more than a steak is junk. The point is, of course, that saturated fats can be eaten but must be eaten in moderation.

If the term *junk food* is taken to suggest food that lacks nutritional value or that may be too high in artificial additives, then there is some possibility that the eating of too much junk food may contribute to behavioral disorders. Attention-deficit hyperactivity disorder is the one most frequently implicated. Assuming that a parent or a caregiver has a well-defined concept of junk food, he or she should see that junk foods are available to children only in limited quantities.

Approximately one-third of the food budget of the average American family is spent on eating out. It is advisable to become familiar with ways of making rational choices designed to maximize the nutritional value of meals that are not prepared at home. This can be done readily enough if some time and trouble are taken to evaluate options. Many family restaurants offer a choice of french fries or baked potatoes, fried chicken or broiled chicken, and so forth. Parents can provide responsible models for their children by frequently picking the most nutritious options for themselves, encouraging similar behavior in their children, and reinforcing with recognition and approval the more responsible choices.

See also *attention-deficit hyperactivity disorder (ADHD); Feingold hypothesis; nutrition.*

juvenile delinquency: A legal term referring to the transgressions, either antisocial or immoral, of minors. Juvenile courts mete out punishment or indicate the necessity for corrective action. Such courts handle about 2,000,000 cases a year.

Juvenile delinquency has been on the increase in recent years. In the past decade, the frequency of recorded delinquent acts has more than doubled. About one-third of robberies are committed by juveniles.

Causal factors in juvenile delinquency are many. Some that have been identified are personal adjustment problems, distressed family relationships, portrayals of violence on television, undesirable companions, and overcrowding in cities. Speaking in broad sociocultural terms, it appears that large-scale changes in traditional values and family life have contributed to feelings of alienation and confusion in many minors.

Correctional institutions, probation programs, and personal counseling are all ways that society has developed in an attempt to cope with the problem of juvenile delinquency in a constructive manner.

See also *adolescent sex relations; alienation; antisocial behavior; conduct disorder; drug abuse in adolescence; identity crisis; running away; stealing; truancy.*

K

kindergarten: See *preschool.*

kinds of reinforcers: See *reinforcer.*

Klein, Melanie (1882–1960): A pioneer in the field of child psycho-analysis who is most well known for introducing the principal innova-tions in technique that made play therapy with children possible. She was born in Vienna and studied psychoanalysis on the European continent. One of her teachers was the eminent Karl Abraham, who also provided instruction for Karen Horney. Most of Klein's subse-quent professional life was spent in London. She and Anna Freud, also a pioneer in child psychoanalysis working in London, had several controversies concerning theoretical concepts.

Klein is considered to be a neo-Freudian because she felt free to comment on, and revise according to her own findings and reflections, a number of classical psychoanalytic concepts. Of particular interest to Klein were anxiety, the Oedipus complex, the superego, the stages of psychosexual development (e.g., oral and anal), and the ego defense mechanisms of fantasy and projection.

A book by Klein is *Envy and Gratitude* (1957).

See also *anxiety; child psychotherapy; ego defense mechanisms; fantasy; Freud, Anna; Freud, Sigmund; Horney, Karen; Oedipus complex; play therapy; projection; psychoanalysis; psychosexual development; superego.*

Klinefelter's syndrome: A set of symptoms characterized primarily by mental retardation and underdeveloped testes. The disorder affects only males. Frequently, there is inadequate appearance of secondary sexual characteristics such as facial and pubic hair. There may be little or no sperm production. Often the body tends toward obesity and the formation of large breasts. The syndrome was first identified in 1942 by H. F. Klinefelter, an American researcher.

The cause of the syndrome is a chromosomal anomaly. The individual with Klinefelter's syndrome has one male chromosome and two female chromosomes in each cell of his body. X is the symbol used to indicate a female chromosome. Y is the symbol used to indicate a male chromosome. The normal male has a chromosome structure that may be identified as XY. The person with Klinefelter's syndrome has a chromosome structure that may be identified as XXY.

Treatment for Klinefelter's syndrome includes prescription of the male hormone testosterone, which often helps the individual have a more normal appearance. A sexual drive, formerly absent, sometimes emerges as a result of hormone therapy.

See also *chromosomal anomalies; mental retardation; testes; testosterone.*

knee-jerk reflex: A reflex that is present in the neonate and that is characterized by an involuntary kicking motion when the neonate is tapped on the tendon just below the patella (i.e., the kneecap). This is one of the signs that the infant is neurologically normal. The knee-jerk reflex is never outgrown, and it retains the described pattern for life.

See also *neonatal reflexes.*

Kohlberg, Lawrence (1927–): An educational and developmental psychologist recognized for his studies of moral development in children. Kohlberg earned a Ph.D. degree from the University of Chicago in 1958. His principal academic affiliation has been with Harvard University.

Kohlberg's work can, to some extent, be seen as inspired by two important antecedents. First, Kohlberg's interest in how moral behavior is acquired in childhood is anticipated by Freud's concept of the superego. Second, Kohlberg extends to moral development some of Piaget's formulations on how children think.

A book by Kohlberg is *The Meaning and Measurement of Moral Development* (1980).

See also *cognitive development; Freud, Sigmund; moral development; Piaget, Jean; socialization; superego.*

L

Lamaze method: A training method designed to reduce the pain and fear associated with childbirth. Instruction is usually offered in a group setting and consists of conditioning exercises and realistic information about childbirth. The participation of a labor coach is part of the method, and the father is encouraged to attend the Lamaze classes along with the mother. The idea is for the father to be a participant in the entire process of pregnancy and to provide both assistance and emotional support to his partner during childbirth. Lamaze classes are offered by a number of clinics, counseling centers, schools, and public health agencies.

The method was introduced by the physician Fernard Lamaze in the 1940s, and he used the phrase "painless childbirth" in the title of a book he authored. To some extent, the introduction of the word *painless* was unfortunate. Today, Lamaze instruction has the more limited goals of reducing pain and anxiety to acceptable levels and to giving the mother a sense of control over what is happening to her body during the birthing process. This is not the same thing as saying that labor and delivery will be "painless." For these reasons, the reference to lack of pain has been dropped in favor of such terms *natural childbirth* and *prepared childbirth*. (The Leboyer method is also described as a kind of natural childbirth.)

Clinical experience suggests that the use of the Lamaze method will often have some of the effects it promises. In many cases, the duration of labor is shortened because the mother knows how to consciously relax and cooperate with contractions, dilation proceeds more rapidly, and less anesthetic is required during delivery. Not only do these effects reduce the discomfort and risk of childbirth for the mother, they also decrease the likelihood that the birthing process will have any adverse effect on the infant. For example, in a long labor, the infant is likely to experience oxygen deprivation. This has been implicated as a factor in minimal brain dysfunction (MBD), which itself is associated with attention-deficit hyperactivity disorder.

The Lamaze method is based on principles of classical conditioning formulated by Ivan Pavlov. Lamaze gave full credit to Pavlov for developing the theoretical viewpoint that inspired Lamaze's clinical work.

See also *attention-deficit hyperactivity disorder (ADHD); birth trauma; cesarean section; classical conditioning; Leboyer method; minimal brain dysfunction (MBD); Pavlov, Ivan Petrovich; Rank, Otto.*

language acquisition device (LAD): As formulated by the linguist Noam Chomsky, an inborn set of cognitive structures making it possible for children to acquire language readily and use it with fluency and facility at an early age. It must be understood that Chomsky does not contend that there is an actual "thing" in the brain that "is" the language acquisition device. Instead, the word *device* is chosen to say that the minds of children act *as if* there were such a device. Chomsky's language acquisition device is a psychological concept, not a physiological one.

Evidence in favor of the existence of a language acquisition device comes primarily from studies of language acquisition in children. They use nouns, verbs, and adjectives correctly long before they can say in any conscious way what nouns, verbs, and adjectives are. They take creative leaps with language independent of observation. Even preschoolers speak in sentences that they have never heard before, that are the child's own invention. Children generalize rules. For example, at first they say they *"goed* to the store," instead of *"went* to the store." They are perceiving, without formal instruction, that the "ed" is usually used for past tense. Errors such as this one suggest that children are thinking for themselves when they learn to speak, not simply copying the speech patterns of adults and older children. These kinds of verbal behaviors, and many more, are universal in children; these usages appear independent of nationality, income, or the country's level of development. All of this suggests that it is as natural for children to speak as it is for birds to fly.

Although it is correct to say that LAD is a psychological concept, not a physiological one, nonetheless physiological structures and processes logically provide an underpinning for it. Consequently, it is often pointed out that there are two brain structures, usually located in the left hemisphere of the brain, dedicated to speech. These are Broca's area and Wernicke's area. If either of these areas is damaged due to a stroke or an accident, speech is often impaired.

See also *Chomsky, Noam Avram; cognitive development; language development.*

language development: Growth in the ability to use language, from the babbling of the infant to the subsequent fluency of most children. Language development implies the maturation of a set of related psychological processes including perception, cognition, and memory. It also implies the biological maturation of the brain and the nervous system pathways that control the voluntary movements of the tongue.

According to Barbara S. Wood, a behavioral scientist who has conducted research on language development, there are six distinct stages in such development.

- Stage 1 is associated with infancy and is characterized by *babbling* or *prespeech*. Although babbling appears to be random and meaningless, it has both structure and pattern.
- Stage 2 is associated with middle infancy and is characterized by the *holophrase*, a single word that stands for a sentence.
- Stage 3 is associated with late infancy and is characterized by *duos*, sentences with two words. (Stage 3 is also known as the *two-word stage.*)
- Stage 4 is associated with early toddlerhood and is characterized by *several-word sentences*, often with a noun and a verb.
- Stage 5 is associated with late toddlerhood and is characterized by *elaborated sentences*, sentences that may include adjectives and prepositions.
- Stage 6 is associated with the preschool period and is characterized by *maturelike speech*, speech that closely resembles the

speech of adults in terms of grammar and overall structure. This kind of speech is, of course, restricted by a lack of vocabulary and adult understanding.

See also *babbling; cognitive development; holophrase; language acquisition device (LAD).*

lanugo: A covering of delicate, fine hair on the body. A lanugo appears on the fetus around the fifth month of pregnancy and is considered to be rudimentary hair. A lanugo is often visible on premature infants and on some full-term neonates.

A lanugo is also one of the several signs and symptoms of anorexia nervosa.

See also *anorexia nervosa; fetal development; neonate; premature birth.*

latchkey children: An informal term describing children who come home to an empty apartment or house after school, usually because the parent or parents are otherwise employed. The term *latchkey* is linked to the observation that some of these children carry a key on a string around the neck. The percentage of latchkey children has been rising. In the 1960s, about one-third of mothers had outside jobs. Today, somewhat over one-half of mothers have such jobs. Also, it is important to note that there are a large number of one-parent families.

If a child is preadolescent, is completely unsupervised, and spends 3 to 4 hours every school day in this manner, the situation is hardly conducive to optimal social and psychological development. The kind of emotional isolation described by the term *latchkey child* may play a causal role in behavioral problems, mental disorders, and juvenile delinquency. Quality day care should be arranged for children if no parent can be present for them after school.

See also *child abuse; day care; juvenile delinquency.*

late childhood: See *child.*

latency stage: In Freud's theory, the fourth stage of psychosexual development, the stage associated with the elementary period, the time from about 6 to 12 years of age. The latency stage is character-ized by little or no conscious interest in sex. In contrast, there is a great deal of interest in the outside world of play and school.

According to Freud, this seeming lack of interest in sex is due *not* to absence of biological interest, but due to guilt and conflict over incest wishes toward the parent of the opposite sex. Thus, libido (i.e., psychosexual energy) is repressed to the unconscious level of the personality and reappears in the modified form of interest in nonsexual objects.

Freud's analysis is open to criticism. Some psychologists argue that he made too much out of the importance of incest wishes in children. Others say that sexual drive is highly immature before puberty because the biological structures involved in the drive are not yet mature. For example, neither the ovaries nor the testes are pro-ducing the high levels of hormones that they will produce in ado-lescence. Also, Freud's conclusions are based on case histories, not well-designed studies and experiments.

In spite of the various criticisms, it would be incorrect to entirely reject Freud's interpretation of the latency stage. It is possible that some of the psychological factors he identifies do in fact operate to some extent in individual cases. Also, his interpretation is believed to be useful to psychoanalysts in dealing with certain kinds of sexual dysfunction in adults. For example, some men have little or no sexual desire for their partners after their partners become mothers. An Oedipus complex, associated with the latency period, may be a contributing factor.

See also *golden age of childhood; Electra complex; incest wish; libido; Oedipus complex; psychosexual development.*

laughter: See *smiling.*

law of effect: As formulated by the learning theorist Thorndike, the proposition that if an act has satisfying consequences for an organism it will be "stamped in" and retained by the brain and nervous system. Thorndike conducted his research about 90 years ago studying the trial-and-error behavior of cats escaping from puzzle-boxes. He ob-served that if a success immediately followed a given action then the action tended to be learned and repeated. Thus, the fact that successes have positive effects is the basis of the law of effect stated as a formal proposition. He also observed that despite the fact that his experimental cats didn't seem to have any conscious understanding of what they were doing, they learned anyway and became quite adept at escaping from the puzzle-boxes. (They were required to pull a string that in turn released a latch on a door.) On the basis of these observations, Thorndike described learning as a process of association between an action and its consequences, not one of comprehension or what the Gestalt psychologists were later to call "insight."

The law of effect is important because it is an early statement of the principle of reinforcement and is considered a forerunner of the kinds of discoveries B. F. Skinner made when he studied operant conditioning. The knowledge of how reinforcers affect behavior plays an essential role in applications of behavior modification and behavior therapy with children.

See also *behavior modification; behavior therapy; insight learning; operant conditioning; reinforcer; Skinner, Burrhus Frederic; Thorndike, Edward Lee.*

learned helplessness: The tendency to overgeneralize failure experiences and develop the negative attitude that one is helpless in situations where one is not in fact helpless. Pioneer research on learned helplessness was conducted by Martin E. P. Seligman, a clinical and experimental psychologist, in the 1960s. To demonstrate learned helplessness, suppose that a rat is subjected to inescapable, painful shock in situation A. It learns that its struggles are to no avail. Now the same rat is placed in a tank of deep water in situation B. Although it *can* swim and is not helpless at all, it will *not* swim and will drown unless rescued. The rat is displaying learned helplessness.

Since Seligman's first observations, the concept of learned helplessness has been extended by him and others to human behavior. It seems reasonable to propose that chronic anxiety and depression in adults may have roots in a series of failure experiences in childhood. Learned helplessness may also play a role in low self-esteem.

Suppose that Emil had difficulty acquiring some of the basic arithmetical skills in the second and third grades. Later, in the tenth grade, he avoids all math courses, thinking, "I'm no good at math." It is quite possible that the 14-year-old adolescent he has become is quite able to comprehend and apply mathematical concepts. But he still thinks as if he were the child he was in grammar school. The problem is not that he *is* helpless in the face of mathematics, but that he *believes* he is helpless.

The tendency toward learned helplessness is a pervasive one and may affect many areas of life.

See also *anxiety; depression; inferiority complex; self-esteem.*

learning: A more or less permanent change in behavior, or a behavioral tendency, as a result of experience. A moment's reflection reveals that learning plays a role in most of what one does. One learns to walk, talk, speak, write, and do arithmetic. Also learned are our attitudes, how to relate to other people, and how to cope with the challenges of life.

John Watson believed that aside from a few inborn reflexes all behavior is learned. His point of view is a reflection of an earlier view proposed by the philosopher John Locke that the mind of the infant is a *tabula rasa,* or "blank slate." This doctrine is associated with *empiricism,* and it is opposed by *nativism.*

In Western culture, so much importance is assigned to the phenomenon of learning that our children are required to spend about 12 years in school receiving formal instruction. Many seek higher education. However, it is important to realize that learning in school, as important as it is, is only one aspect of learning. The learning that takes place in the home, on the street, and in informal settings with friends is every bit as important to the development of the individual as is that presented in the classroom.

In view of the fact that the definition of *learning* says that it is "more or less" permanent, there is hope if undesirable habits are acquired in childhood or adolescence. These can often be extinguished, or unlearned, by experience in the same way that they were initially acquired by experience.

See also *classical conditioning; empiricism; extinction; insight learning; instinct; learned helplessness; learning disability; nativism; operant conditioning; social learning; Watson, John Broadus.*

learning disability: A perceptual or motor problem that impairs one's ability to learn. Common perceptual problems are visual impairments and hearing impairments. Dyslexia, or developmental reading disorder, is another common perceptual problem. A common motor problem is *dysgraphia,* difficulty in learning to write.

The concept of a learning disability, as it is usually used, implies the presence of a physical problem, not an emotional one. Thus, children who suffer from chronic anxiety or depression are not usually said to have a learning disability even though the emotional problem will, of course, interfere with successful performance in school. Also, mentally retarded children are not usually said to have a learning disability. Their low intelligence scores suggest a general problem that goes beyond the concept of a learning disability.

A learning disability sometimes has its roots in minimal brain dysfunction (MBD), which impairs the child's ability to pay attention for sustained periods of time.

Children with a learning disability usually have normal intelligence and are quite capable of profiting from instruction. They need special instruction designed to help them cope with their specific disability. Under these circumstances, their academic performance is often quite satisfactory.

Parents of children with a learning disability need to explore what resources are offered in the child's school or the community at large for their child's problem.

See also *attention-deficit hyperactivity disorder (ADHD); developmental reading disorder; hearing impairment; minimal brain dysfunction (MBD); visual impairment.*

Leboyer method: A method that aims to make the process of birth less of an emotional shock for the neonate. The French obstetrician Frederick Leboyer introduced the method to the United States, and the title of his 1975 book on the subject is *Birth Without Violence.* Leboyer advocates "gentle birth." Some of his specific recommendations are the following:

1. Delivery should take place without bright, glaring lights.
2. Immediately following birth, before the umbilical cord is severed, the infant should be positioned for a time on the mother's abdomen.
3. After separation from the mother, the neonate should be given first a soothing bath in water warmed to body temperature and then a light massage.

In brief, the transition from the cozy inner world of the womb to the harsh outer world of light and sound should be gradual rather than sudden.

Like the Lamaze method, the Leboyer method is sometimes referred to as a kind of "natural childbirth." A key difference between the two methods is that the Lamaze method was initially designed to reduce the pain and anxiety of the mother. The Leboyer method is designed to reduce the trauma of birth for the infant.

The long-term effects of the Leboyer method have been subjected to scientific scrutiny. Leboyer himself believes that children born by his method tend to fare somewhat better than other children in terms of emotional adjustment and ability to learn. However, studies conducted in the United States have not presented convincing evidence that this is so.

Nonetheless, common sense dictates that no unnecessary emotional wounds should be inflicted on the infant at birth. If the use of the Leboyer method does not interfere with good medical practice in general, then, until all of the data are in, it has much to recommend it.

The assumptions of the Leboyer method are similar to ideas proposed by the psychoanalyst Otto Rank in the 1920s and 1930s.

See also *birth trauma; cesarean section; Lamaze method; Rank, Otto.*

libido: In classical psychoanalysis, psychosexual energy. Libido has two aspects: it is the energy (1) that makes the mind work and (2) that resides behind the sex drive. Freud linked it to Eros, the god of love in Greek mythology. He indicated that in infancy and early childhood, libido is immature and finds expression through the oral, anal, and phallic zones of the body. He called these zones, appropriately, erogenous zones. To illustrate, during infancy, the individual experiences a sort of oral sensous pleasure by biting, eating, sucking, and chewing that foreshadows certain aspects of adult sexual behavior.

The concept of libido is somewhat nebulous. This is partly because it is a psychological concept, not a biological one. However, even psychologists have been hard put to define it with any particular precision. Its value as a concept has therefore been frequently challenged.

See also *anal stage; Freud, Sigmund; oral stage; phallic stage; psychoanalysis; psychosexual development.*

limit on behavior: A reality-oriented boundary set by a parent or caregiver allowing a child to recognize what is and what is not acceptable behavior. An example from early childhood is telling a child that he or she cannot cross the street alone. An example from adolescence is telling a teenager that he or she must be home no later than midnight.

Overly permissive parents either do not define limits or make them so vague that the child mistakenly thinks that almost anything is all right. Overly authoritarian parents define limits so arbitrarily and categorically that the child feels confined and is in a sort of psychological prison. Parents who are at once both democratic and authoritative set wide limits that are appropriate for the child's age. Preadolescent children need narrower, more well-defined limits than do adolescents. The general consensus among developmental psychologists is that appropriate limits on behavior help a child to feel both secure and loved. Also, the setting of limits appears to be a contributing factor to self-esteem.

See also *authoritarian parent; authoritative parent; parental style; permissive parent; self-esteem.*

lisping: A speech problem characterized by difficulty in pronouncing *s, z,* or other sibilant sounds. A *th* sound is usually substituted for the difficult sounds. Thus, *soda* might be pronounced *thoda*; and *zipper* might be pronounced *thipper*.

It is important to distinguish developmental lisping from chronic lisping. *Developmental lisping* appears during toddlerhood, is very common, and usually goes away spontaneously if it is not reinforced with too much parental concern and attention. *Chronic lisping* is an entrenched tendency to lisp that may continue into late childhood or puberty. This kind of lisping is seldom corrected successfully by well-meaning parental interventions such as, "Slow down" or "Don't place your tongue against your front teeth." Often the child becomes more self-conscious and anxious about speaking, and the problem becomes worse. In such cases, speech therapy can be helpful.

See also *speech therapy; stuttering.*

lithium carbonate: See *mood stabilizing drugs.*

Little Albert: The subject in a classical experiment on conditioned emotional responses published by John Watson and his assistant Rosalie Raynor in 1920. It was established that Little Albert, age 11 months, had no prior fear of a white rat. When Albert was shown the rat on subsequent occasions, a loud, unexpected gong was sounded behind him. Albert responded by crying. Test trials were eventually conducted in which Albert was shown the rat alone, without the gong. Albert responded to the rat by sniffling, holding back, and generally avoiding the rat. It seems evident that Albert had developed a conditioned fear of the rat.

The experiment fits the general pattern of classical conditioning. The loud gong was an unconditioned stimulus that elicited an inborn response (crying). The white rat become a conditioned stimulus that elicited a learned response (avoidance). Watson and Raynor's work was inspired by their study of Pavlov's experiments.

It was Watson's belief that infants are born without instincts or fears. The aim of the experiment was to demonstrate how human fears can be acquired through learning. Although the experiment was of interest, today such an experiment would be considered unethical because of its lack of regard for the rights of the subject as an individual.

Indeed, Watson and Raynor had plans for extinguishing Little Albert's fear of the rat and described in detail a counterconditioning procedure for doing so. This did not take place for reasons that are not entirely clear.

However, the counterconditioning procedure outlined by Watson and Raynor was used successfully by research psychologist Mary Cover Jones a few years later. She reported that she was able to use the procedure to extinguish a child's fear of rabbits.

See also *classical conditioning; counterconditioning; fear; phobia; Watson, John Broadus.*

Little Hans: The subject of one of Freud's more well-known case histories. Little Hans (not his real name) was a 5-year-old male child with a phobia of horses. Freud never saw Little Hans in person but received all of his information from Hans's father. An interpretation was made of the phobia in terms of Freud's psychosexual theory. The irrational fear of the horse was not an actual fear of the horse itself, but of what the horse symbolized. The horse stood for a fear of the father and what the father might do. Little Hans, feeling guilty over forbidden dawning sexual feelings, imagined that his father might want to punish him, even castrate him, for his fantasies. The case history is particulary important in the history of psychoanalysis because it was an early one and played a pivotal role in Freud's thinking about such subjects as the castration complex, phobias, the Oedipus complex, and psychosexual development in general.

Critics of psychoanalysis assert that Freud's interpretations in the case of Little Hans are overgeneralizations and are too imaginative and not merited by the facts.

See also *castration complex; child psychotherapy; Freud, Sigmund; Oedipus complex; phobia; psychosexual development.*

locomotor development: See *motor development.*

logical consequences: See *response-cost punishment.*

logical thinking: The ability to reason and reach sound conclusions. Logical thinking is an important component of intelligence. Prior to about the age of 7, the thinking of children is *prelogical.* They "reason" with the use of intuition, sense impressions (in contrast to concepts), and a belief in magic.

Mature logical thinking is characterized by the ability to make valid generalizations from groups of facts as well as the capacity make deductions and predictions from the generalizations.

See also *cognitive development; creative thinking; deductive thinking; formal operations; inductive thinking; intelligence.*

longitudinal study: A research method characterized by the investigation of the behavior of a given group of subjects over an extended time period. For example, suppose Professor Marie Q., a university instructor and researcher on developmental psychology, is interested in the question of whether or not temperament tends to be a stable personality trait. She starts with a randomly selected sample of 100 toddlers and objectively evaluates them on such bipolar traits as relaxed-calm and passive-aggressive. Every two years, the children are re-evaluated until they are 18 years old. (Such studies have tended to support the hypothesis that temperament is a more or less stable trait.)

One of the most famous longitudinal studies was conducted by Lewis M. Terman and his coworkers at Stanford University. Using the Stanford-Binet Intelligence Scale, Terman's research team began in 1921 to study the social adjustment of a group of more than 1,000 gifted children. The original group was evaluated until its members were middle-aged and older. On the whole, it was found that gifted children tend to have above average long-term health and social adjustment.

Longitudinal studies are expensive and sometimes require years of waiting for results. For this reason, a different strategy called the *cross-sectional study* is sometimes adopted. The cross-sectional study is characterized by the investigation of the behavior of several different groups of subjects representing different chronological ages. The subjects are observed during the same, relatively restricted time period. For example, it might be possible to conduct research similar to that conducted by Terman by simultaneously investigating the relationship of giftedness to social adjustment in groups of 7-year-old, 14-year-old, 18-year-old, 25-year-old, and 35-year-old individuals.

See also *giftedness; intelligence; Stanford-Binet Intelligence Scale; temperament; Terman, Lewis Madison.*

love: In human relations, an intense feeling of devotion, affection, or attachment to another person. The word *love* is obviously rich in associations and connotations; consequently, no pretense is made that a precise definition has been given. Several kinds of love can be distinguished. The ancient Greeks made a distinction between agape and erotic love. *Agape* is characterized by unselfish caring and is nonsexual in nature. *Erotic love* is characterized by sexual desire.

In Western culture, one often speaks of parental love, romantic love, and the love of an infant for his or her parents. Parental love has a large component of agape in it; people like to think of it as an unselfish, giving love. This is not entirely accurate. Studies on the bidirectionality of influence have shown that an infant's responses to the parents in turn shape the attitudes and affectional responses of parents.

Like erotic love, romantic love has a sexual component. However, it suggests more than sexual desire. In romantic love, the partner is often idealized and placed on a pedestal or in an ivory tower. Often, unrealistic expectations are associated with the relationship, particularly in its early stages.

The love of an infant for his or her parents is a selfish love, if this can be called love at all. The infant is egocentric and sees the parents as sources of psychological and emotional nurturance. This kind of love, or attachment, appears to play an important role in the infant's capacity to thrive and develop a sense of trust.

See also *attachment; bidirectionality of influence; trust versus mistrust.*

love-hostility dimension: See *parental style.*

ludic behavior: Behavior that is enjoyable in and of itself without regard to satisfying a biological need. The word *ludic* is derived from a Latin word meaning "play." Ludic behavior refers to a broad range of behaviors. When children or adults go exploring, act curious, use imagination, participate in games, write a story for pleasure, sing a song just for the sheer joy of singing it, laugh at a joke, and so forth, they are exhibiting ludic behavior.

Although specific ways are learned to display ludic behavior, the behavior itself appears to have an inborn basis. There is good evidence to suggest, for example, that humans have a curiosity drive. It is strong and as much a part of human nature as the hunger drive and the sex drive.

People never outgrow their need to engage in ludic behavior and display that need at all ages. However, it seems to be particularly intense in childhood. Many adults have made the informal observation that children frequently would rather play than eat. They seem to live in a world dominated by toys, imagination, and games.

See also *creative thinking; imaginary playmate; imaginative play; parallel play; play.*

lying: The act of making of a false statement with the intent to deceive another. Lying among preschoolers is common. Their moral sense is not yet well-developed, and they tend to judge behavior in terms of power and success, not right and wrong. Around the age of 7, most children will develop a more or less conventional sense of right and wrong and will usually avoid lying. However, even this statement is a weak generalization. Various studies have suggested that lying is not a stable trait in normal children, and many of them sometimes tell lies for a variety of reasons. *Chronic lying*, a pattern of behavior characterized by almost never telling the truth, is, however, another matter. Children who display chronic lying may be thought of as undersocialized. Chronic lying is antisocial behavior and may be associated with a conduct disorder.

If a child is caught telling a lie, the child should be confronted and informed that such behavior is neither acceptable nor permitted. The child should be made to feel that lying was an unsuccessful strategy and that it is unlikely to succeed in the future. A constructive opportunity should be offered to make amends for telling the lie. The cost in terms of time and effort for making amends will be perceived as a penalty and should act as a deterrent to the telling of future lies. Parents need not use excessive punishment and make long moral announcements. These are likely to alienate the child and have the opposite effect from the one intended.

See also *antisocial behavior; character; cheating; conduct disorder; moral development; superego.*

lysergic acid diethylamide-25 (LSD): A powerful drug belonging to the class of drugs called hallucinogens. LSD is one of the drugs frequently cited in connection with drug abuse in adolescence. LSD is often called *acid*. The popularity of LSD has decreased in the past few years. Nonetheless, it is both available and inexpensive to make. Therefore, it still poses a threat.

LSD is an alkaloid substance derived from ergot (a kind of fungus). Very tiny amounts of LSD can produce large alterations in thinking, perception, mood, and actions. Delusions and hallucinations associated with the use of LSD are common. Neurophysiological research indicates the possibility that the drug produces its effect by interfering with the action of *serotonin*, a neurotransmitter. Some people experience flashbacks (i.e., a repetition of a hallucinogenic experience) after they cease using the drug.

Regular use of LSD produces tolerance, a tendency for the drug to induce only modest alterations in consciousness. The drug does not cause physiological dependence. Thus, the cessation of its use does not produce significant withdrawal symptoms. However, some individuals do develop a psychological dependence on LSD.

The quality of an LSD "trip" varies greatly. Psychotherapists using LSD in research have found that some subjects have vivid transpersonal experiences that may change their outlook on life. However, "bad trips" can and do take place. Panic reactions, suspicion, a sense of alienation, disorientation, and despair are examples of the kinds of experiences that have been reported. Therefore, substantial warnings have been issued against the recreational use of LSD.

In the 1960s, there was a certain amount of enthusiasm for the possibility that LSD might facilitate the process of psychotherapy. Some research reports supported this hypothesis. However, the present consensus is that LSD has not lived up to its early promise, and, at present, it has no medical or psychiatric use.

See also *drug abuse in adolescence; hallucinogens; marijuana; phencyclidine (PCP)*.

M

macrocephaly: A condition characterized by an unusually large head. Macrocephaly is a cranial abnormality. It is associated with an unchecked growth of the brain's *glia cells*, the cells making up the supporting tissue of the brain. Macrocephaly is an uncommon disorder and is usually identified as congenital (i.e., present at birth). Its cause is obscure, and it is believed that it probably has a genetic basis. The condition produces complications such as visual problems, seizures, and mental retardation. There is no cure for macrocephaly. Treatment consists of adequate medical and psychological care.

See also *hydrocephaly; mental retardation; microcephaly.*

mainstreaming: The practice of placing children with a wide range of physical, behavioral, and cognitive impairments in conventional, instead of special, classes. Advocates of mainstreaming say that children with impairments who are segregated from other children have an intensified sense that there is "something wrong" and that they are "not normal." They feel like outsiders, lose self-esteem, and have motivational problems. By moving into the conventional classroom, they can feel that they are regular human beings and that they are not that odd or handicapped; and they can learn to cope with more able peers. Often they can function quite effectively in regular environments.

Opponents of mainstreaming point out that the child with an impairment in a conventional classroom is often at a great disadvantage. For example, a child with a hearing impairment may miss important explanations. Or a mentally retarded child will consistently score lower on tests than do other children and will consequently feel defeated and inferior. A child with a conduct disorder will disrupt the class and make it difficult for other children to work effectively.

A substantial amount of research has gone into the question of the advisability of mainstreaming. Conflicting results have been obtained, and a consensus has not been reached in educational psychology. However, the principle behind mainstreaming, that children with disabilities should be helped to feel as normal as possible, is widely accepted.

See also *conduct disorder; exceptional children; hearing impairment; learning disability; mental retardation; visual impairment.*

major tranquilizers: See *drug therapy.*

maladjusted child: A child who lacks harmony with himself or herself and the external world. The maladjusted child does not adapt readily to the demands of the family, school, and life in general. The concept of maladjustment in psychiatry and clinical psychology is a very broad, general one. Consequently, it expresses itself in a wide spectrum of ineffective behaviors.

Broadly speaking, these behaviors fall in one of three general classes. First, there are a group of behaviors associated with the outward actions of the child. Breaking things, lying, and cheating provide examples of behaviors in this class. Second, there are a group of behaviors associated with the emotional life of the child. Anxiety, depression, and phobias (i.e., irrational fears) provide examples in this class. Third, there are a group of behaviors in which the child's reality contact is impaired. Gross distortion of thought processes, hearing voices that others do not hear, and extreme withdrawal from social contact provide examples in this class.

Loosely speaking, ineffective behaviors involving outward actions are within the domain of *personality disorders.* Ineffective behaviors involving the emotional life of the child suggest the presence of a *neurotic process.* (Note that the term *neurotic disorder* has been avoided. See the *childhood neurosis* entry for an explanation.) Ineffective behaviors involving impaired reality contact are classified as *psychotic disorders.*

Maladjustment can be thought of as a component of every behavioral and mental disorder. Therefore, there are as many causes of maladjustment as there are causes of these disorders. Examples of general causes are: (1) an inadequate developmental history, (2) learned maladaptive habits, (3) frustration of important desires, (4) association with peers who provide maladaptive role models, and (5) lack of opportunity.

A general cause of maladjustment that has been debated at length is genetic predisposition. It is too easy to say that a child or adolescent has "bad blood" or "it's all in the genes." On the other hand, there is evidence from genetic research that certain traits of temperament and behavior may have an inborn basis. The general trend of contemporary professional thought is to agree that genetic factors can *contribute* to maladaptive behavior. However, there is no simple one-to-one link between genes and behavior. Therefore, it is inaccurate to say that a person was "born bad" or "doomed to be neurotic."

See also *childhood neurosis; childhood schizophrenia; genetic predisposition; psychotic disorders; temperament.*

malnutrition: Significant deficits in nourishment usually caused by an inadequate diet. (It is possible for malnutrition to be caused in some cases by a malabsorption problem, that is, an inability to take advantage of the contents of a normal diet.) Children who suffer from malnutrition may display either inadequate mental development, inadequate physical development, or both. Adequate nutrition is important both during prenatal development and after a child is born.

The primary requirements of an adequate diet are sufficient quantities of proteins, carbohydrates, fats, vitamins, and minerals. *Proteins* supply the basic building blocks of the body and are required for muscle and bone. They are also required to repair and rebuild the body. Foods particularly rich in protein include meat, fish, eggs, and milk. However, it should be noted that almost all foods contain at least some protein. *Carbohydrates* provide energy. Foods particularly high in carbohydrates include rice, beans, breads, and potatoes. *Fats* also provide energy. Foods particularly high in fats include eggs, whole milk, butter, margarine, oils, and prime cuts of beef.

Both *vitamins* and *minerals* enter into the body's chemical processes. In general, they play the role of *catalysts*, facilitating the body's ability to take advantage of proteins, fats, and carbohydrates. Trace amounts of both vitamins and minerals are present in most foods. However, this is not to say that all foods contain all vitamins and minerals.

In the United States, it is uncommon for children to suffer from malnutrition because of inadequate diets. However, in many under-developed countries, there is a significant problem. About one-third to one-half of the world's children suffer from malnutrition. Approximately 14 percent of the diet must be protein in order for the brain to develop properly. Children who receive only 8 or 10 percent protein during the developmental years may have smaller brains and, in turn, retarded mental development.

It has become a truism to say that children do not need to take vitamin and mineral supplements if they receive adequate diets. However, it must be remembered that it is possible for a child to be overfed and at the same time malnourished. Even an obese child can be deficient in important vitamins and minerals if most of the foods consumed are in the form of high-calorie soft drinks, candy bars, doughnuts, ice cream, cookies, cakes, and pies. In fact, the overconsumption of foods containing refined sugar may deplete the body of certain important B-complex vitamins because these vitamins are consumed during the metabolism of sugar.

If it is suspected that a child is suffering from malnutrition, it is essential that changes be made in the child's diet.

See also *anorexia nervosa; Feingold hypothesis; junk food; obesity.*

marasmus: See *anaclitic depression.*

marijuana: A hallucinogen obtained from the hemp plant. Marijuana is one of the drugs frequently cited in connection with drug abuse in adolescence. Marijuana is related to hashish. The chemical name for marijuana is *cannabis.* Street names include "grass," "pot," and Acapulco gold. Marijuana cigarettes are referred to as "joints" or "reefers." Sometimes marijuana is called Mary Jane (i.e., "mari" + "juana").

Although it is true that marijuana *is* a hallucinogen, it is usually classified as a mild one. It does not usually produce alterations of consciousness as vivid as those produced by lysergic acid diethylamide-25 (LSD), phencyclidine (PCP), mescaline, and psilocybin. Some of the adjectives used by users to describe the effects of marijuana are "euphoric," "self-confident," "less shy," "exhilarated," "relaxed," and "floating." The use of marijuana tends to make the user less inhibited. Therefore, there may be impulsive acting out of sexual or aggressive feelings. However, it is important to quickly add that a 1972 report of the National Commission on Marijuana and Drug Abuse found no particular link between the use of the drug and violent criminal behavior.

Although the use of marijuana is illegal, this has not stopped its widespread use. It is estimated that about 50 to 60 percent of people between the ages of 21 and 29 have tried marijuana at least once. It should be realized that there is quite a bit of distance between a one-time experimental use of a drug and frequent use or abuse. Many persons who have tried marijuana do not repeat the experience with any great frequency. Although it *is* possible for some people to develop a psychological dependence on marijuana, there is little or no tendency to acquire a physiological dependence. Withdrawal from the drug's use does not present a medical crisis.

There has been much discussion about marijuana's effects on health. Smoking marijuana with regularity does present clear-cut health hazards. Medical problems associated with respiration (e.g., bronchitis and emphysema) are common. People with heart disease may put an undue strain on their hearts by using marijuana. There have been studies that suggest regular marijuana use may (1) have an adverse effect on the immune system, (2) lower testosterone levels in males, and (3) do chromosome damage. However, a general medical consensus does not exist on the results of these studies. At present, the situation is inconclusive. However, the safest approach would obviously be to avoid use of the drug.

On the psychological side, it has been suggested that the regular use of marijuana produces a general reduction in ambition. This is termed the *amotivational syndrome*. Although the amotivational syndrome is a reality, it is not clear what is cause and what is effect. Some researchers have suggested that the use of marijuana causes a loss of interest in goal-oriented behavior. Other researchers have suggested that persons who already suffer from the amotivational syndrome are attracted to the use of marijuana.

See also *drug abuse in adolescence; hallucinogens; phencyclidine (PCP).*

Maslow, Abraham Harold (1908–1970): A research psychologist and a principal founder of American humanistic psychology. In 1934 he received a Ph.D. degree from the University of Wisconsin. For a number of years, he was associated with Brooklyn College and subsequently with Brandeis University. He served as president of the American Psychological Association in 1967.

In his early professional years, Maslow was favorably impressed by behaviorism. However, as his thinking matured, he decided that the inner world of people was too rich a territory to exclude from psychological theory. He decided to study human beings in their fullness—with their hopes, ambitions, and dreams.

His researches led him to the conclusion that human motivation follows a sort of ladder of needs from lower to higher. Low on the ladder's rungs are physiological needs and the need for safety. These are primary and important. However, they are not unique to human beings; they are shared with animals. Although Maslow does not give his hierarchy of needs a developmental focus, it is clear that it does in fact have such implications. The needs lower in rank are most pressing in childhood. The needs higher in rank became increasingly pressing in adolescence and adulthood.

The uppermost rung of the ladder of needs is *self-actualization,* an inborn tendency to maximize one's talents and potentialities. It is the frustration of this need that causes many people to become anxious, depressed, and otherwise troubled. Maslow explored ways to help people become more self-actualizing, to bring forth by their own actions the person they were meant to be. Again, although Maslow does not speak too often of self-actualization in developmental terms, it is evident that what one will become and what one will do with one's life becomes of intense interest during adolescence. It is possible to make a link between self-actualization and Erikson's concept of an identity crisis. The individual who succeeds in becoming self-actualized also tends to have a robust sense of identity.

Maslow's most influential book is *Toward a Psychology of Being* (1968). Another important work is *Motivation and Personality* (1970).

See also *behaviorism; cognitive needs; Erikson, Erik Homburger; identity crisis; psychosocial development; self-actualization.*

masturbation: Self-stimulation of the sex organs, commonly to the point of orgasm. Outdated terms for masturbation are *onanism* and *self-abuse.* The term *onanism* is traceable to *The Book of Genesis* and the sin of Onan. He was commanded by God to marry the wife of his dead brother Er. He was further commanded to procreate. Onan defied God's wishes. He had sexual intercourse with his wife, but he withdrew prior to ejaculation, thus "spilling his seed on the ground." This is the sin of Onan—the wasting of "seed" or sperm. Over the years, this "wasting" came also to be associated with masturbation. Masturbation was considered the same as Onan's sin and, consequently, a sin against God.

The term *self-abuse* is based on the idea that masturbation is harmful. In the past, it was believed that it depleted the body of vital fluids or of energy and therefore weakened it. This in turn left one vulnerable to disease. It was also believed that masturbation made people go mad, that they would lose their minds. Neither of the assumptions associated with the concept of self-abuse is accepted today.

Various surveys and studies suggest that about 80 to 90 percent of male adolescents and about 50 to 60 percent of female adolescents masturbate at least on occasion, many frequently. Therefore, from the statistical point of view, masturbation is a normal activity in both adolescence and young adulthood. The majority of psychiatrists and clinical psychologists also take the position that masturbation is a normal activity. In the vast majority of cases, masturbation is an outlet for sexual tension when an appropriate partner is not available.

Childhood masturbation is self-stimulation of the penis or the clitoris for erotic gratification, usually during the preschool period. The behavior is not at all unusual. It is estimated that about 60 percent of males and about 30 percent of females spontaneously engage in childhood masturbation some of the time. Again, the behavior is considered normal. From the point of view of socialization, the child must be helped to realized that the activity should be confined to private settings.

See also *genitals; libido; psychosexual development.*

maturation: The overall process of growth in both a biological and a psychological sense. The term *maturation* is derived from a Latin word with the meanings of "ripe" or "full age." Maturation takes place over time and is closely associated with the concept of development in general. A mature organism is one that has attained full development, one that is completely grown.

An example of biological maturation is growth in height from infancy to the end of adolescence. The process is largely under the control of the pituitary gland and represents an unfolding in accordance with a biological timetable.

An example of psychological maturation is cognitive development. Adult modes of thought differ quite distinctly from the modes of thought of the preschool child. A person can be spoken of as having "cognitive maturity" when he or she can solve algebra problems, reason in a logical manner, and even reflect on the nature of those processes.

The concept of maturation originated with biology and was extended to the psychological domain with the rise of behavioral science in the 20th century.

The principal contrasting process to maturation is learning. Maturation requires the passage of time. Learning requires experiences. Although for the purposes of discussion and analysis the two processes are kept apart, in fact they are intertwined in life. For example, toilet training requires both biological maturation and learning. The child's nervous system must be mature enough for voluntary control of the muscles in the region of the bladder and the bowel. And the child must be given experiences designed to facilitate the learning of voluntary control.

The fact is that maturation and learning work together in the development of the organism. This is reflected in a wide spectrum of behaviors, ranging from walking to talking and from thinking to sexual behavior.

See also *cognitive development; growth spurt; learning; toilet training.*

mature birth: A birth taking place between approximately 8.5 and 9.5 months of pregnancy. A full-term normal birth weight is a minimum of 5.5 pounds and an average of 7 to 8 pounds.

See also *immature birth; premature birth.*

McCarthy Scales of Children's Abilities (MSCA): A test used to evaluate the intellectual and developmental level of children between the ages of 2.5 and 8.5 years. The overall test consists of six associated scales.

1. The *Verbal Scale* is used to evaluate the child's ability to comprehend and use language.
2. The *Perceptual-Performance Scale* is used to evaluate the child's ability to coordinate actions with sensory information (e.g., what is seen and heard).
3. The *Quantitative Scale* is used to evaluate the child's level of mathematical comprehension.
4. The *General Cognitive Scale* provides a general appraisal of the child's present level of intellectual functioning. The score on the General Cognitive Scale is considered to be similar to an IQ, but not identical to it.
5. The *Memory Scale* is used to evaluate the child's ability to retain and recall cognitive information.
6. The *Motor Scale* is used to evaluate the child's level of motor maturation. Manual dexterity provides an example of a motor skill. This last scale overlaps considerably with the Perceptual-Performance Scale.

See also *Apgar scale; Bayley Scales of Infant Development; developmental quotient (DQ); Gesell, Arnold Lucius; Gesell Developmental Schedules; Stanford-Binet Intelligence Scale; Wechsler intelligence scales.*

meaning in language: One of the principal characteristics of language. A word has meaning when it can be understood, defined, and used correctly in speech or in writing. Sentences are units containing larger meanings. In general, it can be said that a word has meaning if it is understood to stand for something beyond itself. For example, the word *cat* is obviously not an actual cat. The word stands for a living organism, an object of perception. The ability of words to communicate meanings is known as the *semantic* quality of language, and it is what gives language much of its range and power.

In early infancy, very little meaning is attached to words. However, human beings appear to have a great facility for appreciating the semantic quality of language; and by the time children are toddlers, they already demonstrate that they are able to use language to both recognize and communicate various meanings.

See also *babbling; Chomsky, Noam Avram; displacement in language; holophrase; language acquisition device (LAD); language development.*

meiosis: A kind of cellular division characterized by the reduction of 23 pairs of chromosomes in an original cell's nucleus to 23 individual chromosomes in each nucleus of the two newly generated sex cells. The general name for cells produced by meiosis is *gametes.* Gametes produced by females are called *ova,* and gametes produced by males are called *sperm.* The subsequent union of an ovum and a sperm produces a *zygote,* a fertilized cell with a nucleus restored once again to 23 pairs of chromosomes. Meiosis is one of the key underlying biological processes that make sexual reproduction possible.

See also *mitosis; ovum; sex chromosomes; sperm cell; zygote.*

memory: In classical psychology, a mental faculty that gives a person the power to recall or recognize previous experiences. In contemporary terms, memory is a process characterized by the encoding, storage, and retrieval of cognitive information. Three kinds of memory are often identified:

1. *Sensory memory* is a brief impression retained by the eyes, the ears, or other sense organ.
2. *Short-term memory* is a somewhat longer impression retained for a few minutes to a few hours, but certainly not for months and years.
3. *Long-term memory* is a more or less enduring impression. Some long-term memories last for many years; others survive for a lifetime.

Memory development in children appears to be a part of cognitive development in general. Various studies suggest that sensory and short-term memory capacities are similar in young children and adolescents. However, long-term memory operates in a more reliable manner in adolescents and adults than it does in young children. Older children develop memory strategies, strategies that require a fairly high level of cognitive maturity. For example, they may group information into categories, think of examples, or make fresh associations.

Older children often invent *mnemonic devices*, explicit aids to memory. For example, when trying to learn how to spell the word *calendar*, the more reflective child may think, "Calendars keep track of *days*. And the *dar* at the end of calendar makes me think of days. And they both have an *a* in the middle."

Older children and adolescents tend to employ a set of learned memory skills. Memory and learning are related processes. Indeed, it can be said that memory is a kind of learning. So, in a sense, older children not only remember, they *remember to remember*. This is a cognitive skill higher on the developmental ladder than memory itself and is described as *metamemory*.

See also *cognitive development; concept formation; information-processing theory; learning.*

menarche: The first time a female menstruates. The menarche usually occurs between the ages of 11 and 14. The average age is 12.5 years. However, a normal menarche can occur as young as age 9 and as late as age 16.

Studies suggest that the average age for the menarche is one or two years younger today than it was in the early decades of this century. It is believed that this is due to better nutrition and health care. The tendency for maturation to occur at an earlier age than it once did is called the *secular trend*.

There is evidence suggesting that females who participate in a systematic program of exercise such as gymnastics or ballet training around the time of puberty may experience a delay of two or three years in their menarche. One hypothesis advanced to explain this phenomenon is that exercise restricts the development of body fat. And body fat is required in the production of estrogen hormones. The fact that females suffering from anorexia nervosa—and its associated loss of body fat—often experience *amenorrea*, cessation of menstruation, is taken as evidence supporting this hypothesis. In the case of young female athletes, the delay in menstruation in early adolescence is considered to be a normal state of affairs, not one requiring treatment.

See also *anorexia nervosa; estrogen hormones; puberty; secular trend.*

mental age (MA): A measure of intelligence based on the average scores of groups of children of increasing chronological ages. For example, suppose that, for a particular standardized test of intelligence, a score of 24 correct answers is average for 8-year-old children, a score of 29 correct answers is average for 9-year-old children, a score of 36 correct answers is average for 10-year-old children, and so forth. Assume that 8-year-old Pamela takes the test and obtains a score of 36 correct answers. Although her chronological age is 8, her mental age is 10.

The concept of mental age was introduced into psychology by Alfred Binet, the father of the modern intelligence test, and his assistants in France in the 1910s. It was the first practical measure of the intelligence of children. The concept of mental age is meaningful only up to ages of about 15 or 16. Mental ages are unstable measures of intelligence because, by definition, they tend to increase with chronological age. Consequently, the intelligence quotient, a measure that compares mental ages with chronological ages, is preferred.

See also *Binet, Alfred; chronological age (CA); intelligence quotient (IQ); Stanford-Binet Intelligence Scale.*

mental deficiency: An early term for what today is called *mental retardation.*

See also *mental retardation.*

mental disorder: A disorder characterized by a pathology of thought, feelings, or actions. Such terms as *mental illness, abnormal behavior, maladaptive behavior,* and *maladjustment* are used to broadly identify mental disorders. Examples of pathology of thought are illogical thinking, irrational ideas, and delusions. Examples of pathology of feeling are chronic anxiety, anger, and depression. Examples of pathology of action are alcohol abuse, compulsive eating, and extreme agitation.

The list of mental disorders is long, and it includes both organic and functional disorders. The American Psychiatric Association's *Diagnostic and Statistical Manual of Mental Disorders* provides a complete classification scheme. The encyclopedia provides names, explanations, and treatment possibilities for the principal mental disorders that afflict children and adolescents.

See also *alcohol abuse in adolescence; anaclitic depression; anorexia nervosa; attachment disorder; attention-deficit hyperactivity disorder (ADHD); autistic disorder; behavior disorder; bulimia nervosa; childhood neurosis; childhood schizophrenia; conduct disorder; developmental disorders; drug abuse in adolescence; eating disorders; encopresis; enuresis; gender identity disorder of childhood; identity disorder; maladjusted child; mental retardation; oppositional defiant disorder; phobia; psychotic disorders; separation anxiety disorder; sleepwalking disorder; Tourette's disorder.*

mental representation: In Piaget's theory of cognitive development, the sixth and last substage of the sensorimotor stage. During the substage of mental representation, children begin to develop the ability to visualize or otherwise imagine the consequences of their actions. For example, suppose that 22-month-old Kim is presented with the following problem. A desirable object such as a small red ball is placed in a half-open drawer. A child in early infancy would be totally baffled by the problem. But Kim appears to contemplate the problem before acting. Then he tugs on the drawer, appearing to recognize that *sliding* it open is the key to the solution. It can be inferred that Kim has mentally represented the problem and its solution to himself before acting. This is a significant intellectual attainment for an infant. The substage of mental representation is associated with the end of infancy and provides a bridge to the cognitive capacities of toddlers.

See also *cognitive development; object permanence; Piaget, Jean; sensorimotor stage.*

mental retardation: A lack of normal mental ability as measured by a standardized intelligence test. Examples of such standardized tests are the Stanford-Binet Intelligence Scale and the Wechsler intelligence scales.

Subnormal mental ability is defined as an intelligence quotient (IQ) score of about 70 or below. Four categories of mental retardation are identified: (1) Mild (IQ = 50–55 to about 70); (2) Moderate (IQ = 35–40 to 50–55); (3) Severe (IQ = 20–25 to 35–40), and (4) Profound (IQ below 20–25). It is estimated that roughly 1 percent of the population falls into these categories of mental retardation.

The term *mental retardation* is preferred over the older term *mental deficiency.*

There are a number of biological causes of mental retardation. Genetic disorders such as Down's syndrome, Turner's syndrome, and phenylketonuria (PKU) account for a substantial percentage of mental retardation. Other biological causes include rubella (German measles) during pregnancy and antagonistic blood categories between infant and mother.

Mild mental retardation often has little or no organic basis. This kind of retardation is called *familial mental retardation.*

There is no cure for mental retardation. However, the condition can be treated with much success depending on the severity of the retardation. Persons with mild and moderate retardation can often be trained to be quite productive and self-sufficient. Persons with severe and profound retardation often require institutional care. However, even under these circumstances, much can be done through training programs to greatly enhance the quality of life.

See also *Down's syndrome; familial mental retardation; intelligence; Stanford-Binet Intelligence Scale; Turner's syndrome; phenylketonuria (PKU); Wechsler intelligence scales.*

messiness: In children and adolescents, not conforming to adult standards of order and neatness. Messiness tends to be very frustrating to parents and other caregivers, and there is often a large gap between what the child considers satisfactory and what the adult considers satisfactory. It is important to realize that there is no particular meaning in the messiness of toddlers and preschoolers. They initially have little sense of order, of putting things away, or of organizing a room or work space. Saying to very young children "Go straighten up your room" or "Make things neat in this area" does not mean much. The instructions are too abstract to be followed. Instead, the adult needs to give specific instructions such as, "Hang up your clothes the way I showed you yesterday" or "Put your shoes in the closet." Demonstrations are often required in order to induce social learning. Also, children should be reinforced for acceptable behavior with praise or some other form of approval. All of this goes under the heading of training, and its purpose is eventual generalization to later childhood and adolescence.

Unfortunately, even adolescents who have had quite a bit of training as children will often insist on keeping messy rooms and work areas. Three examples of reasons for this follow. First, they want to be like their peers who also have messy rooms. Odd as it may seem, the messiness of the room may be a sort of "badge of honor" when they visit each other. Second, they see themselves as too busy and involved in life, school, homework, and social activities to bother with everyday tasks such as making a bed or hanging up clothes. Third, messiness is a way to declare autonomy, a way of saying, "You can't tell me everything to do; I have a mind of my own."

Giving an adolescent lectures and direct orders will usually make matters worse and will tend to intensify the adolescent's need to express autonomy. Also, the kinds of behavior modification methods effective with younger children are readily understood by adolescents, and they may resent what they perceive as manipulation. On the other hand, parents are human, too, and find it difficult to suppress their natural tendency to react with disapproval when they want to.

The effective parent will express a natural level of disapproval for unacceptable behavior but will avoid overdefining the problem and converting an irritating state of affairs into a war. It is worth remembering that adolescents will respond to negotiation. They are usually willing to enter into verbal contracts in which each party to the contract both gives and gets a little. The vast majority of adolescents are basically socialized and usually have a strong sense of honor concerning the necessity to abide by a contract. The result may not be satisfactory to either the parent or the adolescent but will represent a sort of temporary truce concerning issues that will be of small importance in a few years when the adolescent is an adult. The methods advocated in parent effectiveness training are helpful in coping with a problem such as adolescent messiness.

See also *behavior modification; discipline; parent effectiveness training (P.E.T.); social learning.*

metamemory: See *memory.*

metaneeds: See *growth needs.*

methylphenidate: A stimulant used to treat attention-deficit hyperactivity disorder, drowsiness, fatigue, and narcolepsy. (Two trade names for methylphenidate are Methidate and Ritalin.) The functional action of methylphenidate is to increase alertness and general arousal.

Methylphenidate is often prescribed for attention-deficit hyperactivity disorder in children. The hyperactive aspect of this disorder is associated with an overly high level of central nervous system arousal. However, methylphenidate appears to have a paradoxical effect. Instead of stimulating the child with attention-deficit hyperactivity disorder, the child is frequently calmed. The mechanism by which this takes place is somewhat obscure. However, it is possible to speculate that the relationship between arousal and stimulation is like an inverse *U*. The child who is suffering from attention-deficit hyperactivity disorder may be on the crest of the *U*. A stimulant moves the child off the crest and thereby has a tranquilizing effect.

Like most drugs, methylphenidate sometimes has adverse side effects. Common ones include changes of mood, sleep disturbances, headaches, and loss of appetite. A prescription is required in order to take the drug.

See also *attention-deficit hyperactivity disorder (ADHD); minimal brain dysfunction (MBD).*

microcephaly: A condition characterized by an unusually small head. Microcephaly is a cranial abnormality. Persons suffering from this condition have a brain that is below average in size. The condition is linked to mental retardation, the degree of which is usually more than moderate.

Biological factors play a major part in microcephaly. Some cases are probably caused by a recessive gene. Infection of the mother during pregnancy, such as by rubella (German measles) is another common cause. Exposure during pregnancy to extremely high levels of radiation has also been linked to microcephaly.

The condition is not curable. It is, however, treatable to some slight degree. In most cases, an individual with the disorder is cared for in a supportive institutional environment. Training programs aim at helping the individual develop the maximum amount of self-sufficiency.

See also *hydrocephaly; macrocephaly; mental retardation.*

middle childhood: See *child.*

minimal brain dysfunction (MBD): A general term used to suggest a set of related cognitive and behavioral disturbances. The assumption is that these disturbances are caused by a slight amount of damage in the brain stem, the region of the brain that controls arousal. It is hypothesized that in most cases the damage was caused during the birthing process. An infant deprived of oxygen, for example, may suffer such damage. Slight damage to the brain stem does not affect intelligence, but it does affect attention span and motor activity. Therefore, persons with the problem are somewhat more likely than most persons to have problems in concentration. Also, they tend to be restless and do not like to sit still for very long.

Minimal brain dysfunction is one of the principal explanations of conditions such as attention-deficit hyperactivity disorder and developmental reading disorder.

See also *attention-deficit hyperactivity disorder (ADHD); developmental reading disorder.*

mitosis: The division process by which a body cell reproduces itself. Mitosis takes place when an original body cell splits itself into two cells. A normal body cell has 23 pairs of chromosomes in its nucleus. When mitosis is complete, two final cells remain, both with a full complement of 23 pairs. In essence, the two final cells are identical, and also identical to the original cell.

Mitosis is an asexual form of reproduction. It is essential for growth and for self-repair of the body. Mitosis is possible because deoxyribonucleic acid, the building block of genes, has the unique capacity to replicate itself.

See also *deoxyribonucleic acid (DNA); meiosis.*

model: See *social learning.*

modeling: See *social learning.*

mongolism: See *Down's syndrome.*

monozygotic twins: See *twins.*

Montessori, Maria (1870-1952): An Italian physician and educator. Montessori graduated from the University of Rome and was the first woman in Italy to earn an M.D. degree. In 1907, she was challenged with the responsibility of educating children of the slums in the city of Rome. Because she lacked both funds and trained teachers, she developed methods of instruction that stressed active learning, children helping each other, and self-reliance. Also, she devised educational materials designed to elicit the spontaneous curiosity and interest of children.

In the early 1900s, it was widely believed that slum children were mentally retarded. Much to the surprise of many observers, children taught by Montessori's methods performed academically as well as—and in some cases outperformed—more affluent children taught by traditional methods. These early experiences launched Montessori on a long and successful career as an educational psychologist.

Among books by Montessori are *The Montessori Method* (1912) and *The Advanced Montessori Method* (1917). *The Absorbent Mind,* one of Montessori's most popular works, is based on lectures she delivered in India in 1949 and was published in the United States in 1967.

See also *Montessori method.*

Montessori method: A method of instruction characterized by active learning. In the Montessori method, the child is not thought of as the passive receiver of information and knowledge, but as an active explorer and seeker. Several important features of the method can be identified:

1. The child is provided with various materials designed to invite curiosity at various age levels. Nesting canisters, blocks of ordered sizes, counting beads, and maps that can be assembled and disassembled are examples of such materials. The assump-

tion is that children learn best by a combination of sensory and motor activities.

2. Older children act as mentors for younger children. Therefore, the classroom contains children of varying ages.

3. There is a minimum of formal instruction from teachers in the form of lectures. Instead, teachers react to questions and give guidance.

4. The classroom environment is serious, relaxed, and informal.

Maria Montessori, originator of the method, coined the phrase "the absorbent mind" to describe the child's learning capacities, particularly in early childhood. She believed that a normal child "soaks up" information somewhat like a sponge, that learning is a spontaneous, natural process. The challenge for educational psychology is to take full advantage of the child's initial interest and motivation.

Although the Montessori method can be applied to the teaching of adolescents, it has had its greatest successes with younger children.

The Montessori method has made only modest inroads into the public educational system. As a consequence, advocates of the method have established a number of private schools.

See also *educational psychology; Head Start programs; Montessori, Maria; open classroom.*

mood stabilizing drugs: Drugs that modify an individual's tendency to have excessive emotional reactions. Consequently, mood stabilizing drugs are useful in treating a range of child and adolescent problem behaviors, such as as excessive aggressiveness, conduct disorder, extreme mood swings, depression, impulsiveness, mania (i.e., extreme and irrational excitement), rage, and some seizures. The two principal mood stabilizing drugs are lithium carbonate and carbamazepine.

Lithium carbonate is the principal tranquilizing drug used to treat bipolar disorder in adolescents and adults. *Bipolar disorder* is a mood disorder with two extremes, mania and depression. (An older term for bipolar disorder was *manic-depressive psychosis.*) Lithium carbonate is marketed under several trade names, such as Eskalith, Lithane, Lithonate, and Lithotabs. It is hypothesized that lithium carbonate is effective in modulating both mania and depression by (1) regulating the action of neurotransmitters in the central nervous system and (2) producing beneficial cellular changes in neurons.

Although lithium carbonate is not a habit forming drug, a prescription is required for its use. It has potentially adverse side effects, and the amount taken must be carefully regulated. In very large doses, the drug can be quite toxic.

Carbamazepine functions by modulating the activity of the brain's neurons and also by interfering with pain messages. Also, it has an anticonvulsant action. Carbamazepine is marketed under the trade name of Tegretol. Like lithium carbonate, a prescription is required for carbamazepine.

See also *antidepressant drugs; drug therapy; neuroleptic drugs.*

moral development: A process of learning and maturation centering on one's concepts of right and wrong. Moral development refers to the growth of an ethical sense and a set of values. According to Lawrence Kohlberg, a leading investigator into the subject of moral development, children think quite differently about ethical questions than do adults. Kohlberg proposes three principal stages of moral development—the premoral, conventional, and principled stages.

The *premoral stage* is associated primarily with the preschool years. Children in this first stage see the social world as a power struggle. They are "right" if they can get away with something. They are "wrong" if they get caught. In the premoral stage, right and wrong are more closely associated with physical value than with one's motives for an act. For example, 4-year-old Angela breaks an expensive lamp by accident. It is only partly her fault. Her parents had placed the lamp in an unfamiliar place because they were planning to repair it. Angela bumped into it inadvertently. Her parents let her off with a mild reprimand, even though they feel badly about the lamp. Later in the day, Angela breaks her 2-year-old sister's toy on purpose. It is an inexpensive toy, but her parents are quite cross. How does all of this look to Angela? From her point of view, her parents are incomprehensible. She thinks that breaking the expensive lamp is a greater offense than breaking the inexpensive toy. It is difficult for her to see that she violated her sister's rights. At the premoral level of development, an abstract concept such as "human rights" is not readily accepted by the child.

The *conventional stage* is associated primarily with the school-age and adolescent years. The person in this second stage believes in law and order. But the belief is based more on what one has been taught than on one's own thinking processes. In this stage, there tends to be the feeling that something is right if someone in an important position—an authority figure—says it is right. On the whole, obedience to authority figures is desirable and necessary in a complex society. However, it can sometimes cause problems, particulary if the person in power asks an underling to violate a human right.

The *principled stage* is associated with adulthood. Persons in this last stage have internal codes of conduct based to a large degree on their own reflections and analyses. Their value system places a greater premium on the welfare of other human beings than on an established set of rules. The leadership of India's Mohandas Gandhi, when he led nonviolent protests against British rule in the 1930s and 1940s, provides an example of an individual operating at the principled level.

It should be realized that not all adults reach the principled level. Many remain at the conventional level. Also, persons who are undersocialized or who suffer from personality disorders may be operating at the premoral level that is normally associated with early childhood.

See also *cognitive development; conscience; Kohlberg, Lawrence; Piaget, Jean; superego.*

Moro reflex: One of the reflexes that is present in the neonate and that is characterized by a "grabbing" motion if the neonate is subjected to such stimuli as an unexpected loss of support or a sudden loud sound. The neonate's arms and legs will extend and then come together; also, the back will arch. The Moro reflex is often referred to as the *startle reaction* and is considered to be a primitive, immature form of what will eventually emerge as the complex startle pattern exhibited by older children and adults. The Moro reflex is also sometimes called the *embracing reflex* because its purpose appears to be an attempt on the part of the infant to cling to the parent when there is some possibility of being dropped.

The Moro reflex fades away in infants around the age of 5 to 7 months. The presence of this reflex in a neonate is a sign that the infant is neurologically normal. However, its appearance in an older child is a sign of brain damage, neurological impairment, or motor reflex difficulties.

See also *neonatal reflexes.*

moron: In informal everyday usage, a person who is dull or unintelligent. The word *moron* is derived from a Greek root meaning "stupid" and was coined by the pioneer clinical psychologist Henry H. Goddard. Originally, the designation *moron* was used in intelligence testing to classify persons who were below normal in intelligence but capable of some degree of self-sufficiency and learning. Today. the term has no formal clinical meaning and is considered outdated because of its pejorative character. It has been replaced with the category *mild mental retardation.*

See also *Goddard, Henry Herbert; intelligence; mental retardation.*

morpheme: A meaningful sound, one of the basic building blocks of language. A morpheme is similar, but not identical to, the concept of a word. For example, *cat* is one morpheme and one word; *cats*, however, is two morphemes (i.e., cat + s) but only one word. The added *s* pluralizes the word, changes its meaning, and is consequently a morpheme in and of itself.

The general ability of a child to use grammar is reflected in the number of morphemes that appear in a sentence. For example, Child A might say, "I want go to store." Child B, the same chronological age, might say, "I want to go to the store." Child B's grammatical development is more advanced, as reflected in the greater number of morphemes used. A measure identified as the *mean length of utterance (MLU)* can be used to evaluate a child's level of grammatical development.

Morphemes are made up of smaller speech units called *phonemes.*

See also *babbling; holophrase; language development; phoneme.*

mother: In developmental psychology, a word that has acquired two related meanings, that is, (1) a female biological parent and (2) a female who fulfills the role of parent. An adoptive parent or a stepmother may be clearly identified as a mother in a child's mind. It is widely recognized that playing the role of mother is as important, perhaps more important in some ways, than being a biological parent.

Various studies suggest that the mother is usually the favorite parent of either male or female children. This is probably the case for several reasons. First, many mothers nurse children. The feeding, holding, and affectionate contact with the infant appears to foster a strong mother-infant bond. This is, of course, true even if the infant is bottlefed. And this provides an opportunity for fathers to strengthen the father-infant bond.

Second, mothers tend to spend more time with children than do fathers. In spite of expanded parental roles for both sexes and the fact that many women work out of the household, it is still women who do the majority of the caregiving in both infancy and later years.

Third, traditional gender-biased social roles call for women to be more emotionally involved with children and more nurturing than men. They are expected to be more loving and affectionate. They tend to cook more of the meals, make the arrangements for the holidays and for special occasions such as birthday parties, and so forth.

Fourth, if there is a divorce or separation, it is usually the mother who retains principal custody of children.

Women in general tend to show a greater interest in raising children and in caregiving than do men. Most monthly women's magazines contain at least one article on effective parenting. Men's magazines seldom carry such articles. Most of the buyers of books on child care and development are women.

Although there are many individual exceptions, the larger share of the emotional burden associated with being a parent still tends to rest on women. With a growing awareness of the possible inequities involved in traditional gender-biased social roles, this is changing somewhat. Many of today's fathers are becoming more nurturing and are spending more time with their children. Many of today's mothers are feeling somewhat less guilt for taking an interest in a vocation outside of the home. Nonetheless, the importance of the mother's role continues to be the dominant theme in the development of children.

See also *attachment; authoritarian parent; father; juvenile delin-quency; parental style.*

mother-infant bonding: See *attachment.*

mother's age: A causal factor in birth defects associated with chromo-somal anomalies. One of the most well known of these anomalies is Trisomy 21, the cause of Down's syndrome. Older mothers are somewhat more likely to produce children with chromosomal anomalies than are younger mothers. A possible reason for this is that the process of meiosis, the process by which ova are produced, may be less reliable in the older mother. In general, it can be said that the risk of producing an infant with a chromosomal anomaly increases significantly after the age of 35, and continues to increase after this age. For example, the overall incidence of Down's syndrome is 1 in every 600 infants. The likelihood of having an infant with Down's syndrome at age 40 is about 1 in every 100 infants. At age 45, the risk rises to about 3 in every 100 infants.

See also *amniocentesis; birth defects; chromosomal anomalies; Down's syndrome; meiosis.*

motor development: The development of the ability to move in a coordinated, effective manner. *Locomotor* development refers to the ability to move one's body about in space (e.g., crawling and walking). The basic foundation of motor development is laid down in infancy and is considered to be more or less complete when the child can walk. Both maturation and learning are involved in motor develop-ment.

Motor development follows a predictable sequence for almost all infants:

1. *Holding the head.* Between the ages of 1 and 4 months, most infants can hold their heads in an upright position when they themselves are held in an upright position.
2. *Self-elevation.* Between the ages of 2 and 4 months, most infants can, when in a prone position, use their forearms to lift their chests off, for example, a mattress or the floor.
3. *Rolling over.* Between the ages of 3 and 6 months, most infants can roll over. (The ability to roll from chest to back appears first, followed by the ability to roll from back to chest.)
4. *Sitting with help.* Between the ages of 4 and 7 months, most infants can sit up with some assistance.

5. *Grasping*. Between the ages of 4 and 7 months, most infants can successfully grasp an object such as a small ball or a rattle.

6. *Sitting alone*. Between the ages of 6 and 9 months, most infants can sit upright without assistance, for example, in a high chair or on the floor.

7. *Standing*. Between the ages of 8 and 11 months, most infants can stand when held or when holding on to something.

8. *Crawling and pulling up*. Between the ages of 9 and 12 months, most infants can crawl, or creep, about on all four limbs. Shortly after developing this capacity, most infants will be able to pull themselves to a standing position using, for example, a piece of furniture.

9. *Standing alone*. Between the ages of 10 and 15 months, most infants can stand alone, without help.

10. *Walking*. Between the ages of 11 and 16 months, most infants can walk alone, without help.

Note that the age ranges for normal motor development are quite large. If motor development does not follow the described sequence or does not take place within the usual age ranges, this may be a sign of neurological problems.

See also *Bayley Scales of Infant Development; cognitive development; learning; maturation.*

Murray, Henry A.(1893–1988): A physician, personality theorist, and author of psychological tests. He graduated with a B.A. degree from Harvard University in 1915, earned an M.D. degree from Columbia University in 1919, and graduated with a Ph.D. degree in biochemistry from Cambridge University in 1927. For most of his professional career, he was associated with Harvard.

Murray was inspired by the works of Freud and Jung and combined their insights into the nature of the human personality with his own original ideas. He believed that behavioral traits can be best understood in terms of psychological needs and developed the *Thematic Apperception Test* (see entry *need to achieve*) to investigate patterns of these needs in individuals. The construction of the Thematic

Apperception Test was based on research conducted at the Harvard Psychological Clinic.

Murray made important contributions to the study of both personality development and the nature of behavioral traits.

Two of Murray's books are *Explorations in Personality* (1938) and *Personality in Nature, Society, and Culture* (1953).

See also *Freud, Sigmund; Jung, Carl Gustav; need to achieve; personality development; trait.*

mutation: A variation in genetic structure. If a gene on a chromosome undergoes a transformation, new characteristics may appear in offspring carrying that gene. These new characteristics are permanent and become a part of the hereditary chain. The changed offspring with a new trait is called a *mutant.*

One of the causes of mutations is radiation. For example, fruit flies bombarded with X rays produce many mutants. It is hypothesized that background radiation in general, in addition to high energy subatomic particles originating from outer space, may be involved in human mutations. Some chemicals can cause mutations, particularly *carcinogens,* chemicals that cause cancer. The overall name of agents that can cause mutations is *mutagens.* Often mutations are simply spoken of as "spontaneous," suggesting that they are of unknown causes.

Most mutations are undesirable and tend to die out quickly in a species because they have either no survival value or interfere with effective behavior. Some mutations are desirable and they tend to be preserved because of their survival value. Biologists frequently refer to the process of mutation as one of the principal ways of explaining variation and changes within a species, including human beings.

Mutations are relatively rare and are not a principal cause of chromosomal anomalies and birth defects.

See also *birth defects; chromosomal anomalies; deoxyribonucleic acid (DNA); gene; heredity.*

mutism: A condition characterized by lack of speech. In children, there are several causes of mutism. Children with a hearing impairment are often mute or speak poorly because they have a difficult time hearing and imitating the sounds of words. Children suffering from autistic disorder are frequently mute. It is hypothesized that their lack of social interest also causes them to have little or no interest in speaking. Children suffering from hydrocephaly or other brain pathology may have neurological impairments that interfere with speech. Such a condition is referred to as *akinetic mutism.*

A behavioral disorder due primarily to psychological, not biological, factors is *elective mutism.* The disorder is characterized by a voluntary resistance to talking. Such children *can* speak and understand what is said. The disorder's usual age of onset is about 5. Causal factors in the disorder include a tendency for parents to be overprotective, low intelligence, and other speech pathology (e.g., stuttering). Children who have come to the United States from foreign countries are somewhat more prone to elective mutism than are other children. Psychologically, elective mutism is often interpreted as a form of negativism and hostility on the part of the child. The overall incidence of elective mutism is low. Fewer than 1 child in 100 seen by a mental health professional for behavioral and emotional problems suffers from the disorder. Female children are somewhat more likely to suffer from the disorder than are male children.

See also *aggressiveness; autistic disorder; hearing impairment; hydrocephaly; negativism.*

myelinization: A process characterized by the formation of a fatty covering around the fibers of *neurons,* cells that specialize in the transmission of information. The fatty covering itself is called the *myelin sheath.* The sheath has several functions. First, it insulates a nerve fiber. Second, it provides some nutritional support for the cell. Third, it helps the fiber transmit messages with greater speed. A myelinated fiber sends messages about 20 times more rapidly than does an immature one. Myelinization begins before an infant is born, and the bulk of myelinization takes place during infancy (i.e., the first two years after birth). Toilet training and walking unaided require a high level of myelinization. Although both behaviors involve learning, they also require the kind of maturation associated with myelinization.

See also *infant; motor development; toilet training.*

N

nailbiting: Frequent biting of fingernails that is usually interpreted as an outlet for anxiety, nervous tension, or unexpressed aggressiveness. If chronic, nailbiting in children and adolescents is characterized by ragged nails, tender fingertips, and some bleeding. It cannot be taken for granted that a child will automatically outgrow nailbiting. A survey conducted by researchers V. J. Adesso and J. M. Vargas at the University of Wisconsin suggested that about one-fourth of the college students in their sample had a problem with nailbiting. Children and adolescents who frequently bite their nails are often ashamed of their hands.

It is not easy to break a nailbiting habit. Parental interventions such as nagging, lecturing, punishing, and so forth are usually ineffective. Indeed, they often make the habit worse by reinforcing it with both too much status and attention.

In early childhood, the parent should employ behavior modification strategies. With older children and adolescents, the problem can be discussed and self-modification strategies can be explained. Professional treatment consists of counseling and behavior therapy.

See also *behavior modification; behavior therapy; cognitive-behavior modification.*

narcissism: A kind of ego defense mechanism characterized by self-absorption. Another term for *narcissism*, one that sometimes appears in psychoanalytic literature, is *ego erotism*. The Greek myth of Narcissus tells the story of a youth who fell in love with his own image as it was reflected in a pool of water. He was overcome with longing for the beautiful youth in the pool and he eventually starved to death. The myth contains a warning: excessive self-love can be destructive. A person with a healthy personality cares not only about himself or herself, but also about others.

Here are two examples of adolescents using narcissism. Fifteen-year-old Julia doubts that she is pretty. She spends an inordinate amount of time picking out clothes and worrying about makeup. Sixteen-year-old Mark is short for his age. He is a compulsive body builder and frequently preens and poses in front a mirror when he is alone. Both of the examples reveal that the individuals in question use narcissism to defend the ego against threats to its sense of integrity and worth.

See also *ego defense mechanisms*.

narcolepsy: A tendency to fall suddenly and involuntarily asleep. Usually the period of sleep is brief in duration (e.g., a few minutes). Symptoms often associated with narcolepsy are chronic drowsiness, insomnia, and abrupt loss of muscle control. The condition is relatively rare in children and adolescents. However, if it does occur, it is cause for concern and may require professional treatment.

Narcolepsy can be biological or psychological in origin. A biological cause of narcolepsy is dysfunction in the *reticular activating system*, an arousal control center in the brain stem. (Dysfunctions of the reticular activating system are also a common factor in attention-deficit hyperactivity disorder.) Another biological cause of narcolepsy is encephalitis. A psychological cause of narcolepsy is an unconscious wish to run away from responsibilities. A child who feels overburdened or unable to cope with life may tend to oversleep. Consequently, narcolepsy may be one sign of an underlying depression in the child.

If the cause of narcolepsy is thought to be biological, the treatment is usually drug therapy. Amphetamines are often prescribed. They are stimulants and, in some cases, have a beneficial effect. If the cause is psychological, a common treatment is child psychotherapy. Sometimes antidepressant drugs are prescribed.

See also *attention-deficit hyperactivity disorder (ADHD); child psychotherapy; depressant drugs; drug therapy; epilepsy; sleep patterns.*

narcotic drugs (narcotics): In general, drugs that produce a stupor; more specifically, addictive depressant drugs such as opium, morphine, codeine, and heroin. Sometimes, methadone, a synthetic drug, is also listed as a narcotic. Morphine is derived from opium. Codeine and heroin in turn are derived from morphine. These drugs are among the drugs commonly abused in adolescence.

Opium is derived from the fluid in the pods of the opium poppy plant. Chemical substances derived from opium are also narcotics and are designated *opiates*. As indicated above, these include morphine, codeine, and heroin. Opiates are capable of relieving pain. Consequently, they have legitimate medical uses.

Opiates are also capable of inducing pleasurable states of relaxation and euphoria. For this reason, they are subject to substantial abuse. Unfortunately, a physiological tolerance to the opiates builds quite rapidly, and ever increasing dosages are required to maintain the wanted drug response. As a consequence, an addiction to an opiate tends to cost more and more money, and the body is forced to endure higher toxic levels of the drug. Opium and its derivatives are addictive in both the physiological and psychological sense. The body develops a "need" for the drug. And a craving for the drug may remain even after a physiological dependency is broken.

Methadone, as indicated earlier, is a synthetic narcotic. Methadone is used in some medical and psychiatric programs to help an individual withdraw from an addiction to heroin. The idea is for methadone to provide a supporting bridge as the individual makes an effort to give up heroin. Methadone can sometimes be helpful because it meets the physiological demands of the addicted individual without providing the euphoria of heroin. Therefore, the individual can be an effective student or engage in gainful employment. The psychological dependence on heroin is thus broken first; then the individual proceeds to give up the physiological dependence by withdrawing from the methadone.

Methadone treatment has its opponents and advocates. Opponents point out that methadone is, like heroin, an addictive drug, and that it, too, is subject to abuse. Advocates say that it provides important support during the critical withdrawal period from heroin. At present, there is no professional consensus.

See also *depressant drugs; drug abuse in adolescence; hallucinogens; inhalant drugs; marijuana; sedatives; stimulant drugs.*

National Institute of Child Health and Human Development (NICHHD): A division of the National Institutes of Health (NIH). The National Institute of Child Health and Human Development was established in 1962, has a staff of approximately 260 professional persons, and maintains an active interest in all facets of the welfare and development of children. The staff conducts both basic and clinical research into such topics and areas of concern as high-risk pregnancy, childhood origins of adult diseases, sudden infant death syndrome (SIDS), learning disabilities, and so forth. Results are published in scientific journals. The NICHHD's address is NIH Building 31, 9000 Rockville Pike, Bethesda, Maryland 20892.

See also *birth defects; fetal alcohol syndrome (FAS); fetal development; genetic anomaly; immature birth; learning disability; premature birth; sudden infant death syndrome (SIDS).*

nativism: In philosophy and psychology, the point of view that inborn structures and tendencies play important roles in thinking and behavior. One of the earliest versions of this is the philosopher Plato's doctrine of *innate ideas*, ideas present in the mind at birth. Plato believed that one has inborn ideas of beauty, goodness, and truth. A latter-day version of nativism in philosophy is the philosopher Immanuel Kant's teaching that the mind has inborn conceptions of space and time, consequently imposing its own order on experience.

More recently, the influence of nativism is evident in contemporary developmental psychology in a number of ways. Chomsky hypothesizes that language development in children is facilitated by an inborn language acquisition device (LAD). A number of studies indicate that traits of temperament are to a large extent inborn. Sociobiology teaches that much of social behavior has a genetic basis. These are all nativistic concepts.

Empiricism is the point of view that opposes nativism.

See also *Chomsky, Noam Avram; empiricism; innate; instinct; language acquisition device (LAD); sociobiology.*

natural childbirth: See *Lamaze method; Leboyer method.*

nature: See *nature-nurture controversy.*

nature-nurture controversy: A running controversy over the relative importance of nature (i.e., heredity) versus nurture (i.e., environment) in the determination of behavior. Applied to developmental psychology, the controversy focuses on the relative importance of the two factors in the determination of intelligence, creativity, traits of personality, and other determinants of behavior. Advocates of the importance of nature argue that it is the dominant cause of human abilities. For example, a child who displays ready ability in drawing, writing, or music is said to be a "born artist," suggesting that genetic factors play a significant part in the manifestation of artistic ability. In contrast, advocates of the importance of nurture argue that it is the dominant cause of human abilities. For example, it can be pointed out that children with artistic ability often come from homes where artistic expression is reinforced with encouragement, time to work, and praise. If the parents are themselves artists, social learning (i.e., learning through observation) plays a significant role in the behavior. (On the other hand, advocates of the importance of nature suggest that if the parents are artists, the child may have inherited genes that contribute to artistic ability.)

In the late 19th and early 20th centuries, advocates of the importance of nature had great prestige. Exciting discoveries in genetics and biology in general seemed to suggest that human abilities could be explained primarily in physical and organic terms. With the rise of behaviorism in the 1910s and 1920s, there was a great surge of interest in the environmental approach. The individual's learning history seemed to be the key to unlocking the mystery of the causes of behavior. Freud's emphasis on the importance of the person's developmental history also gave great weight to the environmental viewpoint.

Today, the pendulum of opinion has swung to a middle position between an extreme nature viewpoint and an extreme nurture viewpoint. The contemporary approach is to emphasize the importance of the *interaction* between heredity and environment. They affect each other in a complex way, and a certain amount of weight must be given to both nature and nurture if one wants to obtain a complete explanation of a human ability or trait. Thus, a great deal of wind has gone out of the sails of the traditional nature-nurture controversy.

See also *behaviorism; genetic predisposition; heredity and environment interaction; social learning.*

need to achieve: A more or less stable motivational disposition expressing itself in such behaviors as finishing tasks, reaching goals, and setting a high level of aspiration. Children and adolescents with a high need to achieve will generally work willingly to achieve some well-defined end, such as obtaining good grades, earning a letter in sports, learning to play a musical instrument, or earning a merit badge in a scouting activity. Adolescents with a high need to achieve often have a well-defined identity and seem to have a thought-out future course of action. They give the impression that they know where they are going and how they are going to get there. On the whole, a high need to achieve is thought to be desirable and appears to be associated with self-esteem. (Naturally, even achievement motivation can be excessive. And it is possible for a child to be driven and compulsive.)

The level of an individual's achievement motivation can be evaluated by a projective personality test called the *Thematic Apperception Test.* The scoring category is abbreviated *nAch.* The concept of achievement motivation is often associated with the test and is one of a list of motives drawn up by the test's author, Henry A. Murray.

Several causal factors appear to be involved in a high need for achievement. First, the need for achievement seems to some extent to have an inborn basis. Adler, for example, spoke of an inborn will to power. Others have spoken of an inborn competence motivation. These all seem to be related concepts. Second, as already indicated, children with high self-esteem appear to also have a high need to achieve. Third, if parents model goal-oriented behavior themselves, children tend to engage in similar behaviors because of the social learning process. Fourth, some cultures have a higher level of achievement motivation than do other cultures. The United States has traditionally valued the person of action who strives toward objective accomplishments.

See also *Adler, Alfred; identity versus role confusion; self-esteem; social learning; will to power.*

negative identity: An identity that is unacceptable to one's family and general culture. When a negative identity forms, the adolescent is usually undersocialized, rebellious, and acts out aggressive impulses. In a broad sense, a negative identity represents a sort of mirror opposite of the image of an unformed positive identity, one that would be valued by parents.

In psychoanalytic terms, the positive identity is represented in the superego as the *ego ideal*, the adolescent's incorporated concept of what is expected from a responsible member of society. When moral development is deficient or when there is substantial hostility toward the parents, the adolescent may do a sort of psychological flip, reject the ego ideal, and manifest a negative identity.

In transactional analysis, a negative identity is associated with the *antiscript*, an unconscious life plan that is at odds with parental expectations.

See also *identity; identity crisis; identity disorder; identity versus role confusion; script; superego; transactional analysis.*

negative reinforcer: See *reinforcer.*

negativism: An attitude or behavioral trait characterized by a tendency to resist commands or requests. Two basic kinds of negativism are identified: (1) passive and (2) active. In *passive negativism,* the individual may resist by "forgetting" to do something, by performing a task slowly, or by completing work inadequately. In *active negativism,* the individual does the opposite of what is requested. For example, a toddler may run in an opposite direction when a parent says, "Come here."

Negativism often appears in early childhood and again during adolescence. It is considered to be normal at these times and is interpreted as an expression of the individual's need for autonomy. In most cases, it is the expression of a developmental stage and usually will pass with maturation. If it does not pass, then negativism can become a personality trait. It tends to be a component factor in both a conduct disorder and an oppositional defiant disorder.

See also *aggressiveness; conduct disorder; oppositional defiant disorder.*

Neonatal Behavioral Assessment Scale (NBAS): A psychological test used to assess the quality and range of a neonate's behavior. Aspects of behavior evaluated include reflex responsiveness, reaction to lights, sounds, and other sensory stimulation, attention, interest in social contact, and capacity to be soothed and calmed. Developed by the psychologist T. Berry Brazelton, the NBAS is sometimes referred to as the *Brazelton neonatal scale.*

The NBAS has been used as a research instrument and has revealed that there are significant individual differences in the behavioral tendencies of neonates. In longitudinal studies, it has been found that traits apparent in the infant tend to be stable and are often also present later when the child becomes a toddler and preschooler. One of the values of the NBAS is that it helps parents and other caregivers appreciate the fact that children are individuals from birth.

See also *Apgar scale; Bayley Scales of Infant Development; Gesell Developmental Schedules; McCarthy Scales of Children's Abilities (MSCA).*

neonatal reflexes: Reflexes present in the newborn child. The presence in a neonate of the complete set of expected reflexes is evidence of neurological normality. Neonatal reflexes are presumed to be inborn and have a predictable action pattern. For every reflex, there is an *eliciting stimulus* (e.g., a finger placed against the palm of the neonate's hand) and a *response* (e.g., grasping of the finger). Also, every neonatal reflex has a typical *duration*. Some are permanent; others vanish with maturation.

See also *Babinski reflex; blink reflex; diving reflex; knee-jerk reflex; Moro reflex; Palmar grasp reflex; rage reflex; rooting reflex; sucking reflex; walking reflex.*

neonatal scales: Biological and psychological tests used to evaluate the health and behavioral status of newborn children.

See also *Apgar scale; Bayley Scales of Infant Development; Gesell Developmental Schedules; McCarthy Scales of Children's Abilities (MSCA); Neonatal Behavioral Assessment Scale (NBAS).*

neonate: A newborn child. There is no exact neonatal period. It is usually considered to last from birth until approximately 2 or 3 weeks of age. A more formal criterion is sometimes applied—if there is a weight loss after birth, the neonatal period is not considered ended until the birth weight is attained again. After the neonatal period, the child is referred to as an *infant.*

See also *fetal development; immature birth; infant; mature birth; neonatal reflexes; premature birth.*

nervous tic: See *tic.*

neuroleptic drugs: See *drug therapy.*

neurosis: See *childhood neurosis.*

newborn child: See *neonate.*

night terror *(pavor nocturnus)*: An intense emotional reaction characterized by great anxiety, talking while asleep, erratic movements, agitation, screaming, sitting up, heavy breathing, rapid heart rate, and confusion. (The term *pavor nocturnus* is derived from Latin and is a clinical term for *night terror.*) Sometimes a child experiencing a night terror seems to be seeing something that is not there. Neither completely awake nor asleep, the child will usually respond if spoken to. In most cases, calm reassurance will relax the child, and he or she can go back to sleep. The next day the child often has no memory of the night terror.

A night terror is similar, but not identical to, a nightmare. In a night terror, the emotional reaction is more intense than it is in a nightmare. In addition, a night terror has a sudden onset, is associated with deep sleep, and has little or no dream content.

Night terrors tend to be associated primarily with children around the ages of 3 to 7. Although preadolescents and adolescents sometimes experience night terrors, there is a strong tendency to outgrow them with maturation.

On occasion, a night terror induces an episode of sleepwalking.

Psychological and emotional factors associated with night terrors include a tendency to be anxious and tense during the day, excessive anger, an overexcited state, fatigue, and hyperactivity. In general, it can be said that anything that increases the child's level of emotional arousal during the day to an excessive degree will contribute to the likelihood of experiencing a night terror.

A pattern of night terrors can be diminished in frequency by providing the child with a calm, secure social environment. In particular, the hour or two before going to bed should be relaxing and free of intense stimulation.

In cases of chronic night terrors, sedatives or antianxiety drugs are sometimes prescribed.

See also *drug therapy; enuresis; insomnia; nightmare; sleep patterns; sleepwalking disorder.*

nightmare: A dream that induces an emotional state of fear, terror, or general anxiety. Dream images such as terrifying animals, dangerous strangers, monsters, huge robots, and being trapped in a tunnel or buried alive are typical of the content of nightmares. The onset of the fear is usually gradual, resulting from the buildup of events in the dream. Nightmares are associated with rapid eye movement (REM) sleep.

Nightmares are so common that they must be considered normal. Almost all children and adults have them from time to time. They are most common in preschool children. However, about one-fourth of preadolescent children have fairly regular nightmares.

A child who cries out for a parent after waking up from a nightmare should receive calm reassurance that everything is all right. Scoldings, calling the child silly, and so forth, are counterproductive. The incidence of nightmares can be reduced to some extent if a child is calm and not overly tired before going to bed.

The psychological and emotional factors associated with nightmares are similar to those associated with night terrors. These include anxiety, tension, anger, depression, and hyperactivity. Freud theorized that the function of nightmares is to prevent the breakthrough of something even more terrifying to the individual than the dream content. This was a forbidden wish, often of an aggressive nature in preschoolers and preadolescents, that is counter to what a "good child" would or should do. The fearful dream images are a cloak over the even more fearful repressed impulses. In a very general way, then, if Freud is correct, nightmares are functional in maintaining the child's self-esteem. There is no general consensus concerning the correctness of Freud's explanation.

See also *Freud, Sigmund; insomnia; night terror; sleep patterns.*

norms of development (developmental norms): Norms used to describe the learning and maturation of children over a span of time. In statistical work, a *norm* is a numerical value used to describe a group's central tendency. (*Central tendency* is a measure of the degree to which a group of scores tend to converge or be similar.) The three principal measures of central tendency are the mean, the mode, and the median. The *mean* is the arithmetical average of a set of scores. The *mode* is the most frequently repeated score in the group. The *median* is the score that cuts a distribution of scores in half. Sometimes a short range is used to represent a norm in an informal way and to provide recognition that small deviations from the exact numerical norm are themselves normal. For example, instead of saying that in infants a norm for sitting upright without assistance is 7.5 months, it can be said that most children can sit alone between the ages of 6 and 9 months.

Norms of development can be stated in such forms as height, weight, age, percentile, and IQ scores. Norms of development are useful in (1) longitudinal research studies designed to evaluate changes over a span of time, (2) the standardization of psychological tests (e.g., the Gesell Developmental Schedules or the Wechsler Intelligence Scale for Children), and (3) the evaluation of an individual child's growth, learning, and maturation.

Norms provide standards for comparison. Consequently, significant deviations from such standards suggest the possibility of abnormal development.

See also *abnormal development; developmental quotient (DQ); Gesell Developmental Schedules; motor development; Wechsler Intelligence Scale for Children (WISC).*

nocturnal emission: The release of semen while sleeping. An informal name for a nocturnal emission is a "wet dream." The emission is often the result of an erotic dream accompanied by an orgasm. Almost all males have experienced nocturnal emissions, and they are more common in adolescents than in adults. They are also more common in unmarried than married men, suggesting that nocturnal emissions are more frequent in males who do not have an available partner. Sexual release of this kind is involuntary and has nothing to do with the individual's mental health or moral training. Medical and mental health professionals consider nocturnal emissions to be completely normal.

Although females do not have emissions as such, they can and do experience orgasms in association with erotic dreams. It i estimated that about 35 percent of women have had such dreams. Unlike males, orgasms during sleep take place in a relatively small percentage of adolescent females. Such orgasms are more common in women in their 30s and 40s. Again, nocturnal orgasms are completely normal.

See also *adolescent sex relations; masturbation; psychosexual development; sexual maturity.*

nubile female: A female who has reached a stage of maturity such that she is biologically ready for marriage or reproduction. In most cases, this is about one year following the first time a female menstruates. The majority of females are nubile between the ages of 13 and 15.

See also *menarche; puberty; secular trend.*

nuclear family: A family unit consisting of parents and their child or children. The word *nuclear* is used to suggest that this particular family unit is the core of what is thought of as family structure.

See also *dysfunctional family; extended family; family therapy; one-parent family.*

nursery schools: See *preschools.*

nurture: See *nature-nurture controversy.*

nutrition: See *malnutrition.*

O

obesity: The condition of having an excess of body fat, or being obese. This definition of *obesity* is applicable to all human beings regardless of age. A formal distinction is made between *obese* and *overweight*. *Obese* is a relative term and means that the ratio of a person's body fat (which is measurable) to total body mass is above accepted norms. *Overweight,* on the other hand, means that the measure of a person's weight in a unit such as pounds is above accepted norms. It is technically possible to be overweight without being overfat, or obese. For example, an athletic adolescent who plays football and who exercises in order to build muscle might be overweight in terms of a standard height-weight chart. Nonetheless, if he has only about 15 percent body fat, he is not obese.

The normal male adult has about 15 percent body fat. The normal female adult has about 20 to 25 percent body fat. Developing human beings tend to have more body fat than normal-weight adults. Consequently, these percentages need to be raised somewhat in evaluating whether or not a particular child or adolescent is obese.

In the vast majority of cases, the formal distinction between obese and overweight is of little importance. A rough rule of thumb is that individuals who weigh 20 percent more than stated maximums in standardized charts are probably obese.

Obesity is common among children and adolescents in Western culture. Surveys and clinical reports suggest that about 4 to 9 percent of all children can be classified as obese. About 15 to 20 percent of adolescents are obese. More female adolescents suffer from obesity than do males. About three-fourths of those who suffer from obesity in adolescence will also suffer from it in adulthood.

Biological and psychological factors both contribute to obesity. Several interacting biological factors appear to play a role. First, there is evidence that in a number of instances there is a genetic predisposition to be obese. Second, there is a body type known informally as the *endomorph* that may have more fat cells than other body types. Third, a tendency toward hypoglycemia (i.e., low blood sugar) may make a child excessively hungry. Fourth, a low production of *thyroxin*, a hormone produced by the thyroid gland, may contribute to a sluggish metabolic rate. There are, of course, additional possibilities.

The role of psychological and emotional factors in obesity is believed to be quite significant. Children and adolescents, like adults, often eat because they are worried, angry, depressed, bored, lonely, and so forth. Food acts as a "quick fix" for an unpleasant emotional state. Also, bad eating habits, such as eating too fast, snacking between meals, eating because friends are eating, nibbling while watching television, and so forth, are easy to establish and difficult to modify.

Chronic obesity in a child or adolescent is a difficult condition to treat with success. Help from physicians and mental health professionals, particularly those who employ behavior modification techniques, may be required. Parents should avoid moralizing, lecturing, and the imposition of strict reducing diets. Severe criticism or strict monitoring of eating will usually make the problem worse by lowering the child's self-esteem. Often the child will cheat and overeat. This represents an attempt to declare autonomy and maintain control over one's own behavior.

Prevention is more effective than treatment. Therefore, from a child's earliest years, some attention should be given to the potential problem of becoming obese. In infancy and toddlerhood, the child should not be overfed and stuffed with food. In later years, food should not be regularly offered as a sign of love. Parents themselves should present easily admired role models who eat correctly and in moderation. Food should be presented primarily as a source of nourishment and reasonable pleasure, not an irrational source of emotional satisfaction.

See also *anorexia nervosa; behavior modification; body type; bulimia nervosa; eating disorders; hormone; genetic predisposition.*

object constancy: The tendency to perceive a world of objects with stable shapes, colors, and other attributes, even though these objects project varying patterns of stimulation on the sense organs. For example, suppose that a child is looking at a rectangular 3 × 5-inch index card. If the card is tilted back with the base slightly nearer the child and its top slightly farther away, the child will still perceive a rectangle. However, the sensory impression on the retina is, technically, a trapezoid. (This example demonstrates that sensation is not perception. *Sensation* refers to unorganized information. *Perception* refers to organized, meaningful information.)

Various studies have shown that object constancy makes its first appearance in infancy. It is usually well established by toddlerhood. Both inborn organizing factors, known as *Gestalt laws*, and the learning process work together to make object constancy possible.

See also *cognitive development; object permanence; perceptual development in infancy; sensorimotor stage.*

object permanence: In Piaget's theory of cognitive development, a tendency to think of an object as continuing to exist even when it is not being directly seen or otherwise sensed. For example, first, 3-year-old Angela is shown a dime. Then, while she is watching, it is covered with a paper cup. She is told she can keep the dime if she can find it. This "problem" is no problem at all for Angela and children with normal cognitive development. Angela lifts up the cup and quickly claims her dime. This seemingly simple ability on Angela's part represents object permanence. However, it is not present at birth nor in early infancy. It is a cognitive capacity that develops with maturation and experience.

Piaget's studies suggest that object permanence makes its first appearance in incomplete form between the ages of 4 and 8 months. The capacity to use object permanence in relatively complex problem solving (e.g., searching for a concealed object in more than one place) does not appear until the infant is between the ages of 18 and 24 months. Recent studies suggest that some rudimentary capacity for object permanence may be present even in some 4-week-old infants.

See also *attachment; cognitive development; Piaget, Jean; sensorimotor stage; stranger anxiety.*

obscene language: See *undesirable language.*

observational learning: See *social learning.*

Oedipus complex: In psychoanalysis, a set of unconscious motives and ideas characterized by (1) an incest wish toward the parent of the opposite sex, (2) guilt over the wish, and (3) fear of punishment from the parent of the same sex. According to Freud, the conflict surrounding the forbidden incest wish reached crisis proportions toward the end of the phallic stage (around the age of 5 or 6) and was "solved" by the defense mechanism of repression. Repression brought about a period of psychosexual latency lasting from about the age of 6 to the age of 12.

The term *Oedipus complex* is derived from the Greek tragedy *Oedipus Rex* in which a man inadvertently slays his own father and marries his own mother. Freud believed that the play revealed a universal theme and that all children must cope with their incest wishes. Although the word *Oedipus* suggests a male, the term *Oedipus complex* is appropriately used to refer to either males or females. However, the term *Electra complex* is sometimes used as a synonym for *Oedipus complex* when talking about women.

There is no consensus among clinicians concerning the importance of the Oedipus complex. Many believe that Freud exaggerated its importance. Others argue that it is far from universal.

However, it can be noted that, at least in some cases, patients have incest wishes or incest fantasies toward their opposite sex parents. In these instances, Freud's hypothesis that incomplete repression of an

Oedipus complex can be a factor in sexual disorders certainly seems to be of some value.

See also *Electra complex; Freud, Sigmund; latency stage; phallic stage; psychosexual development.*

one-parent family: A family unit consisting on one parent and a child or children. One-parent families are common. It is estimated that about 50 percent of children are raised by one parent for approximately four or five years. In nine out of ten cases, a mother heads the single-parent household. The three principal causes of one-parent families are (1) death of a spouse, (2) unwed motherhood, and (3) divorce or separation. The third cause is the most common one.

A substantial amount of research has been conducted to evaluate the effects of the one-parent family on children. In general, it can be said that there is a higher incidence of adjustment problems among children in one-parent families than in two-parent families. This has been attributed to a number of factors, such as the absence of a father, low income, and the trauma of divorce. In spite of these findings, it is important to note that the results cited are *statistical* and do not necessarily reflect *individual* status. There are maladjusted children in two-parent families. And there are many well-adjusted children in one-parent families. Such factors as differences in parental effectiveness, temperament of the particular child, and other psychological factors account for these variations among children in both kinds of families.

See also *divorce; extended family; maladjusted child; nuclear family; parental style.*

one-word stage: A stage in language development that usually appears around the age of 18 months. Infants abstract words from the strings of vocalizations they hear and then attempt to imitate these units of meaning. At first, they will often speak simplified versions of more complex words. For example, *spaghetti* might be spoken as "getti." In the beginning, the first words are usually nouns and common objects of perception, such as the parents, food, and toys.

The one-word stage is normal and is to be expected. It appears in virtually all children in all cultures. When one word is used to stand for a whole sentence, this is referred to as a *holophrase.*

See also *babbling; Chomsky, Noam Avram; holophrase; language acquisition device (LAD); language development.*

onlooker play: A kind of play in which a child passively observes other children at play. Indeed, this kind of "play" can hardly be called play at all and often has a wistful, helpless quality to it. It upsets parents and caregivers to see a child looking on, unable to join in. However, it must be realized that it is both normal and common, particularly when a child is a toddler or in the early preschool years. By 5 years of age, onlooker play usually diminishes greatly and gives way to higher levels of associative and cooperative play.

See also *cooperative play; parallel play; play; solitary play.*

only child: A child with no siblings. Research on only children suggests that in general they tend to fare quite well. Attributes associated with only-child status are (1) high achievement, (2) rapid language development, (3) sociability, and (4) above-average IQ scores.

Folklore suggests that an only child will be spoiled, egocentric, neurotic, and maladjusted because he or she will be made to feel "too special." G. Stanley Hall, an early pioneer in the study of child development, said, "Being an only child is a disease in itself." There are no data to support the common idea that being without brothers and sisters handicaps normal development. Indeed, most evidence gathered by behavioral science is to the contrary.

See also *birth order; Hall, Granville Stanley; sibling rivalry.*

ontogenetic development: The development of the individual. The Greek root *onto* means "being" or "existence." *Genetic,* in the present context, suggests "the process of growth or becoming." Thus, *ontogenetic development* refers to the whole process of becoming a person from the moment of conception. During the fetal stage, ontogenetic development is primarily biological in nature. After birth, ontogenetic development has both biological and psychological features. For example, Piaget often spoke of his theory of cognitive development as a kind of ontogenesis.

See also *cognitive development; fetal development; ontogeny recapitulates phylogeny.*

ontogeny recapitulates phylogeny: In biology, a tendency during prenatal development for the organism to go through stages that briefly resemble species of life (i.e., phyla) lower on the evolutionary ladder than human beings. Prior to birth, there are times when the human organism is somewhat like a fish, an amphibian, a reptile, and a nonhuman primate.

The basic idea of *recapitulation* was applied to psychology by G. Stanley Hall in the 1910s. He believed that children go through stages that resemble the social evolution of the human race. Infants were compared to unsocialized savages who cannot control their anger or appetites. Young children like to explore and hunt like cave dwellers. They also have magical ideas and superstitions like stone-age savages. Hall's idea has not won much acceptance, and today the idea of recapitulation at the behavioral level is discounted as being of little or no value.

See also *fetal development; Hall, Granville Stanley; ontogenetic development; socialization.*

open classroom: A learning environment that allows the student a high level of self-directed behavior and a range of choice in activities. Unlike the traditional classroom in which a teacher offers structured information to a group of students who sit at desks, face forward, and listen, in the open classroom children can start and finish tasks at will, help or be helped by other children, and be active without fear of criticism. The teacher roves, answers questions, and gives guidance in a nonauthoritarian manner. In practice, the open classroom has been used primarily in elementary education. (Laboratory hours in high school and college science classes are similar to open classrooms, although they are seldom given the label.)

Advocates of the open classroom assert that it encourages creative thinking and takes advantage of the child's natural curiosity. Self-directed learning tends to be exciting and interesting. Children learn by doing. Opponents of the open classroom say that students often do not adequately acquire basic writing and arithmetical skills, that the unstructured atmosphere encourages a lack of respect for elders, and important personality attributes such as self-discipline are neglected.

Open classrooms have been associated mainly with research programs, Head Start Programs, and the Montessori method. They have not become a major trend in elementary schools. However, variations of the open classroom are often used. It is not unusual for a traditional classroom to employ a period of self-directed activity. Open classrooms are often a part of special programs for gifted children.

Although open classrooms have a number of drawbacks, research does suggest that they do have a positive impact on creative thinking. They also tend to foster cooperative activity among children.

See also *creative thinking; Dewey, John; Head Start programs; Montessori, Maria; Montessori method; progressive education.*

operant conditioning: A kind of learning in which actions are modified by their own consequences. Another way to describe *operant conditioning* is to say that it traditionally involves the shaping of observable actions through the use of reinforcers. The term *operant* is used for any action that has an immediate effect upon the physical or social environment. Operant behavior is a common part of everyday life for both children and adults. A child pulls a string on a talking doll and the operant (i.e., pulling the string) is reinforced by the sound of the doll's voice. A child or adult flicks a wall switch and is reinforced when a light comes on. A college professor tells a joke and is reinforced when the class laughs.

In general, operants that are reinforced tend to increase in frequency. Operants that are not reinforced tend to decrease in frequency (i.e., extinguish). The basic outline for operant conditioning is clearly seen in the early rat and pigeon experiments of B. F. Skinner. A rat presses a lever, and this operant is reinforced with food pellets. A pigeon pecks at a lighted disc, and this operant is reinforced with grain. The training device that Skinner used is called the *operant conditioning apparatus* or, informally, the *Skinner box.*

It is important to appreciate that operant conditioning is a pervasive principle affecting a wide range of behavior. The idea that behavior is modified by its own consequences is a powerful one that lends itself to many applications in areas such as behavior modification with children, teaching machines, and the self-management of behavior.

See also *behavior modification; classical conditioning; conditioning; extinction; reinforcer; Skinner, Burrhus Frederic.*

operational thinking: See *concrete operations stage.*

oppositional defiant disorder: A behavioral disorder that is associated with childhood and adolescence and that is characterized by a negative and hostile attitude toward adults in positions of authority, particularly parents. Examples of specific behaviors that suggest the presence of the disorder are temperamental outbursts, arguing with parents, refusing to do household chores, acting in an annoying manner on purpose, refusing to accept responsibility for mistakes and errors, and using foul language. On the whole, a picture emerges of an extremely troublesome and willful child or adolescent. The disorder is a problem primarily within the family setting.

It is important to realize that the maladaptive behavior is displayed with an intensity and a frequency that is substantially greater than average for children and adolescents of the same age. This needs to be established before a diagnosis of oppositional defiant disorder is warranted.

In children, the disorder is more common in males. In adolescents, the disorder is equally common in both sexes.

Not much reliable data exists concerning the causal factors involved in this disorder. However, it is reasonable to speculate that the causal factors are similar to those involved in conduct disorder. Three factors of particular importance appear to be emotionally cold parents, too much punishment, and absence of a stable home environment. Informally, it appears that parents who are not affectionate and who also rely on an authoritarian parental style are somewhat more likely to induce, or aggravate, an oppositional defiant disorder.

Oppositional defiant disorder is very similar to conduct disorder and, in some cases, progresses into it. A conduct disorder is more severe than an oppositional defiant disorder.

Treatment for oppositional defiant disorder is similar to treatment for conduct disorder. It consists of counseling and psychotherapy. A therapeutic approach in which the troubled child or adolescent is helped to see the adverse long-run consequences of defiant behavior may be helpful.

See also *attention-deficit hyperactivity disorder (ADHD); child psychotherapy; conduct disorder; psychotherapy.*

oral stage: In Freud's theory, the first stage of psychosexual development, the stage associated with infancy, the time from birth to about 18 to 24 months of age. Freud hypothesized that libido (i.e., psychosexual energy) was concentrated in the oral zone during this time period. Thus, this zone is the first erogenous zone (i.e., zone of sexual pleasure).

See also *Freud, Sigmund; libido; psychoanalysis; psychosexual development.*

orienting response: A tendency to respond to a change of stimulation with increased excitement and alertness. The purpose of the orienting response is to increase the individual's level of attention to selected portions of the environment. Informally, people find novelty interesting.

One of the first researchers to identify the orienting response was Ivan Pavlov. When he trained a dog to salivate to a sound, he noticed that when the sound was first introduced, the dog perked up its ears, became more alert, and turned its head in the direction of the sound.

The orienting response is present in human infants. Changes in the level of illumination around an infant, the loudness of someone's voice, the sounding of a doorbell, and the presentation of a new rattle are all examples of stimuli that will elicit the response. An important aspect of the orienting response is adaptation to it. *Adaptation* refers to the gradual lessening of the capacity of a stimulus to elicit a response. Research with infants has shown that if a stimulus is repeated in a predictable manner, the stimulus becomes boring to the infant. However, change the stimulus even slightly and the orienting response will be elicited. For example, say "Plop!" every five seconds to a 3-month-old infant. At first, there will be excitement and interest. But attention will diminish with every repeated "Plop!" Now, after the tenth repetition, say "Blip!" and there will be another elicitation of the orienting response. In studies, the existence of the orienting response is confirmed by changes in heart rate, pupil size, and other similar factors.

As indicated, the orienting response is present in infancy, and it remains with us throughout life.

See also *classical conditioning; neonatal reflexes; Pavlov, Ivan Petrovich.*

orphan: A minor child who has no living parents. Informally, sometimes the word *orphan* is used to refer to a child who has only one living parent. The word is also used to describe a *waif*, a homeless, neglected child.

Various studies of orphans in infancy and early childhood suggest that they usually obtain lower scores on tests of intelligence, motor development, and emotional adjustment than do children in general. Evidence suggests that this is because most orphans, often institutionalized, have to cope with an impoverished environment. If institutional care is improved or if an orphan is adopted by a loving family, the rate and quality of development may improve.

See also *adopted child; adoptive parent; anaclitic depression; feral child; institutionalization; institutionalized children;* parens patriae.

ovaries: The female reproductive glands. The ovaries are so named because they are somewhat "oval" in shape, like almonds. Ovaries are a little over one inch in length and a little under one inch in width. They produce *ova*, egg cells essential to reproduction. These are deposited, when ripe, about once a month into a given ovary's associated fallopian tube. The ovaries also produce estrogen hormones, progesterone, and other important hormones. In some cases, for various reasons, a female may have only one ovary. (Or only one ovary may be functional.) Under these circumstances, it is still possible for her to have children.

Adolescent females begin to produce ripe ova about one year after the menarche. At this time, they are said to be nubile.

See also *estrogen hormones; menarche; nubile female; ovum; testes.*

overanxious disorder: A disorder that is associated with either child-hood or adolescence and that is characterized primarily by persistent anxiety. The young person's mental and emotional life is clouded by irrational apprehension, consternation over real or imagined mistakes, misgivings concerning ability, and dread of coming events. Related symptoms include tension, headaches, and upset stomach. If the disorder continues past the age of 18, it often develops into one of the anxiety disorders.

The disorder occurs with a relatively high rate of frequency. Males are more often afflicted than females. The oldest child in the family is more likely to have the disorder than siblings. Children in large families tend not to display the disorder. It is speculated that a small family in which the child carries a large burden of emotional respon-sibility and in which the parents are overcontrolling and set very rigid high standards contributes to the formation of the disorder. It is also reasonable to hypothesize that inborn traits of temperament may make some contribution to the disorder.

Psychiatric treatment for the disorder includes the prescription of tranquilizing drugs. However, this approach is recommended only if the disorder disables the patient. Often, counseling and therapy de-signed to help the child or adolescent express feelings more openly and to become more assertive are helpful.

See also *anxiety; childhood neurosis; drug therapy.*

overdependent behavior: As exhibited in younger children, a pattern characterized by such individual behaviors as inappropriate clinging, crying, pleading, whining, and shyness. The child seems to be con-stantly turning to a parent or caregiver for emotional support and/or permission to act. Older children and adolescents who are overdependent are often very demanding of their parents, asking that clothes be taken care of, rooms tidied, hair combed, and so forth. They ask for a lot of time, attention, and sympathy. The basic message seems to be "Take care of me" or "I need your help to do anything."

Several factors may coincide to cause overdependent behavior.

1. The child's innate temperament may be an inhibited one, and it is possible that this contributes to lack of self-confidence.

2. Parents may reinforce overdependent behavior by catering to it and giving it increasing strength. Overprotectiveness is related to this factor.

3. Some children may use overdependent behavior as a way to express their need for power; it is a way to control and manipulate parents.

4. Overdependent behavior may be a sign of chronic anxiety in the child.

5. Feelings of emotional deprivation or lack of confidence in parental love may contribute to a child's excessive demands.

Parents can cope with overdependent behavior by avoiding its reinforcement. In order to do this, they have to examine their own behavior and evaluate how it may strengthen the overdependent behavior. Behavior modification skills are very helpful in this regard. Counseling and child psychotherapy may be required in some cases.

See also *anxiety; behavior modification; child psychotherapy; overanxious disorder; overprotection; parental style; reinforcement.*

overprotection: As formulated in psychoanalysis, an attribute of the parent-child relationship such that the parent will attempt to shield the child from the natural risks and hazards of life. One can speak of overprotection only if the parental behavior is excessive and rather obviously pathological. For example, an overprotective parent might not allow a child to learn to roller skate because it is possible to sprain an ankle or break a leg while roller skating. Another overprotective parent might insist that a child wear a sweater if there is the slightest breeze. The *concerned* parent is, of course, protective in a *rational* way.

Psychoanalysis interprets overprotection in terms of a reaction formation, an ego defense mechanism. The basic idea is that the parent in question has repressed hostility toward the child. At an unconscious level, it is possible that the parent wishes the child harm. In order for the parent to protect his or her ego, that is, to maintain a positive self-concept, he or she converts this unconscious hostility to conscious affection. The artificial quality of the affection is betrayed by the compulsive "watchdog" attitude toward the child's welfare.

The psychoanalytic interpretation certainly seems appropriate in some cases. However, it is possible to interpret overprotective behavior in other ways. A car owner is often overprotective toward a new car. This is hardly unconscious hostility toward the car. The excessive care and caution manifested toward the car almost certainly arises from the fact that the car may, for the moment, be overvalued in the owner's eyes. It is also possible for a parent to feel the same way. Parents who have only one or two children, who waited a long time for children, or who had to go through fertility counseling in order to conceive a child may all have a tendency to be overprotective.

Nevertheless, whatever the cause, it has been suggested that overprotection can have an adverse affect on a child's development. Psychoanalysis hypothesizes that it may be a contributing factor to a neurotic process.

See also *childhood neurosis; ego defense mechanisms; reaction formation.*

oversleeping: see *narcolepsy.*

overweight: See *obesity.*

ovum: An egg cell produced by a female's ovary. (*Ova* is the plural form of *ovum.*) An ovum is about 0.04 inch in diameter, or the size of a period at the end of a sentence. Each human ovum contains 23 *individual* chromosomes instead of pairs due to the reduction process called *meiosis.* Also, each 23rd chromosome is an X, or female, chromosome. Therefore, it is sperm cells, which carry either an X or a Y chromosome, that will determine the eventual sex of a child.

A female infant is born with a total of about 2,000,000 ova. Only about 400 of these will become mature, released eggs.

See also *chromosomes; meiosis; mitosis; ovaries; sperm cells.*

P

pacifier: A device made of a combination of plastic and rubber, somewhat similar in structure and texture to the human nipple. Infants who suck, bite, or chew on a pacifier appear to be tranquilized, soothed, or "pacified" by the object—hence its name. Infants who use a pacifier seldom develop the habit of thumbsucking. It is possible that the use of a pacifier throughout infancy and toddlerhood may have a negative effect on the formation of teeth and the child's bite. However, this effect is usually quite slight compared to the effect associated with thumbsucking. Very few children will continue to use a pacifier past the age of 3. In contrast, if there is a thumbsucking habit, it may tend to persist.

Pacifier use has value primarily because it helps to (1) meet an infant's oral needs and (2) prevent thumbsucking.

See also *oral stage; thumbsucking.*

palmar grasp reflex (Darwinian reflex): One of the reflexes that is present in the neonate and that is characterized by the fingers closing around, or grasping, an object such as a finger or a pencil that is placed crosswise on the palm. Charles Darwin, a principal founder of the theory of evolution, suggested that the purpose of the palmar grasp reflex in infancy is to hold on to the mother when there is a threat of being dropped. Therefore, the reflex is sometimes called the *Darwinian reflex.* The reflex has a short developmental time span and will usually be gone around the age of 3 or 4 months. The presence of the reflex is one of the signs that the infant is neurologically normal.

See also *neonatal reflexes*.

parallel play: A kind of play characterized by a lack of meaningful exchange or shared rules between two or more children. Parallel play is associated with toddlerhood and is a stepping stone to the cooperative play exhibited by older children. Although parallel play is in a sense "social," it is only roughly so. For example, assume that two toddlers are together in a sandbox. They are each engaged in their own self-defined play activity and stay out of each other's way. One is pretending that an airplane is taking off and landing, while the other one is making a "mountain" of sand. Parents watching may say that they are "playing together." This is correct only in a physical, not a psychological, sense. In parallel play, each child is in his or her own play world.

See also *cooperative play; onlooker play; play; solitary play.*

parens patriae: A legal term derived from Latin meaning "the parent is the fatherland." It is the power of an individual state, not the federal government, to assume a parental role for individuals who are without a responsible guardian and unable to care for themselves. Applied to children, the power is invoked in cases where parents do not offer appropriate care and custody, thus abusing or neglecting the children. *Parens patriae* can also be invoked when a child is an orphan without adequate protection. Under *parens patriae*, the child becomes a ward of the state, and the state as guardian is charged with doing its best for the child's long-term welfare.

See also *adopted child; adoptive parent; child abuse;* in loco parentis; *orphan; stepparent.*

parent effectiveness training (P.E.T.): As formulated by the clinical psychologist Thomas Gordon, a set of explicit skills designed to bring about no-lose conflict resolution between parents and their children.

Four of the most important skills are (1) defining unacceptable behaviors, (2) identifying problem ownership, (3) active listening, and (4) I-messages.

1. *Defining unacceptable behaviors* requires a parent to divide behaviors into two categories: acceptable and unacceptable. Often parents waste time trying to change behaviors in children that are, after all, more or less acceptable. For example, suppose that a parent is unhappy with a child's table manners. It may not be necessary to adopt the overly general position that "everything that the child does at the table is wrong." Perhaps reflection will reveal that some aspects of the child's table manners are acceptable and other aspects are unacceptable. Efforts to change the child's manners should be directed only to the unacceptable aspects. The child will not then feel "picked on" unfairly for everything and anything.

2. *Identifying problem ownership* requires that parents ask themselves the question, "Who owns this problem?" Is it the child's problem or the parent's problem? If a child has had a falling out with a best friend, it is not the parent's problem. And the parent does not have to struggle to figure out a solution.

3. *Active listening* involves decoding a child's statements and looking for the emotional content. Suppose that 14-year-old Nola says to her mother, "Mrs. Jones is such a jerk! She gave us a surprise algebra test today." A parent who is responding only to the surface content of Nola's complaint might say, "Now, Nola, that isn't nice. I met Mrs. Jones and she's a very lovely person." On the other hand, a parent who uses active listening might say, "You're very angry at Mrs. Jones. She didn't give you time to prepare and study adequately for the test."

4. *I-messages* require that parents state their own perception of an experience. I-messages are contrasted with *you-messages* in which a child is blamed or criticized. For example, a parent can say "I'm tired and don't want to play checkers with you tonight" instead of "You're such a pest. Can't you ever leave me alone?"

Parent effectiveness training courses and workshops have been offered in many areas of the country. Gordon's popular book *P.E.T.-*

Parent Effectiveness Training sets forth a set of basic skills with numerous examples.

See also *communication skills; parental style; self-esteem.*

Parent ego state: See *ego state.*

parental style: The characteristic way or ways a parent interacts with a child. There are two broadly conceived dimensions to parental style: (1) Authoritarian-Permissive and (2) Accepting-Rejecting. Each dimension has bipolar aspects to it.

In the case of the first dimension, an *authoritarian* style at one extreme is manifest in parents who are overcontrolling, possessive, and overprotective. A *permissive* style at the other extreme is manifest in parents who are detached, allow the child too much freedom, and do not set well-defined limits on behavior. The optimal region between the two extremes is called a *democratic* style, which is manifest in parents who allow the child as much autonomy as possible, have well-defined values, and set realistic limits on unacceptable behavior.

In the case of the second dimension, an *accepting* style at one extreme is manifest in parents who give a child unconditional love and who are often overindulgent. A *rejecting* style at the other extreme is manifest in parents who tend to be emotionally remote, hostile, and generally lacking in displays of affection. The optimal region between the two extremes is a combination of unconditional love and the *conditional* giving and withholding of the tokens of love, not love itself. The *tokens of love* are smiles, hugs, kisses, and other social rewards for approved behavior.

The two dimensions and their intersection generate five basic parental styles.

1. *Authoritarian-Accepting.* This style contributes to traits in children such as overdependence, lack of assertiveness, insecurity, lack of creativity, and excessive obedience.
2. *Permissive-Accepting.* This style contributes to traits in children such as lack of impulse control, aggressiveness, self-absorption, and egotism.

3. *Authoritarian-Rejecting*. This style contributes to traits in children such as sullenness, shyness, inability to express hostility effectively, and self-aggression.

4. *Permissive-Rejecting*. This style contributes to traits in children such as disobedience, aggressiveness, defiance, resentment, and delinquent behavior.

5. *Democratic-Accepting*. This style is the optimal one and is the image toward which parents should consider striving. The democratic-accepting style contributes to traits in children such as autonomy, a robust sense of self, assertiveness, and creativity. It is distinctly associated with high self-esteem.

It is important to realize that although parental style is a contributing factor to behavioral traits in children, it is not the only one. Temperament, birth order, peer groups, and other factors also play significant roles.

See also *authoritarian parent; communication skills; discipline; parent effectiveness training (P.E.T.); permissive parent.*

Parents Anonymous (PA): A national self-help organization for abusing parents. Parents Anonymous has a recovery program somewhat similar to those advocated by other self-help organizations, such as Alcoholics Anonymous (AA) and Overeaters Anonymous (OA).

PA assumes that personal recovery from a tendency to be abusive is difficult, if not in some cases impossible, without the help and support of other people. There are about 1,500 PA chapters. Members maintain telephone contacts and visit each other's homes. In group meetings, participants talk over parental styles, attitudes toward children, and ways to avoid abusive patterns. There are no professional fees. The PA approach is quite effective, and about one-half of those who attend meetings report good results.

The telephone numbers and locations of PA groups are available through local directories, mental health clinics, family service agencies, and counseling centers.

See also *abusing parent; child abuse; parental style.*

partial reinforcement: Any method of reinforcing behavior in which a defined action is reinforced some of the time. (*Continuous reinforcement* is the term used to identify the reinforcement of every defined action.) For example, if Nancy, a preschooler, is praised every second or third time she makes her bed on successive mornings, she is receiving partial reinforcement for bed-making. A large body of research has convincingly shown that habits acquired by partial reinforcement have more resistance to extinction than habits acquired by continuous reinforcement. Put another way, habits acquired by partial reinforcement tend to be very strong ones. Therefore, parents are well-advised to build desirable habits in their children by offering reinforcement on a slightly irregular basis.

A practical strategy is to start by reinforcing a desirable defined action every time at first, then every other time, and then somewhat randomly.

See also *behavior modification*; *extinction*; *operant conditioning*; *reinforcer*.

passive vocabulary: The vocabulary that a person is using when listening or reading. Passive vocabulary is used, for example, when paying attention to what someone else is saying, when listening to the radio or watching television, or when studying or just reading in general.

See also *active vocabulary*.

passive-aggressive behavior: See *aggressiveness*.

Pavlov, Ivan Petrovich (1849–1936): A Russian physiologist and researcher into the process of classical conditioning. Pavlov received his medical degree from the University of St. Petersburg in 1833 and won a Nobel prize in 1904 for his research on the physiology of the digestive glands. It was subsequent to the winning of that award that he turned to the experimental investigation of conditioned reflexes in dogs.

In one of his sets of experiments, Pavlov was able to demonstrate that it was possible to create behavioral pathology in previously agreeable dogs by forcing them to make difficult discriminations.

This phenomenon is called *experimental neurosis,* and it has suggested to many students of abnormal psychology that a similar process may operate in human beings. In particular, it was asserted by the anthropologist Gregory Bateson that double-bind communication patterns, patterns in which a parent creates a series of insolvable psychological problems for a child, can induce neurotic anxiety or aggravate a mental disorder such as schizophrenia. Bateson's viewpoint was shared by the British psychiatrist Ronald D. Laing, who made a study of the psychosocial factors contributing to schizophrenia.

Pavlov took the point of view that science alone can bring enlightenment to the human race. He asserted that behavior can be explained without recourse to vague or mysterious forces. On the contrary, he believed that behavior is a part of the natural world and can be understood as such. This outlook on Pavlov's part had a great influence on John B. Watson, the father of behaviorism, and, in turn, on B. F. Skinner, known for his research on operant conditioning.

Pavlov is looked upon as the father of modern learning theory. His work remains an inspiration to behavior therapists.

One of Pavlov's principal works is *Conditioned Reflexes* (1927).

See also *anxiety; behavior therapy; childhood neurosis; childhood schizophrenia; classical conditioning; communication skills; learning; operant conditioning; parental style; Skinner, Burrhus Frederick; Watson, John Broadus.*

pavor nocturnus: See *night terror.*

peer group: A group of individuals who share a common important feature, such as age, sex, intelligence level, or social status. As used in developmental psychology, the term usually applies to children or adolescents who are the same age or who are at the same grade level in school.

Peer groups become a significant factor in development when a child starts grammar school, and they continue to be of importance throughout high school—and often in college. In the preschool years, the impact of the parents on development is paramount. (This is true even if the child spends some time in day care or a preschool.)

In high school, peer groups often appear to exert more power to shape the behavior and attitudes of adolescents than do the parents. Choices made in regard to drug and alcohol use, sexual activity, music, mode of dress, and so forth, are heavily under the influence of peer groups. It should be noted that most adolescents spend substantially more time interacting with their peers than with their parents. Also, adolescents want to be accepted and well-liked. Consequently, they often conform to peer-group values even if these are sometimes at odds with parental values.

It should not be concluded that peer groups encourage only undesirable values. They frequently support such values as courage, friendliness, cooperation, loyalty, and so forth. Peer groups are essential to the socialization process.

See also *adolescence; adolescent sex relations; generation gap; socialization.*

penis envy: An early psychoanalytic concept hypothesizing that women in general have an unconscious wish to have a penis. Freud proposed that the wish has its origin in the phallic stage of development (i.e., during the preschool years). The girl may see the penis of her father or of a brother and develop the idea that something is missing from her anatomy.

A more mature version of *penis envy* is to suggest that the female does not literally wish for a penis but envies the status and power that being a male confers on the individual. She wants not the penis itself but what the penis can bring. This describes a revision of classical psychoanalysis and is not what Freud had in mind.

In psychoanalytic theory, the well-adjusted adolescent female has given up the infantile wish for the penis, has made her peace with the facts of life, and accepts the both the biological and cultural roles associated with her gender.

The concept of *penis envy* has been criticized on several counts. First, it suggests that biological normality is perceived as biological abnormality by the young female. This appears to be a somewhat doubtful idea. Second, it hypothesizes that penis envy is universal among females, which seems highly unlikely. Third, it appears to relegate women to a secondary status. As a consequence of these and similar criticisms, Freud has been accused by some feminists of male chauvinism. Contemporary defenders of Freud argue that he himself was not a male chauvinist, but that the concept of *penis envy* reflects in the psychology of the individual the reality of a sexist culture.

See also *castration complex; Freud, Sigmund; Oedipus complex; phallic stage; psychoanalysis; psychosexual development.*

perceptual development in infancy: The development, during the first 18 to 24 months of life, of the ability to use the senses effectively. Traditionally, there are five external senses and two internal senses, all of which are present in the neonate

The external senses—vision, hearing, taste, smell, and touch—are those through which a person gathers information about the external world. (The familiar term *touch* is somewhat misleading when used to identify a single sense. It is more accurate to speak of the *skin senses.* These include not only touch but also pain and temperature.)

The internal senses are the vestibular sense and kinesthesis. The *vestibular sense* allows a person to maintain a sense of balance while walking; it also makes it possible to be aware of acceleration or deceleration in a vehicle, even with the eyes closed. *Kinesthesis* makes it possible for a person to feel the movements of his or her limbs, fingers, and other body parts.

Both maturation and learning are required to bring sensory processes to full fruition. Research psychologists have been very interested in the sensory capacities of neonates and the subsequent development of those capacities during infancy. By the time normal children are about 2 years of age, their senses are usually functioning very efficiently.

See also *hearing impairment; motor development; visual impairment.*

perfectionism: A trait evident in some children that is characterized by an excessive desire for order, neatness, organization of details, clean things, and so forth. Often, perfectionistic children are unhappy with any test grade less than an *A.* Although perfectionism might seem to be a desirable trait, it is not. The child is in fact overly fussy and compulsive. The behavior can be interpreted as a way of controlling anxiety and is a sign of insecurity. Loosely speaking, perfectionism is associated with childhood neurosis.

The parent can help the child by looking for ways to make the child feel more emotionally secure. Also, in the older child or adolescent, the parent can point out, without criticism of the child's personality, that the child's thinking reflects an overly demanding either-or approach to the world and life. The child should be helped to adopt a somewhat more relaxed outlook. If the problem persists, child psychotherapy may of value.

See also *anxiety; child psychotherapy; childhood neurosis.*

perinatal period: The span of time beginning 28 weeks (approximately 6 months) after conception and ending 1 week after a child is born. The bulk of the perinatal period can also be described as the last trimester of pregnancy. A premature birth is defined as one taking place between the sixth and eighth months of pregnancy, or during the first two months of the perinatal period.

See also *fetal development; gestation period; immature birth; mature birth; premature birth.*

permissive parent: See *parental style.*

personality development: The process, over time, by which an infant becomes an individual with both a character and a sense of self. The character is the set of unique behavioral traits and dispositions seen from an outsider's viewpoint. The self is the person experienced from one's own inner viewpoint. (The ego, or the "I," is the conscious center of this self.) The process is a complex one involving a set of factors that include the effects of genetic predispositions, the family, peers, and cultural attitudes.

The most well-known personality theory is Freud's. It describes both the structure of personality and its development. According to Freud, the infant is born only with the *id*, a set of primitive biological drives oriented toward fantasy and pleasure. Encounters with the world of fact force the formation of the *ego*, the agent of the personality oriented toward reality. The ego is present in most toddlers. They think and say, "I want," "I will," "I won't," and so forth. And they know their own first names. All of these simple facts suggest the existence of an ego. With more experience, the sense of shame develops, and out of this, the sense of guilt. These, in the preschool child, represent the *superego*, the agent within the child representing the values of the family and society. With the formation of the superego, the basic structure of the personality is in place.

Another major theory of personality development, Erik Erikson's psychosocial theory, accepts Freud's basic structural model. However, Erikson describes how such developmental tasks as the formation of trust, autonomy, identity, and intimacy affect one's *social self*, the individual as he or she typically relates to other people.

Although the theories of psychoanalysis have been extremely influential, they do not offer the last word in personality development. As set forth in various entries in this encyclopedia, genetic factors, social learning, reinforcement, and temperament all play significant roles in personality development.

See also *ego; Erikson, Erik Homburger; Freud, Sigmund; genetic predisposition; id; psychosocial development; reinforcer; social learning; superego; temperament.*

pervasive developmental disorders: See *developmental disorders.*

petit mal seizures: See *epilepsy.*

phallic stage: In Freud's theory, the third stage of psychosexual development, the stage associated with the preschool period, the time from about 3 to 5 years of age. During the phallic stage, the child's libido, or psychosexual energy, is concentrated in the phallus. (In anatomy, the phallus is the penis in males and the clitoris in females.) During this stage the child receives erotic pleasure from self-stimulation of the phallus.

All of the preceding is according to Freud. Based on his clinical data, which were primarily reports from his patients, Freud concluded that the phallic stage is a universal one. If this is so, one might expect that all children engage in childhood masturbation during this stage. Research based on interviews with parents give some, but not complete, support to Freud's view. The conclusion is that childhood masturbation is both common and normal during the preschool years, but not necessarily universal.

See also *Freud, Sigmund; psychoanalysis; psychosexual development.*

phencyclidine (PCP): One of the drugs that is sometimes cited in connection with drug abuse in adolescence. Phencyclidine is a hallucinogenic drug, popularly known as "angel dust." Although PCP is classified as a hallucinogen, this is somewhat misleading because the taking of the drug seldom causes hallucinations. It is probably more correct to broadly classify PCP as a *psychoactive drug*. Small doses of PCP produce a reaction in the individual similar to intoxication. The individual becomes somewhat more impulsive, and thinking becomes confused. The problem is with high doses. These are capable of producing a delirium. The individual loses the ability to think clearly and becomes very confused.

There are many reports stating that PCP users become violent. The violence seems to be primarily reactive in nature. If left alone, the user will probably sink into a sort of temporary personal oblivion. However, if frustrated, restrained, or arrested by police officers, then aggressive and assaultive behavior can result. It is also reported that PCP users are "hard to stop" when they are fighting off others. This seems to be correct because PCP has anesthetic properties. The person in a PCP delirium "feels no pain."

Because PCP does not induce euphoria, it has been hard for nonusers to see why anyone would abuse the drug or take it on a recreational basis. The key seems to be related to (1) the drug's ability to blot out consciousness and (2) the lack of subsequent recall of the PCP state. Thus, it can be reasoned that the PCP user is not looking for a "high" or a pleasant experience. He or she is looking for temporary oblivion.

Unfortunately, PCP is an abused drug. It has little practical value for human beings, and it is not used in the practice of medicine. Frequent use of the drug produces significant adverse effects on intellectual abilities. On the hopeful side, one does not acquire a physiological addiction to PCP. Thus, from the organic point of view, withdrawal is not a great problem. However, it should be noted that psychological addiction can be a problem; the person becomes emotionally dependent on the drug. Therefore, counseling and psychotherapy may be required to help the individual stay away from the drug on a permanent basis.

See also *drug abuse in adolescence; hallucinogens; lysergic acid diethylamide-25 (LSD); marijuana.*

phenotype: See *genotype*.

phenylketonuria (PKU): A defect of metabolism that is present in some infants and that is capable of causing mental retardation. (The disease is also known as *phenylpyruvic oligophrenia*.) The neonate with phenylketonuria (PKU) lacks a specific enzyme critical in the digestion of *phenylalanine*, one of the amino acids. If phenylalanine builds up in the blood stream in large amounts, injury to the central nervous system can occur.

Physical signs and symptoms usually become quite evident toward the end of an infant's first year of life. They include an unpleasant smell, digestive upset, and skin problems.

Most states now require that the urine or blood of infants be tested for the presence of *phenylpyruvic acid*, a substance indicating an excess of phenylalanine. If a child has PKU, he or she can be placed on a special diet that is free of proteins containing phenylalanine. In practical terms, this will be a diet that is free of meats and animal products such as milk and cheese. Naturally, consultation with a physician and dietician is important to determine the optimal diet for a particular child.

Research suggests that PKU is a recessive inherited disorder. The incidence of PKU in infants is estimated to be between 1 in 10,000 and 1 in 20,000. About 1 percent of hospitalized patients with mental retardation suffer from PKU.

See also *mental retardation*.

phobia: An irrational, stubborn fear of specific kinds of animals, people, things, or situations. Minor phobias are fairly common in children and adolescents, and their presence alone is not enough to justify the diagnosis of a serious behavioral disorder. The problems associated with the phobia should be either incapacitating or greatly interfere with the course of living before a condition receives a clinical label.

There are three principal kinds of phobia. *Agoraphobia* is characterized by a set of related fears including the fear of being alone, fear of public places, and fear of traveling any significant distance from home. *Social phobia* is characterized by a fear of placing oneself in situations where others have an opportunity to observe or judge one's behavior. Social phobias are usually specific in nature. For example, the individual may be afraid to speak in public, to go to a party and meet new people, to use a public rest room, and so forth. *Simple phobia* is characterized by a given irrational fear.

Some well-known simple phobias are: (1) *acrophobia*, a fear of high places; (2) *claustrophobia*, a fear of confinement or closed areas; (3) *cynophobia*, a fear of dogs; (4) *demophobia*, a fear of crowds; (5) *haptephobia*, a fear of being touched; (6) *hemophobia*, a fear of blood; (7) *hypnophobia*, a fear of sleep; (8) *necrophobia*, a fear of dead bodies; (9) *nyctophobia*, a fear of darkness or the night; (10) *ophidiophobia*, a fear of reptiles; and (11) *zoophobia*, a fear of animals.

Although both sexes can and do develop phobias, they tend to be more commonly diagnosed in females.

Broadly speaking, there tend to be two general approaches to explaining phobias. First, psychoanalysis tends to see them as symbolical representations. The situation or object consciously feared is not what is actually feared. The consciously feared stimulus stands for an unconscious wish, one that has been repressed. The actual fear is that one will act on a forbidden impulse, the one contained in the forbidden wish. Thus, a fear of heights might be a protective mechanism against an adolescent's wish to commit suicide by leaping from a tall building.

Second, behavioral psychology tends to see phobias as having a learned basis. They are generalizations from prior experiences. A fear of dogs, and perhaps other animals, might be based on the fact that one was once injured badly by a dog. The behavioral approach is useful for explaining simple phobias in children.

Although the two general explanations are usually presented as contradictory in nature, they need not be, in specific clinical cases. It is certainly reasonable to say that one child's fear is based on a repressed wish and a second child's fear is based on generalization from a prior experience.

The treatment for a phobia is usually some kind of psychotherapy. Insight-oriented therapy can be helpful if the phobia has a symbolical basis and unconscious roots. On the other hand, most simple phobias in both children and adolescents can be effectively treated with systematic desensitization, a kind of behavior therapy. In fact, this approach to the treatment of phobias has been one of the outstanding success stories of the 20th century. More than one research project has shown the value of treating phobias with desensitization therapy.

See also *anxiety; behavior therapy; psychoanalysis; systematic desensitization.*

phoneme: A basic speech sound. When infants babble and utter such sounds as "ba," "ki," "loo," "ee," "oo," and so forth, they are uttering phonemes. Spoken words are constructed from phonemes, and English uses 45 of them.

The utterance of basic phonemes is a universal phenomenon, and infants all over the world emit the same ones. However, some are not used in the child's native language. For example, some European languages have no "th" sound. Although the infants utter the "th" sound, it is not used in later speech. When adults from these countries emigrate to the United States, they tend to say "dem" instead of "them" and "dey" instead of "they." Apparently, if phonemes uttered by the infant are not reinforced and used, the capacity to employ them subsequently as an adult is severely restricted.

See also *babbling; holophrase; language development; morpheme.*

physical disabilities: Disabilities involving impairment of the sensory processes or motor capacities. Approximately 1 percent of children suffer from a physical disability. Common physical disabilities are visual impairment, hearing impairment, cerebral palsy, epilepsy, muscular dystrophy, asthma, and paralysis of the limbs.

Aside from the actual problems caused by a physical disability, the complications associated with low self-esteem and a poor self-image must be considered. Adler coined the term *inferiority complex* to describe the set of associated negative ideas often formed by children who find their desire to be effective and competent (i.e., the "will to power") frustrated. Often an "I can't do it" attitude functions as a self-fulfilling prophecy in the case of children with significant disabilities.

Although children should not be pressured to exceed their realistic abilities, it is also true that they should be encouraged to use whatever potential they do in fact have. Children with physical disabilities can often compensate in highly adequate ways. And they frequently have cognitive capacities that are *not* impaired. Their eventual achievements often reach, or even exceed, the level of children without physical disabilities.

See also *Adler, Alfred; cerebral palsy; hearing impairment; inferiority complex; self-esteem; visual impairment.*

physical giftedness: Unusual competence in terms of sensory processes, motor capacities, or both. Children with physical giftedness are alert, well-coordinated, and tend to be highly active in an effective, competent way. Often these children make exceptional athletes. Less obvious is the fact that they may have outstanding ability to draw, sing, or play a musical instrument.

Although physical giftedness is desirable, the risk that such children sometimes run is that of overconfidence and self-absorption. They occasionally receive so much attention and recognition for their remarkable qualities that egotism can become a bit of a problem. Parents and caregivers should both value and reinforce physical giftedness. However, they should not be doting. The child who is physically gifted should, like children in general, be presented with as normal an adult attitude as possible.

See also *giftedness; narcissism; physical disabilities; spoiled child.*

physiological needs: In Maslow's hierarchy of needs, the foundation beneath all "higher" needs. Physiological needs fall in the general category of *deficiency needs*, needs that become activated by something necessary for survival. Infants are born with physiological needs, and such needs remain with us for life. The needs in this category most commonly identified are food, water, oxygen, temperature regulation, elimination, sleep, and escape from pain.

Freud theorized that a primitive version of the sex drive was present in infants in the form of the need for oral gratification. In psychoanalysis, the set of physiological needs and their related biological drives is called the *id*.

See also *biological drives; Freud, Sigmund; id; Maslow, Abraham Harold.*

phylogenetic development: See *ontogenetic development.*

Piaget, Jean (1896–1980): A Swiss zoologist, philosopher, and research psychologist who is widely recognized for his studies of cognitive development in children. Piaget obtained his university education in both Zurich and Paris and then pursued postgraduate study under Eugen Bleuler, the psychiatrist who introduced the term *schizophrenia* into clinical language. Also, Piaget worked with Theodore Simon, one of Alfred Binet's associates. (Alfred Binet authored the first modern intelligence test.) Piaget's primary academic affiliation was with Geneva University. In 1929, he was appointed the director of the Jean Jacques Rousseau Institute in Geneva and remained in that post for many years.

Unlike behaviorists such as Watson and Skinner, Piaget, in the classical European tradition, assumed that children are conscious and that they can think. He wanted to study how the content and quality of a child's thought change from early childhood to late adolescence. This, he believed, would grant important insights into *epistemology*, a branch of philosophy that studies the characteristics and limits of human knowledge.

Conducted over a period of more than 40 years, Piaget's explorations into the child's mental life have yielded a rich harvest of important observations and original ideas. Largely ignored in the United States until the 1950s, primarily because of the negative influence of behaviorism, Piaget's approach became within a decade a powerful new trend in American psychology. It was an important contributing factor to what has been called the "cognitive revolution" in psychology, the rediscovery of the importance of human consciousness and the thinking process.

Among Piaget's numerous works are *The Language and Thought of the Child* (1926), *The Child's Conception of Physical Causality* (1927), *The Origins of Intelligence in Children* (1952), and (with B. Inhelder) *The Psychology of the Child* (1969).

See also *anthropomorphic thinking; Binet, Alfred; cognitive development; concrete operations stage; egocentric thinking; egocentrism; formal operations stage; object permanence; operational thinking; Piagetian scales; preconcept; prelogical thinking; preoperational stage; primary circular reactions; schema; secondary circular reactions; sensorimotor stage; syncretic reasoning; tertiary circular reactions; transductive reasoning.*

Piagetian scales: Psychological tests used to evaluate a child's cognitive development in terms of Piaget's theory. On the whole, these tests center on the kind and quality of a child's thought and are not meant to provide well-defined measures of intelligence. Their primary purpose has been research into cognitive development, the way in which the ability to think grows in range and nature from infancy to adolescence.

An example of a published Piagetian scale is the *Concept Assessment Kit* authored by the research psychologists M. L. Goldschmid and P. M. Bentler. This scale is used to evaluate a child's grasp of the concept of *conservation*, the ability to appreciate that changes of form in substances do not affect their total quantity (see *concrete operations stage*). The *Concept Assessment Kit* is applicable to children in the second half of the *preoperational stage*, between the ages of approximately 4 and 7 years.

See also *cognitive development; concrete operations stage; Piaget, Jean; preoperational stage.*

pica: The eating of substances without nutritional value. Examples of such substances are clay, chalk, ashes, dirt, bits of paper or cardboard, peeling paint, tiny rocks, and dry animal feces. The word *pica* is derived from a Latin word for *magpie*, an omnivorous bird that eats with little selection.

Pica also has the status of a specific mental disorder associated with infancy or early childhood. Children afflicted with pica usually also enjoy eating food. In most cases, children spontaneously outgrow the behavior.

The incidence of pica is low, and it seems to affect both boys and girls in about equal numbers. Pica is rare in older children and adults, but it hs been exhibited in some pregnant women and schizophrenic individuals.

Causal factors in pica include low economic status, mineral deficiencies (particularly iron and zinc), mental retardation, and lack of parental supervision.

Treatment of pica involves a combination of behavior modification for the child and guidance for the parents. In most cases, the behavior can be readily controlled.

See also *behavior modification; eating disorders.*

pituitary gland: An endocrine gland located toward the bottom of the brain and attached to the hypothalamus. The pituitary gland is approximately the size of a garden pea (i.e., about one-third inch in diameter) and is informally called the "master gland" of the body because its hormones control the action of other endocrine glands, such as the thyroid gland, the adrenal glands, and the gonads. The action of the pituitary gland is itself controlled by the *hypothalamus*, a part of the lower brain that regulates biological drives.

One of the principal hormones secreted by the pituitary gland is *growth hormone (GH)*, a hormone that induces cellular divisions in the body's tissues at key times during childhood and adolescence. A deficiency of growth hormone can be a cause of short stature in a child. Excessive secretions of growth hormone play a role in a disease known as *gigantism* (or *giantism*), characterized by abnormal height.

A pituitary hormone of particular importance in adolescence and adulthood is *follicle-stimulating hormone (FSH)*. This hormone acts upon the gonads. In females, it stimulates the maturation of ova in the ovaries. In males, it stimulates the maturation of sperm cells in the testes.

See also *gonads; growth spurt; hormone; ovaries; ovum; short stature; sperm cell; testes.*

play: A spontaneous activity engaged in by almost all children and characterized by the fact that the behavior itself is its own reward. Play is *not*, in Skinner's language, an operant act. It is not, in other words, a means to an end but an end in itself from the child's point of view. Words such as *pleasure, joy, laughter, delight,* and *excitement* come to mind when one thinks of play. Nonetheless, play has its serious side. A child playing alone may be engaged in a project such as carefully coloring pictures in a book—yet this is still play.

Play appears to be motivated in large part by a combination of needs and drives, including the activity drive, the curiosity drive, a need for sensory stimulation, and a need for optimal arousal. Although children themselves, as indicated above, have no particular concern for the long-run effects of play, it is clear to behavioral scientists that play has a number of important functions. It helps children to become socialized by interaction with their peers; sharpens perceptual, motor, and cognitive abilities; and often builds self-esteem through the discovery of important abilities and competencies.

Although psychologists usually identify the physiological needs as more fundamental than the need to play, it is a common observation that at times a child—even if hungry—would rather play than eat. As indicated in the following cross-references, there are several different kinds of play.

See also *associative play; cooperative play; imaginative play; ludic behavior; onlooker play; parallel play; solitary play.*

play therapy: A kind of psychotherapy that allows a troubled child to express emotions such as anxiety, anger, or sadness directly through actions instead of indirectly through words. In order to do this, the child is provided with a set of materials such as clay, paint, dolls, crayons and paper, chalk and blackboard, inflated punch-toys, building blocks, and so forth.

A principal assumption of play therapy is that children are less articulate than adolescents and adults. Consequently, they may have a difficult time expressing attitudes and emotional states in a well-defined manner. The play materials allow them to eloquently display their psychological and emotional states. The therapist interprets the child's actions to the child, putting into words the child can understand thoughts and feelings implicit in the play behavior. The therapist's interpretations help the child to attain a better understanding of previously chaotic ideas and emotions.

One of the values of play therapy is that it allows a child a safe way to discharge pent-up emotions.

See also *acting out; child psychotherapy; Freud, Anna; Klein, Melanie.*

pleasure principle: According to Freud, the process that guides the functioning of the *id*, the foundation of the personality. The id operates in terms of fantasy and wishing. No attention is paid to reality. Psychoanalysis assumes that the *ego*, the conscious "I" of the personality, is not present in the neonate. The newborn child experiences tension—distress in terms of unsatisfied biological drives, such as hunger, thirst, and the need to eliminate. Relief from tension in the form of food, water, urination, and defecation is experienced as pleasure. Thus, to Freud, pleasure *is* satisfaction of the biological drives (i.e., the id's impulses).

See also *biological drives; ego; Freud, Sigmund; id; physiological needs; psychoanalysis.*

positive reinforcer: See *reinforcer.*

postconventional stage: See *moral development.*

power assertive discipline: An approach to discipline characterized by a willingness to use force, either physical or psychological, to obtain behavioral compliance from a child. Examples of parental strategies that fall in this category are spankings, giving orders without explanations, harsh warning, taking away privileges, and severe punishments. Power assertive discipline in effect conveys the message to the child that "I'm right because I'm bigger, have more strength, and can use force."

The child who asks "Why?" in response to a seemingly arbitrary order is often given an answer such as, "Because I told you so." Power assertive discipline is associated with an *authoritarian* parental style.

See also *authoritarian parent; discipline; parental style.*

preconcept: According to Piaget, a vague grasp of concepts. This cognitive style, called *preconceptual thought,* is associated with the early portion of the preoperational stage, between the ages of approximately 2 and 4 years. For example, 3-year-old Michael has formed the general idea that animals with the capacity to bark are called "dogs." Upon hearing a seal bark at a marine show, he says to his mother, "Look, Mommy, a dog!" He has taken the characteristic that dogs bark, applied it to all barking animals, and decided that they, too, are dogs. The tendency to *overgeneralize* is one characteristic of preconceptual thought.

Another characteristic of preconceptual thought is to rely on sensory data over reasoning processes. Suppose that 4-year-old Tina is asked to make a choice between taking and keeping a dime or a nickel. She sees the that nickel is bigger and, therefore, perceives that it is worth more. She elects to keep the nickel. The abstract concept of *value* as something that cannot be seen or otherwise experienced, yet still exists, is not contained in Tina's preconcept of value.

See also *cognitive development; Piaget, Jean; preoperational stage.*

preconceptual thought: See *preconcept.*

preconventional stage: See *moral development.*

prehension: In motor development, the ability to grasp and hold objects. Effective prehension usually appears in most infants between the ages of 4 and 7 months.

See also *motor development; prereaching.*

prelogical thinking: See *logical thinking.*

Premack's principle: As proposed by the learning theorist David Premack, a tendency for a high-probability behavior to have a reinforcing effect on a low-probability one. For example, 8-year-old Bradley tends to resist doing homework. For him, this is a low-probability behavior. He enjoys reading comic books, a high-probability behavior. Doing homework can be effectively reinforced by telling Bradley that he must complete a well-defined part of his assignments before he can read a comic book. If this approach is maintained, doing homework will be perceived as an effective way to obtain the opportunity to read comic books. Premack's principle can be a practical and effective way to discover reinforcers when it seems to a parent that "nothing works."

The application of the principle is most effective when the child sees the arrangement as a fair behavioral contract, not an impossible and overly demanding situation. It is sometimes missed that behavior itself has reinforcing properties. Premack's principle corrects this oversight.

See also *behavior modification; operant conditioning; reinforcer.*

premarital sexual activity: See *adolescent sex relations.*

premature birth: A birth taking place between the sixth and eighth months of pregnancy. The average birth weight under these circumstances is between 2 and 5 pounds. About one in ten neonates are premature. In about one-half of cases, it is possible to specify a medical condition in the mother (e.g., high blood pressure, diabetes mellitus, or heart disease) as a reason for the premature birth; in the other half, the cause is obscure. Premature neonates have very little fat in comparison to full-term ones and display a *lanugo,* a covering of delicate, fine hair on the body.

In the United States, approximately eight in ten premature infants win the battle for life. This is due to intensive postnatal care and medical innovations such as the use of an incubator and the use of a stomach tube for nutrition.

Premature infants are subject to a number of problems, such as greater risk of infection, low blood sugar, excessive bleeding, and breathing problems. Such difficulties may play a causal role in behavioral complications that show up in later development as intellectual deficits (including mental retardation) or attention-deficit hyperactivity disorder. Nonetheless, it can be said with confidence that most premature infants will eventually thrive and function normally.

See also *attention-deficit hyperactivity disorder (ADHD); immature birth; lanugo; mature birth; mental retardation.*

premoral stage: See *moral development.*

prenatal development: See *fetal development.*

preoperational stage: The second stage in Piaget's theory of cognitive development, the stage associated with toddlerhood and the preschool period, lasting from approximately 2 to 7 years of age. It is characterized by such features as egocentrism, overdependency on sensory information in contrast to reason, and thinking intuitively rather than logically. There is a conspicuous lack of the concept of *conservation* (see *concrete operations stage*).

Cause and effect in terms of logical mental operations are not appreciated by the child in the preoperational stage. Instead, explanations of events in terms of magic and anthropomorphic thinking are more readily appreciated. If the child is told that airplanes can fly because they have been given such powers by a magician who makes flying carpets, this seems to be more satisfactory than an explanation in terms of drag, gravity, and a partial vacuum over the wing's surface. If a child is told that the leaves of trees turn various colors in the fall because Jack Frost paints them, the humanlike (i.e., anthropomorphic) aspect of the explanation has intuitive appeal.

Children do not appreciate explanations in terms of natural laws until they are in the third stage of cognitive development, the *concrete operations stage.*

See also *animistic thinking; anthropomorphic thinking; cognitive development; concrete operations stage; egocentrism; Piaget, Jean.*

prepared childbirth: See *Lamaze method.*

prereaching: Poorly coordinated attempts in early infancy to reach for and grasp an object. The infant displaying prereaching makes sweeping motions, often with both hands, aimed at the object of interest. Contact is hit-or-miss. By the age of 2 to 3 months, prereaching diminishes, and, between the ages of 4 and 7 months, gives way to the ability to grasp with precision.

See also *motor development; prehension.*

preschool: A school that is designed for the care and education of children before the first grade. (The term *preschool* is something of a misnomer because a school is, after all, a school.) Typically, children in preschool range between the ages of 2 and 6 years. Familiar alternative names for preschool are *nursery school* and *kindergarten.* The literal meaning of *kindergarten* is "children's garden," and the first one was established in 1837 by Friedrich Froebel, a German teacher and educational philosopher.

Preschools vary in their approach to cognitive instruction (i.e., instruction designed to encourage the growth of conscious thinking abilities). Some see themselves as providing experiences that will facilitate the acquisition of reading and arithmetical skills in grammar school. Such preschools provide enrichment in the form of illustrated books, alphabet blocks, items that can be counted (e.g., large wooden beads on a string), nesting cylinders, and so forth. Montessori preschools in particular operate on the assumption that early cognitive development is important.

On the other hand, many, perhaps most, preschools place little emphasis on cognitive development. They take the position that cognitive development will come naturally, in good time, in grammar school. Rather than rushing the child toward academics, they stress the importance of games, music, play, and interactions with peers. The key idea is that these early experiences will help the child overcome shyness, build self-confidence, foster cooperation, and in general encourage socialization. There appears to be a consensus among educational psychologists that the preschool experience has substantial value for children. Consequently, parents are encouraged to provide a preschool experience—even if this is only for a few hours two or three days a week.

See also *day care; educational psychology; Head Start programs; Montessori, Maria; Montessori method.*

prespeech stage: See *babbling.*

primary circular reactions: See *circular reactions.*

primary reinforcer: See *reinforcer.*

primary sexual characteristics: Those biological characteristics that determine the basic gender of the individual. Examples of primary sexual characteristics in males are the penis, the prostate gland, the seminal vesicles, and the testes. Examples in females are the vagina, the vulva, the clitoris, the uterus, and the ovaries. In normal infants, the primary sexual characteristics are present and well-defined at birth.

See also *pubescence; secondary sexual characteristics.*

principled stage: See *moral development.*

procrastination: To defer until a future time an action that should be taken in the present. Examples of procrastination in children are not doing homework when it is supposed to be done, not performing a chore at the time requested, playing instead of dressing for school, and avoiding unpleasant tasks by saying, "I'll do it later." Most children procrastinate on occasion. It can be thought of as a problem only if it can be identified as chronic and habitual.

There is always the possibility that the child has a chronic illness and consequently a low level of energy for responsible tasks. However, if the child has plenty of energy for play and very little for responsibilities, this is a dubious interpretation. If illness is not suspected, several interacting psychological factors can be at work in the case of habitual procrastination.

1. A child, particularly a toddler or preschooler, may have a poorly formed concept of time.

2. Procrastination can represent a power struggle between parents and a child. Delaying tactics can be a child's way of expressing a need for autonomy.

3. Procrastination can represent latent aggressiveness. Recalcitrant behavior allows the child to fight back indirectly without openly expressing hostility.

4. Procrastination can be a way of avoiding unpleasant reality. A child who feels incompetent or anxious when faced with arithmetic problems, for example, will be tempted to run away from this threat to self-esteem.

5. The child may perceive the parent as too demanding and perfectionistic.

6. There are wide individual differences in temperament, and it is possible that some children are, in terms of their own nature, more relaxed and unconcerned about time demands than one or both of their parents.

Parents can cope with procrastination by attempting to understand its psychological and emotional roots, and they need to find ways to avoiding feeding and strengthening, for example, a power struggle or aggressiveness. Then, behavior modification principles should be applied. Tasks and times for tasks should be well-defined in objective terms. Reinforcers should be provided for approved behaviors. Possible applications of *Premack's principle* should be explored. If procrastination is a stubborn problem and is seriously complicating family life, then behavior therapy, counseling, or child psychotherapy are recommended as resources.

See also *aggressiveness; behavior modification; behavior therapy; child psychotherapy; Premack's principle; self-esteem; temperament.*

productive thinking: As formulated by Max Wertheimer, the father of Gestalt psychology, the ability to think effectively and constructively by looking at problems and tasks as organized wholes. (The German word *Gestalt* can be translated variously as "organized whole," "pattern," or "configuration.")

Suppose that a class of eighth-grade children are taught how to calculate the area of a parallelogram. The formula is given as *Base × Altitude = Area.* Assume that the problem is always presented with the Base in a familiar orientation. Now the teacher draws the problem on the board in an unfamiliar orientation. Some of the children will be confused and protest, "We haven't had that." On the other hand, some of the children will realize that changing the position of the parallelogram does not change the basic parts and their relationship to the whole geometric pattern. These children are using productive thinking and will go on to easily solve the problem.

Productive thinking requires at once both an appreciation of novel elements (i.e., divergent thinking) and a grasp of fundamental principles (i.e., convergent thinking). Consequently, productive thinking itself represents a whole with two aspects, or parts, and is regarded as standing high on the ladder of cognitive accomplishments.

See also *convergent thinking; creative thinking; divergent thinking; insight learning; Wertheimer, Max.*

productiveness in language: One of the principal characteristics of language. Language is productive because a relatively small set of words can be used to produce a large set of ideas. This means that language can be used to express new thoughts and concepts. The productive feature of language makes it possible for even toddlers and preschoolers to give voice to thoughts that have both invention and originality. Productiveness makes language one of the prime tools of creative thinking.

See also *creative thinking; displacement in language; meaning in language.*

profane language: See *undesirable language.*

progeria: A disease characterized by premature aging. The variety of progeria associated with childhood is called the *Hutchinson-Gilford syndrome.* Its onset is during the preschool period, and the victim is biologically like an elderly person before puberty. Progeria makes normal development impossible, and life usually ends during the early adolescent years. The causal factors in progeria are obscure, and there is no known cure. Progeria is an extremely uncommon disease in terms of its rate of occurrence.

See also *norms of development; puberty.*

progressive education: As formulated by the philosopher and psychologist John Dewey, a general educational philosophy characterized by an emphasis on the practical, useful aspects of education. Dewey believed that children often become bored in school because they can see very little connection between subjects to be learned and life as it is lived. He asserted that "dead" languages, such as Latin, no more train the mind than do living languages. A child is better off learning German or Spanish, potentially useful languages, than Latin. Similarly, there is no point in the universal teaching of abstract mathematical subjects such as geometry and algebra to children who will never use these subjects in their careers. It is better to teach them applied mathematics. On the whole, Dewey tended to downgrade the importance of a classical education. He did not believe that it "trained the mental faculties" or "improved the mind," as earlier educational philosophers contended. He said that memory, attention, and intelligence were natural attributes of the mind and that they could best be employed in the learning of subjects with potential applications in life.

Progressive education also stresses the importance of individual differences. Children should not be made to learn subjects for which they have little or no aptitudes. Instead, children should follow their own leads and develop those areas that are most compatible with their own personalities.

Dewey's influence was greatest around the early part of this century, and many changes in curriculum were inspired by his writings. Today's schools still reflect the influence of Dewey, although one seldom hears the term *progressive education*. Interestingly, there has been, of late, something of a countermovement against an extreme emphasis on the applied aspects of education. For example, in the last decade, high school curriculum committees have displayed a rebirth of interest in such classical subjects as Latin and geometry.

See also *Dewey, John; educational psychology; Montessori method.*

projection: A kind of ego defense mechanism in which a repressed idea or motive is unconsciously placed upon an external source, such as a person or thing. The name *projection* is aptly chosen. It is as if the mind acts like a slide projector, and the outer world is the screen. What is perceived as external is put there by the individual's psychological and emotional needs.

The ego is defended in the sense that projection allows the individual to deny ideas or motives that are at variance with his or her superego, the agent of moral values. Thus, the ego avoids the criticism of the superego. For example, 10-year-old Justine has repressed hostile feelings toward her teacher. However, she tells friends, "Mrs. Dunlap doesn't like me." Projection allows Justine to maintain a feeling of psychological innocence.

See also *ego defense mechanisms; superego.*

prosocial behavior: Behavior that serves the needs and functions of a social group such as the family, church, tribe, school, club, or, on a larger scale, the nation. Prosocial behavior consists of such attributes as caring about others, cooperation, friendliness, helpfulness, responsibility, trustworthiness, generosity, and lack of self-centeredness. From the point of view of parents and adults in general, prosocial behavior is deemed desirable and is an important sign of general socialization in the child or adolescent. Consequently, caregivers should seek ways to encourage and reinforce it. If they value it, they should themselves be role models of prosocial behavior.

See also *antisocial behavior; social learning; socialization.*

proximodistal development: Literally meaning "near-far" development, a strong tendency in the processes of growth and maturation to proceed from the central (i.e., "near") to peripheral (i.e., "far") bodily regions of the individual. This is evident in infant development. The heart, lungs, and digestive tract are all functioning efficiently long before the individual has control over bodily movements. When some motor control is achieved, it is seen to be effective in the arms and legs before the fingers and toes.

See also *cephalocaudal development; fetal development; motor development.*

pseudohermaphroditism: See *hermaphroditism.*

psychoanalysis: Both a personality theory and a method of psychotherapy created by Sigmund Freud. A principal, underlying theme running throughout psychoanalysis is that there is an unconscious mental life. A secondary theme of substantial importance is that the complexion of the unconscious mental life is shaped primarily by forbidden wishes of a sexual and aggressive nature.

The personality theory states that there are three major agents of the personality. The *id* consists of the basic inborn drives, and it is oriented toward pleasure. The *ego* is in contact with the external world, and it is oriented toward reality. The *superego* represents the values of one's parents and culture, and it is oriented toward morality. Conflicts between the id's wishes and the superego's prohibitions represent a neurotic process, and this neurotic process can be the basis for many psychological and emotional disturbances.

Freud's personality theory is also a developmental theory. The id is present at birth and is dominant in infancy. Around the age of 2 years, the ego emerges from the id in order to help it fulfill its wishes. Around the age of 3 years, the superego begins to form out of the ego and is more or less complete toward the ages of 5 or 6 years.

When the word *psychoanalysis* is used to refer to a kind of psychotherapy, it suggests an approach in which the unconscious aspects of mental life are explored and brought to a conscious level. The patient develops *insight*, meaning that he or she sees into the connections between repressed psychological information (e.g., painful childhood memories and forbidden wishes) and present moods and actions. It is anticipated that insight will relieve the patient of neurotic symptoms, particularly chronic anxiety.

The principal tool used to explore the unconscious aspects of a given patient's mental life is *free association*, a technique requiring that the individual talk at random, without censorship, about anything that comes to mind. Early in the development of psychoanalysis, Freud used hypnosis but eventually gave it up.

Free association and a sophisticated verbal exchange are not practical possibilities with prepubertal children. Therefore, such pioneer psychoanalysts as Melanie Klein and Anna Freud innovated and introduced play techniques as devices providing access to unconscious motives and memories.

The words *psychoanalysis* and *psychotherapy* are not synonyms. Psychoanalysis is a *kind* of psychotherapy. Therefore, the concept of *psychotherapy* is the broader one, and it includes psychoanalysis. However, it should be noted that psychoanalysis is accorded the high status of being historically the first of the modern kinds of psychotherapy.

See also *child psychotherapy; childhood neurosis; ego; Freud, Anna; Freud, Sigmund; id; Klein, Melanie; play therapy; superego; unconscious mental life.*

psychogenic factors: Factors playing a role in development assumed to have a basis in learning, motivation, perception, thinking, emotional reactions, and similar psychological processes. Psychogenic factors are of particular importance in efforts to understand the behavior of troubled children when there is an absence of organic pathology. In other words, children who are healthy and biologically normal can still display mental and behavioral disorders such as enuresis (i.e., bedwetting), stuttering, and various phobias.

Broadly speaking, the two principal viewpoints used to explain behavioral problems in terms of psychogenic factors are psychoanalysis and behavioral psychology. Psychoanalysis sees personal difficulties as arising out of emotional traumata (i.e., wounds) in early childhood, unconscious motives, and emotional conflicts. Behavioral psychology sees difficulties arising out of adverse conditioning experiences, an ineffective reinforcement history, and inadequate social learning experiences. The emphasis in psychoanalysis is on the motivational process; the emphasis in behavioral psychology is on the learning process. In practice, both general approaches are used by mental health professionals to explain the behavior of, and to do therapy with, troubled children.

See also *behaviorism; biogenic factors; psychoanalysis.*

psycholinguistics: The study of the connection between language and behavior. The findings of psycholinguistics have numerous applications in developmental psychology. Here are three examples: they (1) give a better insight into cognitive development, (2) assist in communicating effectively with children at different ages, and (3) improve ability to help children with a developmental reading disorder.

See also *cognitive development; communication skills; developmental reading disorder; language acquisition device (LAD); language development.*

psychopathy: A pathological personality trait characterized by an inadequate moral sense and an absence of either anxiety or guilt feelings for violations of social norms. The term is an old one and considered to be somewhat outdated. Terms with more or less synonymous meanings are *sociopathy* and *antisocial behavior.* In classical psychoanalysis, psychopathy is linked to an underdeveloped superego, the moral agent of the personality.

In children and adolescents, psychopathy is associated with a conduct disorder. In adults, it is associated with an antisocial personality disorder.

See also *conduct disorder; moral development; superego.*

psychopharmacology: See *drug therapy.*

psychosexual development: A maturational process involving both the sexual drive and the general personality. The general idea is that one's thoughts, emotions, and actions from infancy to adulthood are to some extent influenced by sexual needs and interests.

The most famous single theory of psychosexual development was the one proposed by Freud, and it gave great impetus to 20th century study of the sexual life of both the child and the adult. Freud proposed a theory of infantile sexuality, which was a somewhat unsettling notion, particularly around the early part of the 20th century. However, Freud did not mean that infants have full-blown sexual interest as adults understand it. Instead, certain signs and behaviors evident in both the infant and the child foreshadow mature sexuality.

Freud hypothesized that children go through five stages of psychosexual development:

1. *Oral Stage:* At first *libido*, or psychosexual energy, is concentrated in the oral zone. The *oral stage* lasts from birth to the end of infancy (i.e., at about 18 to 24 months of age). During the oral stage, the infant obtains a sort of erotic gratification from sucking, biting, chewing, and other oral activities.

2. *Anal Stage:* Libido moves, because of maturation, from the oral zone to the anal zone. The *anal stage* lasts until the age of 3 or 4 years. During the anal stage, the child obtains a sort of erotic gratification from both the voluntary retention and eventual expulsion of fecal bulk.

3. *Phallic Stage:* In the third stage, libido moves from the anal zone to the phallic zone. The *phallic stage* lasts from the age of 3 or 4 years to about the age of 6 years. During the phallic stage, the child obtains a degree of erotic gratification from self-manipulation of the phallus (i.e., the clitoris in a female and the penis in a male).

   Now a crisis takes place. According to Freud, the child of either sex commonly develops an incest wish toward the parent of the opposite sex. There is almost immediate guilt arising from the punitive side of the child's recently formed superego. Also, there is fear of punishment from the parent of the same sex. The male in particular may develop the fantasy that the father will castrate him. The entire conflict herein described is called the *Oedipus complex.* (Sometimes in females the conflict is referred to as the Electra complex. However, it is correct to use the term *Oedipus complex* in reference to either sex.)

4. *Latency Stage:* As a consequence of the Oedipus complex, the child must repress sexual interest in order to be psychologically comfortable, and libido goes underground. This is the *latency stage*, which lasts from about 6 to 12 years of age. During the latency stage, the child has no conscious interest in sexuality. On the contrary, at a conscious level, the normal child has many external interests manifested in play, avocations, friends, and school. (These are sometimes referred to as "the golden years of childhood.") However, libido still exists, and it continues to work at an unconscious level.

5. *Genital Stage:* When the child reaches puberty (around 12 or 13 years of age), libido surfaces again at a conscious level. The adolescent begins to develop, in most cases, a sexual interest in members of the opposite sex. This eventually expresses itself in marriage, sexual intercourse, the rearing of children, and so forth. Thus, the *genital stage*, which starts at puberty, lasts throughout adulthood.

Freud believed that if libido is fixated due to emotional traumata (i.e., wounds) at one of the early stages of psychosexual development, the result can contribute to a neurotic process and have an adverse effect upon the individual's adult personality.

Freud's theory of psychosexual development is open to criticism. Freud believed that the theory is universal and applicable to all children. This appears to be incorrect. The theory tends to be limited to the description of the development of some, not all, children in intact families with parents who play traditional roles. It cannot be readily generalized to either one-parent families or to families characterized by a permissive parental style. Also, not all children engage in autoerotic activity during the phallic stage. However, it does appear that the behavior is common and relatively normal. Although both sexes exhibit the behavior, it appears with somewhat more frequency in males.

To the therapist with a psychoanalytic orientation, behavioral traits such as excessive eating, sarcasm, and gullibility suggest oral fixations. Traits such as defiance or stinginess suggest anal fixations. Traits such as excessive dominance of others and self-absorption suggest phallic fixations. Thus, the theory can be of some utility in therapy because it suggests to both the therapist and the patient possible explanations for maladaptive behavior. However, most contemporary psychiatrists and psychologists recognize that there are no universal explanations of specific behavioral traits. Thus, alternative explanations to Freud's psychosexual theory are, of course, possible.

See also *anal stage; anal-expulsive character; anal-retentive character; genital stage; latency stage; libido; Oedipus complex; oral stage; phallic stage; superego.*

psychosocial development: The process by which an individual forms a social personality. Human beings move from the relative egocentrism and psychological isolation of early infancy to the rich, complex world of relationships with members of the family, school, club, job, the opposite sex, and so forth. The most well-known single theory of psychosocial development is the one proposed by Erik Erikson, which has given great impetus in the past several decades to research on the socialization process.

Erikson proposes that there are eight stages of psychosocial development. At each stage, the individual is challenged with a developmental task. If the challenge is met successfully, a positive personality trait (e.g., trust) is formed. If the challenge is met with failure, a negative personality trait (e.g., mistrust) is formed.

The eight stages and their approximate associated ages are as follows:

1. Trust versus mistrust (birth to 2 years)
2. Autonomy versus shame and doubt (2 to 3 years)
3. Initiative versus guilt (3 to 6 years)
4. Industry versus inferiority (6 to 12 years)
5. Identity versus role confusion (12 to 18 years)
6. Intimacy versus isolation (young adulthood)
7. Generativity versus self-absorption (adulthood)
8. Integrity versus despair (old age)

(Note that ages in years were not specified for stages 6, 7, and 8. This is because from the point of view of psychosocial development *young adulthood, adulthood,* and *old age* vary considerably from individual to individual. It is probably best to allow these terms to stand alone with their common-sense meanings.)

As can be seen from the above outline, Erikson's theory spans the entire life cycle from birth to death. Descriptions of the stages and their importance to psychosocial development are discussed in the individual entries.

See also *autonomy versus doubt; Erikson, Erik Homburger; generativity versus self-absorption; identity versus role confusion; industry versus inferiority; initiative versus guilt; integrity versus despair; intimacy versus isolation; socialization; trust versus mistrust.*

psychotherapy: Any kind of therapy that attempts to relieve the symptoms of mental disorders or general emotional distress through psychological means. An informal name for psychotherapy is "the talking cure." And this name captures the essence of psychotherapy. It is possible to think of psychotherapy as a special kind of conversation between a therapist and a troubled person.

However, it needs to be noted that this "conversation" *is* indeed special because in practice it includes an array of techniques including free association, dream interpretation, role playing, deconditioning, behavior modification, hypnosis, guided fantasies, and play. Indeed, psychotherapy is one of the most creative and innovative areas of psychiatry and clinical psychology.

The first modern psychotherapy was psychoanalysis, its father was Sigmund Freud, and its birth coincides roughly with the early part of the 20th century. However, it should be understood that today psychoanalysis has the status of only one *kind* of psychotherapy among others.

A perennial question of importance is this one: Is psychotherapy effective? The question, unfortunately, cannot be answered with a simple yes or no. A tremendous amount of research has gone into various attempts to answer the question. However, the effectiveness of psychotherapy depends on too many factors to be able to respond categorically to any question concerning its effectiveness. The personality of the therapist, the nature of the disorder, the severity of the patient's symptoms, and the specific kind of psychotherapy used in a given case all have potent effects on outcomes. However, it can be said with assurance that psychotherapy is *often* effective. It offers real hope to persons with mental health problems. And in many cases, it is an appealing alternative to drug therapy, electroshock therapy, and other somatic approaches.

This book identifies in some detail a number of different kinds of psychotherapies employed with children and adolescents. These are listed in the following cross-references.

See also *behavior modification; behavior therapy; child psychotherapy; cognitive-behavior modification; counterconditioning; play therapy; psychoanalysis; systematic desensitization; transactional analysis.*

psychotic disorders: Mental disorders in which the individual is out of touch with reality as it is usually understood. It is rather clear-cut evidence of a psychotic disorder if a person is plagued with delusions (i.e., irrational beliefs) or hallucinations (i.e., false perceptions). A somewhat less obvious criterion is *greatly disorganized behavior*; signs of such behavior are talking incoherently, great excitement or mania, inability to attend to anything for more than a few moments, and general confusion.

Psychotic disorders can be either functional or organic in nature, or a combination of both. If they are functional, there is no obvious biological process present. Causal factors appear to be basically psychological in nature. If they are organic, there is an apparent biological process at work. There may be an infection, a tumor, a stroke, or a biochemical imbalance. In practice, psychological and biological factors often interact in a complex way. For example, schizophrenia is usually thought of as functional. Nonetheless, there is considerable evidence to suggest that there is also a biological process at work in schizophrenia.

Two of the most striking psychotic disorders afflicting children and adolescents are autistic disorder and schizophrenia.

See also *autistic disorder; childhood schizophrenia.*

puberty: The biological stage associated with the beginning of an individual's capacity to reproduce (i.e., to have children). The onset of puberty is typically around the age of 12 or 13 (i.e., early adolescence).

See also *adolescence; menarche; nubile female; pituitary gland; secondary sexual characteristics.*

punishment: A painful or extremely unpleasant consequence. Usually this highly negative outcome is obtained as the result of an action that is judged to be unacceptable by an authority figure such as a parent. Note that punishment *follows* an offense. For example, a toddler sneaks some cookies before lunch and a parent slaps the child's hand. Or an adolescent receives a speeding ticket and a parent takes away driving privileges for two weeks.

It is important to distinguish corporal punishment from punishment in general. *Corporal punishment* refers to inflicting pain or injury to the body. Examples are slapping a child's hand or face, spanking the buttocks, and whipping the child with a switch.

The principal reason parents punish their children is that they want to eliminate unacceptable behaviors. Does punishment work? The question does not allow an easy answer. A series of experiments in operant conditioning conducted by B. F. Skinner and W. K. Estes suggest that punishment temporarily suppresses an undesirable behavior but does not extinguish it. When the punishing outcome is removed, the unwanted behavior returns eventually to full strength. In particular, when punishment is used in early childhood in the hope of doing away with such habits as thumbsucking, enuresis (i.e., bedwetting), playing with food, procrastination, resistance to toilet training, and temper tantrums, it is seldom effective.

On the other hand, punishment can be an effective way to cope with undesirable behavior that requires suppression at the moment (e.g., running out into the street). In those situations where a parent believes that punishment is called for, it is worth taking note of several guidelines:

1. Punishment "stands out" for a child most clearly between the ages of about 2 and 6 years. Punishment has little meaning to a child younger than 2 years of age; a child older than 6 years of age has some sense of shame and guilt and probably responds

better to reason and logical outcomes than to spankings and harsh restrictions.

2. Punishment should be immediate. If it is not, the connection between the negative outcome and the offense is lost on the child.

3. The punishment should not be too harsh nor create physical injury, or it becomes child abuse. Punishment must be used with restraint and intelligence.

It is important to realize that punishment can have a boomerang effect. A series of experiments conducted by research psychologist N. Azrin clearly demonstrate a link between punishment and aggressiveness. Children who have been punished too often or unfairly experience anger and general hostility toward their parents.

On the whole, it can be concluded that punishment is sometimes an effective technique but under a very limited set of circumstances. As a general way to discipline children, it has many drawbacks. Usually punishment is a last resort and is employed when all other approaches seem to have failed. Frequently, the responsible adult using punishment feels that he or she has failed also. For these reasons, it is probably better to explore more constructive alternatives to punishment, such as behavior modification, the application of Premack's principle, and positive reinforcement.

See also *behavior modification; counterconditioning; discipline; operant conditioning; Premack's principle; reinforcer; response-cost punishment.*

pupillary reflex (iris reflex): One of the reflexes that is present in the neonate and that is characterized by a change in the size of the pupil of the eye if the eye is subjected to change in the intensity of light.

The pupil admits light to the interior of the eye, and its size is controlled by the surrounding iris and its muscles. Increases in light intensity cause the pupil to become smaller; decreases in intensity cause the pupil to become larger. The function of these activities is to maintain a relatively constant level of perceived brightness on the retina. Unlike a number of neonatal reflexes, the pupillary reflex is retained for life. Its presence and proper functioning are one sign that an infant is neurologically normal.

See also *neonatal reflexes; perceptual development in infancy; visual development in infancy; visual impairment.*

Pygmalion effect (Rosenthal effect): As formulated by the research psychologist R. Rosenthal, a strong tendency for positive teacher expectations to have a corresponding positive effect on classroom performance. A number of studies tend to offer support for the reality of the Pygmalion effect. One of the interesting things about the effect is that it is a *self-fulfilling prophecy,* a prediction that tends to be realized primarily because it is made. Generalizing the research findings, it seems reasonable to suggest that when parents and other caregivers expect effective, responsible behaviors from children, there will be a strong tendency for these very behaviors to be realized.

Studies of the Pygmalion effect have also demonstrated that it can produce measurable improvements in intelligence-test scores. This suggests that at least some component of measurable intellectual functioning must be the result of nurture (i.e., an environment that fosters the growth of thinking abilities).

The name *Pygmalion effect* is derived from the ancient tale of Pygmalion, a sculptor of Cyprus, who fell in love with his own work of art—a statue of the goddess Aphrodite. (Legend states that the goddess granted the statue life.)

See also *intelligence; nature-nurture controversy; parental style.*

pyromania: A disorder characterized by an impulse to set fires. If a tendency to start fires is a chronic problem with a child or adolescent, it often signifies a serious emotional disturbance. Males appear to suffer from the disorder more often than do females.

The reason for pyromania depends on the life history of the particular child or adolescent. However, it is possible to speculate in a general way on psychological factors in the disorder. It is possible that some children use fire setting as a way to strike back at adult authority by doing something unacceptable or illegal. Others may be expressing pent-up hostility by doing something destructive. Psychoanalytic theory points out that fire and heat are used in a metaphorical way in connection with sexual drive. For example, we say, "Your kisses set me on fire," "I'm burning with passion," or "He's a hot number." Adolescents with confused or repressed sexual urges might find an erotic pleasure in setting fires.

Because pyromania is a serious disorder, it does not respond well to common-sense parental interventions. Treatment is often required. This usually consists of psychotherapy aimed at helping the disturbed child understand the emotional roots of the disorder. A principal focus of effective therapy is on developing practical ways to gain self-control over irrational impulses.

See also *acting out; aggressiveness; child psychotherapy; psychoanalysis; psychotherapy.*

R

rage reflex: One of the reflexes that is present in the neonate and, if the spontaneous movements of an infant are arbitrarily restrained, is characterized by an effort against the restriction, redness in the face, and crying. The reflex tends to diminish in intensity before six months have elapsed. The presence of the rage reflex is one of the signs suggesting that a neonate is neurologically normal.

The rage reflex is thought to be a forerunner of more complex emotional states in older children, such as anger, irritation, exasperation, indignation, and resentment.

See also *aggressiveness; emotional states; neonatal reflexes.*

Rank, Otto (1884–1939): A psychoanalyst and personality theorist recognized for his introduction of a treatment approach known as *will therapy*. At one time a member of Freud's inner circle of associates, Rank was one of the first "lay analysts," meaning a psychoanalyst without a medical degree. Rank's academic training was in literature and history, and Freud approved of the rich and general background that Rank brought to psychoanalysis.

Rank and Freud parted as professional colleagues over the issue of the importance of the birth trauma. Rank believed that the emotional pain associated with the loss and separation from the mother at the moment that one came into the world was a prototype for anxiety in general; it was also the root of most neuroses seen in patients. Freud thought that the birth trauma might be of some importance, but he refused to assign to it the paramount role given by Rank.

Rank emigrated to the United States in the 1920s, after his break with Freud, and worked out the practical aspects of will therapy.

One of Rank's principal works is *The Trauma of Birth* (1923).

See also *anxiety; birth trauma; child psychotherapy; childhood neurosis; Freud, Sigmund; Lamaze method; Leboyer method; personality development; psychoanalysis; trust versus mistrust.*

rapid eye movement sleep (REM sleep): See *sleep patterns.*

rating scales: Standardized measuring instruments used to evaluate such important attributes in children as intelligence, motor ability, personality traits, creative thinking, social adjustment, and so forth.

See also *Apgar scale; Bayley Scales of Infant Development; creativity tests; Gesell Developmental Schedules; McCarthy Scales of Children's Abilities (MSCA); Neonatal Behavioral Assessment Scale (NBAS); Stanford-Binet Intelligence Scale; Wechsler intelligence scales.*

rationalization: A kind of ego defense mechanism in which either an irrational idea or irrational behavior is made to seem rational through the use of a chain of superficial logic. The basic theme of rationalization is the *making of excuses* in order to maintain self-esteem. For example, suppose that 10-year-old Katherine receives an F on an arithmetic test. One of her parents asks, "What went wrong?" Katherine says, "All of the kids got bad grades on that test. Our teacher didn't give us enough time to study, and there were too many problems on the test." Or, assume that an adolescent engages in sexual relations on a date and that this goes against his or her moral training. The next day he or she thinks, "It's not my fault. We were drinking and I was talked into it." The rationalization is a way of avoiding responsibility for one's own actions.

Two basic kinds of rationalization are *sour grapes* and *sweet lemons. Sour grapes* is characterized by thinking that something that one cannot have is undesirable anyway—"I can't have it" is translated into "I don't want it." (The term comes from one of Aesop's fables in which the fox could not reach a bunch of grapes high on a vine. As he skulked away, he muttered, "They were probably sour anyhow.") For example, suppose 14-year-old Howard makes friendly overtures to a classmate named Debra and is rebuffed. Later he tells a friend, "I don't like Debra anyway. Did you ever notice what skinny legs she's got?"

There is a proverb that states, "When God hands you a lemon, make lemonade." *Sweet lemons* is characterized by trying to convince oneself that an unfortunate event is in fact a fortunate one. For example, 16-year-old Magda is too sick to go on a long-planned school picnic. She rationalizes, "I needed to stay home and study anyway for Monday's English test."

Rationalization is a common ego defense mechanism used frequently by both children and adolescents, and, employed in moderation, it probably helps to maintain mental health. However, the troubled child may use rationalization to excess and, thus, avoids a realistic confrontation with real problems that require practical solutions. Psychoanalytic theory suggests that a chronic dependence on rationalization indicates the presence of a neurotic process.

See also *childhood neurosis; ego defense mechanisms.*

reaction formation: A kind of ego defense mechanism in which a repressed idea reappears at the conscious level in opposite form. For example, suppose that 11-year-old Marsha has a substantial amount of repressed hostility toward her mother. She is also a highly social- ized child who would feel very guilty if she admitted to herself just how much anger she is holding back. Her "good girl" image demands this. The hostility expresses itself at the conscious level in masked form as sweetness and docility. She compulsively and rigidly carries out all of her mother's requests promptly and without fail as a way of proving to herself that she is *not* hostile, that she dearly loves her mother.

A reaction formation can often be useful, helping a child to control impulsive or irresponsible behavior. The danger resides in the fact that reaction formations often break down. Unfortunately, when this happens, the behavior may temporarily be more impulsive and erratic than before. That is why a reaction formation should be looked upon as a psychological crutch, sometimes useful, but not usually an adequate solution to a child's problems of living.

See also *childhood neurosis; ego defense mechanisms.*

reality principle: See *ego.*

reasoning: A cognitive process involving the evaluation of facts, the making of inferences, and the reaching of a conclusion. When adults reason effectively, they generalize correctly, decide whether propositions appear to be true or false, and manipulate symbols such as words and numerals in a way that is congruent with consensual reality. Effective reasoning is a sign of both maturity and intelligence and is linked to a stage of cognitive development called the *formal operations stage.*

In the Western world, the age of 7 years is traditionally taken to be the age of reason. Prior to this time, children reason in highly limited and somewhat ineffective ways. However, the age of 7 is not the end of cognitive development. At approximately this age, children enter a cognitive stage called the *concrete operations stage*, which is itself a forerunner of the formal operations stage.

See also *cognitive development; concrete operations stage; formal operations stage; Piaget, Jean; syncretic reasoning; transductive reasoning.*

Rebellious Child ego state: See *ego state.*

rebelliousness: In children and adolescents, a behavioral trait characterized by an unwillingness to accept adult authority. The trait makes itself manifest in such specific behaviors as talking back, refusing to follow a rule or obey an order (disobedience), displaying behaviors seemingly designed to irritate adults, using illegal drugs, and so forth.

A certain amount of rebelliousness is to be expected. On the positive side, it is a sign that children and adolescents have the capacity to think for themselves. Also, it represents the need for autonomy, the need to have some degree of self-control over events.

However, if rebelliousness becomes chronic and excessive, it is certainly an undesirable personality trait. When this happens, it can become a part of a disorder such as oppositional defiant disorder, and it can play a role in juvenile delinquency.

It should be understood that the stereotype of adolescent rebelliousness in terms of a lost generation of wild young people is completely false. This portrait fits a very small percentage of adolescents. A number of studies have found that the vast majority of adolescents are, on the whole, socialized. They are responsible, respect the law, and accept the majority of social norms.

See also *autonomy versus doubt; ego state; juvenile delinquency; oppositional defiant disorder.*

recessive gene: A gene that exerts its influence on the phenotype only if paired with a second similar gene. In practical terms, what this means is that if an individual has a recessive gene for a given characteristic on the first member of a pair of chromosomes *and* a matched recessive gene for the same characteristic on the second member, the individual will display the attributes associated with the recessive gene.

For example, suppose that Shepley has two recessive genes for blue eyes. This is usually symbolized *bb*. (The lower case letter is used to indicate *recessive*; upper case is used to indicate *dominant*.) Shepley will have blue eyes.

If an individual has one recessive gene and one dominant gene, he or she will not display the characteristic associated with the recessive gene. Nonetheless, such an individual is a *carrier* of the gene. His or her children can display the recessive characteristic if a partner is also a carrier of the recessive gene. This is of particular importance with respect to diseases such as Tay-Sachs disease and sickle-cell anemia, both caused by recessive genes. If two carriers of genes for a recessive disease marry, the statistical probability of a given child having two recessive genes, and the disease itself, is 25 percent. The statistical probability that a given child will be a carrier, and free of the actual disease, is 50 percent. There is only a 25 percent probability that a given child will neither have the disease nor be a carrier. Therefore, persons who suspect that they are carriers of a recessive gene for a disease may wish to consider seeking genetic counseling.

See also *dominant gene; gene; genetic counseling; genotype; phenotype; sickle cell anemia; Tay-Sachs disease.*

reflex exercise: According to Piaget, a spontaneous process associated with the first month of life, during which infants acquire the ability to use their reflexes with greater ability and coordination.

See also *cognitive development; neonatal reflexes; Piaget, Jean; sensorimotor stage.*

reflexes in infancy: See *neonatal reflexes.*

regression: A return to behavior associated with an earlier level of development. Thus, if an 8-year-old child has a tantrum, sucks a thumb, pouts, whines, urinates or defecates in clothing, and so forth, the behavior can be described as regressive.

In psychoanalysis, *regression* is identified as a kind of ego defense mechanism. The basic idea is that when both children and adults are subjected to too much stress, they sometimes go backwards in psychological time seeking old comforts. Thus, if eating brought great satisfaction as an infant, an adolescent who feels somewhat overwhelmed by school work and the demands of social life might find himself or herself looking for food.

See also *ego defense mechanisms; enuresis; tantrum; thumb sucking.*

reinforcer: A consequence, or outcome, of an action that has the effect of increasing the likelihood that similar actions will be repeated in the future. Informally, a reinforcer is a valued "pay-off" for behavior. The basic idea is that the reinforcer "strengthens" the connections involved in a learned response. A knowledge of kinds of reinforcers and how they work is of value when parents and other caregivers make applications of behavior modification to the rearing of children.

The concept of a *reinforcer* is associated to a large extent with the contributions of B. F. Skinner, operant conditioning, and behavior modification.

A reinforcer is in reality a reinforcer only if it has the effect described earlier. It is similar, but not identical, to a reward. A *reward* is valued by the giver and may have little or no effect on behavior. A *reinforcer* is valued by the receiver and, by definition, has an effect on behavior.

Reinforcers can be classified in two principal ways: (1) primary and secondary reinforcers and (2) positive and negative reinforcers. A *primary* reinforcer is one that satisfies a biological drive. Food for a hungry child and water for a thirsty one are examples of primary reinforcers. A *secondary* reinforcer is one that has acquired value through learning. Money, merit badges, grades in school, and so forth are all examples of secondary reinforcers.

A *positive* reinforcer is one that is approached by the individual. Again, examples are food, water, and money. On the whole, the general theme running through the concept of positive reinforcers is that they are valued and actively sought. A *negative* reinforcer is one that is avoided by the individual. Common examples are excessive heat, excessive cold, disliked food, unpleasant persons, and so forth. To be more specific, suppose that a room is too hot and a child learns how to turn on the air conditioner. Assuming that relief from the heat (i.e., a negative reinforcer) is obtained, the child's likelihood of turning on the air conditioner in the future has increased.

It is important to make a clear distinction between a negative reinforcer and punishment. As described above, a negative reinforcer *precedes* a learned response (i.e., the state of being too warm exists in time before the action taken to become more comfortable). On the other hand, punishment *follows* a learned response. For example, a child sneaks a cookie before dinner and has his or her hand slapped. The effect of a negative reinforcer is predictable. It will, by definition, increase the likelihood of a given response. The effect of punishment is variable and may or may not have the intended effect.

The search for effective reinforcers is a challenging one. There are times when "nothing seems to work" with a particular child. Often the problem resides in the fact that the adult confuses rewards with reinforcers. A parent who values money may offer a son in high school $5.00 for every A grade. And the son may be completely unresponsive. The parent says, "I've tried to motivate this kid, but he's hopeless." The parent would be well-advised to think in terms of reinforcers—"pay-offs" for behavior that will be *actually* valued by the son.

It is important to realize that common sense is usually a good guide in the search for reinforcers, but not always. Common sense says that praise is a reinforcer. This is often correct. But some children may go through a stage when they do not respond well to praise. At these times, the parent needs to look for other reinforcers.

One possibility that is often missed is that behavior can be used to reinforce behavior. Premack's principle, described in its own entry, addresses itself to this possibility and offers an innovative approach to the search for effective reinforcers.

See also *behavior modification; operant conditioning; partial reinforcement; Premack's principle; punishment; Skinner, Burrhus Frederic.*

relational concept: See *concept formation.*

reliability of a test: An aspect of a test that is measurable and that is characterized by the capacity of the test to yield a highly similar score on repeated presentations. It is important that psychological tests, such as intelligence tests, be reliable. A psychological test is a measuring instrument and, to be useful, should give stable, predictable measurements. A bathroom scale provides a familiar example. Most bathroom scales are, to a degree, reliable. A first weighing may read 120 pounds. A second weighing a few minutes later may read 123 pounds. A third weighing the next morning may read 119 pounds. Even though the weights are all different, they are still within a few pounds of each other. On the other hand, if the scale were to read 120 pounds on the first weighing and 140 pounds on the second weighing, it would be completely unreliable, and, of course, useless.

The reliability of a test can be assessed by using a statistical tool called the *correlation coefficient*, a measure of the magnitude of the relationship between two variables. For example, suppose that a researcher wants to evaluate the reliability of a new intelligence test. He or she randomly selects items from the test and creates two forms of the test, Form A and Form B. When administered, both forms should yield IQ scores that are similar. If Ilene receives a high IQ score on Form A, she should receive a similar high score on Form B. If Laura receives a low IQ score on Form A, she should receive a similar low score on Form B. If consistent results are obtained for a large group of children, then the two forms have a high positive correlation, and the overall test can be deemed "reliable."

See also *correlation; intelligence tests; validity of a test.*

repression: A kind of ego defense mechanism used by both older children and adults in which unpleasant memories and forbidden motives are directed toward the unconscious level of mental life. Unpleasant memories may include early childhood events that were emotionally traumatic. Forbidden motives often have an aggressive or sexual component.

The basic idea of *repression* is that in terms of the conscious self, certain ideas are threatening to its integrity and status. Therefore, protection of the ego is perceived in terms of attempting to rid oneself of these threatening agents. The entire repressive action is itself unconscious and involuntary.

Freud hypothesized that it is the mechanism of repression that actually creates the unconscious level of the personality. The unconscious dimension may be thought of as a psychological netherworld, a world populated by banished ideas.

However, banished ideas have a way of working their way back to consciousness. Freud spoke of the *return of the repressed.* Thus, repressed psychological material often makes itself known in adverse ways, such as slips of the tongue, disturbing dreams, compulsive behavior, chronic anxiety, and so forth. The concept of childhood neurosis is related to the return of the repressed.

The thrust of psychoanalysis as a form of therapy, as Freud originally conceived it, is to explore repressed material and make it accessible to conscious evaluation. Anna Freud, Sigmund Freud's daughter, applied these ideas to child psychotherapy.

As can be seen from the foregoing, the concept of *repression* has very little meaning for infants, toddlers, and preschoolers. It is not until the superego, the agent of the personality that represents moral standards, forms that the child begins to actively repress in the Freudian sense. In general, this begins around the age of 6 years, and is associated with the latency stage of psychosexual development. Prior to this time, a more primitive defense mechanism, denial of reality, is used by the child's ego to cope with anxiety. In a sense, repression is a rather complex form of denial of reality in which internal, in contrast to external, reality is denied. In other words, the inner world of thought and perception is somewhat distorted in order to protect the ego.

See also *child psychotherapy; childhood neurosis; denial of reality; ego defense mechanisms; Freud, Anna; Freud, Sigmund; psychoanalysis.*

response-cost punishment: A kind of punishment characterized by the loss of a privilege. Another name for this kind of punishment is *deprivation of privileges.* There are two basic kinds of response costs: (1) logical consequences and (2) arbitrary consequences. *Logical consequences* are those that occur naturally as a result of a lapse in responsible behavior. For example, a child who takes too long to dress in the morning may miss the bus and may have to walk to school. Alfred Adler, a principal figure in the early history of psychoanalysis, recommended that logical consequences be allowed to operate whenever it is practical to do so.

Arbitrary consequences are those that are imposed by a parent or other authority figure. Examples include the temporary loss of the right to watch television or the liberty to call friends on the telephone. When arbitrary consequences are applied, it is best to make them both rational and appropriate. The child should be convinced that "the punishment fits the crime." Under these conditions, arbitrary consequences can often be effective.

Response-cost punishment is one of the techniques used in behavior modification.

See also *Adler, Alfred; behavior modification; discipline; punishment.*

retardation: See *mental retardation.*

reversibility: The ability to understand that some physical operations, or procedures, can be inverted or transposed. For example, the water in a (narrow) glass can be poured into a (wide) bowl; the amount of water is the same, but the depth of water in the bowl is less and the level of the surface is lower because the water is more spread out. The child who can think in reversible terms is aware that if the water is poured from the bowl back into the glass, the level of the surface will again be higher. This capacity is absent during the preoperational stage of development. It appears in connection with the concrete operations stage, around the age of 6 or 7.

See also *cognitive development; concrete operations stage; preoperational stage; Piaget, Jean.*

reward: See *reinforcer.*

risk factor: Any factor that increases the likelihood of an undesirable outcome in development or behavior. Risk factors can operate at either a biological or a psychological level and can include genetic predispositions, chromosomal anomalies, infections, exposure to toxic substances, malnutrition, an overly stressful birth, child abuse, lack of affection, and so forth.

Rubella contracted during pregnancy is an example of a biological risk factor because it can be a cause of birth defects. Another example of a biological risk factor is the excessive consumption of alcohol by a mother during pregnancy because it causes fetal alcohol syndrome. On the other hand, a series of failure experiences in a given area of endeavor (e.g., the acquisition of basic arithmetical skills) in childhood is a psychological risk factor because it can be a cause of learned helplessness and low self-esteem. It is evident that there are numerous risk factors that can potentially contribute to adverse outcomes.

See also *birth defects; child abuse; chromosomal anomalies; fetal alcohol syndrome (FAS); genetic predisposition; rubella; learned helplessness; malnutrition; self-esteem; sexually transmitted diseases (STDs); teratogenic agents.*

Ritalin: See *methylphenidate.*

rite of passage: In tribal societies, a ceremony, often involving a challenge to the abilities and skills of a young person, marking the transition from child to adult status. The term has been adapted to contemporary culture to signify the tasks that are associated with an adolescent's acquisition of adult status.

A familiar rite of passage in our culture is obtaining a driver's license. There is the challenge: the adolescent must pass the driver's test. Then there is often a little celebration. And the adolescent with driving privileges often experiences an important rise in self-esteem. Other common rites of passage on the way to adulthood in contemporary culture are going out on a first date, obtaining a first job, acquiring a credit card, and departing for college. These are all important, exciting psychological events and have substantial personal meaning to the adolescent. Effective parents tend to respect the significance of rites of passage.

See also *adolescence; identity versus role confusion; self-esteem.*

rivalry: See *sibling rivalry.*

Rogers, Carl Ransom (1902–1987): An American psychologist, personality theorist, and father of client-centered therapy. Rogers' personality theory and his techniques of therapy both have important implications for child rearing.

Rogers was granted a Ph.D. degree in clinical psychology in 1931 by Columbia University Teachers College. He served for more than ten years on the staff of the Rochester Guidance Center in Rochester, New York, and for a portion of that time as the Center's director. He taught psychology at several universities, including the University of Chicago. In 1946, he was elected president of the American Psychological Association. When he was 54 years of age, the Association honored him with its Distinguished Scientific Contribution Award.

Rogers became disenchanted early in his career with traditional psychoanalysis as a form of therapy. First, he believed that it focuses too much on the past and not enough on the present and the future. Second, it is too deterministic. The person's behavior is seen as reactive, a result of biological forces and painful experiences. Rogers wanted to introduce an element of voluntarism, suggesting that the individual has the capacity to make choices and effect changes. Third, as a kind of therapy it proceeds too slowly because it tends to avoid dealing with the individual's current, actual problems in living. Fourth, the therapist is too much of an authority figure. He or she should be seen as a helper, but not an all-wise judge.

Borrowing to some extent from ideas earlier expressed by Alfred Adler and Otto Rank, Rogers formulated client-centered therapy. One of the key ideas of client-centered therapy is the assertion that human beings have a basic self-actualizing tendency, an inborn inclination toward personal growth and mental health. Rogers held this viewpoint in common with Abraham Maslow. Therapy, according to Rogers, should provide a nurturing environment, making it possible for the individual's self-actualizing tendency to emerge. Rogers's approach to therapy is particulary useful in counseling adolescents who do not have a severe mental disorder, but who are going through a significant life crisis, such as a battle with alcohol or other drugs, a tendency toward sexual promiscuity, a lack of a sense of direction in life, a problem with defining an identity, and so forth.

The therapy techniques employed by Rogers have been applied to recommended communication skills and parent effectiveness training. Rogers has emphasized that it is important for the therapist to have unconditional positive regard for the client in therapy. *Unconditional positive regard* refers to accepting the client as a person even if the individual's behavior itself is immoral or irresponsible. This has suggested to followers of Rogers that unconditional love is an important factor in the nurturance of a healthy personality in the child.

Two of Rogers's books are *Psychotherapy and Personality Change* (1954) and *On Becoming a Person* (1961).

See also *Adler, Alfred; child psychotherapy; communication skills; Maslow, Abraham Harold; parent effectiveness training (P.E.T.); personality development; psychoanalysis; Rank, Otto; self-actualization; unconditional love.*

role confusion: See *identity versus role confusion.*

role playing: Acting in accordance with a set of behaviors associated with a given social role. A *social role* itself is a set of behavioral expectations assigned by a family, other group, or a culture to individuals in particular situations. Examples of familiar social roles are "the student," "the child," "the adolescent," "the teacher," "the parent," "the tough guy," "the sweetheart," "the judge," "the doctor," "the juvenile delinquent," "the prostitute," and so forth. As is implied, social roles can be antisocial or prosocial.

Social roles can be played consciously or subconsciously. If one is aware that one is acting in accordance with a social role and feels that this role does not in fact "fit" one's personality, then the role is being played consciously. This is often a source of emotional distress. If one identifies through processes such as identification, operant conditioning, and social (i.e., observational) learning with a particular role, then one has an identity. This is usually a source of emotional satisfaction. It should be noted that a person can play several roles during the same general time frame. For example, the same individual might at different hours of the same day play the roles of "loving child" to older parents, "parent" to his or her own children, and "attorney" in a law office.

According to Erikson's psychosocial theory of development, the discovery of satisfactory social roles is one of the major developmental tasks of adolescence.

See also *antisocial behavior; Erikson, Eric Homburger; identification; identity versus role confusion; operant conditioning; prosocial behavior; psychosocial development; social learning.*

rooting reflex: One of the reflexes that is present in the neonate and that is characterized by the neonate's head turning toward an object (a nipple or a finger) that stimulates the neonate's cheek. There will also be a sucking response. The obvious purpose of the reflex is to help the infant obtain milk. (One of the meanings of the verb *to root* is to search for something.) The reflex has a short developmental time span and will usually be gone around the age of 3 or 4 months. The presence of the reflex is one of the signs that the infant is neurologically normal.

See also *neonatal reflexes.*

Rosenthal effect: See *Pygmalion effect.*

rubella (German measles): A usually mild illness that is caused by a virus and that causes symptoms such as pains in the joints, a rash on the upper body, swelling of the neck's lymph nodes, and general fatigue. Rubella contracted during pregnancy can be dangerous to the fetus. If the infection takes place during the first four months of pregnancy, it can can cause birth defects such as heart problems, a hearing impairment, a visual impairment, cerebral palsy, and mental retardation.

See also *cerebral palsy; hearing impairment; mental retardation; visual impairment.*

rule-following in games: The capacity to play games and participate in contests in accordance with a set of rules, customs, and regulations. In general, research on cognitive development suggests that children go through four stages in their ability to follow rules:

1. Toddlers cannot play games in any meaningful sense because they simply cannot and will not follow rules.
2. Preschoolers follow some rules but often do not take them seriously. Sometimes they do not understand or remember them.
3. School-age children are able to follow rules, often take them seriously, and realize that rules, in a sense, make the game more fun.
4. Adolescents realize that rules can be rewritten, that they are human inventions and the result of social contracts.

According to Piaget, the ability of children to follow rules in games is an important component in both cognitive and moral development.

See also *cognitive development; moral development; Piaget, Jean.*

rumination disorder of infancy: An eating disorder characterized by bringing back into the mouth previously swallowed food. The disorder obtains its name from a class of animals known as ruminants (e.g., cows, sheep, and camels); these animals swallow food and then regurgitate it. The behavior of chewing this regurgitated food is known as "chewing the cud."

Although the behavior is normal for ruminants, it is certainly not normal for infants. Rumination in an infant can sometimes lead to death due to malnutrition. The disorder is an uncommon one. It appears with equal frequency in males and females.

If regurgitation is due to illness or any organic disorder, it is not rumination disorder of infancy. The disorder is a functional condition and is best thought of as a maladaptive habit.

Sometimes a drug that inhibits vomiting is prescribed to treat the disorder. Another treatment consists of small and more frequent feedings. Overstuffing the infant distends the stomach, and this may become a cue for regurgitation in some children. A combination of medical care and behavior modification is likely to be effective in bringing the condition under control. Although spontaneous recovery from the condition is quite possible, it is unwise to count on this because of the very real danger to the child.

See also *behavior modification; eating disorders.*

running away: The act of leaving home without permission for an extended period of time. When prepubertal children run away it is often a sham behavior without serious intent. Often the act lasts for only a few hours. On their own, they feel threatened and afraid and return home quickly. Seldom do they stay out overnight. The behavior is common and should not be taken as a sign of a serious emotional problem unless it is chronic.

When adolescents run away, they are often quite serious about it, and many of them stay away for weeks and months. Some never return home. Estimates suggest that about 1 in 100 adolescents become runaways in a given year. In terms of sheer numbers, this is close to 250,000 teenage runaways each year. It is encouraging to note that more than one half of runaways take refuge with acquaintances or other family members. However, somewhat over 10 percent depart from their familiar territory and travel for substantial distances. Big cities have become a questionable haven for relatively large numbers of homeless adolescents who survive by theft and prostitution. Drug abuse is often associated with these behaviors. Even the most serious runaways may decide that they are better off at home than on their own, and it is common for them to make contact with the family after several months.

Causal factors in running away include abusing parents, inability to relate to a stepparent, an unwanted pregnancy, poor grades in school, ineffective relationships with peers, the belief or fantasy that parents can be manipulated and made to feel sorry for their failures, low self-esteem, a need for autonomy, feeling unloved and unwanted, and the desire for a more exciting and interesting life.

In the larger sense, running away is a sign that there has been a breakdown in two-way communication between parent(s) and child. Prevention of the inappropriate behavior revolves around dealing with the causal factors identified earlier. Adolescents seldom run away from a functional family in which they feel understood and loved. Respect for the child's feelings is a key factor in keeping the home intact.

When the runaway returns, it is prudent to be as affectionate and forgiving as possible. The child should feel that the parent or parents are genuinely happy and relieved that he or she has come back to the family. A series of sharp lectures, tongue lashings, and moral pronouncements may contribute to driving the child away again.

See also *abusing parent; adolescence; communication skills; drug abuse in adolescence; juvenile delinquency.*

S

safety needs: According to Maslow, a set of needs above physiological needs, or biological drives, and below love and belongingness needs. An example of a safety need is the need to protect the body against injury or harm. Therefore, even infants and toddlers learn to avoid potentially harmful stimuli, such as a burning match or a growling dog. Older children may, due to a combination of safety needs and adverse experiences, develop intense fears or even phobias (i.e., irrational fears).

Safety needs fall into the general category that Maslow called *deficiency needs*, needs that must be met as a condition of survival. They are low in the ladder of needs leading to the highest need, which he called *self-actualization*.

See also *biological drives; deficiency needs; Maslow, Abraham Harold; phobia; physiological needs; self-actualization.*

savant: see *idiot savant.*

schedules of reinforcement: As formulated by B. F. Skinner and his associate C. B. Ferster, different patterns of reinforcement based on either response frequencies or time sequences. Schedules of reinforcement are important because they affect both the rate of acquisition of operant responses and their resistance to extinction. In practical terms, this means that if a desirable habit in a child is reinforced in certain ways, it will tend to be a strong habit and difficult to break. Schedules of reinforcement have many applications in behavior modification.

The basic distinction to be made is between continuous reinforcement and partial reinforcement. In *continuous reinforcement,* the child receives a reinforcer every time the desirable action is performed. For example, a child is given a word of praise every time the bed is made properly. In *partial reinforcement,* the child receives a reinforcer some of the time after the desirable action is performed. For example, a child is given a word of praise every other time the bed is made properly. With exceptions, acquisition of a habit is somewhat slower under conditions of partial reinforcement. However, it will show greater resistance to extinction; it will be a stronger, more entrenched habit.

There are four basic patterns associated with partial reinforcement. These are (1) a fixed-ratio schedule, (2) a variable-ratio schedule, (3) a fixed-interval schedule, and (4) a variable-interval schedule. In a *fixed-ratio schedule,* the child receives a reinforcer according to a predictable pattern, such as every other time, every third time, or every fourth time the desirable action is performed. In a *variable-ratio schedule*, the child receives a reinforcer according to an unpredictable pattern, such as the first time, the third time, the fourth time, and the seventh time a desirable action is performed. Although acquisition of the habit will be slower, a variable-ratio schedule tends to build a habit with greater resistance to extinction than does a fixed-ratio schedule.

In a *fixed-interval schedule,* a child receives a reinforcer for the performance of a learning task each time a given span of time has passed. For example, a child receives a word of praise or milk and a cookie after completing each half-hour of practice on the piano. In a *variable-interval schedule,* a child receives a reinforcer a certain number of times, but with varying spans of time between the occurrences. For example, a child receives a word of praise *on average* every ten minutes from a math tutor during a one hour lesson. Sometimes the reinforcers are only 2 minutes apart; at other times they may be 14 minutes apart. It is evident that the kind of variable reinforcement appropriate depends to some extent on the way time is framed in the learning task.

The key concept of importance is that partial reinforcement, either of a ratio or interval type, tends to build strong, resistant habits. A practical strategy when attempting to build habits in children is to start with continuous reinforcement for the first few performances of the desirable action. Then switch to a fixed schedule (e.g., every other time). And finally switch to a variable, or unpredictable, schedule.

See also *behavior modification; discipline; operant conditioning; partial reinforcement; reinforcer; Skinner, Burrhus Frederick.*

schema (scheme): In Piaget's theory of cognitive development, an abstract mental representation of the experienced world; a conceptual outline. A schema in Piaget's theory is similar to what is meant by the more familiar word *concept.* (The plural form of *schema* is *schemata.*)

Schemata become increasingly complex with age. An individual's schematic system can be made manifest, to some extent, by asking questions. Suppose 4-year-old William is asked, "What is the sun?" Perhaps he answers, "It's a big ball of fire in the sky." And this more or less completes his description. It can be seen that his schema, or idea of the sun, is a simple abstraction from his experience. On the other hand, suppose 19-year-old Eleanor, who has taken a course in astronomy, is asked the same question. She answers, "The sun is a solar furnace. It produces its heat by a process of fusion, not fission. Without the sun, life on Earth would not be possible." Her response suggests that her schema for the sun is rich and complex and is probably much closer to whatever the sun "is" than William's schema.

To a large extent, cognitive development is the process of forming increasingly adequate schemata.

See also *accommodation; assimilation; cognitive development; concept formation; Piaget, Jean.*

scheme: See *schema.*

schizophrenia: See *childhood schizophrenia.*

Scholastic Aptitude Test (SAT): A standardized test used to place and advise students applying for college admission. The Scholastic Aptitude Test can be administered in relatively large group settings and scored by machine. The student receives a verbal score and a mathematical score that are reported on a 200-to-800 scale. Results are also reported in terms of percentiles. A *percentile* is a unit of measurement using the base 100. For example, if a student receives a percentile score of 80 on the Verbal Scale, this means that he or she is in the top 20 percent of students in general for this aptitude; looked at another way, it means the student scored better than 80 percent of those who took the test.

The SAT is extensively used, and relatively recently it has come in for a considerable amount of criticism. There are those who argue that the SAT is not a valid test for students who are members of ethnic and racial minorities. Others assert that it is gender-biased in favor of males. The test has been revised, and continues to be re-evaluated, in response to concerns about its validity.

Although the SAT is not defined as an intelligence test, its scores tend to be correlated with scores obtained on standardized intelligence tests, such as the Stanford-Binet Intelligence Scale or the Wechsler scales.

See also *giftedness; intelligence tests; Stanford-Binet Intelligence Scale; validity of a test; Wechsler intelligence scales.*

school achievement: The ability to function effectively in a formal school environment as measured by such standards as grades, teacher evaluations of ability to cooperate, awards and honors, and so forth. A number of interacting causal factors are involved in school achievement. Birth order is one factor. Studies suggest that firstborn children, all other things being equal, tend to be more achieving than their siblings. A second important factor is intelligence. In general, children with higher IQ scores tend to earn better grades. A third factor is self-esteem. Children with high self-esteem tend to function more effectively in school than children with low self-esteem. Other important factors include size and economic status of the family, whether the family is a one-parent or two-parent one, health of the child, teacher competence, parental expectations, and so forth.

See also *birth order; intelligence quotient (IQ); one-parent family; Pygmalion effect; self-esteem.*

school phobia: See *separation anxiety disorder.*

scooting: A form of locomotion from a sitting position and characterized by pushing motions with the arms combined with lifting, assisting
motions from the legs. Scooting is a stepping stone on the way to
walking, and sometimes takes the place of crawling in the infant's
sequence of motor development.

The behavior appears commonly in children raised in institutions
under conditions of stimulus deprivation. It is hypothesized that this
may be because they are to some extent limited in opportunities to
utilize space in a prone position. But it can and does appear in
children who are not deprived and is sometimes simply a preferred
form of locomotion to crawling. Therefore, it does not necessarily
signify a form of motor pathology or emotional disturbance. If parents
want to encourage crawling instead of scooting, they should allow
the child to spend time reclining in a face-down position with ample
surrounding space. If, in spite of adequate opportunity, infants prefer
scooting to crawling, they should not be discouraged. There is nothing
inherently "wrong" with the behavior.

See also *crawling; motor development.*

script: According to transactional analysis, an unconscious life plan
selected and devised by the Child ego state during the prepubertal
years. Eric Berne, the father of transactional analysis, asserted that
children often decide at an early age whether or not they are going
to eventually be successes, failures, or mediocrities in life's competitive race. Thus, they formulate a rough image of what their life will
become. Berne called this rough image the *script protocol.* The three
basic script protocols are the Winning script, the Losing script, and
the Nonwinning, or Also-ran, script.

Later, in adolescence and adulthood, the script is elaborated and
becomes more complex. This is called the *shooting script* and is cast
with a set of actual people. The point, however, is that in scripts the
individuals are not seen in objective terms but in subjective ones
distorted by psychological and emotional needs.

Scripts are behavioral strait-jackets and are basically undesirable
because they reduce spontaneity and autonomy. They also interfere
with intimacy, or emotional closeness, in relationships. This is true
even of Winning scripts. The Winner is a role in the script. And the
individual who is playing this role may strive compulsively for

objective success in terms of money or outstanding professional recognition without much regard for the rights and feelings of other people, including members of his or her own family.

Note that the concept of a Winner in a script is different than the concept of an actual winner in life. A winner in life has a broader perspective than the person trapped in the role of Winner in a script. Actual winners have high self-esteem and are capable of genuine enjoyment.

Transactional analysis argues that living according to a script is living according to a decision made by the Child ego state. Instead, the individual should seek to replace the power of the Child ego state with the reasonable authority of the Adult ego state, the inner agent of reason. When the Adult ego state guides one's life, choices become open and flexible, self-direction becomes possible, and life loses its compulsive quality.

See also *Berne, Eric; ego state; transactional analysis.*

secondary circular reaction: See *circular reactions.*

secondary reinforcer: See *reinforcer.*

secondary sexual characteristics: Readily identifiable, biologically determined attributes associated with the primary characteristic of one's gender (i.e., the fact that one is a male or a female.) Secondary sexual characteristics first become manifest at puberty and become increasingly evident during adolescence. They help to readily discriminate members of each sex, but they are not in and of themselves essential for the reproductive process.

In males, the penis and the testes grow in size, the voice's pitch becomes lower and has more timbre, a beard forms, and the body becomes somewhat harder with muscle. In females, there is maturation of the breasts, and there is the distribution of somewhat more fat in both the breast and the hip area. In both males and females, pubic hair becomes quite evident, and underarm hair forms.

See also *adolescence; menarche; nubile female; pituitary gland; puberty.*

secular trend: See *menarche.*

security blanket: See *security object.*

security object (transitional object): An object important during late infancy and toddlerhood that helps a child reduce anxiety, sleep, or feel more comfortable and relaxed. Some examples of common security objects are a particular blanket (i.e., a *security blanket*), a certain soft doll or stuffed animal, or a tattered piece of clothing.

There is no need to make a special effort to encourage the child to give up the security object. The item is sometimes called a *transitional object* to suggest that it represents a partial psychological bridge between early and late childhood. Around the age of 6 or 7, the vast majority of children spontaneously lose their intense attachment to the object.

See also *attachment; pacifier; trust versus mistrust.*

sedatives: See *drug therapy.*

self-actualization: As formulated by the personality theorist Abraham Maslow, an inborn tendency to maximize one's talents and potentialities. The need for self-actualization is often first evident in middle childhood when children begin to act on their natural interests, aptitudes, and abilities.

The concept of *self-actualization* was first proposed by the psychiatrist and neurologist Kurt Goldstein in connection with the striving tendencies of individuals with brain damage. However, it is in connection with Maslow's humanistic personality theory that the idea has really blossomed in psychology.

Maslow ranks, in ascending order, the needs that prompt human motivation. Those needs are: basic physiological needs, stimulation needs, safety needs, love and belongingness needs, esteem needs, cognitive needs, and self-actualization. All of the needs, with the exception of cognitive needs and self-actualization, represent deficiency motivation; they are experienced as gaps in human existence. Cognitive needs and self-actualization, on the other hand, represent being needs, or growth motivation. It is a great natural tendency, first evident during childhood, for individuals to *become*, to do something with their lives that takes advantage of their abilities, aptitudes, and interests. For example, 15-year-old Martha feels that her true vocation in life is to become a music teacher. She practices two hours a day, is a member of the high school band, earns good grades, and so forth, all in the interests of her goal. It can be said that much of her behavior is rooted in growth motivation, that she is a self-actualizing adolescent.

Although Maslow believed that the need for self-actualization is inborn, he also believed that it is rather easily thwarted. Parents may unfeelingly criticize an adolescent or young adult's choices and decisions, friends may make arbitrary evaluations, opportunities may be difficult to obtain, or doubts may exist concerning one's talents. All of these obstacles, and more, may derail the impetus of self-actualization.

The concept of self-actualization is an important one in the context of mental health. If the need for self-actualization is frustrated, then the individual can fall into a state of depression. The individual may need to rediscover the path toward self-actualization. Reading inspiring books, taking small steps in the direction of personal growth, and psychotherapy with a humanistic orientation may all be helpful.

See also *cognitive needs; depression; growth needs; Maslow, Abraham Harold.*

self-concept: A set of related ideas that one holds about oneself in terms of intelligence, creativity, interests, aptitudes, behavioral traits, and personal appearance. The self-concept may be generally positive or generally negative. If it is generally positive, then the individual usually feels able and attractive. If it is generally negative, then the individual usually feels inadequate and unattractive.

The self-concept begins to form early in life, probably as early as toddlerhood. In psychoanalytic theory, this is when the ego, the conscious "I" of the personality, first begins to emerge. The self-concept is an important personal issue in adolescence and is associated with the psychosocial stage of identity versus role confusion.

It is important to realize that the self-concept often exists independent of the self as perceived by others. For example, in an extreme case, an individual may have a negative self-concept and be perceived as able and attractive by most other people.

The role of the self-concept plays an important part in Carl Rogers's client-centered therapy, a kind of psychotherapy based on humanistic principles. A principal goal of client-centered therapy is to help an individual develop a more positive self-concept.

See also *ego; identity versus role confusion; Rogers, Carl Ransom; self-actualization; self-esteem; self-expectations.*

self-esteem: An evaluation of the self; an informal self-ranking in terms of personal worth. Obviously the concept of self-esteem is related to the self-concept. Persons with a negative self-concept tend to have low self-esteem. Persons with a positive self-concept tend to have high self-esteem. Studies conducted by the research psychologist Stanley Coopersmith suggest that some of the important antecedents to self-esteem reside in childhood. On the whole, parents who tend to be democratic, authoritative (not authoritarian), and affectionate foster self-esteem in their children. As an adult, a series of failures in important life tasks can undermine self-esteem. Conversely, a series of successes can bolster self-esteem.

William James said that self esteem can be thought of in terms of a formula:

Success *divided by* Pretensions *equals* Self-esteem

Success refers to actual accomplishments. Pretensions refers to goals and dreams. Essentially, James's formula communicates the idea that self-esteem is subjective, not objective. If one has a low level of aspiration, then it does not take much real success to maintain self-esteem. However, if one has a high level of aspiration, then it takes much more real success to maintain self-esteem. As a consequence, odd as it may seem, many people who have substantial accomplishments often suffer from low self-esteem. In terms of James's formula, it is perhaps because they demand too much of themselves.

See also *authoritarian parent; authoritative parent; James, William; parental style; self-actualization; self-concept; self-expectations.*

self-expectations: As applied to children and adolescents, what they expect to accomplish when challenged with a task or responsibility. Children with high self-expectations tend to set their level of aspiration correspondingly high. Conversely, children with low self-expectations tend to set their level of aspiration correspondingly low. For example, if 11-year-old Dorothy is given an arithmetic assignment and expects to do well on it, she probably will. If she runs into difficulty comprehending a certain problem, she sticks with the assignment, thinking, "I can figure this out. I've solved this kind of thing before." Her self-expectations form part of a self-fulfilling prophecy in which what she expects to happen does, in fact, happen.

Studies of children's self-expectations reveal that children tend to assign perceived causes to their own behavior. These are called *attributions.* Children with high self-expectations tend to attribute internal causes to their behavior. They see themselves as competent, skilled, having aptitudes, and so forth. Children with low self-expectations tend to attribute external causes to their behavior. They see themselves as burdened with a general situation characterized by unfair teachers, not enough time to do homework, too many unreasonable requests, and so forth.

See also *Pygmalion effect; self-actualization; self-concept; self-esteem.*

self-injurious behavior: Behavior characterized by bodily harm inflicted by and to oneself. Children who engage in self-injurious behavior often display visible bruises, lacerations, or other wounds. Self-injurious behavior is relatively common and is a sign of an emotional disturbance. It is particularly linked to autistic disorder. However, it is also seen in children who do not have such an extreme, pervasive developmental disorder.

Several causal factors play a role in self-injurious behavior:

1. Guilt may play a role. Children who are perfectionistic and self-demanding may believe, in a pathological way, that they deserve punishment for their failings.

2. The behavior may be a sign of aggression directed inward. The child feels frustrated by parents, other authority figures, inability to achieve in school, or inability to make friends. If a child does not think that there is psychological safety in expressing aggression openly, it can be directed to a psychological underground.

3. The behavior may be linked to depression and feelings of incompetence and inadequacy. Depressed people are at increased

risk for suicide; it is the maximum self-injury. Self-injurious behavior is related to suicide in terms of its psychodynamics.

4. The behavior may be a way of manipulating and controlling authority figures. If it evokes sympathy or helps the child evade responsibilities, it may be inadvertently reinforced by well-meaning parents.

5. The behavior is aggravated if the child is a member of a dysfunctional family, one in which psychological and emotional needs are not effectively met.

Parents can reduce the frequency and intensity of a child's self-injurious behavior by exploring ways to undercut its psychological roots. For example, perfectionistic children should not have excessive demands for excellence and overachievement added to their already heavy psychological burden. A practical approach is to apply behavior modification skills designed to stop supplying self-injury with reinforcement.

A principal treatment for self-injurious behavior is insight-oriented psychotherapy aimed at uncovering the child's motives for the behavior. Play therapy can be used to help the child express repressed aggression. Behavior therapy is usually a part of the treatment plan, helping the child discover more constructive ways to cope with chaotic feelings. In some cases, antidepressant medication may be prescribed.

See also *adolescent suicide; behavior modification; behavior therapy; drug therapy; dysfunctional family; play therapy; psychotherapy.*

self-instructional training: See *cognitive-behavior modification.*

selfishness: A behavioral trait characterized by preoccupation with oneself, one's own interests, and one's own desires. Conversely, the individual has little regard for the welfare of others. Toddlers go through a period of natural selfishness, which is considered to be normal. *Egocentrism*, the ability to perceive and comprehend only from one's own point of view, is a defining feature of the preoperational stage of cognitive development.

However, around the age of 7 or 8 years, children usually are much less selfish. They comprehend the fact that others also have rights, and they respect the needs of others. Children who are excessively selfish in middle and late childhood are not described as egocentric, but as *egotistic*.

It should be understood that around the age of 13 or 14 years, there is frequently a partial return of something like early egocentrism. The individual in early adolescence tends to go through a transitional phase in which preoccupation with the self is very intense.

If selfishness is chronic or excessive in a child, it is a sign of pathological personality development. Causal factors in such selfishness include inadvertent reinforcement of early egocentrism, a neurotic process, lack of effective socialization, giving the child an excessive amount of status or importance, and parental overprotectiveness.

Parents can cope with excessive selfishness in several ways:

1. It is important to avoid reinforcing selfish behavior. The child should not obtain a goal by being selfish.
2. Responsible behavior should be valued and reinforced. The application of behavior modification skills will be helpful.
3. The parents should provide appropriate role models. If parents are themselves excessively selfish, children tend to learn the behavior by imitation. Social learning plays a large part in the acquisition of selfish behavior.
4. The parents need to explore underlying causes. If selfishness is a sign of chronic anxiety and emotional insecurity, this needs to be addressed with understanding and, in some cases, counseling and therapy.

See also *behavior modification; egocentrism; preoperational stage; social learning.*

sensitive period: See *critical period.*

sensorimotor stage (sensory-motor stage): The first stage in Piaget's theory of cognitive development, the stage associated with infancy, lasting from birth to approximately 2 years of age. It is itself made up of a set of developmental substages characterized by such features as exercise of the reflexes, becoming familiar with one's own body (e.g., discovering one's fingers), and reaching for, and physically manipulating, objects. Much of the behavior of the infant is repetitive in nature. Piaget labels this kind of behavior *circular reactions.*

Toward the end of the sensorimotor stage, purposeful behavior makes its first appearance. When, for example, infants are able to look for something that is missing or that has been recently removed, they have acquired a capacity called *object permanence.* This capacity is not present in the early portion of the sensorimotor stage.

Piaget's approach assumes an absence of conscious, well-formed ideas in early infancy. These ideas, called *schemata* (i.e., "conceptual outlines") in Piaget's system, arise from experience and take time to develop. The kinds of sensory inputs, and responses to them, that take place during the sensorimotor period form the foundation that makes conscious, self-reflective thought possible. This appears in the second stage of cognitive development, the preoperational stage.

The term *sensorimotor* is intrinsically meaningful and descriptive. The child senses the environment (i.e., sees, hears, tastes, and so forth) and makes motor movements (e.g., head turning, hands reaching, and so forth) in response to sensations. A familiarity with the external world and a set of expectations is, consequently, acquired. During this stage, the child shows an intense, general curiosity. The infant cannot be said to have interests but is very *interested.*

See also *circular reactions; cognitive development; infant; object permanence; Piaget, Jean; preoperational stage; schema.*

sentences in language development: See *language development.*

separation anxiety: Anxiety associated with separation from a parent or parent surrogate. Separation anxiety is signified by crying, agitation, and general distress. In infancy, separation anxiety is normal and is an aspect of the general phenomenon of attachment. The infant has not yet formed the set of expectations suggesting that separations are temporary and that people return. Therefore, from the infant's point of view any separation may represent a total loss of the parent. Separation anxiety usually appears around the age of 6 or 7 months, becomes more intense until about 18 months, and then begins to decline in strength.

See also *attachment; separation anxiety disorder; trust versus mistrust.*

separation anxiety disorder: A behavioral disorder characterized by intense anxiety associated with separation from a parent or parent surrogate. Separation anxiety disorder is a disorder of childhood or adolescence and is not to be confused with normal separation anxiety displayed during infancy. Examples of specific behaviors that suggest the presence of the disorder are irrational fears that a parent will be injured, overconcern about being kidnapped, resistance to going to bed, excessive homesickness when visiting others overnight, and frequently following a parent around the house for no particular reason.

School phobia, an irrational fear of going to school, is usually interpreted as a sign of separation anxiety disorder. In the case of actual school phobia, the child is neither malingering nor trying to avoid tests and homework. Instead the child is avoiding school in order to stay near a parent or home, feeling safe and secure only under these conditions.

In both children and adolescents, the disorder is equally common in both sexes. It is more common during preadolescence than during adolescence. Separation anxiety disorder is encountered relatively often by counselors and therapists.

Loosely, separation anxiety disorder may be thought of as an indication of a neurotic process in the child. Causal factors in the disorder include a lack of basic trust; overprotective and overattentive parents; overattachment to one or both parents; underlying depressive tendencies; and a highly sensitive, reactive temperament. A specific causal factor that can trigger the disorder is an important loss or significant life change. Examples include moving to a different area, enrolling in a new school, loss of a pet, a sickness, or the death of a close relative.

Parents can cope with separation anxiety disorder by providing gentle encouragement and by allowing, if practical, the child to, at first, control the length of separations. The child should not be criticized or mocked for "being silly." Nor should the child be blamed or made to feel guilty for the symptoms of the disorder. On the other hand, the child should not be allowed to manipulate the parents with the symptoms of the disorder; this will reinforce its associated behaviors. The application of both communication skills and behavior modification skills can be helpful.

Treatment for separation anxiety disorder usually consists of insight-oriented psychotherapy aimed at helping the child or adolescent understand the emotional roots of the problem. This can be combined with behavior therapy designed to explore ways to function more effectively. Desensitization therapy, a kind of behavior therapy, can also be helpful. In some cases low doses, for a defined time period, of antianxiety or antidepressant drugs are prescribed.

See also *attachment; behavior modification; childhood neurosis; communication skills; desensitization therapy; drug therapy; phobia; separation anxiety; trust versus mistrust.*

seriation: In Piaget's theory of cognitive development, the concept that objects can be placed in a consistent rank order (i.e., a series) based on a quantitative attribute, such as size or weight. In a typical seriation problem, a child is randomly given objects from two groups, say five blocks and five balls of varying sizes. The child is asked to separate the objects into two groups (the blocks and the balls) and then to place them in order from large to small within each group. Children in the preoperational stage, approximately between the ages of 2 and 7 years, typically fail at the task. Children in the concrete operations stage, approximately between the ages of 7 and 12 years, typically succeed at the task.

See also *cognitive development; concrete operations stage; Piaget, Jean; preoperational stage.*

sex chromosomes: One pair of the set of 23 pairs of chromosomes in the nucleus of a normal cell. One kind of sex chromosome is designated the X chromosome, which carries the genetic information required to produce a female. The other sex chromosome is designated the Y chromosome, which carries the genetic information required to produce a male. The genetic information on the Y chromosome is dominant in developmental influence, and the genetic information on the X chromosome is recessive.

Consequently, if a fertilized egg cell consists of a pair of X chromosomes, one from the mother's ovum and the other from the father's sperm, the eventual child will be a female. On the other hand, if a fertilized egg cell consists of a mixed pair with one X chromosome from the mother's ovum and one Y chromosome from the father's sperm, the eventual child will be a male. Note that the mother can contribute only X chromosomes. Approximately half of the father's sperm carry an X chromosome; the other half carry a Y chromosome. Therefore, the gender of the child is determined by the specific sperm that unites with an ovum.

See also *chromosomal anomalies; chromosomes; dominant gene; gene; recessive gene; Turner's syndrome.*

sex differences in abilities: The hypothesis that important differences in behavior and aptitudes are associated with one's gender. The hypothesis can take the form that differences are ultimately caused by genes on the sex chromosomes. This is the biological, or nativistic, hypothesis. Or it can take the form that differences are ultimately caused by experience and learning. This is the psychological, or empiricistic, hypothesis.

What differences, if any, exist on the basis of gender? Researchers Eleanor Maccoby and Carol Jacklin sifted through a large number of studies and made an analysis. They concluded that much folklore about sex differences is incorrect and that the following widely held beliefs are without foundation: (1) female children are more "social" than male children; (2) female children are more "suggestible" than male children; (3) female children have lower self-esteem; (4) females are better at rote learning and simple repetitive tasks; (5) male children are more "analytic"; (6) female children are more affected by heredity, male children by environment (not necessarily a widely held belief, but a difference hypothesized by some researchers); (7) female children lack achievement motivation; and, (8) female children are auditory, male children visual (again, not necessarily a widely held belief, but a difference hypothesized by some researchers).

In view of the fact that so many myths have been laid to rest, are there any sex differences that are fairly well established? Maccoby and Jacklin answer yes to this question. They indicate that there are only four traits that seem to be consistently associated with gender. These are that (1) female children have greater verbal ability than male children, (2) male children excel in visual-spatial ability, (3) male children excel in mathematical ability, and (4) male children are more aggressive than female children.

Having noted these four consistent differences, two additional points need to be made. First, an individual may reverse the group trend. For example, Steve might have more verbal ability than Elaine. Marie might be more aggressive than Bert. The differences refer to groups, not individuals. Second, the degree to which the four traits are due to inborn tendencies as opposed to experience and the learning process can be debated. The survey of human research conducted by Maccoby and Jacklin and several other researchers suggests that a number of the pet theories of the nativist, those who favor a biological hypothesis, must be laid to rest.

See also *empiricism; gender identity; nativism; sex chromosomes; sex role.*

sex role: A set of cultural expectations concerning appropriate behaviors for individuals based on their gender. In traditional Western culture, standard sex roles for men have called for them to be assertive, achievement-oriented, thoughtful in contrast to intuitive, brave, oriented toward science and technology, and so forth. Standard sex roles for women have called for them to be submissive, shy, home-oriented, intuitive in contrast to thoughtful, nurturing, and so forth. The tendency to have standard expectations for males and females has led to *sex-role stereotypes*, rigid cultural prejudices suggesting that "normal" men and women fit the standard expectations and that it is pathological to act differently. Fortunately, a number of recent trends suggest that there is more latitude and tolerance in sex-roles crossover today than there was in the past. As recently as two decades ago, it was taken for granted that almost all nurses were women and almost all physicians were men. Today, male nurses are respected and there are many women physicians.

The process by which sex roles are acquired is known as *sex typing*. It is common to dress infant males in blue and infant females in pink, suggesting that differential treatment begins early. When a male child cries after a fall, he may be told, for example, by a parent, "Now be a man, son. You shouldn't cry over a little thing like that." On the other hand, when a female child cries after a fall, she may be told by the same parent, "Come and sit with me a few minutes. Let me hug you." In this particular case, the parent in question is providing differential reinforcement for the same behavior and obviously encouraging standard cultural expectations. A given child's reinforcement history will have much to do with the acquisition of sex roles.

Another factor that is important in sex-role formation is the process of identification. According to psychoanalysis, it is common for children in traditional families, particularly in middle childhood, to unconsciously link their egos to the parent of the same sex. Consequently, males tend to imitate their fathers, females tend to imitate their mothers. This ties in with the widely recognized importance of social learning.

Still another factor involved in the determination of sex roles is the presentation of the various activities of males and females in motion pictures, television, and books. Again, it is generally accepted that social learning is influenced by the mass media.

The role of genetic factors in sex roles has been the subject of much discussion and debate. In the past, folklore had it that "boys will be boys and girls will be girls." The implication was that behavior was to a large extent biologically determined. Although today it is recognized that there are some differences that have a genetic basis, they are neither as well-defined nor as clear-cut as our standard sex-role definitions would suggest.

See also *gender identity; identification; psychosexual development; psychosocial development; role playing; sex differences in abilities; social learning.*

sex typing: See *sex role.*

sex-role stereotype: See *sex role.*

sex-linked disorders: Disorders associated with an individual's sex chromosomes (i.e., the X and Y chromosomes). There are a group of recessive disorders carried only on X chromosomes, and these disorders affect, in the main, only males. This is because males have only one X chromosome. (The male genetic code is XY.) Females, on the other hand, have two X chromosomes. (The female genetic code is XX.) Therefore, recessive genes carried on an X chromosome seldom show up in the female. Dominant genes on one of her X chromosomes will interfere with the expression of the recessive gene on her other X chromosome. The male has no such genetic protection because his Y chromosome does not carry genes for the trait in question.

Examples of disorders caused by a recessive gene, or genes, on the X chromosome are male pattern baldness (i.e., hereditary alopecia), color vision problems, a tendency to bleed excessively (i.e., hemophilia), and certain kinds of muscular dystrophy.

Some disorders are caused by sex-chromosome anomalies. Two of importance are Klinefelter's syndrome and Turner's syndrome. *Klinefelter's syndrome* is caused by an XXY chromosome pattern and afflicts only males. *Turner's syndrome* is caused by a missing X chromosome and afflicts only females.

See also *chromosomal anomalies; dominant gene; genetic counseling; Klinefelter's syndrome; recessive gene; sex chromosomes; Turner's syndrome.*

sexual development: See *secondary sexual characteristics; psychosexual development.*

sexual exploration: In prepubertal children, the showing—usually by two children playing alone—of one's body to the other. Often this involves touching of the genitals. Homosexual acts are fairly common but seldom suggest that this will be the child's eventual primary orientation. Efforts in the direction of actual heterosexual intercourse are less common but sometimes take place.

Although the behavior is distressing to adults, it must be remembered that it falls within normal bounds. A certain amount of sexual curiosity exists prior to adolescence, and children may act on it. Psychoanalysis suggests that between the ages of approximately 6 and 12, there is a period of psychosexual latency. If so, the main motive for sexual exploration is not the sexual drive, or eroticism, but curiosity. And children may act on their curiosity drive.

Because the behavior is motivated primarily by curiosity, it is subject to correction without resort to excessive discipline or emotional overreactions. The child needs to be given guidance in the direction of reality with a rational explanation of why the behavior is inappropriate. Parents and other caregivers should not make children feel ashamed or guilty for normal curiosity, but they should help children realize that sexual activity is to be reserved for future years. A straight-forward statement concerning future expectations and a clear prohibition will be helpful. Children who have engaged in sexual exploration should be closely supervised in order to deprive them of the opportunity for such behavior. If they ask questions about sex, these should be answered correctly without lengthy lectures. Sex itself should not be a taboo topic in the home, but simply another area of information. The parents should display normal affection, but not be openly erotic, in front of their children in order to avoid prematurely stimulating sexual interest.

See also *id; libido; love; ludic behavior; psychoanalysis; psychosexual development; secondary sexual characteristics.*

sexual maturity: The capacity to reproduce. The average age for sexual maturity in females is 12 or 13 years. For males the average age is about 14 or 15 years. However, it is normal for some individuals to attain sexual maturity one or two years above or below the average. The word *nubile* is often used to describe the sexual maturity of females.

Sexual maturity usually follows, without delay, after the adolescent growth spurt. Biologically, females begin to secrete greater quantities of estrogen hormones, develop mature ova, and begin their menses. Males begin to produce greater quantities of androgens and develop viable sperm.

See also *growth spurt; menarche; nubile female; secondary sexual characteristics.*

sexual molestation: As applied to children, the making of sexual advances and/or the performance of sexual acts by an adult. This may include the inducement into sexual activities by promises of candy, gifts, or other rewards. Or it may imply the pressuring of a child into sexual activities by threats, punishments, or other negative coercive means. In the case of either type of approach, seductive or coercive, the adult's behavior is socially offensive, illegal, and emotionally traumatic to the child. The negative impact on the child is often quite considerable and may have an adverse effect on the child's subsequent sexual attitudes and development. Sexual molestation is a form of child abuse.

The actual incidence of sexual molestation is difficult to evaluate because it tends to be underreported by its victims. Various studies suggest that between 5 percent and 10 percent of females have experienced some degree of molestation. The incidence is believed to be quite a bit lower for males.

Although children are told to watch out for strangers, it is important to realize that most molestation is associated with relatives and friends. (When molestation by a relative leads to sexual activity, it is referred to as *incest*.) Children should be told that no one (not even a parent) has the right to touch their body in a way that makes them feel uncomfortable. They should know the difference between "good touches" and "bad touches." They should know to tell a responsible adult if *anyone* touches them in a bad way.

Child molesters present no consistent personality picture. However, common factors that often show up are low self-esteem, ineffective relations with the opposite sex, confusion over sexual identity, immature attitudes toward sexual relationships, an inability to establish emotional closeness with others, excessive attention paid to children, and sexual exhibitionism. Chronic molesters who are attracted to prepubertal children suffer from a mental disorder called *pedophilia*. On the whole, it is difficult to effectively treat child molesters with counseling, psychotherapy, or other educational approaches.

The best way to prevent sexual molestation is to make it difficult or impossible to occur—children should be educated, as previously mentioned, and suspected adults should not be allowed to spend any time alone with susceptible children; nor should they be given the opportunity, through frequent contacts, to build up the child's trust and confidence.

See also *child abuse; incest.*

sexually transmitted diseases (STDs): Diseases that are spread by sexual activity. An outdated term for these diseases is *venereal diseases.* (The word *venereal* is derived from Venus, the goddess of love.) The overall incidence of sexually transmitted diseases is on the rise among adolescents because of their increased sexual activity. Among the principal STDs are acquired immune deficiency syndrome (AIDS), chlamydia infections, genital herpes, genital warts, gonorrhea, and syphilis.

Acquired immune deficiency syndrome (AIDS) is a pathological condition of the immune system attributed to infection by the *human immunodeficiency virus (HIV)*, which is found in bodily fluids, mainly blood. There has been much debate and discussion concerning the way in which AIDS is spread, but it is agreed that the main routes of transmission appear to be anal intercourse in the context of either homosexual or heterosexual activity and the sharing of unsterilized needles when using drugs. Somewhat less usual routes of transmission are conventional heterosexual relations or other forms of contact, even medical procedures, that allow the AIDS virus to enter the human bloodstream. New AIDS cases increased rapidly during the early 1980s. The number of cases is still increasing, but the growth rate is not as great as it was. It is presently estimated that close to 100 in every 1,000,000 individuals in the United States has a clinical case of AIDS. This means that the total number of AIDS cases is about 25,000. More individuals than this are infected with the AIDS virus and are likely to eventually develop the disease.

Chlamydial infections are caused by *chlamydiae*, infectious organisms that are neither bacteria nor viruses. An extremely common STD caused by chlamydiae is *nonspecific urethritis*, an infection affecting the genital organs. Nonspecific urethritis can, if ignored, sometimes create serious fertility problems in both males and females. Fortunately, chlamydia infections usually respond well to treatment with antibiotics.

Genital herpes is caused by the *herpes simplex* virus. Symptoms include discomfort when urinating, blisters and ulcers in the area of the sex organs, and swollen lymph glands in the groin. Genital herpes is associated with an increased likelihood of cancer of the cervix. Attacks come and go, usually with decreasing severity. However, the condition is chronic, and there is at present no drug that will kill the virus. Therefore, the disease can be to some extent managed but not cured.

Genital warts are caused by a kind of virus that is related to the viruses that cause other kinds of warts. Genital warts are spread to sexual partners very readily. The principal sign of an infection is warts on the penis in males or warts near the entry to the vagina in females. Both sexes may have warts in the area of the rectum. There are no obvious symptoms such as pain, itching, or other discomfort. Like genital herpes, genital warts are associated with an increased likelihood of cancer of the cervix. Treatments include surgery and the use of a solution of *podophyllin*, a drug that interferes with the activity of the virus.

Gonorrhea is caused by a bacterium. Signs and symptoms include a sore throat, discomfort when urinating, and a thick discharge from either the penis or the vagina. Symptoms are usually less obvious in females than in males. Gonorrhea is associated with an increased likelihood of eye infections, blood poisoning, damage to the heart valves, and sexual dysfunction in males. Gonorrhea is extremely common. In the United States, there are about 1,000,000 reported cases each year. And perhaps two to three times this many are not reported. Gonorrhea usually responds readily to treatment with antibiotics.

Syphilis is caused by the syphilis spirochete, a corkscrew-shaped bacterium. Signs and symptoms of syphilis are associated with four distinct stages: primary, secondary, latent, and tertiary. The *primary* stage appears a few weeks after sexual contact and is characterized by a chancre (i.e., a sore or ulcer with a firm base) commonly in the genital area. The *secondary* stage manifests itself two to three months after the onset of the disease and is characterized by swollen lymph glands, a rash with red bumps, a headache, and a fever. The *latent* stage follows immediately after second-stage symptoms subside. During the latent stage, the disease does not produce symptoms, and the individual may think that he or she is cured. The *tertiary* stage appears after a latency period lasting generally for a few years. One of the principal conditions associated with this last stage is *general paresis*, an organic disorder characterized by paralysis and dementia. The brain and central nervous system are gradually destroyed by the action of the spirochete.

In the 1970s, general paresis accounted for about 1 percent of admissions to mental hospitals. Its incidence has declined to some extent since that time due to both prevention and early detection of the disease. However, syphilis continues to be a major public health problem. It is presently estimated that approximately 140 in every 1,000,000 individuals in the United States have a case of syphilis.

This means that the total number of syphilis cases is about 35,000. About 5 percent of persons with untreated syphilis will develop general paresis. Antibiotics are used to treat syphilis, and treatment is usually effective.

Infection can take place during pregnancy. Infants infected with the disease are said to suffer from *congenital syphilis*. Fortunately, at present, congenital syphilis is uncommon.

The primary ways to prevent sexually transmitted diseases are to avoid promiscuous sexual contacts and to use condoms.

See also *acquired immune deficiency syndrome (AIDS); adolescent sex relations; birth defects.*

shame: An uncomfortable emotional state involving self-consciousness and embarrassment. A principal cause is being revealed to others as having failed at a task or having engaged in a socially offensive act. In psychoanalytic theory, shame is a forerunner of guilt. Toddlers and preschoolers who violate family rules and standards of conduct are often made to feel ashamed of themselves. Repeated shame experiences become internalized and then translate into feelings of guilt during middle and late childhood. The superego, or moral agent of the personality, forms out of this general process.

See also *guilt; initiative versus guilt; moral development; superego.*

shaping: An operant conditioning procedure characterized by reinforcement of a fractional component of a desired behavior. Shaping has practical value as a behavior modification skill. Suppose that making a bed neatly is not in a given toddler's behavioral repertoire. However, pulling up the sheets and blankets is. The toddler can at first be reinforced with hugs or other signs of approval for this behavior. Once the fractional behavior becomes a well-established habit, it facilitates the learning of the more complex habit.

See also *behavior modification; operant conditioning; reinforcer.*

short stature: A height that is significantly under the mean (i.e., arithmetical average) for a child's or adolescent's chronological age. A short stature can have a benign or a pathological cause. The principal benign cause is heredity, and the child may be a shorter-than-average adult. This is not a pathological condition, although it may be undesirable to the child and the parents. Sometimes, children who seem to be growing slowly show a late spurt and reach average, or nearly average, height.

Pathological causes of short stature include malnutrition (e.g., insufficient protein), a deficiency in the pituitary gland's production of growth hormone, an imbalance in thyroid functioning, chronic illnesses, Down's syndrome, and short extremities due to an inherited bone disease called *achondroplasia*. If it is suspected that a short stature is due to a pathological cause, a physician should be consulted.

See also *Down's syndrome; growth spurt; heredity; malnutrition; pituitary gland.*

shyness: A behavioral trait characterized by a lack of poise or confidence when dealing with others or a tendency to avoid social contact. Words such as *bashful, timid, modest,* and *overly reserved* also suggest the trait. Extreme shyness is sometimes called *social introversion.* It should be realized that in early childhood, and also often in early adolescence, shyness is quite common and does not indicate a behavioral abnormality.

If a child seems to be excessively shy it is possible that one or several causes are involved. Common ones are low self-esteem, chronic anxiety, an unstable body image, a fear of being criticized or judged, ineffective communication skills, an overprotective parental style, and a history of being teased by adults or older siblings.

A survey conducted by social psychologist Philip G. Zimbardo revealed that 80 percent of his subjects, mostly young adults, confessed to being shy some of the time. This is referred to as *situational shyness,* shyness under a given set of circumstances. *Chronic shyness,* discomfort in almost all social situations, is less common. The incidence in Zimbardo's survey was 25 percent.

Mild or moderate shyness in some situations is so common in children that it can be ignored. If the child, however, appears to suffer from chronic shyness, then parents and other caregivers need to be alert and respond appropriately. Several effective parental behaviors are possible: (1) the child should not be criticized or corrected for shyness; (2) the parent should attempt to provide an assertive, relatively confident role model; (3) the parent should attempt to arrange for comfortable situations in which the child can socialize with a maximum of emotional security (e.g., family gatherings); (4) the child should be reinforced with recognition and approval when outgoing behavioral traits are displayed. It should be realized that it is possible that some children are, by temperament, just more socially reserved than others; and this should be respected.

See also *anxiety; introversion; parental style; self-esteem; social learning; temperament.*

sibling rivalry: A tendency for brothers and sisters to compete with each other for attention, affection, and status within the family. For example, a second child is born and the first-born child, a toddler, regresses in behavior (e.g., loses some of the gains made in toilet training or cries more). The regressive behavior of the toddler arises from jealousy of the attention given to the infant.

When children are older, sibling rivalry may motivate a younger child to imitate an older sibling. For example, 9-year-old Tad knows how to ride a bicycle. He learned how only a few months ago. His 7-year-old sister, Monica, seeks to emulate Tad and learns to ride a bicycle at an earlier chronological age than he did. The motive underlying Monica's behavior was identified by Adler as the *will to power*, an inborn striving toward competence and generally effective behavior.

Sibling rivalry does not necessarily end in childhood and may extend into adolescence and adult life. However, it is generally agreed that older children are more cooperative than younger ones, and some of the intensity of the rivalry may diminish. It is important to realize that sibling rivalry is a factor in personal and social development.

There are several ways parents can respond to sibling rivalry: (1) they should accept the rivalry as normal and not, in and of itself, "bad" (just because children are rivals does not mean that they do not love each other); (2) parents should do their best to make all of their children feel loved and to make sure that they do not play favorites; (3) if siblings are engaged in an emotional conflict (e.g., bickering), the parents should allow the conflict to run its natural course without interference, making judgments, or taking sides (an exception to this general recommendation is when there is the possibility that the children might injure one another).

See also *Adler, Alfred; birth order; dethroning; inferiority complex; only child; will to power.*

sickle-cell anemia: A disease that is caused by a recessive gene and that is characterized, during its chronic phase, by a group of related symptoms, including headaches, fatigue, weakness, pains, a proneness to infections, impairment of growth, and ulcers on the skin. In the majority of cases, death results before young adulthood. Although the disease is at present incurable, life can be extended, and its quality improved, by prudent management and medical treatment.

The symptoms of sickle-cell anemia are caused by collapsed red blood cells that look somewhat like sickles. These cells interfere with the body's utilization of oxygen.

Individuals who obtain a recessive gene from each parent are the ones who will have a clinical case of the disease. It is possible for an individual to be a carrier of the genetic information for the disease without having a clinical case. Such individuals have obtained a recessive gene from only one parent. Carriers may have some symptoms of sickle-cell anemia, and this is called *sickle cell trait.*

Sickle cell anemia afflicts primarily black persons. It also, to a lesser extent, afflicts persons with Hispanic or Mediterranean backgrounds. The frequency of sickle cell anemia in black children ranges from about 12 to 15 in every 10,000. Estimates suggest that approximately 8 percent of black persons suffer to some degree from sickle cell trait. Potential parents with the disease or a family history of the disease might want to consider the possibility of genetic counseling. Also, procedures such as amniocentesis and chorionic villus sampling can be employed to evaluate the genetic status of the fetus.

See also *amniocentesis; chorionic villus sampling; dominant gene; genetic counseling; recessive gene; Tay-Sachs disease.*

single-parent family: See *one-parent family.*

silliness: In children, a behavioral trait characterized by clowning, showing off, inappropriate actions, playing the fool to obtain laughter from others, and so forth. Silliness often strikes adults as irrational, shallow, and absurd. The behavior has a regressive quality to it, suggesting that the child who is acting silly is also acting in an immature manner.

Occasional silliness is not a problem, and almost all children will manifest it. Chronic silliness is distressing to adults and indicates difficulties in the socialization process. Children prone to silliness may be disruptive in the classroom and present problems at home.

There are several causal factors that may play a role in silliness: (1) children who feel unloved or unrecognized may use silliness in order to attract attention and feel important; (2) silliness may be a way to express hostility toward parents in an indirect, seemingly "safe" way (if so, some silliness can be understood as a kind of passive-aggressive behavior); (3) children with low self-esteem may use silliness in a futile attempt to obtain higher status with other children; (4) when children confronted with a task feel incompetent or inadequate, they may use silliness as a defensive reaction, attempting to discount the importance of the task (e.g., a homework assignment or a chore); (5) on the positive side, there is some evidence that creative children are somewhat more likely to act in a silly manner than less creative ones—in some cases, silliness may be a sign of boredom with conventional ideas and an attraction to divergent thinking.

Parents can cope with silliness by recognizing that a certain amount of silliness in prepubertal children is normal and to be expected. However, if silliness appears to be excessive, it should not be reinforced with too much attention. Long moral lectures on the seriousness of life and the importance of responsibilities may, paradoxically, give strength to the silly behavior by placing too much value on it. If the child senses that he or she has "gotten the parent's goat," then silliness has been effective.

The parent should realize that often chronic silliness in children is an attempt to obtain attention. If this appears to be the case, the parent should try to give the child spontaneous attention, attention given at times that the child is not seeking it. The parent needs to be the first one to initiate interactions by suggesting games, mutual projects, and other activities.

See also *creative thinking; divergent thinking; passive-aggressive behavior; self-esteem.*

Skinner, Burrhus Frederic (1904–1990): An American psychologist who conducted pioneer work in operant conditioning. Skinner received a Ph.D. degree in psychology from Harvard University in 1931. He subsequently taught psychology and did research, first at the University of Minnesota and then at Indiana University.

Sixteen years after he earned his Ph.D., Skinner returned to Harvard to occupy the prestigious William James Chair in psychology. It is somewhat ironic that Skinner was granted this position in view of the fact that William James was a cognitive psychologist who placed great value on conscious processes such as thinking and perception. Skinner, on the other hand, was a radical behaviorist who denied the importance of consciousness as an explanatory concept.

As indicated above, Skinner's main domain of research has been operant conditioning. In his early research, his principal experimental subjects were rats and pigeons. Later he was able to demonstrate how principles of operant conditioning could be extended to human beings. For example, he invented the teaching machine, a programmed approach to learning that is incorporated into much of today's computer-assisted instruction.

Skinner took the general position that most behavior, including maladaptive behavior, is learned. What is learned can be unlearned or modified. Thus, there is hope for troubled children and adolescents. Their behavior is not fixed and unalterable. Although Skinner was not a therapist himself, his formulations and findings are the foundation upon which behavior modification is built.

Skinner is considered a giant of psychology. His status is similar to that of Freud's. His impact upon the course of contemporary psychology has been profound.

Three of Skinner's books are *The Behavior of Organisms* (1938), *Beyond Freedom and Dignity* (1971), and *About Behaviorism* (1974).

See also *behavior modification; behavior therapy; behaviorism; James, William; learning; operant conditioning; reinforcer.*

sleep patterns: In both children and adults, characteristic changes in levels of consciousness, eye movements, electroencephalographic recordings, respirations, pulse rates, and other physiological signs during sleep.

The key piece of equipment used in the experimental study of sleep is the apparatus for recording the human electroencephalogram (EEG), or "brain waves." EEG patterns display different characteristics when individuals are in varying stages of sleep. A widely used categorization system is the one proposed by sleep researcher Wilse B. Webb. He distinguishes five stages of sleep associated with EEG patterns. These are called Stages 1, 2, 3, 4, and 1-REM. (REM stands for "rapid eye movements.") Wakefulness is obviously not a stage of sleep; so it is called Stage 0 for experimental purposes.

Stage 1 is associated with light sleep. The EEG pattern resembles Stage 0. The amplitude of the waves is slight, but the waves are very frequent. The EEG may be informally described as "busy." As one proceeds through Stages 2 and 3 and arrives at Stage 4, the EEG patterns show increasing amplitude and diminished frequency. Again, informally, at Stage 4, the waves may be described as "large and lazy." Stage 4 is associated with deep sleep.

There is a substantial amount of interest in Stage 1-REM. During Stage 1-REM, the EEG patterns resemble those produced during Stage 1. They have a low amplitude and a high frequency. But something new appears. The eyes move from time to time in short bursts consisting of several movements within a few seconds. These are REMs. REMs are not always present during Stage 1 sleep. That is why a distinction is made between Stage 1 and Stage 1-REM. Sleep researchers have found that Stage 1-REM sleep is the stage most likely to be associated with dreaming. If experimental subjects are awakened during Stage 1-REM, they will report dreams about 70 or 80 percent of the time. This is not the case with other stages of sleep, including Stage 1 without REMs.

Classic psychoanalytic theory proposes that the function of dreaming, associated with Stage 1-REM sleep, is to give emotional expression to wishes and to work out frustrations and conflicts. If this were so, we would not expect much REM sleep in infants. It is dubious that the infant leads the complex mental life described in psychoanalytic theory. Nonetheless, infants spend about 50 percent of their sleeping time in REM sleep. Adults spend about 20 percent of their sleeping time in REM sleep. Also, infants in their first year of life sleep 12 hours or more per day; so they spend about 6 hours in every 24 in REM sleep. Adults sleep about 8 hours per day; so they spend little more than 1.5 hours in every 24 in REM sleep.

These observations do not necessarily refute the contention that dreams are used by human beings to express wishes and work out conflicts. But they do suggest that there may be at least more than one function to REM sleep. Why do infants spend so much time in REM sleep? One hypothesis is that REM activity is a form of self-stimulation and facilitates the growth of the brain and nervous system. Another hypothesis is that REM activity indicates that the infant's brain is busily sorting and categorizing experiences received while conscious. There may be merit to both hypotheses.

See also *insomnia; night terror; nightmare; sleepwalking disorder; states of consciousness in an infant.*

sleepwalking disorder (somnambulism): A disorder characterized by walking about in one's sleep with open eyes and an expressionless face. Sometimes the individual engages in goal-oriented actions such as putting on shoes or obtaining food. The disorder is more common in children than in adults. When it is present in adults, it was also usually present in their childhood.

Episodes take place during deep sleep, and the subject is resistant to being awakened. Contrary to folklore, it *is* possible for a person who is sleepwalking to injure himself or herself. The sleepwalker needs protection.

Biological factors that may play a role in sleepwalking disorder include epilepsy and infections of the brain. A psychological factor that may be operative is chronic anxiety. When this is the case, some psychotherapists identify sleepwalking disorder as a dissociative disorder, a type of behavioral disorder in which the usual integrity of memory, action, or personality is significantly disturbed.

In most cases children who suffer from sleepwalking disorder do not have it when they are adults. Spontaneous recovery from the disorder is common. If treatment is required, anticonvulsive medication or an antianxiety agent is sometimes prescribed. Often psychotherapy with the goal of reducing anxiety is recommended.

See also *epilepsy; insomnia; night terror; nightmare; sleep patterns.*

smiling: A facial expression characterized by an upturning of the corners of the mouth, commonly signifying pleasure or amusement. The smile of primary interest to parents is the *social smile*, a smile given in response to other people.

The development of social smiling typically takes place in three stages. First, an *endogenous smile* appears one or two days after birth. This smile is in essence a reflex and has no social meaning. It appears to be prominently associated with REM (rapid eye movement) sleep episodes. Folklore has it that these smiles are due to accumulations of "gas," and this is probably incorrect. Second, the *transient social smile,* brief and fleeting in nature, appears around the age of 3 or 4 weeks. It is characterized by increased arousal, attention to others, and eye contact. Third, the *mature social smile* appears around the age of 3 or 4 months. This is a sustained smile and the infant's face usually has a bright, alert appearance. The capacity for laughter is associated with the mature social smile.

Ability to smile and laugh appropriately at the expected age is a sign of neurological health and normal social development.

See also *bidirectionality of influence; ludic behavior; play; sleep patterns; socialization.*

smoking: Using tobacco in the form of cigarettes or cigars or in pipes. Tobacco can also be used in other ways, such as chewing it or inhaling snuff. Tobacco contains *nicotine,* an oily, toxic alkaloid, and tars; nicotine is a stimulant to the central nervous system and is physiologically addictive. A large body of evidence suggests that the excessive use of tobacco is a causal factor, or a complicating one, in a number of diseases, including lung cancer, emphysema, and heart disease.

Regular smoking commonly starts during adolescence. Surveys suggest that approximately 40 percent of males and 25 percent of females have the smoking habit by the time they are 17 or 18 years old. Research suggests that adolescent smokers have some distinguishing features: (1) a majority of their peers smoke; (2) they belong to a group whose academic performance is not as high as a comparable group of nonsmokers; and (3) their parents tend to be smokers.

It is much easier to prevent smoking than it is to modify, or break, the smoking habit. The most important thing that parents can do to prevent their children from smoking is to not smoke themselves. Social learning appears to play an important role in the acquisition of the habit. Punishing, lecturing, moralizing, and saying such things as "Don't become a smoker like me" are usually ineffective. The adolescent may simply see the parent as an unfair authoritarian or a hypocrite. Under these circumstances, the act of smoking can symbolize to the adolescent that he or she is autonomous and not under the thumb of the parent.

If an adolescent becomes a regular smoker, the habit can be modified most effectively if the adolescent indicates a desire to quit. Numerous smoking clinics, as well as books recommending effective habit-breaking strategies, exist. Behavior modification skills can be used. A parent can be a friendly, supportive helper under these circumstances.

See also *behavior modification; drug abuse in adolescence; social learning.*

social learning (observational learning): A kind of learning in which a key factor is the learner's observation of the behavior of others. Commonly a parent, older sibling, or admired peer provides a *model*. The child learns by *social imitation*, a process involving the conscious copying of the model's behavior. Many behavioral traits, habits, and social attitudes are acquired in this way. Social learning is thus an important factor in the general process of socialization, a process in which behaviors acceptable to the family and the general culture are developed.

It has been convincingly demonstrated by various experiments that not only prosocial behaviors, but also antisocial behaviors, are acquired by social learning. Children in the presence of a model who exhibits aggressive behavior to attain an end are subsequently more likely to employ similar aggressive behavior.

Social learning, because it *is* learning, is responsive to the same principles that apply in operant conditioning. In particular, reinforcement is important. If the behavior "pays off," it tends to be strengthened. In the case, however, of social learning, because it involves a high level of consciousness, the idea of *vicarious reinforcement* has been introduced. Vicarious reinforcement refers to imaginary satisfactions (e.g., fantasizing that one has defeated an enemy or daydreaming that one is popular and well-liked). These vicarious reinforcers, like objective ones, can have a very real effect on the formation of social habits. This is particularly true in the case of older children and adolescents.

Children often identify with parents and use them as models. Therefore, effective parents take care to exhibit prosocial behavior in their own actions.

See also *aggressiveness; identification; operant conditioning; prosocial behavior; reinforcer; socialization.*

social-emotional giftedness: See *invulnerables.*

social imitation: See *social learning.*

socialization: A learning process characterized by the transmission of a given culture's behavioral norms, beliefs, moral values, and traditions to its children. Behavior patterns approved of by the family and general culture are identified as *prosocial.* Those patterns considered unacceptable to the family and general culture are identified as *antisocial.* According to Erikson, the entire socialization process can be described in eight distinct psychosocial stages.

A number of independent factors, such as operant conditioning, social learning, reinforcement, parental style, discipline, sibling rivalry, psychosexual development, cognitive development, and moral development, are involved in socialization. They are included in the following cross-referenced entries.

See also *antisocial behavior; cognitive development; discipline; moral development; operant conditioning; parental style; prosocial behavior; psychosexual development; reinforcer; sibling rivalry; social learning.*

social play: A kind of play distinguished by interactions with other children. This is in contrast to solitary play and onlooker play. The three subclasses of social play are parallel, associative, and cooperative play. Social play begins to become a significant factor in a child's personality development toward the end of infancy, grows in importance during toddlerhood, and remains important throughout childhood.

See also *associative play; cooperative play; onlooker play; parallel play; play; solitary play.*

sociobiology: The study of the genetic basis of social behavior. On the basis of a large number of studies and observations, many of them focusing on animal behavior, sociobiologists have concluded that a wide spectrum of actions are determined more by innate processes than learned ones. An example of such behavior is altruism. Organisms are *altruistic* when they place the welfare of others, or their social group, above their own individual welfare. The function of altruism, according to sociobiologists, is to guarantee the survival of genes identical to one's own. It therefore follows that altruistic behavior will be common among immediate members of a family because they have many genes in common.

Other behaviors that may to some extent be biologically determined are territoriality (i.e., an impulse to protect and defend one's own territory or "turf"), parental love, aggressiveness, and gregariousness.

Contemporary sociobiology was to some extent anticipated by earlier thinkers, such as Carl Jung and Alfred Adler. Jung postulated the existence of *archetypes*—primitive, inborn images said to guide behavior. Alfred Adler asserted that human beings have an inborn social interest.

The general theme running through sociobiology is that the long-run purpose of all social behavior is to preserve the integrity of the group and guarantee the survival of its genes.

See also *Adler, Alfred; attachment; ethology; imprinting; Jung, Carl Gustav; nativism; socialization.*

sociogram: A graphic measurement technique, devised by the psychiatrist Jacob L. Moreno, that provides a visual display of acceptance-rejection patterns in a small- to medium-sized group. Individuals who have a high level of group acceptance, who are well-liked and popular, are called *stars.* Individuals who have a low level of group acceptance are called *isolates.*

A sociogram can be very readily generated and drawn. For example, suppose that Mr. R., a sixth-grade teacher, passes a slip of paper to each class member. On the paper, each student is to answer two questions: (1) Who would you most like to sit next to? and (2) Who would you least like to sit next to? For convenience, on a large piece of paper, a circle is drawn around the name of each student. One-way and two-way arrows are drawn between the circles indicating both acceptance and rejection. The result is a sort of "map" of the class's general social configuration. The whole process is called *sociometry,* and the resulting display is the sociogram itself. Mr. R. may find the easy-to-interpret result useful in defining and comprehending peer interactions in his classroom.

Sociometry can be a useful tool for conducting research on such subjects in social psychology as attitudes toward others, friendship, gender biases, and interpersonal attraction.

See also *peer group; socialization.*

soiling: See *encopresis.*

solitary play: A kind of play characterized by self-directed activity when a child is alone. (Social play is to be found at the opposite end of the play continuum.) Solitary play is a normal kind of play and allows the child important opportunities for personal discovery, the exercise of motor skills (e.g., bouncing a ball or playing with a yo-yo), and the expression of talents and aptitudes (e.g., drawing, playing a musical instrument, or writing a story). Often, unusually bright or creative children have a preference for large time blocks of solitary play.

Solitary play is a problem only if the child is very withdrawn, excessively shy, or generally dislikes playing with other children. In such cases, focusing almost entirely on solitary play can be a sign of anxiety, depression, or abnormal social development.

See also *anxiety; associative play; cooperative play; depression; imaginative play; ludic behavior; onlooker play; parallel play; play; shyness.*

somatotype: See *body type.*

somnambulism: A term with two related meanings; which are (1) sleepwalking disorder and (2) the state of consciousness associated with a deep trance in hypnosis.

See also *sleepwalking disorder.*

Spearman, Charles Edward (1863–1945): A research psychologist and statistician known for his work on the nature of intelligence. Spearman received his Ph.D. degree at the University of Leipzig in 1897 under the tutelage of Wilhelm Wundt, one of the principal founders of experimental psychology. Subsequently, Spearman was associated for approximately 20 years with the University of London as a professor.

Applying the correlational method to the items on intelligence tests, Spearman concluded that there is a general factor at work in all rational mental activity. He called this general factor *g*. In 1904, he published an influential article called "General Intelligence Objectively Determined and Measured."

Subsequent applications of the correlational method revealed that items tended to fall into clusters, or related groupings. Based on this research, Spearman concluded that intelligence is made up of two factors: the first is *g*, and the second is specific ability, or *s*. The American psychologist Louis L. Thurstone (1887–1955) extended Spearman's mathematical approach, and Thurstone's contribution is called *factor analysis*.

Spearman's theory became very influential. It was modified by Spearman himself, in time, and it has been revised by others. Nonetheless, its general outlines, if not its specific details, tend to be assumed by standardized intelligence tests. In particular, this is true of the widely used Wechsler intelligence scales because these scales explicitly measure specific abilities.

Among Spearman's books are *The Abilities of Man: Their Nature and Measurement* (1927), *Creative Mind* (1930), and *Human Abilities* (1950).

See also *correlation; intelligence; intelligence tests; Stanford-Binet Intelligence Scale; Wechsler intelligence scales.*

special education: Educational services, usually provided by the school, for exceptional children. (The term *exceptional children* includes both gifted children and those with intellectual or cognitive problems.)

Some schools provide special enrichment classes for gifted children, while others provide a separate educational track for the gifted. Unfortunately, numerous schools provide little in the way of special education for gifted children. On the whole, special education for gifted children has not been as well funded as programs for mentally retarded children and children with learning disabilities. The National Association for Gifted Children works to obtain more funding and more effective services for gifted children.

It has been common in schools to provide special classes, reading programs, tutoring, diagnostic testing, and so forth, for exceptional children who are either mentally retarded or have learning disabilities. In recent years, there has been a trend in education called *mainstreaming* that makes an effort to integrate exceptional children with below-average intelligence-test scores or specific learning disabilities into the regular classroom.

See also *exceptional children; giftedness; hearing impairment; learning disability; mainstreaming; mental retardation; visual impairment.*

specific developmental disorders: See *developmental disorders.*

speech therapy: A kind of therapy designed to help clients who have various kinds of problems in articulating words. Examples of such problems in children and adolescents include stuttering, lisping, an inability to correctly voice key phonemes, slurring, garbling, muttering, mumbling, mutism, and so forth.

Causal factors in speech problems can be either biological or psychological. Biological factors include a cleft palate, abnormal tooth formation, an injury to the brain or nervous system, a hearing impairment, and an infection of the vocal chords. Psychological factors include anxiety, maladaptive speech habits, low self-esteem, and passive-aggressiveness (i.e., the use of defective speech to punish or frustrate adults). Children who suffer from autistic disorder, childhood schizophrenia, or mental retardation may also display speech difficulties.

Speech therapy consists of a set of techniques and training methods designed to correct specific impairments. Some key examples follow:

1. Mutism is often associated with autistic disorder. Children are often reinforced for speaking with *direct reinforcers,* such as bits of candy.

2. Anxiety often plays a part in stuttering. The client is given homework assignments involving such seemingly unlikely tasks as "voluntary stuttering" when buying an ice cream cone in order to bring about a *desensitization to anxiety.*

3. Changes in such controlling factors as the pacing of speech can sometimes be modified with the *use of a metronome* as a training device.

4. The therapist provides a *model for effective speech*, allowing the child to imitate and take advantage of social learning.

5. *Amplified auditory feedback* in which a child wears headphones and can better hear his or her own voice is particularly useful in helping children with hearing impairments.

6. *Counseling* aimed at reducing anger can be useful in helping children who use defective speech as an expression of passive-aggressiveness.

A number of other techniques are used by speech therapists. The key point is that speech difficulties can be effectively treated. Therefore, they should not be neglected. This is particularly true because habit formation plays a large role in such disorders, and it is a good idea to treat them in childhood if at all possible.

See also *autistic disorder; hearing impairment; mutism; passive-aggressive behavior; stuttering.*

sperm cell (spermatozoon): A reproductive cell produced by a male's gonad. Sperm cells are invisible to the naked eye and are only about 0.002 inch in overall size. A spermatozoon's structure consists of a head containing genetic information and a tail used for a propelling motion. A normal sperm count in an ejaculate may range from 200 to 500 million sperm cells.

Each human sperm cell contains 23 *individual* chromosomes instead of pairs due to the reduction process called *meiosis*. Also, each 23rd chromosome is either an X (i.e., female) chromosome or a Y (i.e., male) chromosome. Ova contain only X chromosomes. Therefore, it is sperm cells that will determine the eventual sex of a child. If the fertilized ovum is XX, the child will be a female. If the fertilized ovum is XY, the child will be a male.

See also *chromosomes; meiosis; mitosis; ovaries; ovum.*

Spock, Benjamin McLane (1903–): An American pediatrician. Spock earned an M.D. degree from Columbia University's College of Physicians and Surgeons. He was a practicing pediatrician for approximately 14 years and subsequently taught medicine at the Mayo Clinic and other institutions. Spock is widely recognized for his book *The*

Common Sense Book of Baby and Child Care. It was first published in 1945 and is still in print. In its paperback version, it has sold in various revised editions almost 39 million copies.

Spock's general approach to the early guidance and discipline of children has been very influential. He stresses that parents should be nurturing, understanding, and affectionate. It is important for them to recognize individual differences in temperament and ability in their children and, in turn, to make allowances for these differences. On the other hand, he does *not*, as some of his critics have charged, advocate excessive permissiveness. He recognizes that parents need to be authority figures and that they must impose reasonable limits on behavior. Much specific advice is set forth in his famous book.

See also *authoritarian parent; authoritative parent; behavior modification; communication skills; discipline; parent effectiveness training (P.E.T.); parental style.*

spoiled child: As formulated by Adler, a child with a personality characterized by a complex of related traits such as egotism, self-absorption, an inflated sense of importance, a lack of concern for the needs of others, irresponsibility, overdemandingness, and impatience. Adler suggested that the principal cause of spoiling is making the home a child-centered one that focuses almost all of its emotional resources on one child. This is often an only child or a favorite child. The parents treat the child like a little prince or princess, and the child behaves accordingly. Although Adler's views were advanced a number of years ago, recent research indicates that when parents rely on a parental style that is overly permissive and accepting, it will contribute to the kind of personality traits associated with the spoiled child.

See also *Adler, Alfred; birth order; inferiority complex; superiority complex; parental style; will to power.*

stages: Plateaus in development during which there is no obvious change in growth, maturation, learning, or performance. Often, during a stage, there will be a relatively long period of stability. Such flat spots are somewhat deceptive because usually quite a bit of change is taking place at a latent level where it is difficult to observe. These latent changes are the roots of subsequent rather abrupt, well-defined steps upward in development.

Stages need to be distinguished from ages. *Ages* are the chronological periods (e.g., infancy, early childhood, late childhood, and adolescence) over which the stages stretch.

Ages-stages theories, such as Freud's theory of psychosexual development, Erikson's theory of psychosocial development, Piaget's theory of cognitive development, or Kohlberg's theory of cognitive development, provide numerous examples of stages.

See also *ages-stages theories; cognitive development; moral development; psychosexual development; psychosocial development; theories of development.*

stammering: See *stuttering.*

Stanford-Binet Intelligence Scale: A standardized test of intelligence developed at Stanford University by the psychologist Lewis M. Terman in the 1910s. Terman based the Stanford-Binet scales on the original work of Alfred Binet and Theodore Simon in France. The Stanford-Binet scale was the first intelligence test widely used in the United States.

Originally designed to measure the intelligence of children, the Stanford-Binet Scale, because of two revisions, is now capable of measuring the intelligence of both adolescents and adults.

Test items are arranged in order of difficulty from easy to difficult, an approach innovated by Binet and Simon to reveal a subject's mental age. The items themselves consist of questions and short tasks designed to assess vocabulary, memory, reasoning, attention, mathematical ability, social awareness, and perceptual-motor ability. The Stanford-Binet Scale provides an intelligence quotient (IQ), which gives an overall measure of an individual's cognitive functioning.

See also *intelligence; intelligence quotient (IQ); intelligence tests; Wechsler intelligence scales.*

startle reaction: See *Moro reflex.*

states of consciousness in an infant: Semistable changes in attention, arousal, sleep, and activity as indicated by corresponding changes in responsiveness to sights, sounds, and other environmental stimuli.

In accordance with research conducted by P. H. Wolf, Wilse B. Webb, and others, it is possible to identify five different states of consciousness in an infant.

1. *Focused activity* is characterized by a relative lack of awareness of environmental stimuli other than the object of attention. An infant will be busy, for example, concentrating on a *particular* sight or sound, not sights and sounds in general. (This state is also known as an *active awake state*.)

2. *Alert inactivity* is characterized by an open attitude toward environmental stimuli. Under these conditions, it is relatively easy to elicit the infant's attention. (This state is also known as an *active awake state*.)

3. *Drowsiness* is characterized by a low level of arousal and attention. The eyes may flutter, opening and closing. It is usually easy to elicit attention with an unexpected sight, sound, or touch.

4. *Irregular sleep* is associated with REM (rapid eye movement) episodes. Respirations are somewhat irregular, and there is quite a bit of restless activity. Infants spend about 50 percent of their sleeping time in this state. (This state is also known as an *active sleep state*.)

5. *Deep sleep,* or *regular sleep,* which accounts for the other 50 percent of sleeping time, is characterized by a lack of activity and the presence of stable respirations. There tends to be little response to random background environmental stimuli.

The time spent in the five states varies over a wide, normal band from infant to infant. This possibly is due to inborn individual differences in temperament.

See also *sleep patterns; temperament.*

stealing: The taking of someone else's property in a secretive, concealed way and without permission. The fact that stealing is secretive suggests that the offender knows that it is wrong. Consequently, children who steal cannot be excused on the simple basis that they did not realize it was a transgression. (Toddlers who take possession of items without permission or a parent's knowledge may do so innocently; they provide a possible exception.) Common examples of stealing among children and adolescents include (1) taking money from a parent's purse or wallet, (2) taking toys, books, and articles of clothing from peers, and (3) taking various items from stores (shoplifting).

It is important for parents and adults in positions of authority to distinguish between situational stealing and chronic stealing. *Situational stealing* takes place when a child experiences a particular need or desire and is subjected to a temptation. It does *not* suggest that the child has no moral sense at all and that he or she will eventually become a juvenile delinquent or a criminal. Sometimes shoplifting is perceived as a practical joke on a merchant by adolescents. At other times, such theft may be in response to a dare. Many, perhaps most, children will manifest situational stealing a few times while they are growing up. *Chronic stealing* takes place frequently. The child or adolescent may look for, and set up, opportunities to steal. Causal factors in chronic stealing include abnormal moral development, a need to oppose and defy adults, strong aggressive tendencies, a desire to own items beyond the financial resources of the family, and a craving for thrills. In psychoanalytic terms, the child who is a regular thief has an underdeveloped superego.

Parents can cope with situational stealing by an application of behavior modification skills involving reinforcers and response costs. The child needs to return what is stolen and make some amends. It is ineffective to subject the child to lengthy moral lectures. Usually the problem will resolve itself without too much difficulty.

Chronic stealing must be dealt with on a long-term basis. The parent needs to recognize that the problem has roots. Better ways must be sought to meet a child's basic emotional needs and to foster moral development. Insight into the underlying causes of the problem will suggest corresponding ways to cope with it. In general, it is recommended that parents look for ways to encourage social learning and the child's identification with family values. Some children are highly resistant to socialization and may manifest a high level of antisocial behavior. Family therapy, counseling, and psychotherapy are recommended treatments when a parent's best efforts seem to be failing.

Children who engage in any kind of stealing, situational or chronic, should be made to feel by parents and others in positions of authority that they will be caught and that there will be a penalty. Close supervision of a child's behavior is a key factor in reducing the likelihood of stealing.

See also *antisocial behavior; conduct disorder; moral development; oppositional defiant disorder; superego.*

stepparent: A surrogate parent acquired when a child's divorced parent remarries. Approximately 70 to 80 percent of divorced persons remarry eventually. Because of rising divorce rates and the high frequency of remarriage, it is estimated that 25 to 35 percent of all children experience a span of time during which they live under the same roof with a stepparent.

Folklore has given the role of stepparent a bad name. Many children are familiar with the wicked stepmothers in *Cinderella* and *Snow White.* In Vladimir Nabokov's well-known novel *Lolita,* the protagonist marries a woman and becomes a stepfather primarily in order to have sexual access to the woman's adolescent daughter. It is understandable that both children and adolescents approach stepparents with a substantial amount of misgiving. Children are not likely to realize that no easy generalizations can be made about stepparents. It is evident to thoughtful adults that stepparents are individuals and, as such, display the normal range of parental styles from authoritarian to permissive, from accepting to rejecting.

It is important to realize that the child's anxiety and apprehension can be overcome, but gradually. The child must be given time to adapt to the stepparent. Instant affection is unlikely or may be a sham on the child's part. But little by little, a child will usually gain confidence in a well-meaning stepparent.

It is of doubtful value to insist that a child immediately call a stepparent "Mom" or "Dad." The child may feel that this is forced and can become quite hostile and resentful. The child will probably use the stepparent's first name for a while so that he or she will have something to call the stepparent. Children can be invited, as their option, to use a form of "Mom" or "Dad" when it is comfortable for them. This allows them to retain an important domain of control over their own lives.

Stepparents are unlikely to completely replace a natural parent in a child's affections. It is important for stepparents to realize that in most cases the natural parent will occupy a special place in the child's psychological world. The effective stepparent will try to fulfill his or her own special role in the child's life without directly displacing the position of the absent natural parent.

See also *adoptive parent; authoritarian parent; parental style.*

stepping reflex: See *walking reflex.*

stereotypy/habit disorder: A behavioral disorder that is associated with childhood and adolescence and that is characterized by useless behaviors that are repeated over and over. Principal examples include self-oriented behaviors such as biting on fingers, pulling out hair, picking a nasal cavity, rocking the body, scratching on skin, sucking a thumb, banging the head, and so forth. Often there is a substantial amount of self-destructiveness involved. The behaviors can be described as entrenched, abnormal forms of the kinds of circular reactions exhibited by normal infants.

Causal factors in stereotypy/habit disorder include mental retardation, visual impairment, hearing impairment, psychotic disorders, abnormalities in the functioning of the brain, a lack of attention, and sensory isolation.

Stereotypy/habit disorder does not respond to conventional parental coping strategies and requires professional treatment. Often institutionalization is recommended for a period of time. Treatment includes the use of both behavior therapy and drug therapy.

See also *autistic disorder; behavior therapy; childhood schizophrenia; drug therapy; psychotic disorders.*

stimulant drugs: Drugs that increase alertness and central-nervous-system arousal. In drug therapy, stimulants are often used to treat attention-deficit hyperactivity disorder, narcolepsy, and obesity.

It may seem odd that stimulants are used to treat attention-deficit hyperactivity disorder, a disorder in which a chief characteristic is overly high arousal and restlessness. However, clinical experience has discovered that stimulants often, but not always, have the paradoxical effect of acting as tranquilizers in the case of this disorder. For this reason, they are often prescribed and then the child's subsequent behavior is carefully evaluated.

See also *attention-deficit hyperactivity disorder (ADHD); drug therapy; narcolepsy; obesity.*

stimulus-response theory: The general viewpoint that, given accurate knowledge of the characteristics of a stimulus (e.g., something seen, heard, or tasted), it is possible to predict the precise nature of the response to it. Stimulus-response theory, or simply S-R theory, is the basic approach advocated by John Watson, the father of behaviorism. *Behaviorism,* in its early radical form, asserted that the subject matter of psychology is behavior itself, not the mind or human consciousness.

Stimulus-response theory is workable to a point. It is implicit in both classical conditioning and operant conditioning. And operant conditioning is the basis of both behavior modification and behavior therapy.

Stimulus-response theory is particularly useful in understanding the behavior of infants when applied to the study of reflexes and their subsequent conditioning.

Nonetheless, it is widely recognized today that the stimulus-response approach is very limited. In order to deal with the full range of human behavior, even in toddlers and preschoolers, it is essential to introduce the concept of *cognition,* or conscious knowing. The subject's thoughts about, and perceptions of, the stimulus induce variety in response patterns. Consequently, the study of cognitive development has become a key part of contemporary developmental psychology.

See also *behaviorism; classical conditioning; cognitive development; neonatal reflexes; operant conditioning; Watson, John Broadus.*

stranger anxiety: In infancy, anxiety commonly arising from seeing, hearing, or being picked up by an unfamiliar person. Signs of anxiety include crying, agitation, and general distress. Stranger anxiety is normal and appears in many, perhaps most, infants between the ages of 7 and 9 months. Two principal factors appear to be at work in stranger anxiety. First, stranger anxiety tends to occur during the time when an infant is intensely attached to a parent. The infant reacts with distress to anything that appears to threaten the attachment. Second, the infant is old enough to tell the difference between the expected and the unexpected, and large discrepancies from the expected are experienced as unpleasant.

Infants from large families or who have parents who socialize frequently are less likely to experience intense stranger anxiety than are infants who are raised in a restricted, somewhat isolated social atmosphere.

When an infant manifests stranger anxiety, the best course of action is to provide reassurance in the form of contact with a parent or familiar caregiver.

See also *attachment; separation anxiety; trust versus mistrust.*

stress-inoculation training: See *cognitive-behavior modification.*

stroke: In transactional analysis (TA), a unit of recognition. When a parent hugs a child or says, "Good morning," the child has been stroked. According to Eric Berne, the father of TA, strokes are essential for the health of the brain and nervous system. They also play a role in personality development.

There are four basic kinds of strokes.

1. *Unconditional positive strokes* are pleasant forms of recognition that are given freely without having to be earned. When a parent spontaneously pays attention to a child or suggests an activity for the fun of it, the child is receiving this first kind of stroke. Transactional analysis hypothesizes that numerous unconditional positive strokes tend to foster a Child ego state, or emotional self, that is natural and spontaneous.

2. *Conditional positive strokes* are pleasant forms of recognition that are granted on an "if-then" basis. When a parent praises a child for good grades, for doing a chore, or for being polite, the child is receiving this second kind of stroke. It is hypothesized that numerous unconditional strokes tend to foster a Child ego state that is overadapted to the needs and wants of others. This is believed to be the basis for neurotic tendencies in the personality.

3. *Unconditional negative strokes* are unpleasant forms of recognition that are given on an apparently random, meaningless basis. When a parent hits a child unexpectedly and says, "That's just to teach you a lesson so you don't get too sassy or sure of yourself," the child is receiving this third kind of stroke. Such strokes are associated with child abuse. It is hypothesized that

numerous unconditional negative strokes tend to foster a Child ego state characterized by doubt and withdrawal.

4. *Conditional negative strokes* are unpleasant forms of recognition that are received on an "if-then" basis. When misbehavior on a child's part is followed by a penalty or punishment, the child is receiving this fourth kind of stroke. It is hypothesized that numerous conditional negative strokes tend to foster a Child ego state characterized by rebellion and defiance.

It may seem odd to speak of negative strokes and unpleasant recognition. But TA asserts that children do not want to be ignored. If they cannot obtain positive strokes, they may misbehave in order to obtain any kind of stroke, including negative ones.

See also *Berne, Eric; ego state; parental style; transactional analysis.*

stuttering (stammering): A kind of speech impairment characterized by involuntary blocks, repetitions, spasms, and breaks in the normal rhythm of speech. Secondary behaviors often seen along with stuttering include head-jerking, changes in respirations, tightening of the muscles, and blinking. No formal distinction is made between the terms *stuttering* and *stammering*, although in the United states the first term is considered the preferred one.

It is important to distinguish developmental stuttering from chronic stuttering. *Developmental stuttering* appears during toddlerhood, is very common, and usually goes away spontaneously if it is not reinforced with too much parental concern and attention. *Chronic stuttering* is an entrenched tendency to stutter that usually begins prior to puberty. The word *stuttering* used alone, without an adjective, is usually referring to chronic stuttering.

Approximately 3 to 5 percent of children show some tendency to stutter. Males are three to four times more likely to stutter than are females. Most of these children will find a way to modify or otherwise deal with their fluency problems. The incidence of stuttering in adults is about 1 percent. However, it is not just a matter of "growing out of it." Coping with stuttering requires substantial effort, and is not always successful without professional assistance.

Causes of stuttering include genetic, biological, and psychological factors. Evidence in favor of the importance of genetic factors comes from studies of families and identical twins, as well as from the fact that more males than females stutter. There may very well be a partial hereditary disposition to stutter expressing itself in some individuals. If so, the victim of stuttering should not be blamed for the difficulty but should receive both understanding and effective assistance.

Several biological factors have been proposed as playing a role in stuttering. First, there may be a problem in brain functioning. Children with attention-deficit hyperactivity disorder, often linked to minimal brain dysfunction (MBD), are more likely to stutter than other children. Second, there may be a difficulty in interpreting the auditory feedback from one's own speech. This is the *auditory interference theory*, and involves a perceptual problem. Third, there is the possibility that the cerebral hemisphere controlling speech (the left hemisphere in most persons) has not attained a sufficient level of dominance over verbal abilities.

Psychological factors in stuttering are usually divided into the two broad categories of emotions and habits. Emotions can readily aggravate stuttering. For example, it is a common, and accurate, observation that stuttering becomes worse when the individual is made particularly anxious in situations such as speaking before a class or explaining a transgression to the school principal. An adolescent with a tendency to stutter may not stutter when talking to a close friend but may stutter when asking for a date. In psychoanalysis, emotional conflicts are seen as playing a complex role in stuttering. The "nice" child who appears to be polite and socialized may use stuttering as a kind of passive-aggressive behavior. Stuttering is likely to aggravate and upset parents, which may be a way of "getting back" at persons in authority in a "safe" manner.

Stuttering can be looked upon as a maladaptive habit. Behavior therapists tend to think of stuttering as the result of a learning process. The general line of reasoning is that stuttering has received an excessive amount of attention by well-meaning parents and other caregivers and that this has reinforced and entrenched it. This is a very hopeful position. What has been learned can be unlearned (or modified).

As already implied, parents can cope with stuttering by not making too much out of it—by not giving the defective behavior power by reinforcing it with attention and too many corrective statements.

Stuttering should not give the child power over the parents. If stuttering appears to be heading in the direction of a chronic problem, or already has become one, the principal treatment is speech therapy. Speech therapy is frequently quite effective and should be approached with an optimistic attitude.

See also *aggressiveness; attention-deficit hyperactivity disorder (ADHD); behavior therapy; genetic predisposition; minimal brain dysfunction (MBD): speech therapy.*

sublimation: A kind of ego defense mechanism in which an unacceptable primitive impulse is converted into a socially acceptable one. Thus, in childhood and adolescence, aggressive impulses find acceptable expression in sports, games, debating contests, competition for grades, and so forth. And sexual impulses, during psychosexual latency or adolescence, find acceptable expression in music, drawing, singing, dance, poetry, sewing, construction projects, and romance.

The basic theory is that the id is pleasure-oriented. It wants its way now, without regard to reality. However, the superego is morality-oriented and says "No" to instant gratification. The reality-oriented ego mediates between the two and finds a middle road that makes it possible to express the energy of the id's impulse in a way that is acceptable to one's family and culture.

Sublimation is one of the classical defense mechanisms identified by Freud. He described it as the psychological process that makes civilization possible. If people were unable to renounce infantile impulses, they could not build an organized social world.

The individual who is unable to adequately sublimate impulses has mental health problems. He or she will have unpleasant confrontations with parents, members of the opposite sex, friends, and the law. One way to look at adolescent sexual promiscuity, characterized by a number of partners with little discrimination and no particular emotional attachment, is to think of it as a failure of sublimation.

See also *antisocial behavior; ego; ego defense mechanisms; Freud, Sigmund; id; superego.*

substance abuse: The habitual abuse of psychoactive drugs, such as alcohol, amphetamines, barbiturates, inhalant drugs, marijuana, lysergic acid diethylamide-25 (LSD), and phencyclidine (PCP). The word *abuse* refers to using a drug in a way that is either self-defeating or self-destructive.

See also *alcohol abuse in adolescence; depressant drugs; drug abuse in adolescence; hallucinogens; inhalant drugs; lysergic acid diethylamide-25 (LSD); marijuana; narcotics; phencyclidine (PCP); sedatives; stimulant drugs.*

sucking reflex: One of the reflexes that is present in the neonate and that is characterized by repetitive sucking if the neonate's mouth is stimulated by a nipple, pacifier, or even a finger. The sucking reflex is strongest during the first three to five months of life. Its obvious purpose is to make it possible for the infant to receive milk and other liquids in order to meet physiological needs. The presence of the sucking reflex is one of the signs that the infant is neurologically normal. The sucking reflex is closely related to the rooting reflex, in which the infant tends to turn and search for the nipple.

See also *neonatal reflexes; oral stage; rooting reflex.*

sudden infant death syndrome (SIDS): Unexpected death of an infant in the absence of any obvious disease, illness, or injury. Often the infant is discovered dead during or after a time set aside for sleep. The most common time period associated with death is the early hours of the morning. The informal name for sudden infant death syndrome is "crib death." When, for statistical purposes, SIDS is listed as a "cause of death," it is the most common single cause during the first year of infancy. Its highest frequency is around 3 months of age. SIDS is associated with a slightly higher number of male infants than female infants. The overall incidence of SIDS is 2 to 3 deaths for every 1,000 infants.

Strictly speaking, SIDS is a syndrome, or cluster of symptoms, and not a single cause of death. SIDS itself has underlying causes, some of which can be identified. A principal cause of SIDS is respiration problems. These may be due to such difficulties as an undetected infection or to sleep apnea. *Sleep apnea* is characterized by interruptions and stops during the breathing process. A possible cause is an immature nervous system or a neurological defect in a control center in the brain stem. Other possible causal factors in SIDS include a genetic predisposition to develop the syndrome, smoking and/or drug abuse by the mother during pregnancy, botulism (i.e., an extremely virulent kind of food poisoning), low levels of certain B-complex vitamins, stressors in the environment (e.g., a room that is much too hot or stuffy).

If a physician has reason to suspect that a given infant is likely to be a SIDS victim, he or she may recommend an electronic monitoring device. The device is attached to the infant and sends out a highly audible sound if the rhythm of respirations is broken. Also, some authorities suggest that during the first three or four months of life, if there appears to be a risk, the infant sleep in the same room with the parents. It is possible that infants take breathing cues from hearing the sleeping parents, and this can be helpful.

See also *neonatal reflexes; neonate; sleep patterns; states of consciousness in an infant.*

suicide: See *adolescent suicide.*

Sullivan, Harry Stack (1892–1949): An American psychiatrist and psychoanalyst who stressed the importance of interpersonal factors in development and adjustment. In 1917, Sullivan earned an M.D. degree from the Chicago College of Medicine and Surgery. For ten years, he was the president of the William Alanson White Foundation, an important psychoanalytic training institute, which is in New York City. Also, he edited the journal *Psychiatry* for a number of years.

Sullivan asserted that personality could not be studied or understood in a social vacuum. The individual is a result of interactions with important other people, or *significant others.* Examples of these significant others are parents, other caregivers, a spouse, siblings, relatives, friends, and peers. In some cases, even imaginary figures can be important (e.g., "my dream girl" or "my prince charming"). Even a person living in isolation, such as a recluse, may relate to imaginary figures or the memories of persons known in the past.

The approach to understanding the personality recommended by Sullivan does not discredit the importance that Freud placed on biological and sexual factors. However, it does attempt to place them in proper perspective, emphasizing that they exert their influence in the context of a family and other people.

Sullivan's general line of thinking is identified as the principal antecedent to transactional analysis, the personality theory and method of therapy developed by the psychiatrist Eric Berne.

Conceptions of Modern Psychiatry (1947) was published when Sullivan was alive. Other books by him, based on his lectures and notes, were published after his death. Two of these books are *The Interpersonal Theory of Psychiatry* (1953) and *The Psychiatric Interview* (1954).

See also *attachment; Berne, Eric; dysfunctional family; family therapy; parental style; social learning; socialization; stroke; transactional analysis.*

super males: Males with an extra Y chromosome in the nuclei of the body's cells. A normal male has an XY combination on the 23rd pair of chromosomes. A super male has an XYY pattern, a chromosomal anomaly. The overall incidence of the anomaly is approximately 1 male in 1,000.

It is hypothesized that the extra Y chromosome is a causal factor in the ultimate production of abnormally high levels of *androgens*, male hormones. Consequently, super males tend to be hairier, taller, and somewhat bulkier in appearance than the average male. They also are likely to be somewhat below average in intelligence. Behaviorally, it has been suggested that they are prone to act out their aggressive impulses. Several studies indicate that they appear in prison populations with a frequency higher than their frequency of appearance in the general population. This is usually taken as evidence supporting the aggression hypothesis. An alternative hypothesis is that a lower level of intelligence increases the probability that a violator will do something crude or obvious, be caught, and be convicted.

It is clear that having an XYY pattern tends to interfere with normal development and socialization.

See also *acting out; aggressiveness; androgen hormones; chromosomal anomalies.*

superego: According to Freud, the third, and last, part of the personality to emerge during development. (The id and the ego are the other two.) The superego is morality oriented; it is the social self or the "we" of the personality. It comes into being from a series of shame and fear experiences in early childhood; the superego internalizes these experiences and translates them into guilt. The person with a normal superego reflects the cultural norms and codes of conduct of a given family and culture.

The superego has two sides. The *conscience* dictates what is right and wrong. The *ego ideal* sets forth an image of what goals should be achieved in life, what one should become. Both sides reflect the indoctrination patterns and values of the parents, particularly in the first five or six years of the child's life.

According to psychoanalytic theory, a child with an underdeveloped superego will be unruly, aggressive, relatively free of guilt feelings, and may manifest a conduct disorder. A child with an overdeveloped superego will be polite, obedient, responsible to a fault, and may suffer from chronic anxiety, phobias, obsessions, compulsions, and nervous tension. (This is what formerly was called a *childhood neurosis*, now considered to be a somewhat outdated term.)

See also *childhood neurosis; ego; Freud, Sigmund; id.*

superiority complex: According to Adler, an overcompensation for an inferiority complex. Behavioral traits associated with a superiority complex in children include boasting, showing off, egotism, arrogance, hostility, insolence, vanity, and lack of common courtesy. The child does not, of course, actually feel superior. Instead, acting superior is a defense against the inner weakness associated with a buried inferiority complex. The psychological process is aptly summarized in the familiar saying, "A good offense is the best form of defense."

See also *Adler, Alfred; compensation; inferiority complex; self-esteem; spoiled child; will to power.*

surface structure of a sentence: See *deep structure of a sentence.*

swimming reflex: One of the reflexes that is present in the neonate and that is characterized by motions similar to those made in swimming if the neonate is supported in a prone position, face downward. The reflex will tend to fade within several months. The presence of the reflex is one of the signs that the infant is neurologically normal.

See also *neonatal reflexes.*

symbolic mode of thought: As described by the cognitive psychologist Jerome Bruner, a mode of thought in which reality is represented in the form of abstract symbols such as words and numerals. The ability to speak and to count makes its appearance in early childhood and becomes increasingly important with continued cognitive development. The ability to manipulate symbols in an effective manner according to rules (i.e., to *think* logically) is one of the chief characteristics of Piaget's highest stage of cognitive development, the stage of formal operations.

See also *Bruner, Jerome S.; cognitive development; enactive mode of thought; formal operations; iconic mode of thought; Piaget, Jean.*

syncretic reasoning: Reasoning by depending on connections between arbitrary perceptual attributes of objects. For example, 4-year-old William is asked to take three objects from a group of seven objects— he is to take the three that "go together." The first object he picks up is a yellow tennis ball. The second object he picks up is not another ball from the initial group, but a piece of white, fuzzy cloth because it is fuzzy like the tennis ball. The third object he picks up is a white block because it is white like the cloth. William has created a grouping that seems random and meaningless from an adult frame of reference. But if one follows his "logic," based on his sense impressions, one can understand his choices. Syncretic reasoning is obviously an immature form of reasoning and is associated with Piaget's second stage of cognitive development, the preoperational stage.

See also *animistic thinking; anthropomorphic thinking; cognitive development; concrete operations stage; egocentrism; Piaget, Jean; preoperational stage.*

syntax: That division of the rules of grammar concerned with how words are combined into meaningful phrases and sentences. A substantial amount of meaning is communicated in English by syntax, or the order of words. Consider these two sentences: (1) John loves Mary, and (2) Mary loves John. The two sentences only have three words, and in each case all three words are identical. Nonetheless, the meaning of the three words is dictated by the syntax of the sentence. The first sentence does not in any way imply the meaning of the second one, that Mary loves John. She may or may not love him, or she may even detest him.

All of this is, of course, obvious to an adult. Is it obvious to a child? Children comprehend and use syntax fluently by the time they are of preschool age, even though they have no conscious knowledge of its formal rules. This observation, among others, led the linguist Noam Chomsky to suggest that inborn capacities are of substantial importance in the acquisition of language. Others, such as B. F. Skinner, argue that syntax and verbal behavior are acquired by conditioning and reinforcement. The child is simply a rapid learner, and this gives the illusion that inborn factors are at work.

See also *babbling; Chomsky, Noam Avram; cognitive development; holophrase; language development; operant conditioning; Skinner, Burrhus Frederic.*

syphilis: See *sexually transmitted diseases (STDs).*

systematic desensitization (desensitization therapy): A type of behavior therapy designed to help a troubled individual adapt to stimuli that produce maladaptive emotional reactions. Systematic desensitization can be used with cooperative older children and adolescents to treat chronic anxiety and phobias.

The father of desensitization therapy is the psychiatrist Joseph Wolpe, who based the approach on well-known principles of classical conditioning. Essentially, a counterconditioning approach is used in which relaxation is pitted against the unwanted emotional reaction.

For an example of how systematic desensitization works, assume that 12-year-old Patrick has an irrational fear of spiders. In therapy, he is given suggestions that bring about deep muscle relaxation. Then the therapist induces fantasies involving spiders. At first, these fantasies are mild (e.g., from a distance, a spider is seen constructing a web). Whenever Patrick's anxiety rises to an uncomfortable level, the therapist switches back to the relaxation suggestions. Gradually, it is possible to increase the intensity of the fantasies. Eventually, Patrick might be able to fantasize, without anxiety, a harmless spider crawling in his hand. When he can do this, he is essentially over his phobia.

Desensitization therapy is also possible without the use of fantasies. The therapist in the given example could have used pictures of spiders, spiders in a bottle, and visits to a museum to view exhibits of spiders as the fearful stimuli. This approach is known as *in vivo* desensitization. However, it is more time-consuming and cumbersome than the fantasy technique. And research indicates that the fantasy method tends to be quite effective in the motivated subject.

Desensitization therapy is generally regarded as one of the most effective and reliable techniques available to therapists.

See also *behavior therapy; classical conditioning; counterconditioning; phobia.*

T

tabula rasa: See *empiricism*.

tantrum (temper tantrum): An intense rage reaction characterized by such behaviors as screaming or shouting, breath-holding, head-banging, and kicking in a prone position. The most common immediate cause of a tantrum in a child is frustration. The child's momentary wishes or desires cannot be gratified, and the tantrum is a display of aggressive behavior in response to the frustration. Fatigue can be a contributing cause to a tantrum because the child's ability to tolerate frustration is greatly diminished. Occasional tantrums are relatively common in toddlers and preschoolers. Chronic tantrums, particularly in older children, are less common and indicate a behavior problem.

    The aim of a tantrum is to exert control over a parent or other caregiver. It has a social meaning and is a form of communication. In essence, it says, "Give me my way and I will stop this offensive behavior. Refuse me, and I'll keep it up!" Therefore, the tendency for a child to use tantrums in a manipulative way will be reinforced if they are effective. The responsible adult should not allow the tantrum to pay off. When at home or in some other controlled setting, this can be done by walking away from the child. Use of the time-out procedure, a behavior modification skill, can also prove helpful. If the tantrum is taking place in public, the adult can move a short distance away and appear to pay active attention to something else. The child will be taken off balance by this strategy; the child expects to be fussed over and told to stop. Often, the child will stop and run to the adult. In general, tantrums respond well to applications of behavior modification strategies.

As indicated earlier, the most common immediate cause of a tantrum is frustration. In fairness to children, it should be noted that there are times when their frustration tolerance is excessively taxed by some parents. Parents are not always "right" just because they are parents. For example, if a preschooler is expected to "behave nicely" while parents spend several hours going from store to store in a shopping mall, the eventual tantrum that may result can be thought of as a child's protest against an unreasonable demand.

See also *acting out; behavior modification; reinforcer; time-out procedure.*

Tay-Sachs disease: An inherited disease involving a deficiency of the enzyme *hexosaminidase.* The deficiency produces damage to the central nervous system and death in early childhood. Indications of the disease include visual and hearing impairments, poor motor coordination, seizures, and a lack of normal alertness and attention.

The disease is caused by a recessive gene. Individuals who obtain the recessive gene from both parents are the ones who will have a clinical case of the disease. It is possible for an individual to be a carrier of the genetic information for Tay-Sachs disease without having a clinical case. Such individuals have obtained a recessive gene from only one parent.

Tay-Sachs disease is relatively rare and afflicts primarily persons of Jewish heritage. It is most common among a particular subgroup, the Ashkenazi. The frequency of the disease in this subgroup is approximately 4 in 10,000 infants.

Tay-Sachs disease is not at present a treatable or curable disorder. Potential parents with a family history of the disease might want to consider the possibility of genetic counseling.

See also *dominant gene; genetic counseling; recessive gene; sickle-cell anemia.*

telegraphic speech: A kind of speech characterized by short sentences, only essential words, and a lack of such subtle grammatical devices as articles, conjunctions, tenses, plural constructions, and so forth. For example, instead of saying, "Mom and I went to the grocery store," a child using telegraphic speech is apt to say, "I go store." The psycholinguist Roger Brown suggests that children are most likely to use telegraphic speech during late infancy and early toddlerhood. It is a transitional way of talking and provides a bridge leading to elaborated sentences.

See also *babbling; cognitive development; holophrase; language acquisition device (LAD); language development.*

television and aggression: The topic concerning itself with the hypothesis advanced by many parents and caregivers that the watching of violence and acts of aggression on television makes it more likely that children will display and act out aggressive behavior. Comic books and motion pictures are also frequently cited as possibly adverse influences. However, television tends to be targeted in particular because it is available in the vast majority of homes and TV viewing time during middle childhood is estimated to be between 2 and 4 hours a day.

A substantial amount of research has gone into the study of television viewing and its possible link to aggression. A series of experiments, based on social learning theory, conducted by Albert Bandura and his associates supports the hypothesis that watching the behavior of violent models makes it more likely that the observer will act out aggressively. On the other hand, a number of studies have led to inconclusive results when comparing aggressive tendencies among two groups of children: those who spend a relatively small amount of time watching television and those who spend a relatively large amount of time in the activity. A report issued by the U.S. Surgeon General suggests that television can be a causal factor in the short-run acting out of violence. Its long-term effects are more obscure.

It is important to realize that the observation of violence, whether it be in life, on television, in a comic book, or in a movie, is not likely to have the same general, predictable effects on all children. Children are individuals with different temperaments and different developmental levels. Parents and caregivers know from working with children that some of them are more likely to become aggressive than others. Children who suffer from attention-deficit hyperactivity disorder, conduct disorders, mental retardation, sensory handicaps, too many life frustrations, and other personal or social disadvantages are probably more likely to become aggressive than children with more stable emotional lives. It is the responsibility of caregiving adults to attempt to place some realistic limits on the content and duration of television viewed by high-risk children.

See also *acting out; aggressiveness; antisocial behavior; Bandura, Albert; social learning.*

temper tantrum: See *tantrum.*

temperament: A cluster of behavioral dispositions making up the characteristic way in which an individual displays emotions and moods. Such words as *reactive, automatic, spontaneous,* and *involuntary* are often used to describe temperament, suggesting that it is thought of as a more or less primitive part of the personality, not under the control of the conscious will. There has been a strong tendency over the years to think of temperament as basically inborn, a part of one's nature. Carl Jung, for example, believed that extraversion and introversion are innate tendencies. The psychologist-physician William H. Sheldon proposed three basic kinds of temperament linked to three basic innate body types. On the other hand, John Watson suggested that personality, including temperament, is to a large extent acquired by learning. The contemporary consensus appears to be that one's basic temperament is essentially due to inborn factors, but it can be modified by learning. A substantial amount of support is given to this viewpoint by various studies of infants that suggest that they display individual differences in temperament in the first few days and weeks of life. Research with toddlers and preschoolers indicates that temperament tends to be a stable, predictable part of a child's personality.

The four classical dimensions of temperament were set forth by Hippocrates (ca. 460–377 B.C.), the father of medicine: people who are *sanguine* tend to be cheerful and optimistic; people who are *choleric* tend to be angry and irritable; people who are *melancholic* tend to be sad or depressed; and people who are *phlegmatic* tend to be easygoing and relaxed. Hippocrates believed that these four temperaments arose from various mixtures of the four basic *humors,* or body fluids: blood, yellow bile, black bile, and phlegm. (From this rose the expressions that a person was in a "good humor" or a "bad humor.") Although linking temperament to body fluids is considered antiquated, Hippocrates's description of kinds of temperament itself remains a relatively useful starting point.

Research pioneered by the psychometrician Raymond B. Cattell suggests that temperament can be subdivided into significantly more dimensions than four. Cattell's studies indicate that there are 16 personality factors, and a number of these can be thought of as essentially aspects of temperament. Cattell presents traits as bipolar opposites. For example, Reserved-Outgoing is the name given to the source trait from which both extraversion and introversion arise. Examples of other source traits contributing to temperament are Affected by feelings–Emotionally stable, Humble–Assertive, Sober–Happy-go-lucky, Expedient–Conscientious, Shy–Venturesome, Trusting–Suspicious, Practical–Imaginative, Forthright–Shrewd, Self-assured–Apprehensive, Conservative–Experimenting, Group dependent–Self-sufficient, Casual–Controlled, and Relaxed–Tense. A parent or a caregiver looking over this list can see that it is a rich source for identifying and describing the behavior of children.

See also *body type; extraversion; innate; introversion; Jung, Carl Gustav; Watson, John Broadus.*

teratogenic agents (teratogens): Agents that interfere with normal fetal development. Teratogenic agents are often implicated in birth defects. Examples of these substances are alcohol, the bacterium that causes syphilis, the virus that causes rubella (i.e., "German measles"), and thalidomide.

See also *birth defects; fetal alcohol syndrome (FAS); fetal development; rubella; sexually transmitted diseases (STDs); thalidomide.*

teratogens: See *teratogenic agents.*

Terman, Lewis Madison (1877-1956): An American psychologist who introduced practical intelligence testing into the United States. Terman earned a Ph.D. from Clark University in Worcester, Massachusetts, in 1905 under the sponsorship of Granville Stanley Hall, an early pioneer in developmental psychology in the United States. From 1910 until his death, Terman was associated with Stanford University.

Terman adapted the Binet-Simon Intelligence Scale, developed in

France, for English language use. This led to the publication of the Stanford-Binet Intelligence Scale, the first standardized individual intelligence test used in the United States. Terman conducted longitudinal studies of development and intelligence. One of his principal conclusions was that gifted children are, contrary to the folklore of the time, emotionally healthy and socially competent.

During World War I, Terman was a leading figure in the development of intelligence tests used in the assessment and placement of military recruits. The two well-known intelligence tests that resulted from his work, and that of his colleagues, were the Army Alpha and the Army Beta tests. The Army Alpha was used to test persons with conventional reading and language abilities. The Army Beta was used to evaluate persons with reading or language difficulties.

Terman was the author of *The Measurement of Intelligence* (1916). He coauthored, with M. A. Merrill, *Measuring Intelligence* (1937).

See also *Binet, Alfred; Hall, Granville Stanley; intelligence; intelligence tests; longitudinal study; Stanford-Binet Intelligence Scale.*

tertiary circular reactions: See *circular reactions.*

test-tube baby: See in vitro *fertilization.*

testes (testicles): The male reproductive glands. Enclosed in an external sack of skin called the *scrotum*, the function of the testes is to produce sperm cells and androgens (i.e., male hormones).

Adolescent males begin to produce mature sperm cells when they reach puberty, typically around the age of 12 or 13 years (i.e., early adolescence).

See also *androgen hormones; ovaries; puberty; secondary sexual characteristics; sperm cell; testosterone.*

testicles: See *testes.*

testosterone: One of the androgens (male hormones) produced by the testes. Its production increases when a male reaches puberty. It is an active biological factor in muscle and bone development, beard growth, and the lowering of the voice's pitch.

Animal experiments combined with data from the behavior of super males (males with an extra Y chromosome) suggest that testosterone is a contributing cause to aggressiveness. This has led some behavioral scientists to speculate that, in general, males, particularly in their early years, are naturally somewhat more aggressive than females.

See also *androgen hormones; hormone; puberty; super males; testes; virilism.*

thalidomide: A tranquilizing drug. In the 1960s, it was discovered that thalidomide has the unfortunate side effect of producing birth defects, particularly malformed limbs, if taken during pregnancy. Although thalidomide was not approved by the Federal Drug Administration (FDA) and never legally sold in the United States, it alerted physicians and the general population to the great importance of the potential dangers to the fetus from the use of drugs during pregnancy.

See also *birth defects; fetal alcohol syndrome (FAS); fetal development; teratogenic agents.*

Thematic Apperception Test (T.A.T.): See *need to achieve.*

theories of development: Theories that attempt to outline, describe, or explain aspects of development in terms of a specific viewpoint or consistent set of assumptions. Some of the most influential theories of development are Freud's psychosexual theory, Erikson's psychosocial theory, Piaget's cognitive theory, and Kohlberg's moral theory. Each of these is highly specific in terms of ages and stages. Less specific in this regard, but equally influential, are Watson's behaviorism, Skinner's operant conditioning, Chomsky's views on language development, Maslow's emphasis on the importance of self-actualization, ethology, and sociobiology. Each of the theories and general approaches identified is included in the following cross-referenced entries.

See also *ages-stages theories; behaviorism; cognitive development; ethology; language acquisition device (LAD); language development; moral development; operant conditioning; psychosexual development; psychosocial development; self-actualization; sociobiology.*

Thorndike, Edward Lee (1874-1949): A learning theorist and educational psychologist. Thorndike received his M.A. degree from

Harvard, studying under William James, often called the "dean of American psychologists." Subsequently, Thorndike worked with James M. Cattell at Columbia University, a pioneer investigator into the nature of intelligence, and earned a Ph.D. degree. Thorndike was a professor of psychology at Teachers College of Columbia for approximately 30 years. He served as president of the American Psychological Association in 1912.

Thorndike took as the subject matter of his early experiments trial-and-error learning. Using puzzle boxes and cats as his experimental subjects, Thorndike made significant contributions to learning theory. He introduced the concept of *the law of effect*, which states that when actions bring satisfying results, they tend to be "stamped in" and make an impression on the brain and nervous system. The law of effect is the forerunner of B. F. Skinner's emphasis on the importance of reinforcement in operant conditioning and its application to behavior modification. Indeed, Thorndike's whole approach to learning was an inspiration to Skinner.

Thorndike applied his theories and discoveries to educational psychology. He argued that the essence of learning is connections, and his approach is known as *connectionism*. When learning takes place, there are connections (1) between stimuli and stimuli or (2) between stimuli and responses. An example of a stimulus-stimulus connection is *thunder* and *lightning*. An example of a stimulus-response connection is *bell* and *walk to class*. Thorndike's connectionism is very similar to associationism as presented by the British empiricists, 17th- and 18th-century philosophers (e.g., John Locke and David Hume) who stressed that the knowing, conscious mind is made up of links between ideas acquired by experience. Thorndike, like the empiricists, believed that complex learning is built on a base of basic connections. However, unlike the British philosophers, Thorndike minimized the importance of awareness and conscious thought. Consequently, Thorndike downplayed classical mental faculties such as will, reasoning, imagination, and memory. For example, he did not believe that some normal children have a "bad" memory and that others have a "good" memory. Instead, he argued that children who seem to have a bad memory and who perform poorly on examinations may not be making connections between various items to be learned (e.g., a word and its definition) because of ineffective teaching methods. He devised methods designed to increase the effectiveness of learning, methods involving the exercise and repetition of connections that bring satisfaction to the child.

Among Thorndike's books are *Educational Psychology* (1903), *Animal Intelligence* (1911), and *The Fundamentals of Learning* (1932).

See also *behavior modification; Cattell, James McKeen; educational psychology; empiricism; James, William; learning; operant conditioning; reinforcer; Skinner, Burrhus Frederic; stimulus-response theory.*

thumbsucking: Use of the thumb as an oral stimulant and a source of gratification. Thumb-sucking is natural in infancy and is associated with the oral stage of psychosexual development. Approximately 40 percent of infants engage in the behavior. It seems fairly evident that the thumb is a substitute for the human nipple. One interpretation is that infants have strong needs to suck and to receive oral stimulation. If these needs are not adequately met during feeding, the infant will seek an alternative object with some similarity to the nipple, such as a thumb, another finger, or a pacifier.

Thumbsucking is seldom a problem during infancy. If thumbsucking becomes chronic and extends beyond toddlerhood into the preschool years, it can be identified as a behavioral problem. Such thumbsucking can often be prevented by the use of a pacifier during infancy.

Assuming that a preschooler has a problem with thumbsucking, the most effective way to cope with the problem is to apply behavior modification skills. For example, the child can be given some attention, recognition, or other reinforcer when observed to be *not* thumbsucking. Shaming or punishing the child for thumbsucking often has the opposite effect from the one intended; these negative efforts often entrench the thumbsucking. A second possibility is to make available to the child an alternative response. When the child is engaged in thumbsucking, a low-calorie snack can be offered without commenting directly on the sucking behavior. (The use of sugar-free gum or candy is also recommended if there is no fear that the child will choke.) A third possibility is to provide the child with a substantial amount of emotional support and affection. Thumbsucking past toddlerhood can be a sign of emotional insecurity. The parent or caregiver who is trying to help a child break a thumbsucking habit must be patient, kind, and persistent. The habit is highly resistant to modification. However, in the long run, the child will often respond. Even without behavior modification, the vast majority of children with a chronic thumbsucking problem will begin to spontaneously discontinue the habit when they are 6 or 7 years old.

There is often the fear that chronic thumbsucking will lead to a bad bite and abnormal dental development. If thumbsucking is discontinued around the age of 4 or 5 years, it will probably not have an adverse effect. If continued until the age of 6 or 7 years, and then discontinued, the effect on the teeth is real, but often temporary. If continued after the age of 7 or 8 years, when permanent teeth have come in, it can be an aggravating factor in malocclusions, and orthodontic work may eventually be recommended.

See also *behavior modification; oral stage; pacifier.*

tic: An involuntary movement with no evident purpose. Tics are often located in the area of the face or neck. Examples include grimaces of the mouth, twisting of the head, and blinking of the eyes. Most tics have no organic cause. The principal cause is chronic anxiety and nervous tension. Indeed, the ordinary tic is often called a *nervous tic.* It is estimated that in late childhood, just before puberty, approximately 7 to 10 percent of children suffer from tics. Male children are two to three times more likely to suffer from tics than are females. About one-half of children with tics will outgrow them during adolescence.

Parents can cope with tics by doing their best to provide a loving, emotionally secure home. They can help the child learn effective ways to cope with the various stresses of life by their own example and by guidance. If common-sense approaches do not appear to be working, professional treatment can be considered. Behavior therapy is often an effective way to help a child modify a tic. Various habit-modification techniques, including systematic desensitization, can be helpful.

See also *behavior therapy; systematic desensitization; Tourette's disorder.*

time-out procedure: A behavior modification technique characterized by segregating a child for a short span of time so that an unacceptable behavior cannot be reinforced. Suppose that 7-year-old Morgan is acting silly and clowning in class. The teacher can send him to sit quietly in an administrative office, an adjacent empty room, or other suitable area free of other children. The basic idea is to remove Morgan from social reinforcers, such as the attention and laughter of other children. The time-out procedure can also be used in the home when a child's behavior is unacceptable. It might seem that the obvious area of choice would be the child's room. But there are probably toys, books, and so forth, there. It might be better to send the child to a little-used room, an empty hallway, or some other area without a television set, toys, books, a telephone, or other sources of reinforcement.

With toddlers and preschoolers, time-out periods of five to ten minutes are usually sufficient. With older children, the time-out period might be as long as 15 minutes. Although the time-out procedure can be effective, it should be used infrequently with children much older than or 7 or 8 years of age. At these ages it is likely to be perceived as unduly authoritarian and punitive and may foster excessive hostility and resentment.

See also *behavior modification; operant conditioning; reinforcer.*

toddlerhood: A stage of development associated with a span of time immediately following infancy. The chronological limits of toddlerhood are often identified as ages 18 months to 3 years. Toddlerhood receives its name from the word *toddle* meaning "to walk unsteadily with small steps." Obviously, children who have recently learned to walk toddle. Important changes in motor, language, psychosexual, psychosocial, cognitive, and moral development are associated with toddlerhood; these are listed in the following cross-referenced entries.

See also *cognitive development; language development; moral development; motor development; psychosexual development; psychosocial development.*

toilet training: Training a young child to control the bladder and bowels. Such training also includes learning the correct use of the toilet facilities. It is usually best to delay toilet training until a child is about 18 months old because at this time the brain and nervous system are sufficiently mature for some degree of autonomic self-control. Prior to the age of 18 months, elimination is largely involuntary and somewhat resistant to conditioning.

There is a consensus in psychiatry and psychology that toilet training should be as relaxed and pleasant a procedure as possible. Punishment, threats, and other harsh measures are ineffective and counterproductive. They may set off a power struggle in which a child uses resistance to training as a way of displaying autonomy.

The training procedure itself consists of social, or observational, learning combined with positive reinforcement. Ideally, the child should see a parent or older sibling using the toilet bowl. The child can be encouraged to use a potty chair and to imitate the older model. When the child urinates or defecates in the potty chair, a few words of praise, a hug, or other positive social reinforcer can be offered. Various behavior modification skills identified in this encyclopedia can be readily applied by the parent. If complete toilet training requires several weeks or even several months, this is an acceptable rate of learning. There are very large individual differences, all normal, in the time required by various children.

Freud's psychosexual theory postulates that emotional experiences associated with toilet training can have an important long-term effect on personality development.

See also *anal-expulsive character; anal-retentive character; behavior modification; Freud, Sigmund; psychosexual development; social learning.*

tokens and reinforcement: See *reinforcer.*

tough love: A parental or caregiving style characterized by authoritarianism combined with genuine love or affection. The concept of tough love came into existence in the late 1970s out of experiences in self-directed community support groups run by and for parents of adolescents who abused alcohol and other drugs and who displayed other kinds of clear-cut unacceptable behavior, such as sexual promiscuity, teen-age prostitution, shoplifting, running away, and suicidal tendencies. The principal founders of the first tough love support group were Phyllis and David York in cooperation with Ted Wachtel. The Yorks are drug- and alcohol-abuse counselors and family therapists; Wachtel is the founder of a community service agency in Sellersville, Pennsylvania.

The application of tough love requires that a parent challenge unacceptable behavior and set well-defined limits. The adolescent must be convinced that the parent means what is said. If the parent's line is crossed by the adolescent, then the consequences to the adolescent fit the magnitude of the offense. Examples of such consequences include loss of most privileges, loss of financial support, placing the adolescent temporarily with other parents, and making a report to authorities. Tough love support groups attempt to creatively explore effective consequences.

It is important to understand that the concept of tough love came into being as a response by parents who felt that they had experienced a long period of manipulation and abuse by an undersocialized adolescent. It teaches parents self-acceptance instead of self-blame and represents a last-ditch attempt to be effective with an adolescent who seems resistant to conventional parental influence.

Some observers believe that tough love goes too far, that it is not much more than a license for hard, overcontrolling parents to vent their own aggressive and punitive tendencies. Others suggest that extreme situations call for extreme measures, that tough love works sometimes when nothing else seems to work.

The telephone numbers and locations of tough love support groups are available through local directories, mental health clinics, family service agencies, and counseling centers.

See also *authoritarian parent; discipline; dysfunctional family; parental style; response-cost punishment.*

Tourette's disorder: A behavior disorder characterized primarily by various tics, including verbal ones. Examples of verbal tics are involuntary sounds such as humming, squealing, tongue-clicking, and the uttering of obscenities. (The involuntary uttering of obscenities is called *coprolalia.*) The disorder tends to be associated with middle childhood. Male children are approximately two to three times more likely to display the disorder than are females.

Parents can cope with Tourette's disorder in the same way that they would cope with tics in general. Also, parents should not overreact to the utterance of obscenities with evident shock or great distress. This tends to reinforce the behavior. Tourette's disorder often requires professional treatment.

See also *behavior therapy; tic.*

trait: A stable, enduring tendency to behave in a predictable manner. An example is *cleanliness* in a child. Suppose that 8-year-old Rhea has the trait of cleanliness. It can be predicted with confidence that she will demonstrate on a regular and frequent basis such specific behaviors as washing her hands before dinner, taking a bath or a shower, brushing her teeth, wanting to wear freshly washed clothes, and so forth.

Traits can be classified in more than one way. It is possible to distinguish between inborn traits and acquired ones. *Inborn traits* are presumed to be due to a genetic predisposition. It is often suggested that traits of temperament such as aggressiveness or introversion have an inborn basis. *Acquired traits* arise as a result of learning. A trait such as cleanliness is probably a learned one arising from both operant conditioning and social (i.e., observational) learning. It is not always possible to be sure if a trait is inborn, acquired, or the result of an interaction of both factors.

A second way to classify traits is to make a distinction between socially adaptive traits and socially maladaptive ones. *Socially adaptive traits* help people to function effectively in the family, in school, and in other group settings. Examples of socially adaptive traits are cooperation, friendliness, need to achieve, willingness to work, and so forth. *Socially maladaptive traits* interfere with functioning effectively in group settings. Examples of such traits are extreme shyness, antisocial behavior, chronic lying, and so forth. A principal task of parenthood is to help children develop socially adaptive traits.

See also *aggressiveness; genetic predisposition; introversion; lying; need to achieve; operant conditioning; shyness; social learning; temperament.*

transactional analysis: A kind of psychotherapy characterized by a detailed analysis of communication patterns in troubled relationships. Transactional analysis can be readily applied to parent-child relationships. The father of transactional analysis was the psychiatrist Eric Berne (1910-1970). Berne based much of transactional analysis's personality theory on Freud's thought. The importance of interpersonal behavior in transactional analysis was inspired by the work of the psychiatrist Harry S. Sullivan.

The basic personality theory proposed by Berne states that the whole personality consists of three ego states: the Parent ego state, the Adult ego state, and the Child ego state.

Transactions are exchanges of information and recognition between at least two people. Three kinds of basic transactions are identified. *Parallel transactions* take place when people agree (or seem to agree). *Crossed transactions* take place when people disagree by arguing or bickering. *Ulterior transactions* take place when communication patterns have two levels, one of them evident and the other hidden. Ulterior transactions have a "sneaky" quality, allowing one person to snipe at a second person.

Although parallel transactions are free of obvious conflict, they are not necessarily desirable. For example, in a family, a particular parent might be very dominating and critical, constantly sending negative messages from the Parent ego state to the Child ego state of a child. (The capitalized terms refer to ego states, not actual parents or children.) The child, wanting love and acceptance, may not fight, regularly sending apologetic messages back from the Child ego state to the Parent ego state of the mother or father. The child may eventually pay a heavy price in the form of chronic anxiety or depression. The parent pays a less obvious price in the form of becoming emotionally alienated from the child.

Berne believed that the greatest danger in parent-child relationships resides in ulterior transactions. Berne labeled complex recurrent patterns involving ulterior transactions *games*, and this became the basis of his best-selling book *Games People Play* (1964). Games are self-defeating in nature. Played over and over, they undermine a family, making people become increasingly distant and remote from each other. In households plagued by game-playing, the parents tend to lose the sense that their children are real persons, not things to be manipulated.

When transactional analysis is used to help a troubled family, two principal goals exist. The first goal is to assist each family member to develop greater *autonomy*, the conviction that one is really in charge of one's own life. The second goal is to assist the members to develop greater *intimacy*, a sense of emotional closeness and authentic communication.

Transactional analysis is an important approach to mental and emotional problems because it recognizes that many of our troubles do not arise in a social vacuum. Other people are involved, and there are times when a troubled child is reacting adversely to the behavior patterns of a parent who is exerting too much arbitrary psychological power. This insight is not, of course, exclusive to transactional analysis. It is also contained in family therapy.

See also *authoritarian parent; Berne, Eric; ego state; family therapy; Freud, Sigmund; parental style; psychoanalysis; stroke; Sullivan, Harry Stack.*

transductive reasoning: Overgeneralizing from a single case of an event or a single characteristic of an object. Transductive reasoning is a kind of preconceptual thought. It is associated with the early portion of the preoperational stage, between the ages of approximately 2 and 4 years.

For an example of transductive reasoning, suppose that 3-year-old Loretta slips and falls, bruising her hip, on a rainy day. Two weeks later, it rains and she announces to a parent as she looks out a window, "Look, it's raining. I'm going to get hurt." Or suppose that 4-year-old Kenneth notes that birds have wings. He sees a picture of a bat in a book and says, "Look at the bird." He has ignored differences between the appearance of bats and birds (e.g., the absence or presence of feathers) and focused on the single attribute of wings.

See also *cognitive development; Piaget, Jean; preconcept; preoperational stage; syncretic reasoning.*

transitional object: See *security object.*

transsexualism: A kind of gender identity disorder characterized by unhappiness with one's biological gender. The person suffering from transsexualism wishes that he or she could have the genitals and social role of the opposite sex.

Although this disorder has received a great deal of publicity, it is relatively uncommon. It is estimated that about 1 in 30,000 men and 1 in 100,000 women suffer from the disorder. The individual with the disorder is often depressed and suicidal.

Adult transsexuals often have a history of gender identity confusion in their early years. Prepubertal children who consistently display behavioral traits and interests that are the opposite of their own sex fit in this general category.

Although it is possible that genetic factors play a role in this disorder, it seems relatively unlikely that they are its principal cause. As far as is known, the person suffering from transsexualism is, in most cases, genetically normal. On the other hand, there is almost always a history of significant problems between parents and the child.

It seems reasonable to assume that conventional gender identity forms to a large extent out of identification with the parent of the same sex. If, for example, a male child finds it difficult to emotionally bond with his father, or if no father is present in the household, he may identify more strongly with his mother. If the identification is strong enough, his wish will be to be a woman, not a man. The same statements can, of course, be made about female children. However, it is clear from a large body of child development research that the favorite parent of either sex, male or female, is usually the mother. In view of this fact and in view of the fact that many contemporary households consist of a single female parent, this may explain in part why transsexualism is more common in males than in females.

There are two basic general approaches to the treatment of transsexualism in adults. The first is sex-change surgery. The second is psychotherapy. Although the successes of sex-change surgery have been popularized, it must be remembered that transsexualism is a disorder and that sex-change surgery is often an unsatisfactory treatment. Many persons who have had the surgery complain of dissatisfaction with the outcome of the surgery and of continuing problems in adjustment. A number of researchers who have studied the pros and cons of sex-change surgery consider it a last resort when no other treatment has been effective.

Psychotherapy is usually insight-oriented with two principal aims. First, the individual is helped to understand the psychological and emotional roots of his or her transsexualism. Second, ways are sought to help the individual foster identifications and emotional bonds with persons of the same sex. Some research suggests that group therapy consisting of persons with similar problems may be particularly helpful in the case of transsexualism. Although therapy does not necessarily cure transsexualism, it may help the individual live with the problem with less emotional discomfort.

See also *gender identity; gender identity disorder of childhood; identity; Oedipus complex; psychosexual development.*

trauma: See *emotional trauma.*

trisomy: A chromosomal anomaly characterized by three chromosomes where there is usually a pair. Normally, chromosomes arrange themselves into pairs, and a trisomy condition can cause developmental problems. An extra chromosome in the 21st pair (i.e., Trisomy 21) is the principal cause of Down's syndrome. An extra female chromosome in the 23rd pair is the principal cause of Klinefelter's syndrome. An extra male chromosome in the 23rd pair is the principal cause of super males.

See also *chromosomal anomalies; Down's syndrome; Klinefelter's syndrome; super males.*

Trisomy 21: See *Down's syndrome; trisomy.*

truancy: Being absent from school without permission. Infrequent or occasional truancy is not a behavioral problem. Most children decide to "play hooky" at least once or twice in their school careers. Chronic truancy, on the other hand, is a significant problem. Unfortunately, chronic truancy is on the rise in our society, and it affects both children in grammar school and adolescents in high school. Truancy rates in various communities range from 10 percent to as high as 30 percent in some city schools. A pattern of chronic truancy often starts in grammar school. Males are quite a bit more likely to be truants than are females.

Causal factors in chronic truancy include lack of parental interest in school, single-parent households, being a latchkey child, lack of academic ability or preparation, boredom with uninteresting classes, a fear of threatening peers, and a wanderlust.

There is no single formula for coping with truancy. Parents need to be interested in school progress, know the whereabouts of their children during the day, and have insight into the emotional lives of their children. Realistic and appropriate consequences should follow truancy; the long-run cost of the behavior should be more than its short-term pleasures. Behavior modification and communication skills are important keys to effective discipline. The tough love approach can be explored. In many cases, chronic truancy will require working with school authorities and a professional counselor.

See also *behavior modification; communication skills; discipline; latchkey children; tough love.*

trust versus mistrust: In Erikson's theory, the first stage of psychosocial development, the stage associated with the neonatal period and infancy, the time from birth until 18 to 24 months of age. If the majority of the physiological, psychological, and emotional needs of infants are met, they will develop the desirable personality trait of *trust,* a preverbal assumption that one can expect positive outcomes and feel well in a rewarding world. On the other hand, if many needs go unmet or half satisfied, this will produce the negative personality trait of *mistrust,* the viewpoint that one is helpless and a victim in a hostile world.

Erikson assumes that the trait formed during infancy, positive or negative, will have an important long-range effect on the infant's future psychosocial development. Therefore, the creation of a sense of trust is a great responsibility, and it falls squarely upon the infant's parents or other caregivers in a parental role.

See also *anaclitic depression; attachment; Erikson, Erik Homburger; infant; psychosexual development; psychosocial development.*

Turner's syndrome: A set of symptoms caused by a chromosomal anomaly in which there is a missing X chromosome on the 23rd pair in the female (i.e., monosomy 23). (The syndrome is named in honor of original research conducted by the physician H. H. Turner.) Children with the syndrome usually display lack of development of the ovaries; in some cases the ovaries are absent. Other signs and symptoms include stunted growth, webbing of the neck, a flattened nose, and impaired hearing. In adolescence, there will be infantile sexual development (e.g., small breasts and little or no pubic hair), and lack of menstruation. Diabetes is more common in people with Turner's syndrome than among people in general.

Mental retardation is associated with about 20 percent of the cases of Turner's syndrome. In the balance of cases, the individual with Turner's syndrome has normal, or nearly normal, intelligence.

An important treatment for Turner's syndrome is the administration of estrogen hormones prior to adolescence. Under these circumstances, although the female will remain sterile, other aspects of development will be close to normal.

See also *chromosomal anomalies; estrogen hormones; mental retardation; secondary sexual characteristics.*

twins: Siblings who came into the world at the same birth. *Identical twins* develop from the same fertilized ovum. This original ovum splits into two ova, and then mitosis proceeds as usual. The resulting neonates will have identical genetics, be of the same sex, and, from the biological point of view, are almost the same organism.

Fraternal twins develop from two unique fertilized ova. The resulting neonates are no more or less genetically similar than siblings in general. They can both be male, both be female, or be one male and one female.

There is a great deal of lore surrounding twins that suggests that identical twins in particular have a mystical connection, that they have a telepathic union, particularly during times of stress, and so forth. Attempts to support these ideas with laboratory experiments on paranormal phenomena have met with mixed, inconclusive results. At present, there is no consensus, and the majority of psychologists are skeptical about the existence of "wild talents" in twins.

On the other hand, there is a good deal of evidence to suggest that identical twins often show remarkable similarities in personality and behavior. This is true even if they were separated in infancy or early childhood and raised by different families. Such findings suggest that genetics do in fact play a significant role in determining behavior.

Studies of twins separated in early childhood have been particularly useful in the investigation of such subjects as alcohol abuse, intelligence, and schizophrenia because it is usually argued that strong similarities in the behavior of twins who have been raised apart have to be attributed to genetics, not environment. This is because they have identical genes but different environments.

Numerous studies of separated identical twins have consistently obtained high correlation coefficients on the various traits and behaviors studied. (A *correlation coefficient* is a measure of the magnitude of the relationship between two or more variables.) When correlation coefficients obtained on fraternal twins reared apart are compared with correlation coefficients for identical twins reared apart, the former frequencies are usually much lower than the latter ones.

Critics of twin studies note at least two difficulties. First, studies using the correlational design tend to favor a genetic hypotheses. It is simply an artifact of the way in which data are gathered and analyzed. Second, twins reared apart do not necessarily have widely differing home environments. Both twins, for example, might have been raised in a middle class home with nurturing parents.

In spite of criticisms, there is a growing conviction among contemporary developmental psychologists that biological factors, including genetics, play a significant role in human behavior. This conviction is based on a large body of evidence, including twin studies.

The rearing of twins presents a unique set of challenges. This is particularly true in the case of identical twins. Fraternal twins are not that different from ordinary siblings. They do, of course, pose all of the problems of sibling rivalry—sometimes in intensified form. However, the rearing of identical twins does metit special consideration. In general, it can be said that they should be assisted to feel like individuals instead of clones of each other. They are, of course, genetically identical. Nonetheless, they are separate persons. Therefore, practices that intensify the identity, such as constantly dressing them in the same clothes and giving them similar names (e.g., Tim and Tom, Evan and Kevin, or Gladys and Gloria), are probably best avoided. Although such practices are "cute" and delight parents, they do not help the formation of a robust sense of identity. In some cases, if practical, parents may want to consider sending identical twins to different schools. This is, of course, an individual decision and will have pros and cons in a given family. In brief, it can be said that the biological sameness of identical twins should be neither denied nor reinforced. It should be perceived as a normal and natural part of their lives.

Principles of behavior modification, communication skills, and parent effectiveness training applicable to children in general can also be used effectively in the rearing of both identical and fraternal twins.

See also *alcohol abuse in adolescence; behavior modification; childhood schizophrenia; communication skills; correlation; genetic predisposition; intelligence; mitosis; parent effectiveness training (P.E.T.); sibling rivalry.*

two-word stage: See *language development.*

U

unconditional love: An absolute, unqualified love that does not have to be earned by any particular effort or specific behavior. When applied to parent-child relationships, a number of psychologists (e.g., Berne, Maslow, and Rogers) assert that unconditional love fosters a strong sense of emotional security and a healthy personality. The child does not learn that love will be present *if* he or she acts in a certain approved way. Instead, the child simply learns that he or she *is* loved, and there are no strings attached. Critics of the unconditional love approach to child rearing say that this kind of love provides no information concerning acceptable and unacceptable behavior, and it may make a child egotistical and self-absorbed. Adler speaks of the spoiled child.

It is possible to resolve the contrasting viewpoints, and to remove apparent contradictions, by making a distinction between love itself and the tokens of love. It can be argued that *love itself* can be unconditional and independent of a child's actions. However, the *tokens* of love (e.g., hugs, kisses, smiles, praise, and so forth) can he given or withheld on a conditional basis for acceptable and unacceptable behavior. Most parents and caregivers would find it difficult to relate to children in any meaningful way if they did not feel able to exert some control over the tokens of love. Behavior modification is based on the general idea that the tokens of love act as powerful reinforcers of behavior.

See also *Adler, Alfred; behavior modification; Berne, Eric; Maslow, Abraham Harold; parental style; reinforcer; Rogers, Carl Ransom; spoiled child; stroke.*

unconditioned reflex: See *classical conditioning.*

unconditioned stimulus: See *classical conditioning.*

unconscious mental life: According to Freud, ideas, motives, and memories existing in the personality at a level not accessible to normal conscious processes of memory, reflection, and will. The unconscious level is created by the ego defense mechanism of repression and, from a developmental point of view, does not become significant until the superego (i.e., the personality's moral agent) has formed around the fifth or sixth year of life. At this time, incest wishes may be repressed, as well as emotional wounds experienced during toddlerhood and the preschool years.

The concept of an unconscious mental life is a key one in classical psychoanalysis. It is assumed that a struggle between unconscious motives, often forbidden and half understood, and the prohibitions of the superego represent a neurotic process. The fear that one may violate one's moral code and impulsively act out antisocial aggressive or sexual desires is experienced as anxiety. One way to explain the presence of emotional distress and chronic anxiety beginning with middle childhood is to refer to this process.

Psychoanalysis as a form of therapy basically involves the exploration of the unconscious level of the personality. The idea is to escape being the victim of unknown forces. A basic assumption of psychoanalysis is that if an idea, a memory, or a motive is consciously understood, then the individual has a good chance of gaining greater voluntary control over both emotions and actions. Some of the methods of psychoanalysis have been adapted to the needs of children.

See also *child psychotherapy; ego defense mechanisms; Freud, Sigmund; incest wish; psychosexual development; repression; superego.*

underachievement in school: Consistent academic performance below a child's aptitude and ability. The term *underachievement* does not refer to learning disabilities, such as developmental reading disorder, or to other problems such as mental retardation. Underachievement implies a lack of motivation, or a low need to achieve in contrast to a high need to achieve. Various studies suggest that underachievement is a common problem affecting from 10 percent to

30 percent of all children. Male children are more likely to underachieve than are females.

Causal factors in persistent underachievement include lack of parental enthusiasm for school, single-parent households, being a latchkey child, boredom with classes, low self-esteem, chronic anxiety, depression, and inability to see the long-range value of education. Factors contributing to underachievement are very similar to those contributing to truancy. In a sense, the underachieving child is a psychological truant—the child's attention and interest is absent. It should be noted in passing that creative children, often children with a substantial amount of ability, are more likely to be bored by classes than less creative children.

There are several ways parents can cope with underachievement. They need to take an interest in school progress and have insight into the emotional lives of their children. Ways to help children with personal and emotional problems should be explored. There should be recognition and other social reinforcers for doing homework and earning good grades. The long-range value of education should be made evident in family discussions without directly moralizing to the child. Parents should take advantage of behavior modification and communication skills. In many cases, persistent underachievement may require consultations with a school psychologist and a counselor.

See also *anxiety; behavior modification; communication skills; creative thinking; depression; need to achieve; self-esteem.*

undesirable language: The frequent and persistent use of language that is disapproved of by parents, teachers, and other responsible adults. Usually this implies the utterance of obscenities or curses. Most children will use undesirable language from time to time. They are experimenting and testing the limits of what is and what is not socially acceptable behavior. This kind of language usage is not a behavioral problem.

A distinction should be made between the voluntary and the involuntary use of undesirable language. The voluntary use of such language suggests that its production is under the control of the child's will. The involuntary use of undesirable language is called *coprolalia* and is associated with Tourette's disorder. The concern in this entry is with voluntary behavior.

Causal factors in the chronic use of undesirable language include feelings of hostility toward authority figures, a desire to shock and receive attention easily, lack of adequate socialization, a need for emotional expression, an attempt to act "grown up," and the belief that "bad" language will win the admiration of certain peers. Psychoanalysis suggests that the use of obscenities referring to elimination and the sex organs can be a sign of transient regression to the primitive pleasures associated with the anal and phallic stages of development.

Parents can cope with the use of undesirable language in several ways.

1. Parents need to provide positive role models and themselves avoid the use of obscenities. Children will not take seriously reprimands from those who seem to live by the maxim, "Do as I say, not as I do."
2. It is not a good idea to act too shocked or offended when a child uses a foul word. This provides the unacceptable behavior with too much attention and recognition.
3. The child should be provided with expressive slang alternatives that may be used as substitutes for obscenities.
4. If the chronic use of unacceptable language is a sign of an aggressive response to frustration in a child's life, the parent can explore ways to remove arbitrary obstacles to a more satisfying emotional life.
5. A rational discussion should be held with the child pointing out the long-run shortcomings of the use of language that offends others.
6. The child should be taught the difference between social settings. Language that is acceptable with one's peers may not be acceptable with grandparents.
7. The time-out procedure can be used.

Parents can expand on the above possibilities by applying the principles identified in the entries for behavior modification and communication skills. In some cases, the chronic use of undesirable language may require professional counseling or psychotherapy.

See also *behavior modification; communication skills; language development; time-out procedure; Tourette's disorder.*

V

validity of a test: A measurable attribute of a test, characterized by the capacity of the test to measure what it is supposed to measure. If, for example, an intelligence test actually measures intelligence, then it is valid. If, on the other hand, it only *seems* to measure intelligence but in fact measures the motivation of the child taking the test, then it is invalid.

It is important that psychological tests, such as intelligence tests, creativity tests, and various scales of development, be valid. A psychological test is a measuring instrument and, to be useful, should measure what it claims to measure.

The reliability of a test can be assessed by using a statistical tool called the *correlation coefficient,* a measure of the magnitude of the relationship between two variables. For example, suppose that a researcher wants to evaluate the validity of a new intelligence test for children. He or she needs first to select an outside criterion, one taken to be already established as valid. Such criteria include an already standardized intelligence test, such as the Wechsler Intelligence Scale for Children (WAIS), or the grade point averages of children who take the test. (Grade point averages are believed to be at least a partial reflection of intelligence.) Then the researcher, using a standard formula, runs correlation coefficients comparing scores on the outside criterion with scores on the new test. If high positive correlations are obtained, the test is taken to be valid.

See also *correlation; creativity tests; intelligence tests; reliability of a test; Wechsler intelligence scales.*

values: Applied to moral development, those ideas, attitudes, and norms of behavior to which a particular culture attaches particular merit or worth. Examples in our culture include cooperation, kindness, cleanliness, ambition, heroism, patience, and so forth. If no adjective is placed before the word *value*, then a positive value is assumed. However, it is possible to speak of negative values, such as defiance, cruelty, filthiness, laziness, cowardice, and impatience. From the examples given, it is evident that values are in fact bipolar in nature, each value implying its logical opposite.

Children and adolescents acquire values through a socialization process that involves both operant conditioning and social (i.e., observational) learning. In the case of operant conditioning, one tends to retain values that are reinforced (i.e., that "pay off") and give up values that have no positive consequence. Consequently, teachers give a mark of "Excellent" or "Satisfactory" to a category such as "Gets along well with others" on report cards in order to reinforce cooperation. Unfortunately, defiance in a child may be inadvertently reinforced by the approval of peers and by too much recognition and attention from adults.

Also, children tend to imitate the behaviors of those they admire. If these are the parents and if the parents represent the larger community, then positive values will be acquired. The opposite is, of course, true if children lose respect for their parents and begin to identify with individuals who exhibit negative values.

Erikson's fifth psychosocial stage, identity versus role diffusion (associated with adolescence), spans a time period when conventional values are often questioned and reevaluated. A number of high schools have instituted as a part of the general curriculum *values clarification* projects. During a values-clarification discussion, students sit in a group of approximately 7 to 11 members and, with the help of a group leader, attempt to sort out their own thinking about values. The idea is not to impose a single pattern of traditional values on all students, but to encourage adolescents to think about their basic assumptions—who they are, where they are going, what they believe is and is not worth doing, and so forth.

See also *identity versus role confusion; moral development; social learning; socialization; superego.*

values clarification: See *values.*

venereal diseases: See *sexually transmitted diseases (STDs)*.

vicarious reinforcement: See *social learning*.

Vineland Social Maturity Scale: A psychological test used to assess, as its name indicates, social maturity. *Social maturity* refers to an individual's capacity to take care of personal needs, to be responsible in general, and to behave appropriately in settings involving other people. The test sets forth a developmental timetable ranging from infancy to early adulthood. Items on the timetable are assessed in a particular case by interviews. Persons interviewed may include a parent, other caregiver, and the subject of the test. Categories of behavior assessed include the capacity to dress oneself, the capacity to feed oneself, and the capacity to cooperate with others.

The overall scoring of the test yields a *social quotient (SQ)*, an index number that can be used to evaluate a subject's level of social maturity with regard to others of the same chronological age. An SQ of 100 is considered average for a subject's age. SQs lower than 100 suggest below-average social maturity; SQs higher than 100 suggest above-average social maturity.

The Vineland Social Maturity Scale has been particularly useful in helping clinicians make decisions concerning a diagnosis of mental retardation. The Vineland, along with standardized intelligence tests, gives a more complete picture of an individual's functioning than does an intelligence test alone.

See also *Apgar scale; Bayley Scales of Infant Development; Gesell Developmental Schedules; intelligence quotient (IQ); intelligence tests; McCarthy Scales of Children's Abilities (MSCA); mental retardation.*

virilism: A relatively rare pathological condition, characterized by the presence of male secondary sexual characteristics in a female. Examples of such characteristics are a beard and a deep voice. Other symptoms may include lack of breast development and absence of menstruation.

Virilism often becomes first evident in early adolescence, and the condition has psychological and emotional ramifications. Females with the disorder may suffer from gender confusion, depression, shyness, and lack of sexual interest.

The cause of virilism is an imbalance in hormones. There appears to be an excessive production of androgens, probably because of malfunctioning of the pituitary gland. In the majority of cases, the recommended medical treatment is hormone therapy administered by an endocrinologist. In some cases, a tumor on the pituitary gland is discovered, and surgery is sometimes employed. In almost all cases, adjunct psychotherapy is recommended to assist the female in coping with the difficulties presented by the virilism.

See also *androgen hormones; estrogen hormones; pituitary gland; testosterone.*

visual impairment: A significantly below-average ability to perceive and discriminate patterns of light, brightness, or color. Examples of specific visual defects include blurred vision, poor night vision, double vision, poor depth perception, and color blindness. Color blindness usually involves either the loss of the red-green sensations or the yellow-blue ones. Developmental reading disorder is not a visual impairment in and of itself, but can be a complicating factor in such disorders.

The term *visual impairment* is preferred to the more informal *blind.* *Blind* is a categorical word, suggesting that an individual either can or cannot see. Cases are usually not this clear-cut. For example, the majority of children and adolescents who are blind in terms of the law do in reality have some useful vision. (One definition of *legal blindness* is to have no better than 20/200 vision even if corrected with glasses. This means the individual must be within 20 feet of a stimulus to see it as well as a person with normal vision can see it at 200 feet.) *Visual impairment* suggests a range of individual differences in the kind and quality of impairment experienced by different persons.

There are a number of causes of visual impairments in children. These include a deficiency of vitamin A, wounds, infections, juvenile diabetes, complications associated with premature birth, birth defects, disorders of the retina, tumors, meningitis, and retinitis pigmentosa. (Retinitis pigmentosa is a hereditary disorder that at first adversely affects night vision and later involves a degeneration of the retina's neurons.)

If the visually impaired child is provided with an effective special education program, then it is possible to compensate to a large extent for the impairment. Depending on the impairment and its nature, most children with an impairment can learn to read and function effectively in school settings. If the impairment is severe, learning Braille, a system of writing made up of raised dots felt by the fingers, provides an effective way to read and learn. A number of schools, based on the philosophy of mainstreaming, attempt to have the visually impaired child spend a substantial amount of time in normal classrooms.

Visually impaired children often make an excellent personal adjustment because their impairment does not exclude them from the social world. Talking and hearing, abilities not affected by the visual impairment, are the main avenues by which individuals relate to others.

See also *birth defects; developmental reading disorder; hearing impairment; mainstreaming; perceptual development in infancy; special education.*

W

walking alone: See *motor development*.

walking reflex (stepping reflex): One of the reflexes that is present in the neonate and that is characterized by stepping motions reminiscent of walking when the infant is held upright with contact between the feet and a resisting surface. One interpretation of the reflex is that it represents a genetic program foreshadowing the subsequent ability, when maturation allows, to actually walk. This will typically take place between the ages of 11 and 16 months. The neonatal walking reflex itself has a short developmental time span and will usually be gone around the age of 2 or 3 months. The presence of the reflex is one of the signs that the infant is neurologically normal.

See also *motor development; neonatal reflexes*.

Watson, John Broadus (1878–1958): An American psychologist and father of the school of psychology known as behaviorism. In 1903, Watson received his Ph.D. degree in psychology from the University of Chicago. At the age of 30, he began teaching and doing research at Johns Hopkins. In 1915, he was elected president of the American Psychological Association. In 1922, he resigned from his position at Johns Hopkins and followed a career in the advertising industry. He was a principal founder of advertising psychology.

Watson had a strong grounding in academic philosophy and, early in his career, became convinced that psychology as then practiced was based on a false set of assumptions. One of these false assumptions was the importance of a subjective frame of reference, an individual's own distinctive way of perceiving the world. Another false assumption was the great value placed on consciousness, or self-awareness. Watson asserted that these and similar assumptions were leading psychology down a pathway toward sloppy science.

Watson argued that it is impossible to rigorously study inner experience and consciousness, key factors in what most people call "the mind." Thus, the study of the mind is impractical because it relies too heavily on personal and private observation. Instead of studying the mind, Watson recommended that psychologists study observable behavior. Behavior itself is a legitimate object of study and has none of the drawbacks of the investigation of consciousness or mental life. The actions of an organism are open to public observation. Two or more observers can agree, for example, that a rat, monkey, or child actually did, or did not, execute a given action.

This general line of thinking underlies behaviorism as a school of psychology, and it was a breath of fresh air for psychology in the 1910s. It encouraged many young scientists to follow psychology as a career because they became convinced that it could eventually be a discipline as rigorous as physics or chemistry.

Watsonian behaviorism was inspired to a large extent by the earlier work of researchers such as Ivan Pavlov in Russia. Indeed, Watson took the conditioned reflex as the basic building block of acquired behavior. Obtaining his lead from Pavlov, Watson tended to focus his own research projects on the learning process. And this trend continued among behaviorists. For example, B. F. Skinner, a leading behaviorist, conducted most of his research in the area of learning.

Watson exerted a tremendous influence on psychology. The two leading forces in academic psychology in the United States for many years were psychoanalysis and behaviorism. The behavioristic point of view is the one that resides behind behavior modification and behavior therapy.

In one of the most famous statements ever made in psychology, Watson said, "Give me a dozen healthy infants, well-formed, and my own specified world to bring them up in, and I'll guarantee to take any one at random and train him to become any type of specialist I might select—doctor, lawyer, artist, merchant, chief, and, yes, even beggarman and thief, regardless of his talents, penchants, tendencies, abilities, vocations, and race of his ancestors." With this statement, Watson asserted the great importance of learning and experience in shaping a child's personality. Although learning is still regarded as important, today's psychology also recognizes the importance of innate, or inborn, factors in development. Contrary to Watson's assertion, these can be neither downgraded nor discounted.

Three of Watson's books are *Psychology as the Behaviorist Sees It* (1913), *Behaviorism* (1925), and *The Psychological Care of the Infant and Child* (1928).

See also *behavior modification; behavior therapy; behaviorism; classical conditioning; developmental psychology; empiricism; nativism; Pavlov, Ivan Petrovich; psychoanalysis; Skinner, Burrhus Frederic.*

Wechsler, David (1896–1981): A clinical psychologist known for his research on the nature and measurement of intelligence. Wechsler was born in Rumania, received a Ph.D. degree from Columbia University in 1925, and for a number of years was chief psychologist at the Bellevue Psychiatric Hospital in New York City. He is the author of a group of widely used psychological tests known as the Wechsler intelligence scales.

Among Wechsler's publications are *The Measurement and Appraisal of Adult Intelligence* (1958), *Manual for the Wechsler Preschool and Primary Scale of Intelligence* (1967), and *Manual for the Wechsler Intelligence Scale for Children* (1974).

See also *Wechsler intelligence scales.*

Wechsler intelligence scales: A group of standardized tests of intelligence developed by the clinical psychologist David Wechsler (1896–1981). These tests are the Wechsler Preschool and Primary Scale of Intelligence (WPPSI), the Wechsler Intelligence Scale for Children (WISC), and the Wechsler Adult Intelligence Scale (WAIS). The WPPSI is intended for children between the ages of 4 and 6. The WISC is intended for children and adolescents between the ages of approximately 6 and 16 years. For older adolescents and adults, the WAIS is the test of choice.

The Wechsler scales have been developed and revised over a number of years. Their forerunner was the Wechsler-Bellevue Intelligence Scale, first published in 1939. The tests are administered individually and are widely regarded as instruments with a high degree of validity and reliability.

One of the principal advantages of the Wechsler tests is that they are divided into two ability areas: verbal and performance. The Verbal Scale for each test is divided into a set of subtests with titles such as *Information, Comprehension, Arithmetic, Similarities,* and *Vocabulary.* The Performance Scale for each test is divided into a set of subtests with titles such as *Picture Completion, Block Design, Picture Arrangement, Object Assembly,* and *Mazes.* It possible to obtain a Verbal IQ, a Performance IQ, and a Full Scale IQ.

What is the distinction between verbal and performance intelligence? The distinction is, of course, not precise, but general. Nonetheless, it is a distinction of some value. A high level of verbal intelligence suggests the individual has ability to think in abstract terms using both words and mathematical symbols. A high level of performance intelligence suggests the individual has ability to perceive relationships and to fit things together into organized wholes. Of course, the two kinds of intelligence are not mutually exclusive, and a child may have a high level of both kinds.

Because the Wechsler scales make a distinction between verbal intelligence and performance intelligence and because of the subtests, these scales are of particular value to school psychologists in making assessments of specific learning disabilities. The scales can also be used to identify gifted children; conversely, they can be used to make a diagnosis of mental retardation in other instances.

See also *exceptional children; giftedness; intelligence; intelligence quotient (IQ); intelligence tests; learning disability; mental retardation; reliability of a test; Stanford-Binet Intelligence Scale; validity.*

Wertheimer, Max (1880–1943): An experimental psychologist recognized as the father of Gestalt psychology and known for his research on perception and thinking. Wertheimer was born in Prague, Czechoslovakia, and earned a Ph.D. degree at the University of Würzburg in Germany in 1904. Subsequently, he taught psychology and pursued his research interests at the University of Berlin and later at the University of Frankfurt. He left Germany in 1933 and was associated with the New School of Social Research in New York for nearly ten years.

A principal assumption of Gestalt psychology is that organized wholes in perception and thinking cannot be understood by an analysis into psychological parts. (The German word *Gestalt* is usually translated as "configuration," "pattern," or "organized whole.") An example of an organized whole in perception is the transposition of a melody. A melody played in the key of C is the same melody when played in the key of F. Nonetheless, all of the "parts," meaning the individual notes as sensory experiences, are different in the two keys. Therefore, the parts do not explain the whole and are not the key to its nature. The explanation of the whole is contained in its pattern or organization.

Finding the answer to the problem

$$1 + 2 + 3 + 4 + 5 + 6 + 7 + 8 + 9 + 10 = x$$

is an example of an organized whole in thinking. Most persons presented with the problem will add the numbers in a logical manner and recognize that the answer is 55. However, a few individuals will perceive the Gestalt. They will recognize there is a key to the problem in its pattern: $1 + 10 = 11$, $2 + 9 = 11$, $3 + 8 = 11$, and so forth. There are 5 sets of 11; therefore, the sum must be 55. Although it is cumbersome to explain this pattern in words on paper, individuals who detect it perceive the correct answer very quickly. This sudden perception of a correct answer combining a group of elements is called *insight*. Wertheimer conducted a series of investigations demonstrating how insight learning can be used to improve the grasp and retention by children of mathematical concepts.

Wertheimer's findings and recommendations have become a recognized part of educational psychology. His viewpoint is set forth in the book *Productive Thinking*, published in 1945 shortly after his death.

See also *cognitive development; concept formation; educational psychology; insight learning; learning; productive thinking.*

will to power: According to Alfred Adler, an inborn need to become effective and competent. In some cases, the will to power can express itself as a desire to dominate and control the behavior of others. The concept of the will to power is not unique to Adler. He derived the concept from the writings of the philosopher Friedrich Nietzsche and made applications of it to psychiatry and clinical psychology. Adler believed that the will to power is quite strong from early childhood and plays an important role in such behavioral phenomena as sibling rivalry and the inferiority complex.

See also *Adler, Alfred; inferiority complex; spoiled child; superiority complex.*

withdrawal behavior: A tendency to avoid certain situations and persons. The aim of such behavior is to reduce anxiety evoked by an actual or perceived threat. If a child or adolescent regularly withdraws from situations or persons that most other children react to with relative comfort, then the behavior suggests the presence of a neurotic process or a behavioral disorder. Withdrawal is a descriptive aspect of a wide range of behavior patterns manifested by troubled children. These are indicated in the following cross-referenced entries.

See also *anxiety; autistic disorder; avoidant disorder; childhood neurosis; childhood schizophrenia; introversion; learned helplessness; phobia; separation anxiety; separation anxiety disorder; shame; shyness; stranger anxiety.*

word blindness: See *developmental reading disorder.*

Z

zygote: A prenatal organism in its first stage of development. A zygote comes into being when an ovum (i.e., an egg cell) and a sperm cell unite. The normal human zygote contains 23 pairs of chromosomes and, consequently, all of the genetic information required to eventually produce a neonate. The stage of the zygote precedes the second stage of prenatal development, the stage of the *embryo*.

See also *embryo; fetal development; fetus; neonate; ovum; sperm cell.*

INDEX OF AUTHORITIES

Boldface numbers indicate biographical sketches.